Tolley's VATwise 2001–02

by

Nick Lawrence BA, International VAT Consultant

Arnold Homer FCA ATII

and

Rita Burrows MBA ACIS ATII

Tolley
LexisNexis

Members of the LexisNexis Group worldwide

United Kingdom	Butterworths Tolley, a Division of Reed Elsevier (UK) Ltd, 2 Addiscombe Road, CROYDON CR9 5AF
Argentina	Abeledo Perrot, Jurisprudencia Argentina and Depalma, BUENOS AIRES
Australia	Butterworths, a Division of Reed International Books Australia Pty Ltd, CHATSWOOD, New South Wales
Austria	ARD Betriebsdienst and Verlag Orac, VIENNA
Canada	Butterworths Canada Ltd, MARKHAM, Ontario
Chile	Publitecsa and Conosur Ltda, SANTIAGO DE CHILE
Czech Republic	Orac sro, PRAGUE
France	Editions du Juris-Classeur SA, PARIS
Hong Kong	Butterworths Asia (Hong Kong), HONG KONG
Hungary	Hvg Orac, BUDAPEST
India	Butterworths India, NEW DELHI
Ireland	Butterworths (Ireland) Ltd, DUBLIN
Italy	Giuffré, MILAN
Malaysia	Malayan Law Journal Sdn Bhd, KUALA LUMPUR
New Zealand	Butterworths of New Zealand, WELLINGTON
Poland	Wydawnictwa Prawnicze PWN, WARSAW
Singapore	Butterworths Asia, SINGAPORE
South Africa	Butterworths Publishers (Pty) Ltd, DURBAN
Switzerland	Stämpfli Verlag AG, BERNE
USA	LexisNexis, DAYTON, Ohio

A CIP catalogue record for this book is available from the British Library.

ISBN 0 75451 292-4

Typeset by Letterpart Limited, Reigate, Surrey
Printed in Great Britain by Hobbs the Printers Ltd, Totton, Hampshire

Preface

Most businesses are registered for VAT, either compulsorily or voluntarily. Their owners are unpaid tax collectors but because VAT is a self-assessing tax, they need to have a good working knowledge in order to minimise the risk of error and financial penalties.

Many publications exist which provide a complete in-depth analysis of the UK VAT system, often using language only understood by those who are continually working with the tax. Tolley's VATwise is a general guide to VAT compliance for those who simply require an overview of the tax. It provides an explanation of how the tax works for those responsible for completing VAT returns and their professional advisers and uses language designed to be understood by the layman. There are over 140 practical examples of points explained in the narrative.

This Fourth Edition includes the law and practice up to July 2001.

Readers should use Tolley's VATwise to obtain guidance on compliance issues but if more detailed information is required, they should seek further advice from the usual sources.

Comments and suggestions for improvements are always welcomed.

BUTTERWORTHS TOLLEY

About the Authors

Nick Lawrence used to be an officer of HM Customs & Excise and subsequently a senior VAT manager with a top accountancy firm. He was a director of VAT Advice & Training Services Limited from 1 January 1995 until 30 April 1999. From 1 May 1999 he has run his own VAT consultancy and training business which incorporated on 1 April 2000. He is also a member of the national VAT Practitioners Group. Consequently, he has considerable experience of VAT compliance issues.

Apart from his role as a VAT consultant, Nick is a regular contributor to the professional press and lectures extensively on VAT issues in the UK and abroad, thus having the ability to address key issues and explain them with clarity.

Arnold Homer and Rita Burrows are Chartered Tax Advisers.

Their experience as tax practitioners gives them a detailed understanding of the day-to-day difficulties encountered when dealing with the UK tax system. They know the problems that you are likely to face, the solutions that are available, and can help you identify the best tax planning opportunities.

As respected lecturers in taxation and regular contributors to the professional press, their flair for simplifying even the most complex of subjects allows them to pass on their extensive knowledge in a distinctively clear and straightforward style.

Their unique skills, together with the editorial expertise of the top UK publisher to the tax profession, combine to provide information that is easy to read, practical, accurate and up-to-date.

Arnold Homer and Rita Burrows are joint authors of companion publications Tolley's Taxwise I and Tolley's Taxwise II – which use detailed tax computations to explain current law and practice – and also Tolley's Tax Guide and Tolley's Partnership Taxation.

Contents

		Page
1.	**An Introduction to Value Added Tax**	1
	Background	1
2.	**Registration and Deregistration**	11
	Introduction	11
	Notification procedures	17
	Ending a business — deregistration	27
3.	**VAT on Outputs**	31
	Introduction	31
	Tax points	33
	Other outputs issues	37
	Tax invoices	39
	Refunds of VAT on bad debts	43
	Mixed and composite supplies	48
	Delivery charges and postage	50
	Packaging and containers	50
	Sales of second-hand goods	51
	Part-exchange transactions	51
	Business gifts	51
	Loss of goods	53
	Theft of goods and cash	53
	Hire purchase and similar transactions	53
	Use of business stocks and assets	54
	Payphones and phonecards	55
	Cancellation charges, booking fees etc.	55
	Tips and donations	55
	Change of rate	55
	Agents	58
	Fuel scale charges	61
4.	**The Zero and Reduced Rate**	63
	Introduction	63
	The Zero Rate	64
	Group 1 — Food	64

		Page
	Group 2 — Sewerage services and water	68
	Group 3 — Books, etc. and Group 4 — Talking books for the blind and handicapped and wireless sets for the blind	70
	Group 5 — Construction of buildings etc. and Group 6 — Protected buildings	78
	Group 7 — International services	78
	Group 8 — Transport	79
	Group 9 — Caravans and houseboats	85
	Group 10 — Gold and Group 11 — Bank notes	86
	Group 12 — Drugs, medicines, aids for the handicapped etc.	87
	Group 13 — Imports, exports, etc.	94
	Group 14 — Tax-free shops	95
	Group 15 — Charities	96
	Group 16 — Clothing and footwear	102
	Supplies subject to 5% VAT	104
	Other supplies subject to VAT at 5%	107
5.	**Exemptions**	109
	Introduction	109
	Group 1 — Land	110
	Group 2 — Insurance	110
	Group 3 — Postal services	116
	Group 4 — Betting, gaming and lotteries	117
	Group 5 — Finance	120
	Group 6 — Education	126
	Group 7 — Health and welfare	132
	Group 8 — Burial and cremation	137
	Group 9 — Subscriptions to trade unions, professional and other public interest bodies	138
	Group 10 — Sport, sports competitions and physical education	139
	Group 11 — Works of art etc.	141
	Group 12 — Fund-raising events by charities and other qualifying bodies	142
	Group 13 — Cultural services etc.	143
	Group 14 — Supplies of goods where input tax cannot be recovered	144
	Group 15 — Investment gold	145
6.	**VAT on Expenditure**	147
	Introduction	147
	Definition of input tax	148
	Non-deductible input tax (VAT (Input Tax) Order 1992, SI 1992/3222)	152
	Documentary evidence required to support input tax claims	162

Page

7. Partial Exemption and the Capital Goods Scheme 167
Introduction to partial exemption 167
The mechanics and consequences of partial exemption 170
The de minimis limits (Reg 106) 178
Annual adjustments (Reg 107) 179
Change of use or intended use (Regs 108 and 109) 181
Introduction to the capital goods scheme (Regs 112 to 116) 183
Mechanics of the capital goods scheme in detail 184

8. Land, Property and Construction 193
Introduction 193
The capital goods scheme 193
VAT liability of typical land, property and construction transactions 197
Further comment regarding construction services 197
Change of use 205
Property sales 206
Leases 208
Civil engineering works 211
Land (Sch 9 Group 1 Item 1) 211
Listed buildings (Sch 8 Group 6) 213
The election to waive exemption (the 'option to tax') (Sch 10 paras 2 to 3A) 216
New reduced rate for conversion, renovation and alteration of dwellings 225
New zero rate for sales of renovated houses 227
Annex 228

9. Margin Schemes for Second-hand Goods 235
Introduction 235
Record-keeping requirements 237
Sales and sales invoices 239
Use of a margin scheme by agents 239
Global accounting 241
The auctioneers' scheme 243
Margin schemes and international trade 246
Second-hand cars 247
Horses and ponies 252

10. The Tour Operators Margin Scheme 253
Introduction 253
Mechanics of TOMS 253
Specific exclusions from TOMS 256
How to calculate VAT due under TOMS 260

		Page
11.	**Trading in Goods within the EC**	267
	Introduction	267
	EC trade in goods — general	268
	Triangulation	276
	Distance selling (SI 1995/2518, Reg 98)	277
	New means of transport (VATA 1994, ss 40 and 95; SI 1995/2518, Regs 146 to 155)	279
	Tax representatives (VATA 1994, s 48; SI 1995/2518, Reg 10)	282
	Record-keeping and reporting requirements for trading in goods within the EC	283
	EC Sales Lists (VATA 1994, Sch 11 para 2(3) and SI 1995/2518, Regs 21 to 23)	284
	Intrastat and supplementary statistical declarations (SSDs) (SI 1992/2790)	287
	Intrastat Simplification	293
12.	**Imports, Exports and International Services**	295
	Introduction	295
	Imports	296
	Exports	304
	International services	312
	The reverse charge for imported services (s 8)	320
	Special treatment of telecommunications services	321
	Internet services	322
13.	**Recovery of Foreign VAT**	325
	Introduction	325
	How the claim procedure works	326
	Specific rules for each member state	328
	Claims in the UK by businesses from outside the EC	338
	Recent developments concerning recovery of foreign VAT	339
14.	**Keeping Records and Accounts**	341
	Introduction	341
	General information required by Customs	341
	Additional requirements for particular trades, activities and special schemes	349
15.	**Completing VAT Returns**	355
	Introduction	355
	Tax periods	355
	The cash accounting scheme (SI 1995/2518, Regs 56 to 65)	369
	The annual accounting scheme (SI 1995/2518, Regs 49 to 55)	376

Page

Monthly payments of VAT on account by larger businesses (s 28 and SI 1993/2001 as amended and SI 1995/2518, Regs 44 to 48) 379
Recent developments 382

16. Assessments, Penalties and Appeals, Interest on Repayments 383
Introduction 383
Customs' powers — failure to make returns, etc. (s 73) 384
Interest on VAT recovered or recoverable by assessment (default interest) (s 74) 385
Other powers — ss 75 and 76 386
Types of assessment 387
Time limits for assessments 392
Penalties 395
VAT account monitoring and voluntary disclosures 404
Appeals procedure 406
Grounds on which to defend assessments 408
Errors following incorrect rulings from previous visiting officers — 'misdirection' 410
Tribunal appeals (ss 82 to 85 and SIs 1986/590 and 2288) 410

Supplementary Example 1: Mixed Supplies 415
Supplementary Example 2 : Zero-Rating, Exemption and Partial Exemption 417
Supplementary Example 3 : New Business Venture 421
Supplementary Example 4: General Compliance Issues 423
Supplementary Example 5 : Motor Vehicles 429
Supplementary Example 6 : Groups of Companies and Group Registration 433

Table of Cases 437
Table of Statutes 439
Table of Statutory Instruments 443
Index 445

Table of Rates

Standard rate (from 1/4/91) 17.5%		
Reduced rate 5%		
Registration threshold taxable supplies	from 1/4/00	from 1/4/01
— in last four quarters	More than £52,000	More than £54,000
— in next 30 days	More than £52,000	More than £54,000
Supplies from other member states	More than £70,000	More than £70,000
Acquisitions from other member states	More than £52,000	More than £54,000
Deregistration limits taxable supplies	from 1/4/00	from 1/4/01
— in the next year	£50,000 or less	£52,000 or less

Fuel scale rates — private motoring (from VAT return periods beginning on or after 6/4/01)

Return period	Car's cc	Scale benefit (VAT inclusive)	VAT @ 17.5%
Petrol		£	£
Quarterly	to 1,400	242	36.04
	1,401–2,000	307	45.72
	over 2,000	453	67.46
Monthly	to 1,400	80	11.91
	1,401–2,000	102	15.19
	over 2,000	151	22.48
Diesel			
Quarterly	to 2,000	225	33.51
	over 2,000	286	42.59
Monthly	to 2,000	75	11.17
	over 2,000	95	14.14

Interest payable (default interest)

From 6 May 2001	7.5% p.a.
From 6 February 2000	8.5% p.a.
From 6 March 1999 to 5 February 2000	7.5% p.a.
From 6 January 1999 to 5 March 1999	8.5% p.a.
From 6 July 1998 to 5 January 1999	9.5% p.a.
From 6 February 1996 to 5 July 1998	6.25% p.a.

From 6 March 1995 to 5 February 1996	7% p.a.
From 6 October 1994 to 5 March 1995	6.25% p.a.
From 6 January 1994 to 5 October 1994	5.5% p.a.
From 6 March 1993 to 5 January 1994	6.25% p.a.
From 6 December 1992 to 5 March 1993	7% p.a.
From 6 November 1992 to 5 December 1992	7.75% p.a.
From 6 October 1991 to 5 November 1992	9.25% p.a.

Chapter 1

An Introduction to Value Added Tax

1.1 Many have asked why value added tax (VAT) is necessary in the United Kingdom. It is often seen as nothing more than an additional cost and an unfair administrative burden. But how exactly does it work? What are its origins? How does its effectiveness compare with alternatives such as cascade taxes and purchase tax which it replaced?

1.2 This book is a general guide to VAT and its scope and application in the UK with a particular emphasis on compliance. It answers some of the above questions and sets out how the tax is controlled.

1.3 The visit of the 'VATman' is often unnecessarily feared, the main reason being a misunderstanding of the way Customs operate and a mistaken concept of what they are looking for.

This book clarifies the obligations of the taxpayer in dealing with Customs.

1.4 There is no doubt that Customs' powers are wide-ranging, perhaps even greater than those of the police, but normally severe action is only taken where significant amounts of revenue are at stake. Taxpayers operating small to medium-sized businesses are often disadvantaged through ignorance of the law and the purpose of a visit by Customs. It has recently been announced that the periodic inspections by Customs are in future to be for the assurance of taxpayers and this book also seeks to redress the balance.

The basic UK VAT law is in the *Value Added Tax Act 1994* and references are to that Act unless otherwise stated. Various changes have been made in other Finance Acts and there are also numerous Statutory Instruments (see Tables at the back of the book).

Background

1.5 The UK was obliged to introduce a VAT system as one of the conditions of joining the European Economic Community (EEC), which is now known simply as the European Community (EC).

1.6 The EEC was established from 1 January 1958 by the Treaty of Rome. There were six members: France, Germany, Belgium, the Netherlands, Luxembourg and Italy. The six became nine from 1 April 1973 when the UK, the Republic of Ireland and Denmark joined after signing the Treaty the previous year.

The main effect in the UK at the time was perhaps little more than a new 50p coin, the 'tails' of which constituted nine hands joined in a circle. However, the relatively quiet changeover from purchase tax to value added tax concealed the birth of an animal, simple at first, but which has grown in complexity as tax mitigation and avoidance schemes over the years have been repeatedly blocked by new legislation.

1.7 The VAT of the new Millennium is in many respects unrecognisable from what it was in 1973. But the onus still rests on the taxpayer to pay the right tax at the right time and, to add to the burden, most errors, innocent or not, are now subject to financial penalties.

1.8 The Treaty of Rome was designed to facilitate the free movement of goods between member states and establish common policies on investment, transport and agriculture. While a single tariff system was also planned, so far as it relates to VAT it has only succeeded in part because each member state has different reasons for interpreting EC legislation in a slightly different way and the more member states there are, the less likely is unanimous agreement on a fully harmonised system.

1.9 The number of member states has continued to increase since 1973. Greece joined from 1 January 1981, Spain and Portugal from 1 January 1986 and Sweden, Finland and Austria from 1 January 1995. The fifteen current members may be joined in the short term by a number of others, notably several of the former Eastern Bloc countries. As the number of members increases, so the likelihood of unanimity on key issues will decrease.

What is VAT?

1.10 VAT is a tax on turnover, consumption, and on imports of goods from inside and outside the EC (*s 1(1)*). It is not a tax on profit, and is best understood by comparing it with similar taxes.

Purchase tax

1.11 VAT replaced purchase tax, which was borne by the consumer on certain categories of goods and did not apply to services. Under what was known as the 'representation' system, no tax was paid on transactions between registered traders at the various stages from raw material to final product. Only when relevant goods were sold to a non-registered person did tax become due and only then if the goods fell within the taxable category.

Purchase tax was fraught with problems, such as:

(*a*) only certain goods were covered giving dealers in tax-free goods an advantage;

(*b*) services were tax free so service industries traded at an advantage;

(*c*) limited coverage meant that rates had to be relatively high;

(*d*) some goods never reached the taxable stage;

(*e*) some goods were made into other goods which often resulted in double taxation.

Despite its name it was to all intents and purposes a sales tax functioning similarly to taxes operated elsewhere, in particular the United States.

Cascade taxes

1.12 As the name suggests, this tax cascades through the level of each transaction, for example, sale of raw material through to sale of the finished product to the consumer.

It has been used in European countries such as Germany but, as with purchase tax, there are a number of inherent weaknesses, such as:

(*a*) from the second transaction onwards, tax is charged on tax;

(*b*) the final consumer pays varying amounts of tax depending on the number of taxable transactions preceding his purchase;

(*c*) if groups are formed to integrate each process so avoiding the charge to tax, resulting rates are often increased.

VAT compared with other sales taxes

1.13 VAT is distinct from purchase tax and cascade taxes in that it covers both goods and services. The uneven playing field has been levelled to a certain extent because the scope of the tax extends to almost all business activities.

VAT is charged on all transactions (other than exempt transactions) in the course or furtherance of business ('output tax', see 1.22) but it differs from other taxes in one significant way: where the buyer of goods or services uses or intends to use them in the course of his own taxable activities, he can recover the VAT paid to the supplier ('input tax', see 1.22) when accounting to Customs for VAT payable.

Businesses making supplies on which VAT has to be charged are known as 'taxable persons' (*s 3(1)*). This is a confusing title, since all the VAT they collect from their customers is paid over to Customs and all the VAT they pay to their suppliers is normally reclaimed from Customs, so the government receives no actual VAT from their business activities. It is the final consumer who bears the tax which the government receives (often known as 'sticking tax'). Final consumers are the general public or businesses which, for whatever reason, cannot reclaim VAT they have paid on their expenditure.

Example 1

Transaction chain comparing cascade tax with VAT (based on 10% tax rate for illustration, although current standard rate of VAT in the UK is 17.5%)

(*a*) *Cascade tax*

(i) A sells raw material to B for £1,000 + £100 tax.

(ii) The cost to B is £1,100. B makes widgets out of the raw material and applies a 50% mark-up on cost when selling them to wholesaler C for £1,650 + £165 tax.

(iii) The cost to C is £1,815. C sells the widgets to retailer D and applies a mark-up on cost of 40%. Therefore, his selling price is £2,541 + £254 tax.

(iv) The cost to D is £2,795 which is so high that margins are squeezed. D can only sell the widgets to the consumer for £3,500 (a mark-up on cost of around 25%) + £350 tax = £3,850.

(v) The total tax through all stages is £869.

(*b*) *VAT*

(i) A sells raw material to B for £1,000 + £100 VAT.

(ii) The cost to B is £1,000 because it can reclaim the VAT. B makes widgets out of the raw material and applies a 50% mark-up on cost when selling them to wholesaler C for £1,500 + £150 VAT.

(iii) The cost to C is £1,500 because it can reclaim the VAT. C sells the widgets to retailer D and applies a mark-up on cost of 50%. Therefore, his selling price is £2,250 + £225 VAT.

(iv) The cost to D is £2,250 because it can reclaim the VAT. Like the other two, D applies a mark-up of 50% on cost and sells the widgets for £3,375 + £337 VAT = £3,712.

(v) The total tax is only £337, the wholesaler and retailer have increased their profit margins and the consumer has paid less.

1.14 A further advantage of the VAT system is that any of A to D in *Example 1* could buy in services for business purposes and reclaim the VAT, although the administrative burden is higher for VAT registered businesses because they are acting as unpaid government agents, collecting tax on its behalf and accounting for it to Customs.

1.15 The term 'value added tax' is itself somewhat misleading because there may be no value added on the next transaction but VAT would still have to be charged by a registered business.

Example 2

ABC sells televisions. A supplier promotes a new make and ABC takes into stock 10 sets at £200 each also paying VAT at 17.5% which is reclaimed from Customs. The sets do not sell. In order to avoid a heavy loss, ABC holds a special sale and slashes the retail selling price from £282 (including VAT of £42) to £188 including VAT of £28, losing £40 on each set.

VAT is still due even though each set is sold at a loss. ABC reclaims from Customs £350 VAT on the original purchase and pays to them only £280 VAT on sales.

1.16 The scope of VAT is much broader than other taxes in that it applies not just to sales of goods and services, but to any transaction deemed to be a 'supply' in VAT law.

Example 3

A parent company makes a management charge to its subsidiaries, which is left owing by the one to the other. VAT must be added by the parent if the companies are separately registered, leaving each subsidiary to reclaim it from Customs. (Groups may avoid having to charge VAT on intra-group transactions by registering as a VAT group — see 2.25.)

1.17 VAT is therefore a tax on supplies of most goods and services made in the course or furtherance of business by VAT registered persons (*s 1(1)*).

If it is paid on expenditure by VAT registered persons, it can be reclaimed from Customs so long it has been incurred in making taxable supplies (*s 26(2)(a)*).

1.18 Those businesses which can or must register for VAT are considered in Chapter 2.

1.19 There are at present three taxable rates of VAT in the UK: the standard rate of 17.5%, the zero rate and the reduced rate of 5% (applicable to sales of fuel and power for residential use and certain associated supplies; women's sanitary products and certain building works connected with urban regeneration schemes). Certain works of art and antiques are also charged at an effective rate of 5% (see 12.5).

1.20 About 1% of all business transactions are exempt from VAT.

Exemption sounds beneficial but, in fact, almost the converse is true when applied to VAT. On the one hand, no VAT is due when exempt supplies are made but any VAT paid on expenditure incurred in arranging those supplies may not normally be reclaimed. Therefore, the costs incurred by the provider of exempt supplies are potentially 17.5% higher than if those supplies were chargeable to VAT at the standard, reduced or zero rate with the VAT paid being recoverable.

Example 4

John runs a business supplying exempt services.

Jane, his sister, runs a business supplying zero-rated goods.

Neither charges any VAT to customers though both have a turnover of £55,000 pa.

Their VAT positions differ as follows:

(i) Since John supplies only exempt services he is not liable to be registered for VAT, nor will he be able to recover VAT charged to him other than by increasing his prices to his customers.

(ii) Supplies that are zero-rated are nonetheless taxable supplies, so Jane will normally be registered for VAT since her turnover exceeds the registration limit.

No VAT will be charged by her on the zero-rated supplies which she makes but Jane will be able to recover from Customs any tax charged to her, reducing her costs accordingly.

Customs in fact have a discretion not to register a person whose taxable supplies are all zero-rated if that person does not wish to be registered but the trader will then not be able to recover the VAT on supplies received, and will thus be financially disadvantaged, although administration costs will usually be less (*Sch 1 para 14(1)*).

If such exception from registration is claimed, it is conditional upon there being no loss to the Exchequer, and the trader is required to notify any change in circumstances to Customs within 30 days of when it occurred or, if no particular day is identifiable, within 30 days of the end of the quarter in which a material change occurs (*Sch 1 para 14(2)*).

For further details on registration, see Chapter 2.

1.21 All sales of goods and services in the course of business are subject to the standard rate of VAT unless they are specifically relieved.

1.22 Sales and income are known as 'outputs' and any VAT arising therefrom is 'output tax' (*s 24(2)*) whereas purchases and expenses are 'inputs' and all VAT paid out is 'input tax' (*s 24(1)*).

1.23 Other forms of income are outside the scope of VAT e.g. non-business income such as most grants and donations and income from supplies of goods and services made outside the UK. VAT incurred on expenditure in generating this type of income is also not normally recoverable (but see Chapter 12 on international services).

1.24 'Taxable persons' embrace any type of business (e.g. sole traders, partnerships, limited companies, charities and pension funds). The usual method of payment and reclaim is the VAT return issued by Customs. This is a form of self-assessment completed in most cases every three months.

1.25 If a business provides supplies all of which are exempt, it cannot normally register for VAT and therefore it cannot reclaim VAT on expenditure. If some of its activities are taxable and some exempt, logic prevails and so long as it is VAT registered it can claim a proportion of VAT on its expenditure. This is known as 'partial exemption' and is covered in detail in Chapter 7. Where the irrecoverable proportion is below certain limits, there is no restriction on the VAT which may be recovered.

Why the UK has VAT

1.26 The tax was introduced in the UK on 1 April 1973 as one of the conditions of joining the EC. VAT in the UK should be consistent with the provisions of the overriding EC law, principally Directive 77/388 which is commonly known as the Sixth Directive. However, there are minor differences in its application in each of the member states of the EC so businesses involved in EC trade should ensure they check the national legislation of the relevant country.

It should also be understood that most major countries of the world have introduced a form of VAT (with the notable exception of the USA) so the same care should be taken by businesses involved in trade with non-EC countries.

International trade is covered in Chapters 11 and 12.

Scope of VAT

1.27 VAT being a tax on the supply of goods and services in the course or furtherance of business by a taxable person, there are essentially four sets of circumstances under which VAT is payable:

(1) on the supply of goods and services made in the UK (see Chapter 2). This includes anything which is treated as a supply under VAT law but is not necessarily a sale;

(2) on the acquisition in the UK of any goods from other member states of the EC. In general, this means imports from other EC countries but different terminology is used to distinguish the VAT treatment from imports of goods from non-EC countries (see Chapter 11);

(3) on the importation in the UK of goods from places outside the EC (see Chapter 12); and

(4) on the 'importation' of services from outside the UK (*ss 1 and 4*).

This category causes particular problems because of the complexity of the legislation. (See Chapter 12.)

1.28 The first category makes sense but, as to the others, it appears at first sight strange that a business buying goods or services from abroad should itself have to pay VAT on their value. The main reason for this is that the current EC system applies VAT on most international trade where the relevant goods or services are used. This helps the tax authorities in each country to maintain greater control over their own revenue, avoids the potential administrative burden of each country having to register large numbers of foreign businesses, and saves the huge task of converting tax paid into the currency of the country to whom it ultimately belongs.

1.29 The business which has to pay the VAT is also responsible for ensuring that the amount on which the tax is calculated is correct and that the tax is paid at the right time. In the case of imports, the VAT is treated as an import duty so on most goods the importer must pay both import duty and VAT. The import duty cannot be reclaimed from Customs. The VAT is either paid to clear the goods into circulation in the UK as soon as they arrive or is deferred under a special scheme and paid on the fifteenth day of the following month. The VAT paid by the importer then becomes input tax and can be reclaimed on the next VAT return so long as the business is registered and entitled to reclaim all its input tax.

1.30 Putting it another way, the importer pays import VAT to its own Government rather than paying it to the supplier, and then reclaims it from Customs in the normal way.

1.31 The VAT paid by the acquirer of goods from other EC countries is entered in Box 2 of the VAT return for the period in which the purchase was made and the input tax is reclaimed on the same return. The treatment is the same for imported services, although the VAT payable is entered in Box 1 rather than Box 2 (see Chapter 15).

1.32 The basic principles introduced in this chapter are examined in greater detail in later chapters.

Chapter 2

Registration and Deregistration

Introduction

2.1 VAT compliance is essential when starting a new business, the first essential being knowing when to register for VAT.

Thresholds

2.2 Registration is compulsory if certain thresholds have been exceeded. From 1 April 2001 a taxable person must register if:

(*a*) at the end of any month, the value of his taxable supplies in the period of one year then ended has exceeded £54,000 (*Sch 1 para 1(1)(a)*); or

(*b*) at any time, there are reasonable grounds for believing that the value of his taxable supplies in the period of 30 days then beginning will exceed £54,000 (*Sch 1 para 1(1)(b)*).

If, however, the taxable person can satisfy Customs that taxable supplies in the period of one year then beginning will not exceed £52,000, he is not liable to be registered (*Sch 1 para 1(3)*).

Taxable turnover should therefore be monitored on a month by month basis.

Example 5

A business starts trading on 1 May 2001 and early sales figures are as follows:

2001	**Month Turnover**	**Cumulative Turnover**
	£	**£**
May	9,600	9,600
June	7,200	16,800
July	8,800	25,600

August	9,100	34,700
September	12,000	46,700
October	11,500	58,200

At the end of September 2001, aggregate turnover is £46,700 so it has not exceeded £54,000 in the last 12 months, nor is there a realistic expectation that turnover for the next 30 days will exceed £54,000. However, the cumulative turnover increases to £58,200 at the end of October so the first threshold has been exceeded at that point.

2.3 Procedures for first notifying Customs and then registering are described later in this chapter.

2.4 The liability to register is usually obvious, but if there is any doubt, a request for a written ruling from Customs should be sought, Customs' public notices and leaflets always being a good initial point of reference.

2.5 Should compulsory registration be inapplicable, it is wise to consider whether a voluntary registration would be advantageous. Voluntary registrations are usually requested for the following reasons:

(*a*) although no taxable supplies have yet been made, VAT has been incurred on start-up costs (*Sch 1 para 9(b)*);

(*b*) taxable supplies have commenced but VAT on expenditure exceeds VAT on income (*Sch 1 para 9(a)*);

(*c*) customers will only deal with VAT registered suppliers;

(*d*) waiting until turnover has exceeded the registration threshold may put the business at a commercial disadvantage in that customers serviced during pre-registration will know that the turnover is below the limit.

Example 6

Basil commenced a part-time self-employed building trade consultancy while still in employment.

He expects his fees chargeable to clients to be £40,000 excluding VAT for his first year of operation.

However, if he does not register for VAT he would have to add approximately 8% to his fees chargeable to cover VAT which is charged to him by those of his suppliers that are VAT registered.

All his clients are large businesses supplying goods liable to VAT.

From 1 April 2001 the turnover limit for VAT registration is **£54,000** (previously **£52,000**) so clearly Basil is not required to register. But since his customers are all taxable persons he will be in a less competitive position if he is not VAT registered because his customers cannot recover the addition which he has made to his fees to cover the VAT he has suffered.

He could therefore apply for voluntary registration, which will mean that VAT will have to be added to his charges, but he will be able to recover any input tax charged to him. The comparative position is as follows (assuming the VAT charged to him is £3,200):

If he does not register for VAT

His total charges will be £43,200, leaving him with a net £40,000 after allowing for the VAT he has suffered on supplies and services to him. His customers will have no VAT recovery and thus will bear the full charge of £43,200.

If he does register for VAT

His total charges will be £47,000, including VAT at 17.5%. His customers will be able to recover the VAT of £7,000, reducing their cost to £40,000, and he will have to account to Customs for the £7,000 VAT, leaving him with £40,000 from his sales. In accounting to Customs for the £7,000 he will, however, be able to deduct the £3,200 VAT which has been charged to him. His net position will thus be the same as before, but he will have improved that of his clients by £3,200, and therefore improved his own competitive position in the market place.

2.6 Certain supplies may be disregarded when determining whether or not registration thresholds have been exceeded:

(*a*) supplies made when a business was previously registered provided that Customs had access to all necessary information to approve the cancellation of the original registration and it was not itself invalid from the beginning (*Sch 1 para 1(5)*);

(*b*) supplies of capital assets other than a positive rated supply of land (*Sch 1 para 1(7)*) (see Chapter 8);

(*c*) any taxable supplies which would not be so if it were not for *s 7(4)* which deems certain supplies of goods to be made in the UK where:

   (i) the supplier directs them to be brought into the UK,

(ii) the supplier is either registrable in the UK under the distance selling rules (see 11.13) or would be so registrable were it not for the fact that he is already registered under the normal rules, *and*

(iii) the supply is not a new means of transport or the disposal of business assets or the moving of business assets from one member state to another.

2.7 Overseas businesses selling goods and arranging delivery to non-registered customers in the UK must register here if, in any calendar year, the aggregate of such sales has exceeded £70,000 or if £70,000 worth of such sales is expected in the next 30 days. This provision is known as distance selling (see 11.13 *et seq.*). Prior to the threshold being exceeded, the overseas supplier should have been adding his own domestic VAT to charges.

Registration for those using margin schemes

2.8 A margin scheme exists for tour operators who pay VAT on the difference between the buying and selling price of designated travel services. For registration threshold purposes, the value is not the full selling price but the difference between the buying and selling price.

Example 7

ABC Tours Ltd starts trading on 1 January 2001 and sells 60 package holidays between 1 January and 30 June 2001 for £1,000 each. Therefore, total turnover to 30 June is £60,000. ABC only sells this type of holiday which consists entirely of designated travel services (see Chapter 10). ABC buys in each package for £500. Therefore, the total cost to 30 June is £30,000. ABC need not register yet because the margin between the aggregate selling and buying prices is only £30,000.

By the end of November 2001, ABC has sold £110,000 worth of package holidays and its total costs are £55,000. The margin is now £55,000. This is above the registration threshold of £54,000 so ABC must now register.

2.9 For certain sales of second-hand goods, VAT is paid on the margin between buying and selling prices, but for registration threshold purposes the value is the full selling price of the goods.

Example 8
Five Star Cars Ltd starts trading on 1 January 2001 selling only second-hand cars. By the end of June, sales have reached £55,000. Therefore, the business must now register even though, once registered, it will pay VAT only on the difference between the buying and selling prices subject to the conditions explained in Chapter 9.

Going concern transfers

2.10 Many businesses are not started from scratch, instead being taken over as a going concern. If this is the case, the threshold rules work as follows:

Where a business or part of a business is transferred as a going concern, the transferee becomes liable to be registered (if not already registered) if:

(*a*) the value of the business supplies for the last year has exceeded £54,000 (note that the transferor's taxable supplies are treated as having been made by the transferee in accordance with *s 49(1)(a)*; or

(*b*) he expects his taxable turnover in the next 30 days to exceed £54,000.

Providing certain conditions are met, the transfer of the going concern is not itself a taxable supply and VAT must not be charged on it by the transferor nor reclaimed by the transferee (see 2.16).

Who must register?

2.11 The 'taxable person' is the legal entity, not the particular business with which it is concerned. Therefore, if a sole trader is involved in more than one business activity, he must aggregate his taxable turnover to decide whether registration is necessary.

Example 9
A sole trader sells computer games from a shop but also acts as a computer consultant based at home. If after, say, 3 months of trading, the shop has taken **£17,000** and the consultancy has invoiced **£38,000**, he has exceeded the threshold at that point.

2.12 Other legal entities for registration purposes include: partnerships, companies limited by shares and guarantee, trusts, limited partnerships, joint ventures (in certain circumstances), charities, clubs, associations, co-operatives and pension funds.

Business splitting

2.13 It has been common practice for business activities to be split and channelled through a different legal entity so that the turnover of at least one entity is kept below the registration threshold. For some time, Customs have had the power to direct that such businesses be treated as one with the conditions for the direction becoming progressively more strict.

Initially, Customs had to demonstrate that 'the main reason' for splitting was the avoidance of registration, which was difficult. The rule was then changed to read 'one of the main reasons', but it was still fairly easy for businesses to claim valid commercial reasons for the structure. Avoidance continued so Customs are now able to issue a direction in any situation where they perceive a threat to the VAT yield (*Sch 1 paras 1A, 2*).

Example 10

Martin runs a launderette from Monday to Thursday each week. His turnover for the last 12 months amounted to £28,000. Molly also runs the same launderette on Fridays, Saturdays and Sundays and her turnover for the last year amounted to £27,500.

A VAT registration covers all of the taxable activities carried on by one person, so that neither Martin nor Molly has an obligation to register for VAT. However, Customs have the power to direct that where two or more persons are carrying on business activities separately and Customs perceive a threat to the VAT yield, the two businesses are to be deemed one for VAT purposes. Accordingly, the registration limit (**£54,000** from 1 April 2001) would then apply to the whole business and since the current turnover is £55,500 (£28,000 + £27,500) Martin and Molly would be obliged to register the joint business from the date of the direction by Customs or such later date as is specified in the direction.

The direction that two businesses be deemed one is always from a current date but where Customs are able to demonstrate that attempts to create two businesses were unsuccessful and that there has only ever been one business, they are able to assess retrospectively. The typical example is where members of a family run a public house in partnership and register for VAT and one member sets up a separate catering business but does not register. If Customs can demonstrate that the catering activity was always part of the partnership business, they can assess for VAT on its takings.

Notification procedures

2.14 When one of the registration thresholds has been exceeded, the business has 30 days to *notify* Customs of the requirement to register. This is best achieved in a letter requesting the Form VAT 1 on which formal notification is made. Alternatively, Form CWF1 addressed to the Inland Revenue (for direct taxation and national insurance contribution purposes) and Customs can conveniently be used as a joint notification. The subsequently received *application for registration* should reach the local VAT office no later than the 30th day after the threshold was exceeded. Customs must then supply a VAT registration number, theoretically prefixed with the internationally recognised two-letter prefix (GB for the UK) but in practice the prefix is only used on invoices involving international trade.

Example 11

Trading starts on 1 June 2001. At the end of October 2001, taxable turnover goes over the **£54,000** threshold. A completed Form VAT 1 must reach Customs by 30 November 2001 and the effective date of registration will be 1 December 2001.

Example 12

Trading starts on 1 June 2001. The first two invoices for taxable supplies cover contracts worth £5,000 each. However, on 18 June a large contract is received worth £55,000. The work is scheduled for completion two weeks later on 2 July. Therefore, on 18 June, taxable supplies in the next 30 days are expected to exceed **£54,000** so a completed Form VAT 1 must reach Customs by 17 July. In this case, the effective date of registration will be 18 June 2001.

Example 13

2001	**Sales**
	£
June	52,000
July	52,000
August	52,000
Total	**156,000**

In this case, the **£54,000** limit has not been exceeded until 31 July 2001 so Customs must be notified by 30 August and the effective date of registration is 1 September 2001. In effect, £156,000 of taxable sales have been made VAT free. This may also be useful if Customs challenge the date on which registration should have been effected.

2.15 Should the past turnover threshold be the only one affecting the date for compulsory registration (for example where a small professional practice is sold as a going concern), it may be possible to time supplies to maximise VAT free sales where that would be to the benefit of the customer base.

Going concern transfers

2.16 The purchaser of a business transferred as a going concern must notify Customs within 30 days of the completion date, either registering for VAT with a new number or taking over the vendor's VAT registration number by completing Form VAT 68. In the latter case, all outstanding VAT liabilities are taken over, so that the successor may well seek appropriate indemnities from the vendor.

The transfer of a going concern is not a supply for VAT purposes if certain conditions are met (see 6.28–6.29). In such circumstances, the vendor must not charge VAT on the positive rated elements of the sale, and consequently there is no input tax for the purchaser to claim.

Other notification matters

2.17 Partnership registration applications must be accompanied by Form VAT 2 completed by all the partners (see 2.22) and applications for group registrations are submitted using Forms VAT 50 and 51 (see 2.26).

If a VAT registered person dies or individuals become bankrupt or a company goes into receivership, liquidation or administration, Customs may continue the registration until somebody else is registered to carry on the activities. The person taking over has 21 days from appointment to notify Customs.

Any changes to the details covering registration for VAT must be notified to Customs in writing within 30 days of the events causing the change (for example, if a sole trader changes his principal place of business, a partner is introduced or retires, or a company is taken over by another).

Receiving a VAT registration number

2.18 Shortly after receipt of the application Form VAT 1, Customs will either send a request for further information or issue a registration number followed by the certificate of registration.

During the time between the effective date of registration and the date the number is received, those issuing invoices and offering credit terms need to allow for the VAT which will have to be accounted for on their first return. This is usually achieved by issuing a pro forma invoice including the VAT element but stating clearly, 'this is not a tax invoice'. A proper tax invoice can then be issued when the number is available. This problem does not affect retailers but they should ensure that in their selling prices they allow for the VAT for which they will be accountable.

How to recognise a valid VAT number

2.19 When calculating how much input tax is recoverable, it is the responsibility of the registered person to obtain and keep valid tax invoices for inspection by visiting officers. Customs are able to confirm if a particular number is valid but it is not always so easy to confirm whether the number available belongs to the supplier using it.

A VAT number can be checked using the system known as 'Modulus 97'. This is how it works:

A VAT number has a '3-4-2' format i.e. three digits, a gap, four digits, another gap, then two digits. The first seven digits are multiplied by eight, seven, six, etc. down to two and the last two digits should be the difference between the seven totals added together and 97 or multiples of 97.

Example 14

487 1312 40

4 × 8 =	32
8 × 7 =	56
7 × 6 =	42
1 × 5 =	5
3 × 4 =	12
1 × 3 =	3
2 × 2 =	4
Total =	154

2 × 97 = 194 so the difference is 40 as per the check digits.

312 6033 58

3 × 8 =	24
1 × 7 =	7
2 × 6 =	12
6 × 5 =	30
0 × 4 =	0
3 × 3 =	9
3 × 2 =	6
Total =	88

1 × 97 = 97 so the check digits should be 09 not 58. The number is invalid.

Intending traders

2.20 Under EC law, any person engaged in an economic activity may be treated as a taxable person. There have been many cases on this subject and Customs must be satisfied that real plans are in place to make taxable supplies some time in the future before they will register the person concerned as an 'intending trader'.

Now that input tax can be claimed at the latest three years after it was incurred, the timing of such registrations has become critical. Input tax recovered is provisional and is only confirmed once taxable supplies are made.

However, the economic activity need not be successful for input tax to be deductible. Thus in the *Merseyside Cablevision Limited* tribunal case (*MAN/85/327, No 2419*) input tax attributable to a failed research and development project was still recoverable even though no taxable supplies were ever made.

This should be contrasted with making exempt supplies. If a business registers on an intending basis but makes exempt rather than taxable supplies, Customs have the power to claw back input tax previously repaid.

Waiver of registration

2.21 If taxable supplies in the last 12 months have exceeded **£54,000** (from 1 April 2001) but taxable turnover is not expected to exceed **£52,000** *in the next 12 months* (from 1 April 2001), Customs can be asked to waive registration and they will usually oblige.

Also, if either threshold has been exceeded but it is clear that input tax will regularly exceed output tax, while the business concerned must still notify Customs that the limits have been exceeded, it may again request that registration be waived, although this is a clear disadvantage unless the amounts involved are nominal and it is not worth the administrative burden of completing VAT returns.

Partnerships

2.22 Where there is a partnership of two or more individuals, a Form VAT 2 signed by each partner must accompany the registration application showing their details as described in 2.17. In the case of limited partnerships, the Form VAT 2 is completed by general partners only.

Each partner is jointly (in Scotland, jointly and severally) liable for the partnership VAT liabilities whilst he is still a partner and this is still the case if he has left the partnership but failed to notify Customs in writing.

Customs should be notified in writing each time a partner joins or leaves the partnership.

The notification should be made within 30 days of the change. New partners should complete a supplementary Form VAT 2 but only a letter is required if a partner leaves.

Limited partnerships ('LPs') and limited liability partnerships ('LLPs')

2.23 Limited partnerships are governed by the *Limited Partnerships Act 1907* and consist of at least one general partner and one limited partner. In certain circumstances, it is possible to register each or a combination of the partners separately because the partner with limited liability cannot be held responsible for the liabilities of general partners.

A new *Limited Liability Partnership Act 2000* received Royal Assent on 20 July 2000. LLPs could be formed under this Act from 6 April 2001.

Under the new provisions, an LLP has a legal status distinct from its members and can enter into contracts in its own right. The members of an LLP must obtain a certificate of incorporation from the Registrar of Companies. Therefore, an LLP is a corporate body and is registered for VAT purposes as such. The members do not normally have to register for VAT separately because they are not seen as supplying their services to the LLP.

Where an unlimited partnership is changed to become an LLP, the going concern transfer rules apply (see 2.16). LLPs may also become part of a group registration provided all the normal conditions are met (see 2.25–2.28).

Co-owners of land (s 51A)

2.24 Where rent is received from commercial property, the 'landlord' has the option to charge VAT. This is done by waiving exemption from VAT in respect of a particular property (see Chapter 8). The election must be made contemporaneously by all the co-owners or not at all, the joint owners together being regarded as 'the property owner' for VAT purposes and a single taxable person with joint and several liability applying.

No change to the constitution of 'the property owner' is effective until Customs have received written notification and any notice served on 'the property owner' includes any party no longer having an interest in the relevant property but who had an interest in the period covered by the notice.

Where several properties are owned by the same persons, the option to tax can be exercised on a property by property basis.

Group registrations

2.25 If certain criteria are met, two or more corporate bodies may be grouped together under a single VAT registration (*s 43*). This is an optional provision specifically designed to relieve administrative burdens rather than to create major opportunities for tax mitigation, although many VAT groups have been set up principally for the latter reason.

Not all of the companies within a commercial group need be included in the VAT group, some being registered separately or not at all, or the formation of a new company for inclusion in a VAT group or the removal of a company from a VAT group being timed for maximum tax benefit.

There is anti-avoidance legislation to counter artificial structures (*Sch 9A*) (see 2.27).

Under *section 43*, two or more corporate bodies may be grouped for VAT purposes if:

(1) one of them controls all the others; or

(2) one 'person' (which could be an individual) controls all of them; or

(3) a partnership business controls all of them.

A 'corporate body' includes:

(*a*) companies limited by shares or guarantee,

(*b*) unlimited companies,

(*c*) companies created by any other legal means e.g. Royal Charter, Acts of Parliament,

(*d*) building societies,

(*e*) industrial and provident societies,

which are registered under relevant company legislation.

One body is 'controlled' by another if:

(i) that other body holds a majority (more than 50%) of the voting rights in it; or

(ii) the other body is a member of it and has the right to appoint or remove a majority of its board of directors (i.e. those who hold the majority of control); or

(iii) that other body is a member of it and controls alone, pursuant to an agreement with other shareholders or members, a majority of the voting rights in it; or

(iv) it is a subsidiary of a company which is itself a subsidiary of that other company.

Applications to form VAT groups

2.26 Forms VAT 50 and 51 must accompany the application for a group registration.

One member of the group is nominated as the 'representative member' and all subsequent taxable supplies are then deemed to be made by that member. Sometimes Customs will agree to a provisional group registration before legal control is obtained. Any figures within a VAT return then become confirmed as and when the legalities are concluded.

Properly controlled companies (see 2.25) can be added to the group at a later date and companies in the group may leave at any time.

Unless Customs use one of their anti-avoidance powers contained in *Sch 9A*, supplies between members of a VAT group are disregarded, with no VAT being added to intra-group charges. This can be especially useful if one or more of the group members is partly exempt and would otherwise incur an amount of irrecoverable input tax.

All supplies outside the group are deemed to be made by or to the representative member but all group members are jointly (and severally) liable for VAT due.

Example 15

PRS Holdings Ltd has two subsidiaries: PRS (Birmingham) Ltd and PRS (Manchester) Ltd. A group registration is formed with PRS Holdings Limited as its representative member. All VAT returns will be in the name of PRS Holdings Ltd but will include the output tax and input tax of the subsidiaries as well.

At 30 June 2001, PRS Holdings Ltd issues a management charge of £100,000 to both subsidiaries. Neither will carry VAT as the group is regarded as a single taxable person.

PRS Holdings Ltd has a third subsidiary, PRS (Newcastle) Ltd but this company is not part of the VAT group and is separately registered. PRS Holdings Ltd issues it with a management charge of £100,000 but this time adds VAT at 17.5% (£17,500).

VAT groups — anti-avoidance provisions

2.27 *Schedule 9A* gives Customs wide-ranging powers to counter avoidance schemes using VAT groups. For example, they can refuse to allow a company to be part of a group, order an existing group member to leave a group, cancel the provision disregarding VAT on intra-group supplies and order a particular company to be the representative member where it appears necessary to do so for the protection of the revenue.

The action will normally take the form of a direction issued by Customs to the affected party but the recipient is entitled to ask for that direction to be reconsidered.

In Business Brief 1/2001, 10 January 2001, Customs announced further anti-avoidance action against group registrations in which the control criteria had been artificially contrived.

2.28 It used to be possible for foreign businesses without a fixed establishment in the UK to be part of a VAT group registration if at least one director with full voting rights was present or resident here and regularly attended directors' meetings.

Recent changes included the replacement of the resident director rule to a requirement for a foreign business to have a fixed establishment here.

Companies becoming ineligible to be part of a group registration should have made alternative arrangements by 1 January 2000. If they have not done so, they face expulsion.

Other changes are as follows:

- Customs have 90 days from the date of an application from a company to join a group to approve or refuse it.
- Appellants to Tribunals against adverse decisions have to prove that Customs acted unreasonably.
- Customs have the power to remove a company from a group if it becomes ineligible (this can be retroactive) or if it appears necessary to do so for the protection of the revenue.

Divisional registrations

2.29 Companies often divide up their business activities into divisions. If certain conditions are met, Customs will allow each division to have a separate registration for VAT (*s 46*). The conditions are as follows:

(*a*) all divisions must be registered even if their stand-alone taxable turnover is below the thresholds;

(*b*) each division must have separate internal accounting and be operated from a separate location;

(*c*) the partial exemption *de minimis* limits for the company as a whole must not be exceeded (see Chapter 7);

(*d*) each VAT return stagger must be the same e.g. each division submits returns for the quarters ending 31 March, 30 June, 30 September and 31 December, albeit Customs can approve return periods ending on the company's internal accounting date. Customs can allow monthly returns where input tax recoverable by the company as a whole will regularly exceed output tax due;

(*e*) VAT invoices must not be issued for transactions between the divisions.

Farmers

2.30 Qualifying farmers need not be VAT registered, instead adopting the UK version of the flat rate scheme set out in EC law (*s 54* and Customs Leaflet 700/46).

In that event they cannot reclaim input tax, but as a form of compensation, the flat rate scheme entitles them to add 4% to their sales to VAT registered businesses. This amount is kept and not paid over to Customs.

Form VAT 98 has to be completed in order to register under the flat rate scheme.

Racehorse owners

2.31 The activities of racehorse owners were originally considered outside the scope of VAT. However, a unique arrangement has applied to them since 16 March 1993. Since that date, they have been allowed to register subject to certain conditions. They must first confirm that they plan to receive income from sponsorship and appearance money (business income) as well as receive prize money (non-business income). This is done in writing to Weatherbys, Sanders Road, Wellingborough, Northamptonshire NN8 4BX.

Thereafter, registration is effected in the normal way but output tax due and input tax recoverable are in accordance with the Memorandum of Understanding agreed between Treasury Ministers and the thoroughbred horseracing and breeding industry. Practice is explained in Customs Leaflet 700/67.

A review of the original scheme resulted in the following changes:

(*a*) future registrations are only allowed if sponsorship is already in place, and

(*b*) sole traders can only apply the scheme to horses in which they hold at least a 50% share.

Distance sellers to the UK

2.32 Where foreign businesses have made distance sales to the UK exceeding £70,000 in a calendar year, they must notify Customs of the requirement to register on Form VAT 1A and also complete Form VAT 1TR if they are appointing a tax representative to handle their future VAT affairs.

Distance sales are covered in greater depth at 11.13 to 11.17.

European Community acquisitions by non-registered persons

2.33 If non-registered businesses make EC acquisitions exceeding **£54,000** in a calendar year, the requirement to register must be notified on Form VAT 1B.

EC acquisitions are covered in greater depth at 11.3 to 11.4.

The Crown and local authorities

2.34 Special rules apply to government departments under *s 41*.

The Treasury can direct that non-business supplies by government departments, which would be taxable if supplied by a normal business, are taxable supplies.

If a local authority makes taxable supplies, it must register for VAT. Input tax may be recovered on certain standard-rated external costs even if they are not directly attributable to business activities. The special legislation applicable to local authorities is in *ss 33 and 42*.

Ending a business — deregistration

2.35 If a VAT registered business closes down or stops making taxable supplies for whatever reason, it should notify Customs within 30 days, after which Customs will effect deregistration. There is no specific form for this notification, a detailed letter sufficing.

Other circumstances requiring deregistration are as follows:

(*a*) the business changes its legal status e.g. a partnership becomes a limited company (but special rules apply to the transfer of a going concern and the existing VAT registration number may be transferred provided both parties agree and complete Form VAT 68) — see 2.16;

(*b*) registration as an intending trader no longer applies i.e. the intention to trade no longer exists;

(*c*) registration was allowed because taxable supplies were made outside the UK which would have been taxable if made in the UK *and this no longer applies*, or such supplies were intended but the intention no longer exists;

(*d*) registration was allowed solely on the grounds of supplies of disregarded warehoused goods and such supplies have ceased. Warehoused goods are dealt with in Chapter 12.

Optional deregistration

2.36 Businesses may opt for deregistration if taxable turnover in the next 12 months is not expected to exceed **£52,000** or if input tax will regularly exceed output tax. Clearly, the latter option would leave the business worse off unless the administrative cost of completing VAT returns is higher than the net repayments it would receive.

2.37 In order to quantify expected taxable turnover in the next 12 months, businesses may ignore supplies of capital assets other than positive rated supplies relating to land (which includes property) and any taxable supplies which would not be taxable apart from *s 7(4)*, such as deeming the bringing of goods into the UK as supplies made in the UK.

Stocks and assets on hand at deregistration

2.38 A final return is usually required covering the time from the end of the previous tax period to the date of deregistration. The final return is Form VAT 193 (VAT 197 in Wales) which embraces output tax on the open market value of certain stocks and assets on hand at deregistration.

Where the VAT on such stocks and assets on hand exceeds £1,000 (from 1 April 2000, previously £250), output tax must be accounted for. The value of the stocks and assets is as follows:

(*a*) the price one would expect to pay for them in their current condition; or

(*b*) if that cannot be established, the price one would expect to pay for similar goods; or

(*c*) if that cannot be established, the cost of producing the goods at the point of deregistration.

Example 16

Centreville Cycles Ltd consists of a shop selling bicycles and is VAT registered. It is struggling, so the directors decide to cease trading on 31 October 2001. It has a closing down sale and in the last VAT quarter (1 August to 31 October) it receives income of £4,700 including VAT and incurs a few sundry costs totalling £1,175 including VAT. On 31 October, the open market value of unsold bicycles and fixed assets is £7,050 including VAT.

The amount due to HM Customs & Excise is as follows:

Output tax on sales — £700, plus

Output tax on stocks and assets on hand at 31 October — £1,050 (payable because the VAT amount exceeds £1,000)

Total output tax due = £1,750, less

Input tax recoverable — £175

Net tax payable = £1,750 – £175 = £1,575.

> Note that whilst the standard rate of VAT is 17.5%, the gross value of assets below which output tax need not be paid over is £6,714.28 (because the VAT included in £6,714.28 is 7/47ths, i.e. £1,000).

2.39 Given that all the conditions of the *VAT (Special Provisions) Order 1995 (SI 1995/1268), Article 5* as amended are met, the transfer of a going concern must not be treated as a supply for VAT purposes (see 2.16). In such cases, no VAT would be charged on any assets of the business being transferred including goodwill.

Distance selling — deregistration

2.40 Foreign businesses registered under the distance selling provisions may deregister if their relevant supplies in the preceding calendar year did not exceed £70,000 and will not do so in the next calendar year. This does not apply if the business has exercised its option for relevant supplies to be treated as made outside its own member state (see 11.13 to 11.17).

EC acquisitions — deregistration

2.41 Businesses registered because their EC acquisitions in the UK exceeded £54,000 are no longer liable to be registered if EC acquisitions in the preceding calendar year did not exceed that figure and will not do so in the next 12 months.

Registration void 'ab initio'

2.42 Where a business registers but it subsequently transpires that it was not liable or entitled to register, Customs may effect deregistration from the original registration date.

Where businesses complete the compulsory registration boxes of Form VAT 1 in error (for example, believing registration was due because trading had commenced, albeit taxable turnover had not reached the threshold), they might request cancellation '*ab initio*' but the request would probably be refused because the business has collected VAT from its customers.

Post-deregistration input tax

2.43 VAT on purchase invoices dated prior to the deregistration date but not included on earlier returns and input tax on services received after deregistration relating to the time the business was registered (e.g.

professional fees) may be recovered by completing Form VAT 427. Claims are subject to a three-year time limit.

Retention of records after deregistration

2.44 Normal business records should be retained for six years after deregistration. In certain circumstances, businesses which have acquired standard-rated commercial property subject to capital goods scheme adjustments over ten years may have to keep them longer to provide a clear audit trail for inspection if required (see 7.22–7.35).

Chapter 3

VAT on Outputs

Introduction

Taxable supplies

3.1 The supplies made by a business are referred to as its outputs, hence the VAT charged by a business on taxable supplies is called its output tax. This chapter examines the accountability to Customs of that output tax (*ss 4–5*).

A taxable supply is any supply of goods or services made in the UK in the course or furtherance of business other than an exempt supply (*s 4*). Types of supply are examined in greater depth in later chapters.

There are special 'place of supply' rules to determine whether a supply is made 'in the UK' (*s 7*). These are as follows:

Goods

3.2 Goods are normally supplied where they are physically located when allocated to a specific customer order (*s 7*).

Example 17
An exporter of machine tools from the UK to the United States who sends consignments once customer orders have been received is making taxable supplies in the UK (even though exports are usually zero-rated — see Chapter 12). However, if a UK supplier of the same goods has a branch or distribution centre in the US and sends quantities of stock over at regular intervals, the place of supply would be the US because the goods would be in the US when customer orders were received.

Services

3.3 The basic rule for services is that a supply takes place where the supplier 'belongs', which effectively means where the business is established. If a business has fixed establishments in more than one country, the place of supply is the country containing the fixed establishment most closely associated with the service in question.

As with most rules, there are exceptions:

(*a*) services relating to land are supplied where the land is situated;

(*b*) cultural, artistic, sporting, scientific, educational and entertainment services are supplied where they are physically performed; and

(*c*) intangible, professional type services, e.g. advertising, services of accountants, lawyers, consultants etc., banking and financial services, certain telecommunications services and the supply of staff, are supplied where the recipient of the service belongs and the latter normally accounts for VAT using the 'reverse charge' mechanism described in Chapter 12.

Other relevant supplies

3.4 These include imports, EC acquisitions and imported services (see 12.40), car fuel scale charges (see 3.76) (or the actual value of fuel used for private purposes) and self-supplies (see 3.19).

Values

3.5 The value applicable to a supply of goods or services is usually the price shown on the invoice or the price agreed by the parties involved. There are, however, different methods of valuation for certain types of business such as tour operators (see Chapter 10).

When output tax is due

3.6 Goods and services are usually supplied in return for money, but not necessarily so. Payment or part payment could be in the form of other goods as in part-exchange transactions (see *Example 27* at 3.56). The tax added to the supply is then declared to Customs on the VAT return. There are, however, certain other circumstances in which output tax is due (e.g. on imported goods or services (see Chapter 12), the fuel used for private purposes in business cars (see Supplementary Example 5) and 'self-supplies' (see 3.19)) so it is dangerous to define 'output tax' as simply the VAT due on sales of goods or services (*s 5*) (see also 'Tax Points' at 3.9–3.18).

Rates of VAT

3.7 UK output tax is charged at 17.5% on all taxable supplies by registered businesses unless the law specifically states otherwise. The law provides for a special 5% rate for a limited number of supplies such as domestic fuel and power, women's sanitary products (from 1 January 2001) and certain construction services connected with urban regeneration schemes (from 12 May 2001) and for a zero rate on a significant number of items (zero-rated items being listed in *Schedule 8*). Under EC law, some zero-rated items should be subject to a positive rate of at least 5% but changes will be effected only if all EC Member States agree and with the UK always likely to vote against, the zero rate is likely to remain in place.

Supplies not subject to VAT either at a positive rate or at the zero rate are exempt and are listed in *Schedule 9*.

3.8 Zero-rating and exemptions are covered in Chapters 4 and 5, this chapter concentrating on how businesses determine when to charge standard-rated VAT and when to pay it over to Customs. The rules regarding tax invoices, refunds of VAT available on bad debts, and the principle of 'self-supplies' are also explained.

Tax points

3.9 The time of supply is called a tax point (*s 6*).

The time when VAT must be charged differs for goods and services although there are basic tax points for both unless overridden.

Basic tax point — goods

3.10 The basic tax point for a supply of goods is when they are 'removed' from the seller to the buyer. This usually means when they are delivered by the seller to the buyer either directly or through some form of agent; or when they are collected by or on behalf of the buyer. Where the goods are not physically moved but a transaction still takes place, the basic tax point is when they are first 'made available' to the buyer.

Example 18

1. Goods 'removed' to a customer

A firm of accountants orders a new photocopier which the supplier delivers. The basic tax point is when the machine is 'removed' to the firm of accountants on delivery.

2. Goods 'made available' to a customer

ABC Ltd buys steel from a stockholder to sell on immediately to its own customer and engages the services of a haulage company to pick up the goods and deliver them. The basic tax point is the time ABC Ltd acquires the right to dispose of the steel as owner.

Actual tax point — goods

3.11 Basic tax points are overridden by 'actual' tax points.

The issue of a tax invoice or the earlier receipt of full (or part) payment, are actual tax points.

Payments may be received or tax invoices issued before or after the basic tax point so particular care is needed where a transaction allows for advance payments or early invoicing.

It is possible for VAT to be due before goods (or services) are actually supplied where an invoice is issued early or a deposit is paid.

Once a basic tax point has been created, goods having been removed or made available to a customer, a tax invoice must normally be issued no more than 14 days later. This means that unless special rules or concessions apply, VAT must be charged on the sale of goods at the latest 14 days after the customer acquires ownership of them even though payment is not likely to be received until a much later date under normal commercial credit terms.

A later tax point applies if the seller has a concession to extend the 14-day period for issuing tax invoices (see 'accommodation tax points' at 3.17) or if he is using the cash accounting scheme and only declares output tax when payment is received (see 15.27–15.35).

Basic tax point — services

3.12 Unless the cash accounting scheme is being used (see Chapter 15) the basic tax point for a supply of services is the time when all work except invoicing the supply has been completed. This is normally referred to as when the service is 'performed'. The issuing of an invoice is not regarded as part of the work itself.

Example 19

An engineering company instructs a business consultant to carry out a review of its management systems and recommend how they can be improved. The work starts on 15 March and lasts 3 weeks. The basic tax point is 5 April when all work except invoicing is complete.

Actual tax point — services

3.13 As for goods, the basic tax point is overridden by an actual tax point which is the issue of a tax invoice or the receipt of payment, whichever is the earlier. Again, unless concessions or special rules apply, the tax invoice must be issued no later than 14 days after the basic tax point.

Example 20

If the consultant in *Example 19* completes VAT returns for the quarters ending 31 March, 30 June, 30 September and 31 December and he issues his tax invoice on 19 April (14 days after the work was completed), he will not actually have to pay over the VAT until he submits his June return. If he were to issue an interim invoice on, say, 26 March, the VAT element on that invoice would have to be declared on the March return if he were not using the cash accounting scheme.

Continuous supplies of services

3.14 Certain types of service are continuous and are never actually 'performed' unless the agreement between the parties involved is terminated. In such cases, there cannot be a basic tax point so the actual tax point is triggered by invoicing or earlier payment.

Example 21

An owner of commercial property has opted to charge VAT on the rent (see 8.40 *et seq.*), which is due for payment on each of the quarter days (25 March, 24 June, 29 September and 25 December). If rent is payable in advance, and a tax invoice is issued on each quarter day, the property owner must declare output tax according to the date of the invoice even though he may not have received payment from his tenants (assuming he does not operate any special scheme).

He might consider issuing a request for payment rather than a tax invoice on the quarter days which should include the words 'this is not a tax invoice'. The tax point would then be the date payment is received, at which time the tax invoice can be issued. By so doing, he would avoid the cash flow disadvantage of having to pay output tax before it had been collected from the tenants.

This principle can apply to businesses providing ongoing services and which issue invoices periodically, e.g. certain services of accountants and consultants.

Other tax point issues

Goods supplied on sale or return, approval or similar

3.15 It is not known when goods supplied on sale or return, approval or similar terms will actually be sold. Therefore, the basic tax point occurs when the customer indicates he wishes to keep them permanently. The actual tax point rules then follow. However, if the potential buyer has not indicated a desire to keep the goods at the end of 12 months from their being supplied, the tax point is then automatically created and VAT must be accounted for by the supplier.

Deposits

3.16 Where a deposit represents advance payment of part or all of the purchase price, VAT is due on the amount of the deposit when it is actually paid over or a tax invoice is issued, whichever is the earlier.

Certain other types of deposit do not represent supplies and so do not trigger tax points, viz.:

(*a*) forfeit deposits (e.g. a charge by a hotel for failure to take a booked room);

(*b*) security deposits (e.g. a charge levied to ensure the safe return of loaned goods);

(*c*) most charges for returnable containers.

Where an advance payment is received and output VAT is declared but the agreed sale falls through, the VAT paid may be recovered from Customs as there has not been and will not be a supply. The VAT can be recovered even if the deposit is not paid back.

Accommodation tax points

3.17 Under certain circumstances Customs will allow taxpayers to apply earlier or later tax points, but only where applying the normal rules would cause excessive difficulty. Taxpayers wishing to make use of this facility should apply to Customs in writing. A typical example would be a business which does all its invoicing at the end of each calendar month. Approval to extend the 14-day rule for issuing tax invoices would be required for all services completed up to the 16th or 17th of each month (or 14/15 February).

Zero-rated and exempt supplies

3.18 Although there cannot be a tax point for zero-rated or exempt supplies, nor tax payable because of the issue of a tax invoice for a zero-rated supply, it is still important to apply the 'time of supply' rules to such transactions, since both will have an impact on how much input tax is recoverable in any tax period for partly-exempt businesses (see Chapter 7) and the timing of zero-rated transactions is crucial for unregistered businesses in determining aggregate turnover and the correct date to register.

Other outputs issues

Self-supplies and goods taken for private use

3.19 Self-supplies are certain designated goods or services acquired or performed by a business from its own resources. They must be treated as a sale by and a supply to the business.

This particularly applies to self-supplies of stationery and construction services and prevents distortion of competition.

Example 22

1. Powell provides totally exempt services.

Thus any VAT charged to him by his suppliers is irrecoverable.

He prints his own stationery at a cost of £100,000.

He must account to Customs for VAT of £17,500, being equivalent to what he would pay to an outside supplier (and be unable to recover as deductible input tax).

2. Jones is a building contractor.

He builds a new office block and workshops for himself at a cost of £500,000.

> He must account to Customs for VAT of £87,500 just as if he had worked for and billed a third party.
>
> He can treat the same amount as deductible input tax unless the business is partly exempt causing a restriction in the recovery.

3.20 In both cases the transactions with VAT thereon are entered in the accounting records as sales and purchases.

With self-supplies, VAT is due when the basic tax point is triggered because no tax invoice is issued nor actual payment made. For goods, this effectively means the date they are put to the specific use which created the supply, and for services, the end of the accounting period in which they were deemed to be performed.

3.21 Where goods are taken out of stock for private or personal use, VAT is due on the cost to the business when they were bought.

Purchases of goods from other EC Member States

3.22 Businesses registered for VAT in the UK which buy goods from suppliers in other EC Member States ('EC acquisitions') must account for VAT on their purchases by including it in their returns within the amount due to Customs. It is declared to Customs in Box 2 and claimed back in Box 4.

The tax point for the acquisition is the 15th day of the month following the one in which the goods are dispatched to the UK buyer or the date the invoice is issued, whichever is the earlier (*ss 10–14*). For further information on intra-EC trade, see Chapter 11 .

Services 'imported' from abroad

3.23 VAT registered businesses which import services from abroad must account for VAT in a similar way to EC acquisitions, although the output tax is aggregated with other output tax for the period and entered in Box 1 of the return, whereas VAT on acquisitions is shown separately in Box 2.

VAT is due on the date payment is made, unless payment is not made in money, when VAT is due on the last day of the accounting period in which the services were performed (*s 8*). For more information on imported services, see Chapter 12.

Land, property and construction services

3.24 Special rules apply for determining the tax point for supplies of goods and services in connection with land, property and construction services. These are covered in detail in Chapter 8.

Tax invoices

3.25 Whenever a VAT registered business supplies goods or services to another VAT registered business in the UK, a tax invoice must be issued so that the customer holds a document which entitles him to reclaim input tax from Customs (*Sch 11 para 2*). Certain exceptions apply which are explained below.

A tax invoice need not be issued to unregistered customers (e.g. businesses with turnover less than the registration threshold or members of the general public) but, as it is not always obvious whether or not a customer is VAT registered, it is usually safer to issue a tax invoice to all customers unless the seller is a retailer dealing with the general public. It is also sound policy to issue a tax invoice whenever the customer asks for one.

A tax invoice is different from a simple invoice in that it must contain certain information to be classified as a tax invoice.

Characteristics of a tax invoice

3.26 Certain information is compulsory for a tax invoice to be valid (*regulation 14* of the *VAT Regulations 1995, SI 1995/2518*). Strictly, if any of it is missing, Customs may disallow the purchaser's input tax claim. This type of tax invoice is often referred to as a 'full' tax invoice to distinguish it from less detailed or modified tax invoices described later.

The required information is:

(*a*) a unique identifying number;

(*b*) the supplier's name, address and VAT registration number;

(*c*) the tax point;

(*d*) the date of issue (which may not necessarily be the same as the tax point);

(*e*) the customer's name and address;

(*f*) the type of supply (this will usually be a 'sale' but could be a lease, hire-purchase etc.);

(*g*) a full description of the goods or services supplied;

(*h*) the net value of each supply if there is more than one on the invoice;

(*j*) the rate and amount of VAT for each supply;

(*k*) the total amount before VAT is added;

(*l*) the total VAT and the gross amount of the whole invoice in sterling.

Businesses involved in international trade may have a commercial arrangement requiring them to invoice in a foreign currency. This is acceptable provided that a conversion to sterling is also shown and VAT where applicable is calculated on the sterling value. Where goods are sold to customers in other member states of the EC, zero-rating applies where the customer's two-letter country code and VAT registration number are also shown on the invoice. In such cases, the supplier must also prefix its own VAT registration number with 'GB'. Many businesses selling to customers in the UK and other member states prefer to have all invoices printed with the GB prefix. Chapters 11 and 12 cover international trade in detail.

Where invoices contain zero-rated or exempt supplies, they should show clearly that no VAT is payable and distinguish between the two types of supply.

Less detailed and modified tax invoices

3.27 If an invoice is to be issued for a supply the charge for which is £100 or less (including VAT), only the following information is required:

(*a*) the supplier's name, address and VAT registration number;

(*b*) the tax point;

(*c*) a description of the goods or services supplied; and

(*d*) the rate of VAT and the amount charged including VAT (this should be split if there are charges at different VAT rates included e.g. £25 for books at zero rate and £70 for stationery including VAT at 17.5%).

Again, all amounts must be in sterling but no exempt supplies can be included on such invoices. If the VAT-inclusive charge exceeds £100 or the customer asks for a VAT invoice, a full or modified tax invoice must be issued.

Modified tax invoices only show the tax-inclusive value of each standard-rated supply and the following aggregate information:

(i) the total value of standard-rated supplies including VAT;

(ii) the total VAT payable;

(iii) the total value excluding VAT;

(iv) the total value of any zero-rated supplies;

(v) the total value of any exempt supplies.

Credit card vouchers

3.28 Credit card sales vouchers may be adapted to serve as less detailed tax invoices.

Receipts for fuel purchases

3.29 A less detailed invoice may be issued for VAT-inclusive sales of £100 or less and, if the total is more, the vehicle registration number may be used instead of the customer's name and address. The type of supply and volume of fuel supplied are not required.

Cash and carry wholesalers

3.30 Till rolls can be used as tax invoices provided the following conditions are met:

(*a*) products must be coded using a system involving at least two digits;

(*b*) code lists must be prepared and maintained and up-to-date copies given to customers;

(*c*) till rolls must contain all the information required on a full tax invoice;

(*d*) copies of till rolls and code lists must be kept for at least six years unless the local VAT office agrees otherwise.

Failure to meet any of the above means a full tax invoice must be issued.

Pro forma invoices

3.31 Some businesses issue such invoices before it is clear whether the potential customer will actually buy the goods or services shown. The actual supply usually depends on payment being made. Pro forma invoices are not acceptable evidence for input tax claims so the words '**this is not a tax invoice**' should be added. If and when the goods or services are actually supplied, a proper tax invoice must be issued subject to the normal rules explained above.

Self-billing

3.32 In certain circumstances, it is acceptable for a customer to make out the tax invoice to itself. A copy is then issued to the supplier with payment. Prior written approval from the local VAT office, agreement from the customer and an undertaking from the supplier not to issue tax invoices for the same supplies are prerequisites for self-billing.

Customs will always require businesses operating self-billing to keep regularly updated lists of suppliers which have agreed to the arrangement and insist, for obvious reasons, that all suppliers included are VAT registered.

Authenticated receipts

3.33 These are alternatives to tax invoices allowed under certain circumstances in the construction industry (see Chapter 8). They are issued under contracts for services where stage payments are made.

They must:

(*a*) contain all the information required on a full tax invoice;

(*b*) be signed by the supplier i.e. 'authenticated';

(*c*) be the only document issued i.e. no other form of tax invoice must be issued.

Computer invoicing

3.34 Computer invoices, issued by whatever medium, must contain all the normal information required. The intention to issue and receive invoices on magnetic tape, disk or any other electronic means requires one month's written notice to the local VAT Business Advice Centre and the approval will contain certain fully explained conditions.

Faxed invoices

3.35 These are acceptable, especially via plain paper fax machines, but since the shiny, flimsy paper produced from thermal-paper machines fades over time, this should be borne in mind considering that records must be kept for at least six years.

E-mail invoices

3.36 While these are acceptable, Customs have discerned a potential problem with self-billed e-mail invoices in that not all messages passed via this medium are legible when they reach the recipient. Therefore, the person issuing the self-billed invoice should advise the supplier to contact him immediately if this problem occurs.

Annual invoices

3.37 For certain supplies which are made on a continuous or successive basis, an invoice may be issued up to a period of one year in advance showing:

(*a*) the date each payment is due;

(*b*) the net amount due on each payment date;

(*c*) the rate and amount of VAT due on each payment date.

This type of invoice is often used for supplies of gas or electricity, or for leasing of goods such as equipment or cars.

Refunds of VAT on bad debts

3.38 For several years now, VAT registered businesses have been able to claim a refund of output tax included in bad debts although the conditions for making claims have changed frequently, the most recent significant changes being made in November 1996.

The scheme provides relief for those businesses which issue tax invoices in advance of payment, declare output tax accordingly and which are unable to take advantage of accounting schemes delaying output tax accountability until their customers have paid them. If customers fail to pay them within a given period of time, the output tax already declared on an earlier VAT return may be reclaimed with input tax in Box 4 of the VAT Return.

Relief is now available six months after the due date of payment compared with six months after the tax point under the earlier rules.

Example 23

(*a*) A construction company which completes VAT returns for the quarters ending 31 January, *et seq.* issued a tax invoice to a customer on 30 April 1996 for £10,000 + £1,750 VAT and paid the output tax on the April 1996 return. Payment had still not been received by the end of October, so assuming all other conditions were met, bad debt relief could be claimed on the October 1996 return. (Note that this is an example of the old rule. This claim would now be barred as it is over three years old.)

(*b*) The same company issued an invoice to a different customer on 30 April 2001 for £10,000 + £1,750 VAT. Payment terms are 30 days from the tax point so settlement should have been received by 30 May. However, payment had still not been received by the end of October. Under the new rules bad debt relief is available six months from 30 May rather than 30 April so it would not be due until 30 November. The claim itself would be made on the January 2002 return.

3.39 The conditions that must be fulfilled for a refund claim to be valid are as follows (*s 36*):

- VAT must have been paid to Customs on the relevant supplies;
- the debt must have been written off in the claimant's accounts and transferred to a separate bad debt account — satisfied by a memo account or list of all refund claims each quarter which can be cross-referred to the original payment of output tax;
- at least six months must have elapsed since the due date for payment.

FA 1999, s 15 amended *VATA 1994, s 36* and *Sch 11* to close a loophole formerly allowing certain businesses to claim too much bad debt relief. The definition of 'receipt of payment' now includes someone to whom the right to receive a payment has been assigned. The time of supply (tax point) is therefore now the same for receipt of payment by the supplier or an assignee.

3.40 The November 1996 changes also provided that:

- for supplies made on or after 26 November 1996, where the debtor is a VAT registered business, the claimant must notify the debtor in writing within seven days of making a claim and the debtor must repay to Customs the input tax claimed if he has not paid his supplier in the six-month time limit and has received the written notification from the supplier;
- ownership of goods need no longer have passed to the customer or through the customer to a third party;
- a claim cannot be made on a VAT return prior to that in which entitlement to the refund arose, but those operating the annual accounting scheme (see 15.36) may declare output tax and claim a bad debt refund on the same return where appropriate;

- a purchaser of a business as a going concern (see 6.28) may claim relief on supplies made by the seller so long as the purchaser takes over the same VAT registration number and all the debts and liabilities of the business;
- claims must be made within three years and six months of the tax point or due date for payment, whichever is the later;
- the debtor must make appropriate adjustments to his VAT account to reflect the input tax no longer reclaimable.

3.41 In addition, because of a European Court of Justice ruling in *Goldsmiths Jewellers Ltd (Case C-330/95)* — issued on 3 July 1997, Customs now accept that they were wrong in applying a previous condition, that the debt must have been due in money. Therefore, there is now scope for retrospective claims where businesses have not claimed relief because 'payment' was due in the form of other goods or services which have failed to materialise (*FA 1998, s 23*). The conditions for such claims are set out in Customs' Business Brief 21/97 issued on 3 October 1997.

Bad debts — records and documentation required

3.42 The identifying number and date of each invoice should be listed in the claim, supported by a copy of the invoice or, if no invoice was issued, documentation showing all the relevant information.

There must be a reference to the tax period in which the output tax was originally included in the VAT return and, alongside it, the tax period in which the refund is claimed. Part payments received should also be shown (see 3.43 below for the effect on a claim).

The bad debt account must also show all amounts included in each claim, identifying the goods/services and the VAT element separately.

Receipt of part payment before or after entitlement to a bad debt refund arises

3.43 The amount of the claim is the debt outstanding six months after the due date for payment. Usually this is the whole of a particular invoice but not always. If a part payment is received, the refund available is the VAT included in the amount still outstanding. If customers pay on account and more than one invoice has been issued, payments must be allocated to the earliest invoices first.

Example 24

Thomson is a trader who makes both standard-rated and zero-rated sales. He has made the following sales:

Date of Supply 2000	Due Date for Payment 2000	Rate	Price excluding VAT	VAT	Total
			£	£	£
14 April	31 May	Standard	2,100	367	2,467
18 May	30 June	Zero	1,430	–	1,430
20 June	31 July	Standard	1,212	212	1,424
1 August	30 September	Standard	1,520	266	1,786
30 August	30 September	Zero	800	–	800
			7,062	845	7,907

Thomson received the following payments on account:

2000	£
18 July	1,800
7 September	850

At a meeting of the creditors on 1 November 2000 the debt due to Thomson was proved and a resolution to wind up the company was passed.

Thomson submits his VAT returns quarterly for the periods ending 31 January, 30 April, 31 July and 31 October.

The bad debt relief that Thomson may claim for VAT purposes is as follows:

Bad debt relief claimable under VATA 1994, s 36

Tax point	Payment Date	Gross Debt	Payment Received (FIFO*)	Unpaid	VAT Fraction	VAT
		£	£	£		£
14.4.00	31.5.00	2,467	2,467	–	–	–
18.5.00	30.6.00	1,430	183	1,247	–	–
20.6.00	31.7.00	1,424	–	1,424	7/47	212
1.8.00	30.9.00	1,786	–	1,786	7/47	266
30.8.00	30.9.00	800	–	800	–	–
			2,650	5,257		478

Bad debt relief claimable:

Input Tax	**Payment Due Date**	**Relief Claimable From**	**In Quarter Ended**
£			
212	31.7.00	31.1.01	31.1.01
266	30.9.00	31.3.01	30.4.01
Debt to be claimed from liquidator			£5,257

* FIFO = 'first in, first out'

3.44 If a payment is received from the debtor after a refund has been claimed, the VAT element must be repaid to Customs by inclusion in Box 1 of the VAT return for the period in which it is received. If the VAT-inclusive amount of the debt is recovered under a bad debts insurance policy, no repayment to Customs is necessary.

Bad debt relief — mutual debts

3.45 If an entitlement to a bad debt refund arises but the supplier also owes an amount to his customer (perhaps other types of goods or services are supplied by the customer to the supplier), a refund is only available on the difference between the two.

Example 25

Y Ltd supplies services to Z Ltd for £1,000 + £175 VAT on 30 April and the due date for payment was 31 May. Z Ltd supplies goods to Y Ltd on 15 June for £200 + £35 VAT. If Z Ltd has not paid by the end of November, Y Ltd may claim a refund of £175 less the £35 VAT within the amount it owes to Z Ltd i.e. £140.

3.46 Annexes A to C of Customs' Leaflet 700/18 'Relief from VAT on Bad Debts' provide useful examples of how to calculate refunds in part payment and mutual debt situations.

Refunds to deregistered businesses

3.47 Clearly, deregistered businesses cannot use Box 4 of VAT returns for making claims. However, they may claim by writing to the local VAT office supplying the following information:

- the VAT number they had when registered;
- names and addresses of debtors;

- the amount claimed;
- copies of relevant invoices or the equivalent;
- proof that the six-month time limit has passed and evidence of a suitable bad debt ledger account.

Bad debt relief — insolvent customers

3.48 If, after a claim to Customs for bad debt relief, a customer becomes formally insolvent, creditors should still claim the tax-inclusive amount of the debt in the insolvency. If an amount is subsequently received from the liquidator, the business should pay back to Customs the VAT recovered by inclusion in Box 1 of the next return.

Group registrations and bad debt refunds

3.49 Although all business activities are deemed to be channelled through the representative member of a VAT group as explained in Chapter 2, each member must keep its own separate bad debt account. Refunds due on each return are aggregated by the representative member and claimed accordingly.

Credit notes

3.50 Credit notes may only be issued to reflect a genuine mistake or overcharge. Therefore, they may not be issued for debts written off in suppliers' accounts.

Mixed and composite supplies

3.51 When a business sells a mixture of goods and/or services, it is important to decide whether each element of the sale should be treated separately for VAT purposes (a 'mixed' supply) or whether only one supply is being made, albeit made up of two or more parts (a 'composite' supply).

Example 26

(*a*) A wholesaler sells goods regularly to a supermarket. The latest invoice is for food items, wines and tobacco products. This is a mixed supply which must be split between the items sold at different rates. Most of the food items are zero-rated (except perhaps crisps and chocolate biscuits) but the wines and tobacco products are standard-rated. Often the products will be coded, say 1 for standard-rated and 2 for zero-rated goods, so a total for each rate will be shown.

(*b*) See Supplementary Example 1 in the examples at the end of this book for the application of this rule to retail schemes.

If it is not possible to split the price of a mixed supply, the total must be split on a pro rata basis using a method accepted by Customs as fair and reasonable.

Composite supplies

3.52 These must be distinguished from mixed supplies.

The most well-known example of a composite supply is the *British Airways* case (*[1990] STC 643*).

Passenger transport is zero-rated, whereas catering is standard-rated.

Customs tried to make a case for there being a mixed supply, meaning VAT would have been due on the catering element of ticket prices. However, it was decided that BA were only supplying passenger transport of which the catering was an integral part.

Therefore, the whole of each ticket price was zero-rated.

For a further example see 4.30.

Where there is any doubt as to whether a supply is mixed or composite, the matter should be cleared through Customs.

A recent ECJ case, *Card Protection Plan,* which was subsequently heard further by the House of Lords (*[2001] STC 174*) involved the principles of mixed and composite supplies. The ECJ decided that in most situations where a single charge covers more than one thing, the VAT treatment of the main supply should prevail. As a result, Customs will normally consider there to be only one supply in many cases where, in the past, they have accepted mixed supplies. The VAT treatment will be determined by the principal goods or services supplied.

How the principles laid down in the ECJ case will work in practice is uncertain but the changes could affect many businesses. For example, if there is only one supply by opticians it might be the standard-rated spectacles rather than the exempt eye test.

Businesses are required to apply the ECJ principles by 1 June 2001 in deciding whether they are making mixed or composite supplies although they are not required to make retrospective adjustments to the period before 1 June 2001 if they relied on the incorrect UK treatment at the time. If retrospective application of the ECJ principles results in less VAT due, businesses may request a refund subject to the three-year cap.

By concession, non-profit-making membership bodies may continue to split subscriptions, allocating a certain proportion to the benefits supplied such as an amount attributable to a zero-rated publication for members. They are not required to treat each subscription as a single exempt supply as would be the case if the ECJ case principles were enforced.

Delivery charges and postage

3.53 If a business supplies goods to its customer and makes arrangements for them to be posted or delivered in return for an extra charge, the amount relating to the delivery or postage is standard-rated unless they are sent abroad, in which case it is zero-rated. This applies even though the charge to the supplier by the Post Office is exempt.

If the agreement with the customer requires the business to deliver or post the goods, the element relating to the postage or delivery takes the same VAT liability as the goods themselves. If the goods are standard-rated, so is the delivery charge, but if the goods are zero-rated (e.g. books), the delivery charge is also zero-rated.

There are significant precedents on the subject of delivery charges. The issues are complicated, and this chapter only provides an overview of outputs issues, the following being relevant:

— *C&E Commrs v British Telecommunications plc HL,* [*1999*] *STC 758*;

— *C&E Commrs v Plantiflor Ltd CA,* [*2000*] *STC 137*.

Customs have sought leave to appeal the Court of Appeal decision in *Plantiflor* to the House of Lords (Business Brief 7/2000, 18 May 2000).

Packaging and containers

3.54 Any normal amount of packaging used to send goods to a customer can be ignored. For example, the sale of a packet of digestive biscuits is zero-rated even though the packaging on its own would be standard-rated. Effectively, the purchaser is only paying for the contents of the packet.

There are two sets of circumstances when VAT is due on the packaging:

(*a*) when the amount of packaging is more than is normal or necessary (but see 4.12 re food packaging). Customs cite the example of storage containers in their Public Notice 700 'The VAT Guide' para 3.3; and

(*b*) where a separate charge is made. This applies if the charge is made when the packaging or containers are sent out or returned although, in the case of refundable deposits, the VAT element may also be refunded.

Sales of second-hand goods

3.55 Special schemes exist for second-hand goods. These are covered in detail in Chapter 9. Essentially, providing certain conditions are met, no input tax is claimed on the purchase of such goods but output tax is only paid on the difference between the buying and selling price.

Part-exchange transactions

3.56 These are treated as two transactions: a sale and a purchase.

Example 27

A transport company buys a new lorry for £20,000 + £3,500 VAT. The supplier takes an old lorry in part exchange and allows £5,000. Therefore, the transport company only pays £18,500.

The supplier has made a sale for £20,000 + VAT and a purchase for £5,000 *including* VAT (assuming the transport company is registered for VAT).

The supplier should issue a tax invoice for £20,000 + VAT and the transport company should issue a tax invoice for £4,255.32 + £744.68 VAT (= £5,000), although both transactions are often set out within one document.

Business gifts

3.57 To come within this definition goods or services must be provided of one's own free will with no conditions attached.

If the value of *goods* supplied to each recipient is no greater than £50 (from 8 March 2001, previously £15), no output tax is due (*Sch 4 para 5(2)*). If the value exceeds £50, output VAT must be paid on the cost to the giver.

Example 28

(i) ABC Ltd buys 150 bottles of whisky and gives 3 each to 50 customers as Christmas gifts. Each bottle costs £15. ABC Ltd may recover input tax in full on the purchase and no output tax is due because the value to each recipient is less than £50.

(ii) DEF Ltd buys 100 bottles of whisky and gives 4 each to 25 customers as Christmas gifts. Each bottle costs £15. DEF may recover input tax in full on the purchase but as the value to each recipient is more than £50 (i.e. £60), output tax is due on the cost. DEF must pay as output tax the same amount as has been claimed as input tax.

To come within this *de minimis* provision, the goods must not be part of a series or succession of gifts to the same person.

Exceptionally, while free meals provided to employees count as gifts, they are not counted as within a series of transactions.

3.58 New *subparagraphs 5(2A)* and *5(5A)* were inserted into *VATA 1994, Sch 4* with effect from 16 March 1998. The change ensured that where businesses give away goods they have acquired without VAT as a result of a transfer of a going concern, they must calculate the cost on which to pay output tax by reference to the original cost to the business that bought them. This might be the immediate transferor or even an earlier owner of the goods if there has been more than one going concern transfer. Prior to this date, there would have been no cost to the donor in such a situation and no output tax would have been payable.

3.59 Zero-rating applies to gifts of goods to charities for sale or export by them, or to sales by VAT registered businesses which covenant all their profits to a charity (see 4.61).

3.60 Services supplied free of charge are not supplies for VAT purposes and no output tax is due provided that the supplier provides them of his own free will and they are not inextricably linked to an obligation on the part of the recipient to do something in return.

Loss of goods

3.61 If goods are lost, destroyed or stolen, whether or not output tax is due depends on the agreement between supplier and customer.

If the goods have been supplied, VAT is due by the supplier.

Where goods are lost en route to a customer and the agreement states that the supplier is responsible for any loss before delivery, output tax is due as is the case where the customer is responsible but a tax invoice has already been issued. However, where the customer is responsible and a tax invoice has not been issued, there has been no supply and no output tax is due by the supplier.

If an insurer is entitled under the terms of a policy to acquire the damaged goods, no VAT is payable by the insured person on their value.

Theft of goods and cash

3.62 If goods are stolen before they are sold, no VAT is due because there has been no supply, but if cash held from the sale is stolen, no reduction of output tax is permitted because the cash originally taken has triggered the tax point.

Hire purchase and similar transactions

3.63 Where goods are made available to a customer who, having the option to purchase them, becomes the owner after a certain time or owns them immediately but pays for them by instalments, there is a supply when the customer takes delivery of the goods or they are made available.

Output tax is due on the full taxable value at that point.

If finance is provided, a part of the transaction will relate to the provision of credit. Sometimes this is provided by the supplier of the goods but more often they are sold to a finance company which in turn sells them to the customer.

For a supply of credit to be exempt from VAT, the credit amount must be disclosed separately in writing to the customer. Without the separate disclosure, the full amount paid by the customer is subject to VAT at the appropriate rate even if there is a credit facility within the sale agreement.

The supplier should ensure the tax invoice is issued to the right person. The finance company should receive the invoice if it takes ownership of the goods but in certain circumstances such as loan arrangements, the customer takes the title direct and should receive the invoice.

The above should not be confused with arrangements in which the supplier retains title to the goods but they are used by his customer, e.g. operating leases, contract hire and equipment rental, where output tax is payable on each stage payment as and when it falls due (see 'Annual invoices' at 3.37).

Use of business stocks and assets

3.64 VAT is not normally due where goods or services made or acquired by a business are *used in the business* rather than being sold or provided to customers.

There are exceptions:

(i) certain stationery produced and used by partly exempt businesses;

(ii) cars used by motor manufacturers, vehicle dealers or vehicle converters in their business, although output tax is still not due on the sale of certain cars if recovery of input tax was blocked in the first place, e.g. on demonstration cars sold by dealers under the second-hand margin scheme (see Chapter 9);

(iii) cars put to another use by businesses which were entitled to claim input tax on their purchase for a qualifying use e.g. for a driving school or for private hire;

(iv) houses and certain other types of residential property constructed or extended by more than 10% by reference to floor area by a partly exempt business using its own labour.

All these situations create a 'self-supply' whereby output tax is payable on the value of the supply and input tax is recovered to the extent allowed by the partial exemption apportionment calculation (see Chapter 7).

Where goods are used privately by the owner, or perhaps by his friends or by relatives, VAT is due on the cost of the goods calculated as follows:

$$\text{depreciation on the goods} + \text{other costs related to the use of the goods} \times \frac{\text{private use element}}{\text{total use}}$$

Special rules apply for calculating the private use of fuel for motor cars (see 3.76).

Payphones and phonecards

3.65 Businesses with payphones on their premises may recover input tax on payphone bills received.

The amounts received for the calls belong to the business and output tax is due.

Some retailers act as agents for BT in the sale of phonecards. Output tax is due on the commission they receive. The method of accounting depends on the method of recording takings used by the agent and on which retail scheme is operated (see 14.22 and Supplementary Examples 1 and 3).

Cancellation charges, booking fees etc.

3.66 In certain types of business, especially where supplies are made by ticket sales or reservations, it is not uncommon for cancellation charges or booking fees to be levied.

Cancellation charges are not subject to VAT because there has been no supply. Booking fees are levied whether or not the supply takes place and they are subject to VAT.

If a guarantee or insurance is provided against a customer having to pay cancellation charges, any actual charge to the customer remains subject to VAT.

If arrangements are made for a specific supply of insurance from a permitted insurer, any commission received is exempt from VAT.

Tips and donations

3.67 A tip or donation is usually outside the scope of VAT provided that it is given voluntarily and there is no obligation to give it nor any obligation on the part of the recipient to do anything in return.

Change of rate

3.68 Where there is a change in VAT rate, or VAT liability, tax is charged in accordance with the normal tax point rules. It is therefore essential to determine the time of supply for any given transaction. In particular, it is important to note that a VAT invoice must be issued (i.e. sent to the customer) to create a tax point. The mere preparation of a

VAT invoice does not create a tax point. Nor does the issue of a zero-rated or exempt supply invoice create a tax point.

If a taxable trader wishes, he may adopt special rules on a change of rate (*s 88*). This permits the adoption of the basic tax point for a supply rather than the normal tax point. This means that the rate of VAT charged on goods removed or services performed before the date of the rate change can be the previous rate even though the tax point would normally be established by the issue of a VAT invoice after the date of change.

Example 29
Say the 17.5% rate of VAT is increased to 20% on 1 April 2002 and the following circumstances applied: 26 March 2002 goods removed, 5 April 2002 VAT invoice issued. Under the normal rules the date of issue of the VAT invoice would be the tax point and therefore 20% VAT would apply. Under the special provisions the basic tax point applies, i.e. time of removal 26 March 2002, and VAT will be charged at 17.5%.

In the case of a reduction in VAT, the charge may be at the new rate on goods removed, or services performed, after the date of change, and at the old rate on goods removed or services performed before the date of change, even though payment has been received or a VAT invoice issued before the date of change.

A credit note must then be issued within 14 days after the change containing the following details (*SI 1995/2518, reg 15*):

(*a*) identifying number and date of issue of credit note;

(*b*) supplier's name, address and registration number;

(*c*) customer's name and address;

(*d*) identifying number and date of issue of original invoice;

(*e*) description which identifies the goods or services;

(*f*) amount of VAT credited.

> *Example 30*
>
> Say the VAT rate of 17.5% is reduced to 15% from 1 April 2002 and the following circumstances applied: 26 March 2002 VAT invoice issued (or payment received), 5 April 2002 goods removed.
>
> Under the normal rules the VAT charged would be at 17.5%, i.e. the old rate. Using the special provisions the basic tax point applies and VAT is due at only 15%, a credit note being issued for the difference.

Where services are involved, it is necessary under the special rules to apportion the services between those taking place before the date of change and those after the date of change. This can be done on the basis of:

(i) measurable work;

(ii) normal costing or pricing systems.

Under the special provisions it is then possible to charge the work done prior to the date of change at the old rate and that done after the date of change at the new rate, with the issue of a credit note as above if the VAT is reduced.

Where a VAT invoice has been issued for continuous services (for a period of up to one year ahead) then that invoice is no longer valid in respect of payments due after the date of change and a new VAT invoice must be issued for such payments. The new invoice must refer to and cancel the appropriate parts of the original VAT invoice. Such a revised invoice can also incorporate the special provisions mentioned above, apportioning the service that spans the date of change.

Care must be taken in the case of clubs or associations. It is normally considered that the tax point for the supply of facilities by member subscription is the time that the subscription is received, or the VAT invoice is issued, whichever occurs first. Accordingly, apportionment is not normally available. However, if payment is accepted in instalments or separate invoices are issued then the rules for continuous services set out at 3.14 above apply.

If a contract is made for a supply of goods or services and there is a change in the VAT rate before the actual supply then, unless the contract provides otherwise, the consideration for the supply is increased (or decreased) by the change in rate (*s 89*).

A taxable trader will complete his VAT return for his normal accounting period. There will be no division shown between the old and new rates.

Cash accounting (see 15.27–15.35)

3.69 Where a trader is using cash accounting, similar rules apply to the above. However, having worked out the VAT payable at the appropriate rate, the trader does not account for the VAT until it is received. It is therefore necessary to analyse receipts carefully between supplies made before the change and those made after the change.

Retail schemes (see 14.22) and second-hand schemes (see Chapter 9)

3.70 Now that traders have to compute takings based upon the normal date of supply, the provisions at 3.68 and 3.69 above will apply. The change of rate rules are set out in Appendix C to Notice 727 for each individual scheme.

In the case of second-hand schemes the margin is determined by the tax point of the sale. This is either the date of removal of the goods, or the date of payment, whichever is the earlier. The special change of rate provisions are available and VAT can be accounted for at the rate at the date of removal (basic tax point) if preferred.

Input tax is recovered at the rate charged on the invoice. If it is a less detailed VAT invoice, then the rate is computed by using the fraction for the appropriate tax point.

Agents

3.71 Not every business that calls itself an agent for particular activities is an agent for VAT purposes. A pure agent:

- enters into a contractual agreement (which can be written or oral) with his principal to arrange supplies of goods or services on his behalf,
- never takes title to goods supplied by the principal,
- never uses services supplied by the principal, and
- only receives commission for his services to the principal.

Therefore, businesses such as employment agencies and distributors usually act as principals rather than agents whereas, for example, solicitors can act as agents in arranging search fees or Land Registry fees for clients.

Agents acting in the name of their principals

3.72 Where an agent acts in the name of his principal, the sales invoice should be completed showing the principal as the supplier of goods or services to the ultimate customer. The agent then invoices his principal for his services and adds VAT if he is registered.

Agents acting in their own name

3.73 Sometimes, however, agents act in their own name. This is often because the supplier does not wish to be known to the customer. The term normally used is 'an agent acting for an undisclosed principal'. Sales in these circumstances may be treated as a sale by the principal to the agent and by the agent to the customer provided that:

- the principal and the agent are both VAT registered, and
- the supplies involved are taxable.

In Business Brief 9/2000, 30 June 2000, Customs announced changes to the treatment of supplies by agents of undisclosed principals from 1 July 2000. The changes apply to agents involved in intra-community and non-EC transactions.

Previously, UK agents of undisclosed principals could not be involved in the main supply of goods or services from their principal to the final customer. The agent would simply pass on the charge from the principal to the final customer and then make a separate supply of his own services to the principal. Under certain circumstances, this put UK agents, governed by UK common law, at a competitive disadvantage compared to most foreign agents, governed by Roman civil law. The changes enable UK agents to act in the same way as those governed by civil law. In practice, this means that they can now become involved in the main transaction and take their commission by charging the final customer a higher price rather than having to make a separate charge to the principal.

Invoicing between agents, principals and customers

3.74 The correct way to invoice and declare VAT is slightly different according to whether the agent is acting for the seller or buyer and whether he is acting in the name of the principal or in his own name as follows:

3.75 *VAT on Outputs*

Agent acting for seller in seller's name

The sales invoice is made out from the seller to the buyer and is sent direct to the buyer or through the agent. The agent issues his own separate invoice to the seller for his commission and adds VAT if he is registered.

Agent acting for seller in his own name

Assuming the supplies involved are standard-rated, the seller invoices the agent and adds VAT; the agent then invoices the buyer for the same amount and adds VAT. The agent then pays output tax and claims input tax on the appropriate VAT return. He must not claim the input tax before he has paid the output tax. Normally, the tax is paid and claimed simultaneously. Finally, the agent invoices the seller for his commission and adds VAT if he is registered.

Agent acting for buyer in buyer's name

The sales invoice is made out from the seller to the buyer and the agent issues his own separate invoice to the buyer showing VAT if he is registered.

Agent acting for buyer in his own name

In a similar way to a selling agent acting in his own name and assuming the supplies involved are standard-rated, the seller invoices the agent and adds VAT. The agent then invoices the same value for the supplier's goods or services to the buyer but shows his own commission separately on the same invoice. The agent then claims input tax and pays output tax in the same way as before, as in the following example:

Seller's invoice to agent: Goods £2,000 + £350 VAT = £2,350

Agent recovers £350 input tax

Agent's invoice to buyer: Goods £2,000 + £350 VAT; Commission £200 + £35 = £2,585

Agent pays £385 output tax.

Disbursements

3.75 Sometimes, incidental costs that a business incurs in making a supply of goods or services to its customer (usually called 'disbursements') are not subject to VAT. If certain conditions are fulfilled, the supplier does not claim input tax on the disbursement or pay output tax on the value recharged to the customer. The conditions are as follows:

- the supplier acts as agent of the customer when he pays the third party;
- the customer actually receives and uses the goods or services provided by the third party (this normally means that the agent's own travelling, subsistence and similar costs cannot be treated as disbursements for VAT purposes);
- the customer is responsible for paying the third party;
- the customer authorises the supplier to make the payment on his behalf;
- the customer knows that the goods or services paid for by the supplier will be provided by a third party;
- the supplier's payments on the customer's behalf will be listed separately when he invoices his customer;
- the supplier recovers only the exact amount he pays to the third party; and
- the goods or services which the supplier pays for are clearly additional to the supplies he makes to his customer on his own account.

All of the conditions must be fulfilled for the treatment to apply. As there is no entitlement to input tax and no output tax payable, the most beneficial time to treat relevant costs as disbursements is when there is no VAT on the third party supplies or the customer is not VAT registered.

Fuel scale charges

3.76 Businesses that claim input tax on car fuel must pay a set amount as output tax known as the 'fuel scale charge' if the car is used for private as well as business motoring. This amount is deemed to cover the amount the vehicle is used for private purposes during the relevant tax period. It should be noted that journeys from home to office are private.

The charge applies to sole traders, partners, employees and anybody else where private use is involved. It is possible to avoid the charge in two ways:

- by notifying Customs that no input tax at all will be claimed on fuel, or

- by keeping a detailed analysis of business journeys and claiming a mileage rate agreed with Customs. (Most businesses find this method an administrative burden and prefer to pay the scale charge.)

The rates are revised from time to time, the last change applicable from tax periods beginning on or after 6 April 2001 (see Table of Rates). These rates vary according to bands of engine size and according to whether the vehicle runs on petrol or diesel. Tables covering annual, quarterly and monthly returns are available from local VAT offices and in VAT leaflet 700/64 'Motoring Expenses'.

Where a car is made available to employees for the purposes of their employment and fuel is provided for them by their employer for less than it has cost him, the employer can reclaim input tax on the original fuel cost and pay the scale charge. This UK treatment has been questioned in the EC because the fuel is not supplied to the taxable person, but no changes are expected in the short term.

The scale charge is added to output tax in Box 1 of the appropriate VAT return. The value producing that amount of VAT is included with other net outputs in Box 6 e.g. the scale charge on a petrol driven car with an engine size between 1400cc and 2000cc is £45.72 per quarter. £45.72 is entered in Box 1 and £261 in Box 6. See Supplementary Example 4.

Miscellaneous issues

3.77 Many other areas of business activity will raise issues as to whether or not VAT is due on outputs and where there is doubt Customs should be asked for written clarification.

Chapter 4

The Zero and Reduced Rate

Introduction

4.1 The EC Sixth Directive does not recognise zero-rating as such but allows exemption from VAT with the right to claim input tax on associated expenditure for certain types of transaction, notably exports.

4.2 Allowance is also made for certain goods or services considered to be basic necessities or which should be subject to some form of relief for the common good, e.g. certain supplies to and by charities, but under EC law, those supplies should be subject to VAT at a minimum rate of 5%. Most of these items are taxed at 0% in the UK, the 'zero rate', and as any change requires a unanimous vote from all member states, there is unlikely to be any change in the short term.

4.3 As well as the zero rate, a reduced rate applies to a limited number of goods and services. The main reduced rate supplies are domestic supplies of gas and electricity (or more generally, fuel and power); women's sanitary products (from 1 January 2001) and certain residential renovations and conversions (from 12 May 2001). All reduced rate supplies have now been consolidated into a new *Schedule 7A* to *VATA 1994*.

4.4 Clearly, it is important for businesses to charge the correct rate of VAT on their outputs and extra care is required if there is a possibility of more than one rate applying. Businesses that make zero-rated supplies benefit because they are entitled to recover all VAT on associated standard-rated expenditure, whereas those that make exempt supplies cannot normally recover the VAT on associated costs.

4.5 This chapter analyses the general rules for each group of zero-rated supply in the order they appear in *Sch 8* and then describes each type of reduced rate supply.

The Zero Rate

Group 1 — Food

4.6 Food and catering must be distinguished. A supply of catering involves some form of preparation service in making food available to customers. Therefore, takings of cafés, restaurants and other eating establishments are not supplies of food and are standard-rated.

Hot take-away food is also standard-rated because a process has been applied to the food before sale in the form of heating, whereas cold take-away food is zero-rated.

Example 31

A local café situated near an industrial estate also supplies a range of sandwiches, hot pies etc. to be taken away. Hot pies and hot sandwiches sold to be taken away are standard-rated whereas cold take-away sandwiches are zero-rated. Any food or drink it sells for consumption on the café premises is a standard-rated supply of catering.

Some factory workers buy frozen pies from a supermarket or other products which they cook themselves using a microwave oven in their factory staff room. These purchases are zero-rated.

Where food is delivered for a function, the supply is of standard-rated catering unless the customer has to perform further preparation, in which case the supply is of food and zero-rated. If there is a nominal amount of further preparation, such as arranging delivered food on plates, the zero rate still applies.

4.7 Anything in the list of general items at 4.8 is zero-rated unless within the list of exceptions at 4.9. The legislation is confusing, its understanding being assisted by Customs Leaflet 701/14 'Food'.

4.8 The main zero-rated items comprise *four general categories*:

- food for human consumption
- animal foodstuffs
- seeds or other means of propagation of plants comprised in either of the above categories
- live animals which are themselves used as food for human consumption or which yield or produce the same, e.g. lambs which themselves are eaten, or chickens which produce eggs etc.

Customs use the expression 'held out for sale' to refer to the way a product is described. The term means the way the particular item is described on packaging, labelling, invoices, signs or adverts or in any form of promotional material including catalogues and price lists. The way it is held out for sale determines whether or not zero-rating applies. The customer must be in no doubt as to what he is buying at any given time. Subject to the exceptions at 4.9, if items in the main list in this paragraph are held out for sale as such, they are zero-rated.

4.9 The exceptions which are standard-rated are:

- ice cream and ice cream products including lollies, frozen yoghurts and mixes for making these products;
- confectionery — this includes biscuits wholly or partly covered in chocolate or 'some product similar in taste and appearance' and has historically caused problems concerning interpretation — for example, Jaffa cakes are cakes and not biscuits following a long drawn out case to decide the issue;
- beers, wines and spirits;
- fruit juices, bottled waters and products used to make them;
- snack products made from potatoes or cereal products (prawn crackers are standard-rated when potato based but zero-rated where the basic ingredient is tapioca);
- salted or roasted nuts but not nuts in their shells;
- canned, prepared or packaged pet foods, including packaged foods for birds (other than poultry or game) and biscuits and meal for cats and dogs;
- any goods in the first three of the main zero-rated categories at 4.8 which are canned, prepared, bottled or packaged for use in brewing beer, making cider or perry, or producing wine or made-wine *at home*.

4.10 Some of the exceptions to zero-rating are themselves overridden, Customs' Leaflet providing a fairly extensive list of common products involved. For example:

(1) In the ice cream category, similar products including mousses which have to be thawed thoroughly before they can be eaten are zero-rated.

(2) In the confectionery category, chocolate eclairs and chocolate spread are both excluded and thus zero-rated. On the other hand, cereal bars remain standard-rated although it is arguable whether they should be.

Mixtures and assortments

4.11 Here the value of each part needs to be calculated where the sale includes standard and zero-rated goods, unless the standard-rated element is small and hence can be ignored.

Thus the following are zero-rated:

- biscuit assortments — provided the weight of standard-rated chocolate biscuits does not exceed 15% of the total net weight;
- fruit and nut mixes — provided the standard-rated element does not exceed 25% of the total net weight;
- petits fours assortments containing standard-rated chocolate biscuits or sweets — provided:

  (*a*) the net weight of chocolate biscuits or the combined net weight of chocolate biscuits and sweets does not exceed 15% of the total net weight, or

  (*b*) if sweets are the only standard-rated product included, their net weight does not exceed 25% of the total net weight.

Where these weight percentages are exceeded, it is possible that the current treatment may change as a result of the *Card Protection Plan* case (see 3.52).

Packaging

4.12 The general treatment of packaging is explained at 3.54. If packaging over and above that which is necessary is used with zero-rated food items, the whole supply can still be zero-rated so long as the cost of the packaging to the supplier is 15% or less of the cost of the packaging and contents together.

Food for animals

4.13 For animal food to be zero-rated, it must be recognised as such, particularly by the trade and by farmers (pet food not being regarded as animal food — see 4.16). Ingredients which have no significant nutritional value are standard-rated. Most importantly, the product must be held out for sale as animal food (see 4.8). Specific inclusions and exclusions are listed in VAT Leaflet 701/15 'Food for Animals'.

Keep of animals and grazing rights

4.14 Although those who supply the service of keeping animals also feed them, the keeping of animals is an example of a composite supply (see 3.51–3.52) and is standard-rated. The supplier cannot charge for the food separately and apply the zero rate.

The grant of grazing rights is regarded as the provision of animal food in the form of grass and is zero-rated unless there is also an element of care of animals provided by the person granting the grazing rights, in which case the whole charge is standard-rated.

Leaflet 701/15 provides clear examples of 'care' bringing the charge within the standard rate:

- turning the animals out to graze
- feeding
- mucking out, spreading straw or other bedding
- exercising
- taking *on behalf of the owner* any responsibility for the welfare of the animal(s) beyond a minimal 'seen daily' or 'twice daily' arrangement.

'DIY livery'

4.15 If stables are rented out and the animal care is provided by the person paying the rent, the rent is exempt from VAT as a licence to occupy land (see Chapter 8). If the person charging the rent also provides animal food, the food element may be identified separately and zero-rated but if that person in any way supplies care as well, the whole charge is standard-rated.

Pet food

4.16 Pet food should be distinguished from animal food covered at 4.13 above. Pet food which is canned, prepared or packaged, packaged food for wild birds, and biscuits and meal for cats and dogs are standard-rated.

There are, however, notable exceptions to what might normally be regarded as a pet:

- rabbits
- greyhounds (but not other dogs)
- mice and rats bred for laboratory purposes

- chinchillas.

Food for these is zero-rated unless it is held out for sale for pets generally (cats, dogs, cage birds, gerbils, hamsters etc.) in which case it is standard-rated.

Group 2 — Sewerage services and water

4.17 Zero-rating for supplies of sewerage services and water depends on the status of the customer, relief essentially applying to domestic customers. Standard-rating applies to supplies to industrial customers listed under Divisions 1-5 of the Standard Industrial Classification (SIC). Customs have produced their own leaflet on the subject: Leaflet 701/16 'Sewerage Services and Water'.

Sewerage services

4.18 The following supplies are always zero-rated, whatever the status of the customer:

- the provision of sewerage services against payment of an unmeasured charge, standing charge or other availability charge for the supply of those services;
- the provision of sewerage services for which a specific charge is made, e.g. the reception into the sewerage system and treatment of effluent which is charged for by reference to the volume and the nature of the effluent, and domestic sewerage services which are charged for by volume.

The following supplies are always standard-rated:

- the cleaning, maintenance, unblocking etc. of sewers and drains;
- the removal of industrial or farm waste not discharged into the sewer.

The following supplies are standard-rated if made to an industrial customer:

- the removal, conveyance, treatment or disposal of the contents of cesspools, septic tanks or similar receptacles.

Water

4.19 The items at 4.18 are sewerage services, whereas supplies of water are supplies of goods.

The following supplies are zero-rated except when made to industrial customers:

- supplies of water, ice and steam;
- the provision of water against payment of an unmeasured charge, standing charge or other availability charge for those supplies;
- charges for the abstraction of water by licence;
- specific charges for the supply of water for hosepipes, swimming pools and garden ponds, sprinklers and sprinkler licence fees;
- disconnection and reconnection charges arising as a result of the non-payment of the bill;
- opening and closing of stopcocks at the request of the water supplier;
- the charge made by a contractor to a customer for the supply of steam.

The following supplies are always standard-rated whatever the status of the customer:

- distilled or deionised water and water of similar purity;
- mineral, table and spa waters in bottles or similar containers held out for sale as a beverage.

The following supplies are always zero-rated whatever the status of the customer:

- sterile water including water which is both sterile and distilled or deionised, except where additives alter the nature of the product.

Civil engineering works

4.20 The general treatment of civil engineering works is covered in Chapter 8 (land and property), those linked with supplies of sewerage services and water being dealt with in this paragraph.

Charges for the installation of communication pipes are zero-rated civil engineering services if made wholly in the course of construction of a zero-rated building and the works are within the site being developed. Water companies can also zero rate civil engineering services necessary in the development of a new permanent residential caravan park. 'Infrastructure' charges made by water companies under the *Water Act 1989* are standard-rated.

Water meters

4.21 Zero-rating is limited to the following situations:

- where the supply and installation constitutes part of a civil engineering work supplied in the course of construction of a new zero-rated building;
- where the supply and installation is part of a civil engineering work supplied as part of a zero-rated approved alteration to a listed building; or
- where the supply is made to a non-industrial customer at the request of the water supplier.

Miscellaneous issues

4.22 Zero-rating is not available just because certain supplies of goods or services may be loosely associated with supplies of sewerage services or water, the following always being standard-rated:

- fluoridation charges
- pressure testing of fire sprinkler systems
- installation and repair of fire hydrants
- reconnection of a water supply (at the consumer's request)
- testing private pipework (at the consumer's request)
- temporary disconnection of supply (at the consumer's request)
- permanent disconnection of supply (at the consumer's request)
- the opening or closing of a stopcock (at the consumer's request)
- rewashering ball valves and taps
- hire of standpipes, irrespective of the liability of the water supplied
- hire of water bowsers, irrespective of the liability of the water supplied.

Group 3 — Books, etc. and Group 4 — Talking books for the blind and handicapped and wireless sets for the blind

4.23 There are six categories of printed matter which are zero-rated:

(1) Books, booklets, brochures, pamphlets and leaflets.

(2) Newspapers, journals and periodicals.

(3) Children's picture books and painting books.

(4) Music (printed, duplicated or manuscript).

(5) Maps, charts and topographical plans.

(6) Covers, cases and other articles supplied with Items 1 to 5 and not separately accounted for.

Items 1 to 6 do not include plans or drawings for industrial, architectural, engineering, commercial or similar purposes.

4.24 The six categories at 4.23 seem clear but since VAT was introduced and new types of printed matter have been developed, there have always been differences of opinion concerning interpretation.

The basic characteristic of a book or booklet is text or illustrations on pages bound by a cover of stiffer material. For this reason, the supply of information on CD-Rom format would not qualify for zero-rating even though the book version of the same material would.

The following are standard-rated:

- exercise books with spaces for insertion of written material, unless the provision of the spaces is 'incidental to the essential character of the publication'
- books of plans or drawings for industrial, architectural, engineering, commercial or similar purposes
- picture card and stamp albums, but if there is a considerable amount of reading material and no more than 25% of the album is for cards or stamps, the whole album may be zero-rated
- completed stamp albums.

4.25 Many disputes have centred around the definition of a leaflet. Customs' view is that to be zero-rated it must be a single sheet of paper (maximum A2 folded down to A4 or smaller if printed on both sides or maximum A4 folded down if printed on one side only) designed to be held in the hand (thus excluding certificates or similar which are for display) and containing information for reading. It must be complete in itself and supplied for distribution in multiples of at least 50. No more than 25% of the whole can be space for completion, which is of particular relevance where a leaflet contains a tear-off form to be sent somewhere. If the whole leaflet is to be sent somewhere, it is standard-rated.

Sometimes, the thickness of the material used to make the leaflet or brochure has been questioned because it is arguably card rather than paper. If in doubt, it is best to confirm the content of the latest agreement between Customs and the appropriate trade body.

Leaflet 701/10 Annex B provides a helpful list of zero-rated and excluded items and is reproduced below:

'Leaflet 701/10 Annex B

Liability of some common items of printed matter

These are examples of standard-rated items. You should not assume that an article is zero-rated just because it is not in this list.

Acceptance
Account books
Address books
Albums
Amendment slips
Announcement cards
Appointment cards
Autograph albums
Badges
Ballot papers
Bankers' drafts
Bills of quantity (blank)
Bingo cards
Biorhythm charts
Book tokens
Bookmakers' tickets
Business cards
Calendars
Certificates
Cheque books
Cloakroom tickets
Colour cards
Compliment slips
Copy books
Correspondence cards
Coupon books
Coupons
Credit cards
Delivery notes
Diaries (unused)
Dividend warrants
Draft forms
Dressmaking patterns
Duplicator matters
Engineers' plans
Envelopes
Exercise books
Fashion drawings
Flash cards
Folders
Football pool coupons
Form letters
Forms
Framed maps
Games
Globes
Greetings cards
Index cards
Insurance cover notes
Invitation cards
Invoices
Labels
Letter headings
Letters (handwritten)

Log books (blank)

Lottery tickets

Manuscript paper

Manuscripts

Medical records

Memo pads

Menu cards (with space for completion)

Microfiche

Microfilm

Microform copies

Music rolls

Note books

Order books

Parts of books

Pattern cards (unless they contain substantial printed matter)

Photograph albums

Photographs

Plans

Playing cards

Postcards (whether completed or not)

Posters

Printed pictures

Questionnaires

Receipt books

Record books

Record labels

Record sleeves

Registers

Rent books

Reply-paid coupons

Score cards

Scrap books (blank)

Scrolls (handwritten)

Seals

Shade cards (unless they contain substantial printed text)

Stamp albums (whether completed or not)

Stationery

Stationery books

Stickers

Swatch books

Swatch cards (unless they contain substantial printed matter)

Sweepstake tickets

Tags

Tickets

Transcripts

Transfers

Transparencies

Visiting cards

Vouchers

Wall charts

Wastepaper

Wills

Winding cards

Wreath cards

These are examples of zero-rated items. You should not assume that an article is standard-rated just because it is not in this list.

Accounts (fully printed)

Advertising leaflets

Agendas (fully printed)
Almanacs
Amendments (loose leaf)
Annuals
Antique books
Antique maps
Articles of association (complete in booklet form)
Astronomical charts
Atlases
Autograph books (completed)
Bibliographies
Bills of quantity (completed)
Booklets
Books (fully printed)
Brochures
Bulletins
Catalogues
Charts (geographical or topographical)
Cigarette cards
Circulars
Colouring books (children's)
Comics
Company reports
Cookery cards
Crossword books
Diaries (completed)
Dictionaries
Election addresses
Encyclopaedias
Fixture lists
Football programmes
Geological maps
Handbills
Holiday & tourist guides
Hydrographical charts
Hymn books
Instruction manuals
Journals
Knitting patterns
Leaflets
Loose-leaf books
Luncheon programmes
Magazines
Mail order catalogues
Manuals
Maps
Memoranda of association (complete in booklet form)
Menu cards (fully printed)
Missals
Monographs
Music
Music scores
Newspapers
Painting books (children's)
Pamphlets
Part works
Periodicals
Picture books
Poll cards
Poster magazines
Prayer books
Price lists (fully printed)

Programmes

Race cards

Rag books

Recipe books

Road maps

Scrap books (completed)

Ships' logs (completed)

Sports programmes

Staff journals

Text books

Theses

Timetables (in book or leaflet form)

Topographical plans

Tracts

Trade catalogues

Trade directories

Travel brochures

Wine lists (fully printed)'

Services associated with the production of printed matter

4.26 If a zero-rated item under one of the six categories at 4.23 is produced but is only an incidental part of a service, the normal treatment of the service applies.

Example 32

(*a*) A writer sends his finished manuscript to his publisher in London. The whole writing service is standard-rated even though the manuscript on its own would have been zero-rated.

(*b*) A consultant provides a written report of his findings to his VAT registered client in France. The whole service is free of UK VAT but the client pays TVA (French VAT) in France. The international service dictates the VAT treatment, not the report (see Chapter 12 covering international services).

4.27 If a process is applied to another person's goods to produce a different product, the service is zero-rated if the finished product is zero-rated, because the supplier of the service is deemed to have supplied the goods themselves.

Example 33

A book publisher engages the services of a printing company to perform preparatory work for a new loose-leaf publication. The publisher supplies all the binders (which on their own would be standard-rated) and the printer adds the protective cover, the spine and the section separators, then prints the title of the work on the cover. As the final product is treated as a zero-rated book, the printer's service is also zero-rated.

4.28 The key point to remember is that the processing service must produce a different class of goods from the original, and the final product must be zero-rated for the service to be zero-rated.

Book tokens

4.29 Book tokens are normally sold for their face value. Where this is the case, no VAT is due. The same applies where the token is sold for less than its face value. If it is sold for more than its face value, VAT is due on the difference between the face value and the selling price.

The service of printing book tokens is standard-rated.

Mixed supplies including zero-rated printed matter

4.30 A mixed supply of goods or services consists of several items. Where printed matter is one of them, the part of the overall price relating to the printed matter may be zero-rated. However, where all the items together constitute one composite supply, the liability of that one supply prevails.

Example 34

(i) Subscriptions to certain professional bodies are exempt but if the subscriber receives certain things in return for his subscription such as a handbook, the subscription is a mixed supply and the zero rate applies to the proportion of the subscription relating to the handbook.

(ii) Compare (i) with a supply of passenger transport on board an aircraft. The whole service is one composite supply of zero-rated passenger transport even though it includes catering which, on its own, would be standard-rated.

Taxpayers should ensure Customs agree with their interpretation in individual cases, especially following the BSkyB case.

BSkyB supplied standard-rated cable TV services to its subscribers and the subscription included a free TV listings guide. However, BSkyB took the normal value of the guide off the total subscription and charged VAT on the balance. The Tribunal agreed with Customs that VAT should be paid on the full subscription.

The issue is further complicated by the *Card Protection Plan* case explained at 3.52. It may now be more difficult to justify mixed supplies.

Talking books for the blind etc.

4.31 This specific relief only applies to supplies to the RNIB, the National Listening Library and 'other similar charities'.

Inclusions within Item 1 of Group 4 are listed below:

> **'ZERO-RATED SUPPLIES TO THE RNIB, THE NATIONAL LISTENING LIBRARY AND SIMILAR CHARITIES**
>
> Item 1 of Group 4 Schedule 8 to VATA 1994
>
> 1. The supply to the Royal National Institute for the Blind, the National Listening Library or other similar charities of–
>
> (a) magnetic tape specially adapted for the recording and reproduction of speech for the blind or severely handicapped;
>
> (b) apparatus designed or specially adapted for the making on a magnetic tape, by way of the transfer of recorded speech from another magnetic tape, of a recording described in paragraph (f) below;
>
> (c) apparatus designed or specially adapted for transfer to magnetic tapes of a recording made by apparatus described in paragraph (b) above;
>
> (d) apparatus for re-winding magnetic tape described in paragraph (f) below;
>
> (e) apparatus designed or specially adapted for the reproduction from recorded magnetic tape of speech for the blind or severely handicapped which is not available for use otherwise than by the blind or severely handicapped;
>
> (f) magnetic tape upon which has been recorded speech for the blind or severely handicapped, such recording being suitable for reproduction only in the apparatus mentioned in paragraph (e) above;
>
> (g) apparatus solely for the making on a magnetic tape of a sound recording which is for use by the blind or severely handicapped;
>
> (h) parts and accessories (other than a magnetic tape for use with apparatus described in paragraph (g) above) for goods comprised in paragraphs (a) to (g) above;

(i) the supply of a service of repair or maintenance of any goods comprised in paragraphs (a) to (h) above.

There is a second item in this Group comprising the supply to a charity of wireless receiving sets, or apparatus solely for the making and reproduction of a sound recording on a magnetic tape permanently contained in a cassette, so long as they are for loaning out to blind people free of charge.

Both Items 1 and 2 refer to supplies to specific charities or charities in general of specific goods. This normally means sales but it also includes letting the goods on hire.'

Group 5 — Construction of buildings etc. and Group 6 — Protected buildings

4.32 Along with partial exemption and international services, this area of VAT legislation is considered to be one of the most difficult to understand and apply. The potential problem is exacerbated by the fact that many transactions in land, property and construction involve large sums, making the cost of a mistake high.

The whole subject is dealt with in Chapter 8. Suffice it to say here that zero-rating is restricted to certain supplies, most connected with construction and sales of residential property, all of which have conditions attached.

Group 7 — International services

4.33 The following are zero-rated:

(1) Services of work carried out on goods that have been obtained in, acquired in or imported into any one of the EC member states for the specific purpose of having that work carried out, and are subsequently exported outside the EC:

  (*a*) by or on behalf of the supplier, or

  (*b*) where the recipient of the services has established its business outside the EC, by or on behalf of the recipient.

(2) Services of making arrangements for:

  (*a*) the export of goods outside the EC,

  (*b*) a supply of services as described in Item 1 above, or

  (*c*) any supply of services made outside the EC.

Other international services are standard-rated, exempt or outside the scope of VAT and are covered in Chapter 12.

Group 8 — Transport

4.34 There is frequent conjecture as to whether this relief will remain because of EC law, but given that the removal of UK zero rates depends on a unanimous vote from member states including the UK, it is safe for the time being.

The Group is divided into 16 items although they are only numbered up to 13 because Items 2A, 2B and 6A were inserted after the legislation was originally drafted. The main theme is the zero-rating of goods and services in connection with certain types of ship and aircraft including the ship or aircraft itself; passenger transport in the UK, and certain types of freight transport. There are several references to supplies made in the UK, Chapter 2 referring.

Transport Items 1 and 2 — qualifying ships and aircraft

4.35 Zero-rating applies to the sale, repair, maintenance and modification or conversion of 'qualifying' ships and aircraft although, in the case of modification or conversion, the ship or aircraft must still be in the 'qualifying' category after the work is completed.

'Qualifying' means:

- any ship weighing not less than 15 tons (gross tonnage) which is not designed or adapted for recreation or pleasure (thus pleasure yachts are excluded from zero-rating)
- any aircraft weighing not less than 8,000 kgs which is not designed or adapted for recreation or pleasure.

Services supplied include those under a charter and letting on hire, but in the case of charter services, zero-rating does not apply where such services consist entirely of any one (or more) of the following and are performed wholly in the UK:

- transport of passengers (but see Item 4 below)
- accommodation
- entertainment
- education.

The normal VAT treatment of each of these applies.

Transport Items 2A and 2B

4.36 These two items took effect from 1 January 1996.

2A zero rates the supply of parts and equipment for installation or incorporation in the propulsion, navigation or communication systems, or general structure of qualifying ships or aircraft.

2B is more concerned with safety and rescue equipment and zero rates the supply of life jackets, life rafts, smoke hoods and similar safety equipment for use in qualifying ships or aircraft.

Included within these items is the letting on hire of specified goods but the supply of parts and equipment to a Government department is excluded from zero-rating unless:

(*a*) they are installed or incorporated as part of a supply to the department in its business capacity, or

(*b*) they are to be installed or incorporated in ships or aircraft used for providing rescue or assistance at sea.

Transport Item 3 — Supplies to charities providing rescue or assistance at sea

4.37 Many charity activities are either exempt from or outside the scope of VAT which can actually cause them to lose out, since input tax attributable to those activities can not be reclaimed. In certain circumstances, reliefs are introduced for supplies *to* charities so that they do not suffer irrecoverable input tax. This is one example.

Zero-rating applies to the supply and repair or maintenance of:

- lifeboats
- carriage equipment and tractors used for the launching or recovery of lifeboats
- winches and hauling equipment used for recovery of lifeboats

where the recipient is a charity providing rescue or assistance at sea and gives the supplier a certificate confirming its name and address and that the supply qualifies for zero-rating under this item. Thus, it is the charity's responsibility to confirm eligibility for zero-rating to the supplier in writing.

These charities may also receive the following at the zero rate:

- services — the construction, modification, repair or maintenance of slipways used to launch or recover lifeboats

- goods — spare parts or accessories provided in connection with any of the goods described in the rest of this item (e.g. lifeboats, slipways etc.).

'Lifeboat' means any vessel used or to be used *solely* for rescue or assistance at sea.

Transport Item 4 — passenger transport

4.38 This is zero-rated to the extent it is enjoyed in the UK.

There are four categories covering transport:

- in any vehicle, ship or aircraft designed or adapted to carry not less than 10 passengers
- by the Post Office
- on any scheduled flight
- from a place within to a place outside the UK (or vice versa) but only to the extent it takes place in the UK.

The following are excluded from zero-rating:

- the transport of passengers —

  (*a*) in any vehicle to, from or within a place of entertainment, recreation or amusement; or a place of cultural, scientific, historical or similar interest, by the person who sells the admission to these facilities or grants a right to use them, or by a person 'connected' with him;

  (*b*) in any motor vehicle between a car park and an airport passenger terminal or between land adjacent to either by the person (or person 'connected' with him) who supplies the car parking facilities; or

  (*c*) in an aircraft where the flight is for the purpose of —

    (i) providing entertainment, recreation or amusement; or

    (ii) the experience of flying either generally or in that particular aircraft and not *primarily* for the purpose of passenger transport.

The term 'connected' refers to people with whom it may be possible to arrange a service the value of which is not at arm's length, the definition within *section 839* of *ICTA 1988* applying.

While passenger transport is only zero-rated to the extent that it takes place in the UK, the whole journey may be zero-rated if it starts and finishes in the UK but includes a part outside without putting in or landing in that other country.

The difference between providing passenger transport and the means of transport itself is important and depends upon whether or not there is a driver, skipper, crew etc. If they are provided, the supply is of passenger transport. Simply supplying means of transport is standard-rated (e.g. the hire of a coach by one transport company to another).

When deciding whether or not a vehicle is designed to carry more than 10 passengers, the driver and crew count as passengers, and if the capacity is less than 10, the service is standard-rated unless the form of transport qualifies under one of the other headings.

There is a special concession for the transport of disabled people which under certain circumstances is zero-rated and ambulance services are exempt (which means associated input tax is normally irrecoverable).

As taxis and private hire cars are designed to carry less than 10 passengers, fares for their use are standard-rated.

Where a journey takes place partly in the UK and partly outside, an apportionment is necessary to determine the zero-rated element. It may then be necessary to register and account for VAT in the other country depending on their treatment of passenger transport and registration rules. If registration is required, the supplier may have to appoint a tax representative based in that country to handle VAT affairs there. This is covered in Chapter 11.

The subject is covered in depth in Customs' Public Notice 744A.

Passenger transport was redefined as relevant vehicles, ships and aircraft with 10 or more seats (including the driver) from 1 April 2001 (previously 12 or more seats). Vehicles that are designed to carry more than 10 passengers but which in fact carry less because they are adapted for wheelchair access, are also included in the changes from 1 April 2001. The changes were enacted by the *Value Added Tax (Passenger Vehicles) Order 2001* which made the changes to *Item 4(a)* of *Group 8*.

Transport Item 5 — freight transport

4.39 The transport of goods from a place within the EC to a place outside the EC (or vice versa) is zero-rated to the extent that it takes place within the UK.

Freight includes:

- goods and cargo
- mail
- documents
- unaccompanied vehicles
- vehicles transported on ships and charged at a 'driver accompanied' rate although without passengers (e.g. buses, coaches etc.).

There are three types of freight transport:

- domestic (wholly within the UK)
- international (from a place in the EC to a place outside or wholly outside)
- intra-community (between places in the EC).

Domestic supplies are standard-rated.

International supplies take place in the country of departure and any others through which the journey passes and the liability is zero-rated for the UK part only (registration may be applicable in other EC countries if the journey passes through them).

Where a UK business supplies freight transport to a customer in another EC member state, it must charge VAT unless the customer is registered for VAT in its own country or any other EC Member State apart from the UK and gives his registration number to the supplier who shows the number on its invoice, in which case no VAT is due. The customer pays output tax in the country of its registration using the reverse charge procedure explained in Chapter 12.

The subject is explained in greater depth in Customs' Public Notice 744B.

Transport Items 6 to 9 and 11 — ancillary and associated services

4.40 These items cover the types of service which are directly connected with the other zero-rated items in the Group. The ancillary or associated services included are as follows:

Item 6

Services provided for:

(*a*) the handling of ships or aircraft in a port, Customs and Excise airport or outside the UK; and (*b*) for the handling or storage of goods carried in a ship or aircraft, in a port or Customs and Excise airport or on land adjacent to a port.

Letting on hire of the relevant goods is excluded from zero-rating.

Item 6A

Air navigation services.

Item 7

Pilotage services.

Item 8

Salvage or towage services.

Item 9

Services in connection with surveying or classifying ships or aircraft for any official register.

Item 11

The handling or storage of goods, or their transport to or from a place at which they are to be exported to or have been imported from outside the EC, and the handling or storage of such goods in connection with such transport is zero-rated.

Also zero-rated under this item is the supply to a person or business which 'belongs' outside the UK (i.e. has established its business abroad or the establishment most closely connected with the supply in question is abroad) of any service described in Items 6 (part (a) only), 6A or 9 above, and Item 10(a) (see below) provided that the customer receives the service for business purposes.

Other than in the circumstances described in this item, the provisions of Items 6(a), 6A, 9 and 10(a) only relate to qualifying ships or aircraft.

Transport Item 10 — agents and business services

4.41 Zero-rating is available for agents or businesses that provide a service which brings about one of the other supplies in the item. The widely used term for this type of activity is 'making arrangements for'.

The making of arrangements for the following is zero-rated:

- Item 10(a) — the supply of, or space in, any ship or aircraft,
- Item 10(b) — the supply of services described in Items 1, 2, 3 to 9 and 11 above, or
- Item 10(c) — the supply of any goods covered by Items 2A and 2B above.

Transport Item 12 — designated travel services

4.42 These are zero-rated to the extent that they are enjoyed outside the EC. A 'designated travel service' is a service from a specified list provided by tour operators and subject to a different method of calculating output tax using a special scheme known as the 'tour operators' margin scheme' or 'TOMS'. The specified list also covers activities that would not normally be associated with tour operators, e.g. corporate hospitality services, so businesses should carefully check the list to determine whether TOMS applies.

TOMS is covered in Chapter 10.

Transport Item 13 — intra-community transport associated with the Azores and Madeira

4.43 The final zero-rated item in Group 8 covers transport services supplied in connection with freight transport to or from the Azores or Madeira (or between those two places) but only to the extent that those services are supplied in the UK.

4.44 Ancillary and associated services in connection with ships and aircraft are covered in depth in Customs' Public Notice 744C.

Group 9 — Caravans and houseboats

4.45 This group has limited application.

The 'supply' of a caravan includes sale, leases for more than one year where the lessee is allowed to take it to a caravan park of his own choice, loan, and private use by the trader.

The liability is zero-rated if the caravan is either more than 7 metres (22.9 ft) long or 2.3 metres (7.5 ft) wide excluding any equipment for attaching it to a vehicle e.g. towbars.

Any other type of caravan is standard-rated.

The zero rate extends to fixtures and fittings such as toilets, sinks and baths but not to removable items such as furniture.

Seasonal pitches and holiday lets are standard-rated but pitch fees or rents charged to caravan owners in permanent residential caravan parks or on sites designated for 'travellers' are exempt.

A houseboat is any boat or any other type of floating decked structure so long as it is only for permanent habitation and cannot be easily adapted for self-propulsion. Sales and lets are zero-rated so long as the customer can tow the boat away to a mooring of his choice.

Mooring charges are not zero-rated. They are exempt if provided for a houseboat and standard-rated if for any other type of vessel.

Customs' Leaflet 701/20 refers.

Group 10 — Gold and Group 11 — Bank notes

Gold

4.46 There are only two items in the zero-rated gold group:

- The supply by a Central Bank to another Central Bank or a member of the London Gold Market of gold held in the UK;
- the supply by a member of the London Gold Market to a Central Bank of gold held in the UK.

The term 'gold' includes gold coins and the supply includes the granting of a right to acquire a quantity of gold.

The zero rate does not extend to imports of gold from EC or non-EC countries but Central Banks may import gold free of VAT under special relief orders.

There is a special way of accounting for VAT on supplies of gold because of the widespread problem of smuggling and fraud. The seller issues a tax invoice to the purchaser but it carries wording to the effect that the output tax is to be paid by the purchaser, shifting the responsibility to account for VAT to the purchaser who also includes input tax on his VAT return.

Customs' Leaflet 701/21 refers.

Bank notes

The issue by a bank of a note payable to bearer on demand is zero-rated.

Group 12 — Drugs, medicines, aids for the handicapped etc.

4.47 Although charities are generally treated in the same way as other taxpayers, certain legislation does provide reliefs, this being designed to ensure that members of the public suffering from a particular handicap or charities specifically established to assist the handicapped, do not suffer the additional burden of irrecoverable VAT on necessary costs.

The relief provided by the Group is often relevant to individuals or organisations to whom Group 15 (Charities) applies. The Group runs to 20 items.

Handicapped Item 1 — goods dispensed on prescription

4.48 Prescriptions are zero-rated so long as they are dispensed by a registered pharmacist from a prescription written by a registered doctor or dentist. Doctors include those who under their own legislation only have limited registration in the register of medical practitioners and visiting doctors from the EC who perform urgent cases without formal registration but are entitled to be registered.

Handicapped Item 1A — other goods

4.49 The supply by doctors of any goods in accordance with a requirement or authorisation under certain NHS and Health and Personal Social Services legislation.

Items 2 to 20 — various supplies to handicapped persons or to charities for use by handicapped persons

4.50 These items constitute the main body of Group 12. It is crucial to understand the definition of 'handicapped persons' in order to discern whether or not relief is available, and Customs' own guidance notes are not particularly helpful. They are at pains not to offend by their use of words and so refer to people with disabilities rather than the handicapped.

Their note defines 'handicapped' as the chronically sick or disabled, leaving room for differences of interpretation.

'Chronically' means long term, so a brief illness or incapacity (such as a broken leg) would not count.

Handicapped Item 2

4.51 Zero-rating applies to the following supplies for domestic or personal use by the handicapped:

- medical or surgical appliances which are only for use in relieving a *severe* abnormality or injury
- electrically or mechanically adjustable beds designed for invalids
- commode chairs, commode stools, devices incorporating a bidet jet and warm air drier, and similar devices
- chair lifts and stair lifts which *must* be designed for use in conjunction with wheelchairs (this does not mean the wheelchair has to go up the stairs but the invalid should be able to get easily from the wheelchair onto the lift and vice versa)
- hoists and lifters designed for use by invalids
- motor vehicles designed or substantially and permanently adapted to carry an invalid or a person on a stretcher along with no more than five other people e.g. invalid carriages, ambulances
- other equipment or appliances not specifically mentioned above but which are designed for use by invalids *only*
- any parts and accessories which are only for use with or in the above goods
- boats designed or substantially and permanently adapted for use by the handicapped.

The legislative notes to Group 12 exclude from zero-rating:

- hearing aids (except those designed for hearing training for deaf children)
- dentures
- spectacles
- contact lenses.

But included for zero-rating are:

- clothing, footwear and wigs
- wheelchairs and invalid carriages other than mechanically propelled vehicles intended or adapted for use on roads

- renal haemodialysis units, oxygen concentrators, artificial respirators and similar apparatus.

The meaning of supply within Items 1, 1A and 2 above includes letting on hire.

From 1 April 2001, the conditions for zero-rating vehicles adapted for disabled persons have been modernised. Eligible disabled people can now obtain vehicles carrying up to 12 people at the zero rate. Also, the condition that the disabled person must be able to travel whilst seated in a wheelchair or lying on a stretcher has been removed. Now those needing a wheelchair or stretcher can have any adaptation they like to suit their condition and still benefit from zero-rating.

4.52 Handicapped zero-rating also applies to the following items:

Item 3 — Services supplied to a handicapped person of adapting goods to suit his condition.

Item 4 — The supply to a charity of services described in Item 3 so long as they are made available by the charity to the handicapped person.

If the services in Item 3 or 4 take place before their supply to a handicapped person, an apportionment is necessary to determine how much is zero-rated. This must be fair and reasonable, Customs' own guidelines in their Public Notice 700 referring.

Item 5 — The supply to a handicapped person or charity of repair or maintenance services to goods described in Items 2, 6, 18 or 19 in the manner described in those items.

Item 6 — Goods supplied in connection with the services described in Items 3 to 5 above.

Item 7 — The services of installing equipment or appliances described in Item 2 when supplied to the handicapped person direct or via a charity, including parts and accessories.

Item 8 — The service to a handicapped person of constructing ramps or widening doorways or passages so that he can get into or move around his home more easily.

Item 9 — As Item 8 but to a *charity* and applicable to *any* building.

Item 10 — Services to a handicapped person of providing, extending or adapting a bathroom, washroom or lavatory in his home where necessary because of his condition.

Item 11 — As Item 10, to a charity for the benefit of handicapped residents in a residential home.

From 1 April 2000, the relief is extended to bathrooms in charity day centres where at least 20% of the users are chronically sick or disabled, and in sheltered flats and houses where a charity is the landlord of disabled people who have their own accommodation.

Item 12 — As Item 10, to a charity in any building used principally by a charity for charitable purposes for the benefit of the handicapped.

Item 13 — Goods supplied in connection with Items 8 to 11 inclusive (but *not* Item 12).

Item 14 — Motor vehicles let on hire to handicapped people receiving 'disability living allowance' which includes a mobility element for a period of not less than three years and where the main business activity of the business letting the vehicles is the provision of them to handicapped people.

There is a further condition in that the vehicle must be unused when the letting period starts and payment for the mobility element of the disability living allowance is from the DSS or MOD on behalf of the handicapped user.

Item 15 — The first sale of a vehicle used in accordance with Item 14 after the letting period has ended.

Item 16 — Services supplied to a handicapped person in connection with the necessary installation of a lift between the floors of his home.

Item 17 — As Item 16, to a charity which provides permanent or temporary residence or a day centre for handicapped people. The lift must facilitate their movement between the floors of the building run by the charity.

Item 18 — Goods supplied in connection with the services described in Item 16 or 17.

Item 19 — Supplies to handicapped people or to charities for onward supply to handicapped people of alarm systems which must be for the domestic or personal use of the handicapped person. He must be able to operate it himself and be able to alert a contact person at a control centre.

The contact person at the control centre must be specifically appointed to receive such calls and retain information about the handicapped people under his control which enables him to act appropriately in the event of illness, injury or any other type of emergency.

Item 20 — The services of a control centre in receiving and responding to calls from systems described in Item 19.

4.53 Where the above supplies are to charities, the recipient must either be registered as such with the Charity Commissioners (or have similar status) and all the conditions of a specific item must be met in order that the supply may be zero-rated.

Some of the supplies covered will be made to hospitals, nursing homes, health authorities, NHS trusts etc. which may or may not have charitable status. If they do not, the supply can only be zero-rated if it is made direct to the user (usually the handicapped person) and is paid for from their own funds.

Customs will accept that the institution looking after the handicapped person may hold those funds as trustee.

4.54 In all cases, the supplier needs evidence that his supply qualifies for zero-rating, so the recipient is required to confirm eligibility by giving the supplier a certificate in a format acceptable to Customs.

Annex D to Customs' Leaflet 701/7 sets out a pro forma declaration by an individual and is reproduced below:

> **'Annex D**
>
> Goods and services for disabled persons: eligibility declarations by an individual
>
> [(referred to in paragraphs 5-7, 9, 10, 17-20, 22 and 23 of the public notice)].
>
> I (full name)
>
> of (address)
>
> declare that I am chronically sick or disabled by reason of:
>
> (give a full and specific description of your condition)
>
> and that I am receiving from: (name and address of supplier)
>
> ⋆ the following goods which are being supplied to me for domestic or my personal use: (description of goods)

⋆ the following services to adapt goods to suit my condition: (description of services and goods)

⋆ the following services of installation, repair or maintenance of goods: (description of services and goods)

⋆ the following alterations to my private residence: (description of alteration — see VAT Notice 701/7 paragraph 19)

⋆ the services of monitoring a personal alarm call system

⋆ the services of leasing a motor vehicle

and I claim relief from value added tax under Group 14 of Schedule 5 to the Value Added Tax Act 1983 [this should now refer to Group 12 of Schedule 8 to the Value Added Tax Act 1994].

(Signature)

(Date)

⋆ Delete words not applicable

Note to Supplier

You must keep this declaration for production to your VAT office. The production of this certificate does not automatically authorise the zero-rating of the supply. You must also ensure that the goods and services you are supplying qualify for zero-rating.

Note to Customer

If you are in any doubt as to whether you are eligible to receive goods or services zero-rated for VAT you should consult your local VAT office before signing the declaration.

Warning: Section 39.2 of the VAT Act 1983 [this should now refer to Section 72.3 of the VAT Act 1994] provides for severe penalties for anyone who makes use of a document which they know to be false for the purposes of obtaining VAT relief.'

Annex E is a pro forma declaration by a charity and is reproduced below:

'Annex E

Goods and services for disabled persons: eligibility declaration by a charity [(referred to in paragraphs 14 and 24-27)]

I (full name and status in charity)

of (name and address of charity)

declare that the charity named above is receiving from: (name and address of supplier)

⋆ the following goods which are to be made available to a specific disabled person or persons for domestic or their personal use: (description of goods)

⋆ the following services to adapt goods to suit the condition of a disabled person to whom the goods are to be made available: (description of services and goods)

⋆ the following services of installation, repair or maintenance of goods: (description of services and goods)

⋆ the following building alterations at (address of building) to enable a disabled person to enter or move within the building: (description of alterations — see VAT Notice 701/7, paragraph 26).

⋆ the services of monitoring a personal alarm call system

and I claim relief from value added tax under Group 14 of Schedule 5 to the Value Added Tax Act 1983 [now Group 12 of Schedule 8 to the Value Added Tax Act 1994].

(Signature)

(Date)

⋆ Delete words not applicable

Note to Supplier

You must keep this declaration for production to your VAT officer. The production of this certificate does not automatically authorise the zero-rating of the supply. You must also ensure that the goods and services you are supplying qualify for zero-rating.

Note to Customer

If you are in any doubt as to whether you are eligible to receive goods or services zero-rated for VAT you should consult VAT Notice 701/7 or seek advice from your local VAT office before signing the declaration.

Warning: Section 39.2 of the VAT Act 1983 [now Section 72.3 of the VAT Act 1994] provides for severe penalties for anyone who makes use of a document which they know to be false for the purposes of obtaining VAT relief.'

4.55 If the disabled or handicapped person cannot sign a declaration, it is acceptable for a parent, guardian or doctor to do it.

If the supplier takes all reasonable steps to ensure that the declaration is accurate, Customs will not normally penalise an error but the annexes state clearly the consequences of deliberate error.

Imports of eligible goods from outside the EC

4.56 Eligible individuals or charities importing the goods mentioned in Items 1 to 20 do not have to pay VAT provided that the import entry declaration is accompanied by a suitably adapted declaration. Annexes H and J of Leaflet 701/7 give a suitable form of words for this purpose (see Chapter 12 for further information on imports).

Acquisitions from other EC countries

4.57 Charities bringing in eligible goods from another EC country may account for tax at the zero rate (see Chapter 11). However, individuals buying from other member states may have to bear a VAT cost as zero-rating hardly ever applies elsewhere. In such cases the supplier would have to charge his own country's VAT because the supply would be subject to domestic rather than UK law.

Group 13 — Imports, exports, etc.

4.58 These are covered extensively in Chapter 12, normal imports and exports not being covered by this Group.

There are three items in the Group, each with limited application. The following are zero-rated:

Item 1

The supply before the delivery of an entry (as defined by Customs regulations on imported goods) under an agreement requiring the purchaser to make such an entry of goods imported from outside the EC.

Item 2

The supply, by or to an overseas authority, overseas body or overseas trader (i.e. an import or an export) charged with the management of any defence project which is the subject of an international collaboration arrangement or under direct contract with any government or government-sponsored international body participating in a defence project under this type of arrangement, of goods or services in connection with the arrangement.

Item 3

The supply to an overseas authority, overseas body or overseas trader of jigs, patterns, templates, dies, punches and similar machine tools used in the UK *solely* for making goods for export outside the EC.

Several terms within the item require further definition and are so defined in the notes to Group 13. An 'international collaboration arrangement' is any arrangement between the UK government and one or more other governments or government-sponsored bodies creating a joint project for research, development or production; and which includes provision for participating governments to relieve the project cost from taxation. 'Overseas authority' means any country other than the UK and any part of or place within that country, or the government there. 'Overseas body' means a body established outside the UK. 'Overseas trader' means any person in business whose principal place of business is outside the UK.

Item 3 does not apply zero-rating where the overseas authority, body or trader is:

- a taxable person,
- another member state,
- any part of or place in another member state,
- the government of any other member state, part of or place within it,
- a body established in another member state, or
- any business with activities carried on in another member state.

Group 14 — Tax-free shops

4.59 Group 14 previously zero-rated goods within certain limits for those travelling to another EC country. Duty free goods ceased to be available for persons travelling within the EC with effect from 1 July

1999. Group 14 was accordingly deleted by the *Value Added Tax (Abolition of Zero-Rating for Tax-Free Shops) Order 1999 (SI 1999/1642)*.

Group 15 — Charities

4.60 As explained under Group 12, charities do not benefit extensively from VAT reliefs.

Many of their supplies may be exempt (see Chapter 5) and a significant amount of their income is usually from grants and donations which are normally outside the scope of VAT.

This means a significant proportion of their input tax may not be recoverable, so the only real benefit charities receive is from zero-rating applicable to them exclusively and not to 'normal' businesses.

Group 15 is a more general list of zero-rated supplies made by and to charities than those already explained in Group 12. Customs Leaflet 701/1 (Charities) refers.

Sales or exports of donated goods

4.61 The supply by a charity, or by a VAT registered business which covenants all of its profits to a charity, of goods which have been donated for sale is zero-rated.

The donation of goods by registered traders for sale or export under the same circumstances is also zero-rated.

The most obvious example of zero-rated sales is from charity shops.

Example 35
If a private individual decides to clear out an overstocked wardrobe, putting all unwanted clothes in a bag and delivering it to an Oxfam shop, the sale of those clothes by Oxfam is zero-rated. If the Oxfam shop were to buy in goods for resale, such as adults' clothes and greetings cards, sales would be standard-rated.

Where a business covenants *all* its profits by deed to charity, it does not matter which charity receives the profits.

The same principles apply to exports of donated goods.

Abuse of the relief led to a change from 26 November 1996, zero-rating now only applying if:

- the supply is a sale of goods donated to that charity or VAT registered business;
- the sale takes place as a result of the goods having been made available to the general public for purchase (this could be in a shop or elsewhere); and
- the sale must not relate to any arrangement between the people involved in the sale which existed before the goods were made available to the general public (whether or not that arrangement was legally binding).

From 1 April 2000, this provision is amended further as follows:

- the zero rate also applies if relevant goods are made available to disabled people or to those receiving means tested benefits, rather than to the general public;
- the transfer of profits from the sale of donated goods by other organisations to charities no longer has to be by deed of covenant but simply by some form of written agreement or other obligation to transfer the profits (such as a trust);
- the zero rate now also applies to the hire of donated goods provided their sale would be zero-rated;
- the zero rate no longer applies to supplies which, by special references in law, are deemed to be of goods e.g. freehold interests in land.

Other exports by charities

4.62 Exports of any goods outside the EC by charities is zero-rated (see Chapter 12).

Supplies of 'relevant goods' to nominated 'eligible bodies'

4.63 Zero-rating applies where:

- relevant goods are for donation to a nominated eligible body and are bought with money provided by a charity or from voluntary contributions; and
- relevant goods are supplied to an eligible body which pays for them with money provided by a charity or from voluntary contributions, or to an eligible body which is a charity providing care, medical or surgical treatment for the handicapped.

Legislative notes (3) and (4) to the Group state the meaning of 'relevant goods' and 'eligible body', viz.:

'Note (3) **"Relevant goods"** means —

(a) medical, scientific, computer, video, sterilising, laboratory or refrigeration equipment for use in medical or veterinary research, training, diagnosis or treatment;

(b) ambulances;

(c) parts or accessories for use in or with goods described in paragraph (a) or (b) above;

(d) goods of a kind described in item 2 of Group 12 of Schedule 8;

(e) motor vehicles (other than vehicles with more than 50 seats) designed or substantially and permanently adapted for the safe carriage of a handicapped person in a wheelchair provided that—

(i) in the case of vehicles with more than 16 but fewer than 27 seats, the number of persons for which such provision exists is at least 2;

(ii) in the case of vehicles with more than 26 but fewer than 37 seats, the number of persons for which such provision exists is at least 3;

(iii) in the case of vehicles with more than 36 but fewer than 47 seats, the number of persons for which such provision exists is at least 4;

(iv) in the case of vehicles with more than 46 seats, the number of persons for which such provision exists is at least 5;

(v) there is either a fitted electrically or hydraulically operated lift or, in the case of vehicles with fewer than 17 seats, a fitted ramp to provide access for a passenger in a wheelchair;

(f) motor vehicles (with more than 6 but fewer than 51 seats) for use by an eligible body providing care for blind, deaf, mentally handicapped or terminally sick persons mainly to transport such persons;

(g) telecommunication, aural, visual, light enhancing or heat detecting equipment (not being equipment ordinarily supplied for private or recreational use) solely for use for the purpose of rescue or first aid services undertaken by a charitable institution providing such services.

Note (4) **"Eligible body"** means —

(a) a Health Authority or Special Health Authority in England and Wales;

(b) a Health board in Scotland;

(c) a Health and Social Services board in Northern Ireland;

(d) a hospital whose activities are not carried on for profit;

(e) a research institution whose activities are not carried on for profit;

(f) a charitable institution providing care or medical or surgical treatment for handicapped persons;

(g) the Common Services Agency for the Scottish Health Service, the Northern Ireland Central Services Agency for Health and Social Services or the Isle of Man Health Services board;

(h) a charitable institution providing rescue or first-aid services;

(i) a National Health Service trust established under Part I of the National Health Service and Community Care Act 1990 or the National Health Service (Scotland) Act 1978.'

4.64 The definition of 'handicapped' is the same as under Group 12 (see 4.47–4.57). 'Care' is not specifically defined by the legislation but Customs give their interpretation of its meaning in paragraph 10(b)(iii) of Leaflet 701/1 which states:

'(iii) meaning of "care"

Care means some form of continuing personal contact in looking after, helping or supervising people.'

The legislative notes to Group 15 also provide further clarification for charities 'providing care or medical or surgical treatment'. They do not qualify as providing such services to the handicapped *unless*:

- they provide those services in a 'relevant establishment', and
- the majority of people receiving such services in that establishment are handicapped.

A 'relevant establishment' is a day centre which does not cater mainly for social or recreational activities or an institution which is:

(i) approved, licensed or registered under any enactment or Northern Ireland legislation, or

(ii) exempted from approval, licensing or registration under such legislation.

The purpose of this particular definition is to ensure consistency of treatment in all parts of the UK.

The repair and maintenance of relevant goods owned by an eligible body and the supply of goods associated with repair and maintenance services are also zero-rated so long as the service is paid for with funds provided by a charity or from voluntary contributions and, where the owner of the goods being repaired or maintained is not a charity, it has made no financial contribution.

4.65 None of the zero-rated parts of the heading — 'supplies of relevant goods to nominated eligible bodies' — applies to charities covered by Note (4)(f) at 4.63 unless the relevant goods are to be used by the charity in a relevant establishment in which it provides care or medical or surgical treatment predominantly to the handicapped. Note, however, that the clarification of providing care or medical or surgical treatment above and the narrow application described in this paragraph do not apply where the handicapped receive care in their own homes; the goods are in the category at Note (3)(a) at 4.63 and they are used to provide that care. In other words, the charity can still zero rate the goods listed in Note (3)(a) if the recipient is a handicapped person in his own home. Parts and accessories for those goods also qualify.

4.66 The supply includes letting on hire as well as sale, relevant supplies also including the provision of computer software *solely* for use in medical research, diagnosis or treatment.

Charity advertising

4.67 Prior to 1 April 2000 certain advertising services supplied to charities were zero-rated as follows:

(*a*) TV, radio or cinema broadcasts of charity adverts;

(*b*) adverts published in any newspaper, journal, poster, programme, annual, leaflet, brochure, pamphlet, periodical or similar publication; or

(*c*) any goods or services provided in connection with preparing adverts at (*b*) above.

With TV, radio and cinema adverts, only the charges for screening them were zero-rated, not any other charges for making them.

From that date, the zero rate is extended to supplies of almost all charity advertisements in all media. This includes design and production services connected with zero-rated advertisements. However, the following are excluded from zero-rating:

- general marketing addressed to individuals e.g. direct mailing and tele-sales;
- supplies made in connection with a charity's own website;
- charity overheads for producing its own advertisements.

The existing concessions for certain paper-based goods were formalised and extended to include collection boxes, lapel badges and pre-printed planned giving envelopes.

Perhaps most notably, the zero rate now covers the previously excluded recruitment advertisements.

As with certain reliefs under Group 12, the supplier needs to know when his charity customer qualifies for a zero-rated advert so the charity must confirm eligibility by giving him a written declaration.

Annex H of Leaflet 701/1 is a pro forma of an acceptable declaration and is reproduced below:

> '**Annex H**
>
> Charity advertising
>
> I (full name)
>
> (Status in organisation)
>
> of (Name and address of organisation)
>
> declare that the above named charity is
>
> *buying from/importing from
>
> (Name and address of supplier)
>
> the following goods or services eligible for relief from VAT under item 8 of Zero Rate Group 15 (description of goods or services)
>
> (Signature)
>
> (Date)

*delete as appropriate

There are severe penalties for making a false declaration. If you are in any doubt about the eligibility of the goods or services you are buying, you should seek advice from your local VAT office before signing this declaration.

You should retain this certificate for production to your VAT officer. The production of this certificate does not authorise the zero-rating of the equipment. It is your responsibility to ensure that the goods or services supplied are eligible before zero-rating them.'

Supplies of medicinal products etc. to charities

4.68 Charities which provide care, medical or surgical treatment for humans, or which are engaged in medical or veterinary research, may buy medicinal products zero-rated for use in that work. They may also buy substances directly used for synthesis or testing in the course of medical or veterinary research at the zero rate.

The term 'medicinal product' means any substance or article but not instruments, apparatus or appliances, to be used wholly or mainly as follows:

- by being administered to one or more humans or animals for a medicinal purpose, and/or
- as an ingredient in the preparation of such a substance or article.

The other key terms in this heading have the same definition as in the *Medicines Act 1968*.

Group 16 — Clothing and footwear

4.69 Clothing and footwear for young children and not suitable for older people is zero-rated. A child is deemed to be young until the eve of his or her 14th birthday. Items such as belts, hats and caps count as clothing but haberdashery and items like cyclists' armbands or armbands to assist children learning to swim do not. It is often difficult to discern if an item of clothing suitable for a 13-year-old is not suitable for a 14-year-old and thus zero-rated so further guidance is given by reference to sizes. Customs have now even issued a supplementary Public Notice to deal only with maximum sizes for zero-rating. Public Notice 714 covers the principles and 714A lists the maximum sizes.

Clothes 'held out' (advertised) for sale or labelled for children over 13 are standard-rated as are all clothes exceeding these measurements:

Height:	158cm	(62 inches)
Chest:	84cm	(33 inches)
Waist:	71cm	(28 inches)
Hips:	86cm	(34 inches)

If a business selling bigger clothes still thinks they are suitable for under 14s only, they are required to contact their local VAT office for approval.

Clothing does not include anything made partly or wholly of fur skin except for headgear, gloves, buttons, belts and buckles. A garment with a fur skin trimming is excluded from zero-rating if the area covered by the trimming exceeds 20% of the area of the outside material or in the case of a new garment, if the cost to the manufacturer of the fur skin part is greater than the cost of the rest.

'Fur skin' is any skin with fur except rabbit skin, woolled sheep or lamb skin, and the skin (if neither tanned nor dressed) of bovine cattle (including buffalo), equine animals, goats or kids (other than Yemen, Mongolian, or Tibetan goats or kids), swine (including peccary), chamois, gazelles, deer or dogs.

Most baby clothing is zero-rated but the following are excluded from zero-rating:

- pram and pushchair covers not designed to serve as a rain cape outside the pram or chair i.e. if the baby can wear the item when it is not on the pram or buggy, it is zero-rated
- disposable nappy material sold in a continuous roll from which are cut individual nappies
- 'mother-and-baby' shawls intended to wrap around both mother and baby
- sleeping bags not designed with sleeves and/or legs.

Hire or loan of clothes can be zero-rated if the clothes themselves would otherwise qualify for zero-rating e.g. costumes, bridesmaids' dresses.

The rules for footwear are essentially the same as for clothes with published maximum sizes. All kinds of footwear are included. The only notable exclusions from zero-rating are platform type roller skates for fitting onto normal footwear, the blades themselves and other attachments when sold on their own. Some footwear is held out for sale as unisex, such as wellington boots and gym shoes for school PE lessons. In such cases, the maximum size for 13-year-old girls is used as the cut-off for zero-rating.

In Business Brief 12/2000, 8 September 2000, Customs announced a review of the zero rate for children's clothing involving the British Retail

Consortium, the main reason for it being that certain children under 14 were not benefiting from the zero rate because of their size.

In Business Brief 6/2000, 18 April 2001, Customs announced that the rules for zero-rating had been updated and simplified from 1 April 2001. Details are in an Information Sheet available from Customs direct or via their website www.hmce.gov.uk.

Zero-rating applies for clothing and footwear designed and suitable for young children. The design test essentially remains the same although suppliers may now ignore maximum sizes where they can clearly demonstrate a garment was designed for young children. Also, some styles of girls' shoes sized 3½ to 5½ are now not zero-rated where they are clearly not designed for younger children. The suitability test can be met by labelling to ensure relevant clothing and shoes are 'held out for sale only to young children'.

Protective boots and helmets

4.70 Sales of protective boots and helmets for industrial use are zero-rated so long as the buyer does intend them for use by his employees, and motor cycle helmets are also zero-rated for the driver or pillion passenger. These goods must be made to BSI or EC approved standards and be marked accordingly. Further details about how to discern whether protective boots and helmets qualify for zero-rating are in Customs Leaflet 701/23 in which Annex C gives BS specifications and their European equivalents.

This group also zero rates motor cycle crash helmets conforming to UK and EC regulations and pedal cycle helmets used by both children and adults.

Supplies subject to 5% VAT

VATA 1994, Schedule A1 — fuel and power

4.71 Supplies of fuel and power (the most common forms being gas and electricity) are supplies of goods. They are subject to VAT at the standard rate unless they qualify for relief in which case they are subject to the reduced rate (currently 5%).

Supplies qualifying for relief are essentially supplies for domestic use and to charities for non-business use. Supplies to the following are for domestic use:

- a house, flat or other dwelling;

- some types of communal residential accommodation (these are listed at *paragraph 3(2)* of *Schedule A1*);
- self-catering holiday accommodation;
- a caravan; or
- a houseboat.

4.72 Charities must give the supplier a written declaration confirming eligible use where applicable. If their activities from a particular building are wholly non-business, their bills are subject to VAT at 5% provided they issue the declaration.

Most charities have some form of business income even if it is exempt from VAT. If so, they must confirm the extent to which the supplies will be used for non-business activities. If the non-business element is 60% or more, the whole bill is subject to VAT at 5%. If the non-business element is less then 60%, only the non-business percentage is subject to VAT at 5%, the rest being at 17.5%.

Wherever there is mixed use of fuel and power supplies (not just by charities), the onus is on the user to provide confirmation of the extent of qualifying use.

Automatic reduced rate for small quantities

4.73 Where fuel and power is supplied in small quantities, the 5% rate automatically applies and no declaration is required because usage should be clear from, for example, meter readings. Customs stress that 'supplied' in this case means delivered, and that evidence of delivery should be available in the form of invoices. The definition of 'small quantities' is clear from paragraph 2 to Schedule A1 which is reproduced below:

> '2. The following supplies are always for domestic use —
>
> (a) a supply of not more than one tonne of coal or coke held out for sale as domestic fuel;
>
> (b) a supply of wood, peat or charcoal not intended for sale by the recipient;
>
> (c) a supply to a person at any premises of piped gas (that is, gas within paragraph 1(1)(b) above, or of petroleum gas in a gaseous state, provided through pipes) where the gas (together with any other piped gas provided to him at the premises by the same supplier) was not provided at a rate exceeding 150 therms a month or if the supplier

charges for the gas by reference to the number of kilowatt hours supplied, 4,397 kilowatt hours a month;

(d) a supply of petroleum gas in a liquid state where the gas is supplied in cylinders the net weight of each of which is less than 50 kilogrammes and either the number of cylinders is 20 or fewer or the gas is not intended for sale by the recipient;

(e) a supply of petroleum gas in a liquid state, otherwise than in cylinders, to a person at any premises at which he is not able to store more than two tonnes of such gas;

(f) a supply of not more than 2,300 litres of fuel oil, gas oil or kerosene;

(g) a supply of electricity to a person at any premises where the electricity (together with any other electricity provided to him at the premises by the same supplier) was not provided at a rate exceeding 1,000 kilowatt hours a month.'

4.74 Since 1998, the 5% rate has also applied to certain supplies of energy saving materials associated with domestic supplies of fuel and power. From 1 April 2000, Schedule A1 is extended to include:

- the installation of energy saving materials in all homes;
- the grant funded installation, maintenance and repair of central heating systems and home security goods in the homes of qualifying pensioners; and
- the grant funded installation of heating system measures in the homes of the less well off.

Also from 1 April 2000, the 5% rate applies to qualifying security goods installed in the homes of qualifying pensioners at the same time as energy saving materials or central heating systems. 'Qualifying security goods' are:

- locks and bolts for windows
- locks, bolts and security chains for doors
- spy holes, and
- smoke alarms.

Supplies by and to landlords

4.75 Supplies to landlords are subject to the reduced rate with the appropriate declaration for qualifying use. If his tenants then put money into meters, the landlord's receipts are also chargeable to VAT at 5% even if he makes a profit on the recharges. However, if he merely makes a charge for unmetered supplies or adds an amount to the rent, the liability follows that of the rent, which for domestic properties will be exempt.

Schools

4.76 Charges to schools are standard-rated unless they qualify as charities using the supplies for non-business purposes. Customs accept that the following qualify to receive supplies at 5%:

- Voluntary aided schools
- Grant maintained schools
- Schools which have opted out of local authority control
- City technology colleges.

Forthcoming changes to the structure of schools, in particular to the grant maintained system, mean the relevant VAT clauses will also need changing.

Other schools can still receive supplies at the 5% rate to the extent that they relate to residential accommodation for their pupils provided they give the supplier a declaration.

Other supplies subject to VAT at 5%

Imported and reimported works of art, antiques and collectors items

4.77 An effective reduced rate applies to these items (see 12.3). However, the rate of VAT for such items is not 5%. The value for VAT purposes is reduced so that when VAT is added at the 17.5% rate, the effective rate is 5%.

Women's sanitary products

4.78 From 1 January 2001, the supply of women's sanitary products is subject to VAT at 5% instead of 17.5% under *paragraph 6* of *Schedule A1*.

Residential renovation and conversion services

4.79 From 12 May 2001, the reduced rate applies to a number of services connected with the renovation and conversion of residential property. These reliefs were introduced as part of the Government's encouragement of urban regeneration programmes and are described in detail in Chapter 8.

Children's car seats

4.80 From Royal Assent to the Finance Bill 2001, the reduced rate applies to children's car seats. The term includes safety seats, booster seats and cushions, and 'travel systems' such as car seats that can also be used as pushchairs or prams.

Consolidation of reduced rate legislation

4.81 From 1 November 2001, all reduced rate provisions will be clarified, simplified and moved from *Schedule A1* into a new *Schedule 7A* to *VATA 1994*.

Chapter 5

Exemptions

Introduction

5.1 Certain supplies are exempt from VAT (*Sch 9*). The exemptions are largely in the public interest but the consequence is that there is a restriction on the VAT recoverable on associated purchases and expenses.

A business that has a mixture of taxable and exempt activities is partly exempt and may not normally recover all its input tax. The way the recoverable amount is calculated is covered in Chapter 7 dealing with partial exemption.

There are 15 categories of exemption as follows.

Group 1 — Land

Group 2 — Insurance

Group 3 — Postal Services

Group 4 — Betting, Gaming and Lotteries

Group 5 — Finance

Group 6 — Education

Group 7 — Health and Welfare

Group 8 — Burial and Cremation

Group 9 — Trade Unions and Professional Bodies

Group 10 — Sport, Sports Competitions and Physical Education

Group 11 — Works of Art Etc.

Group 12 — Fund-Raising Events by Charities and other Qualifying Bodies

Group 13 — Cultural Services Etc.

Group 14 — Supplies of Goods Where Input Tax Cannot be Recovered

Group 15 — Investment Gold

5.2 *Exemptions*

The conditions under each group must be fulfilled for that supply to be exempt. If they are not, the supply is normally standard-rated unless it can be categorised under any of the zero-rated groups of *Schedule 8* or reduced-rated groups of *Schedule A1* (*Schedule 7A* from 1 November 2001) (Chapter 4).

Group 1 — Land

5.2 As stated at 4.32 in relation to certain zero-rated supplies in this area, land, property and construction issues have historically caused problems because of the complexity of the legislation and the large sums that can be involved.

This Group covers those types of supply which are exempt.

The subject is covered in depth in Chapter 8.

Group 2 — Insurance

5.3 The legislation was completely rewritten in 1997 because of differences of interpretation and abuse. It now contains four items:

(1) The provision of insurance or reinsurance through an insurance business authorised to undertake such activities under *section 3* or *4* of the *Insurance Companies Act 1982*, or through a business which is specifically exempted from having to be so authorised under *section 2* of the same Act.

(2) Provision by an insurer or reinsurer who belongs outside the UK of insurance against any of the risks listed in *Schedules 1* and *2* to the *Insurance Companies Act 1982*, or of reinsurance against the risks in those schedules or any other things.

(3) The provision of insurance or reinsurance by the Export Credits Guarantee Department.

(4) The provision of the services of an insurance intermediary by an insurance broker or insurance agent whilst acting in that capacity and in connection with any of the supplies of insurance or reinsurance described in Items 1 to 3 above whether or not a contract between insurer and insured is finally concluded.

5.4 Customs have produced detailed guidelines on insurance in Leaflet 701/36.

Businesses permitted to provide exempt insurance

5.5 The term 'insurance' is used widely in business but the scope of the exemption is restricted as permitted by the Sixth Directive. Customs have the power to set conditions to ensure the 'correct and straightforward application' (Dir 77/388 Article 13 (B) para 13) of the exemption so as to prevent evasion, avoidance or abuse.

They have used that power to allow the exemption only where insurance or reinsurance is provided by a business authorised to do so under the *Insurance Companies Act 1982* or by other specifically named types of person which do not have to be authorised under that Act. These are:

- members of Lloyd's of London
- friendly societies
- trade unions or employers associations where the insurance is only for the benefit of their members
- insurance companies which only provide benefits in kind insurance.

If it is not clear whether or not an insurer is authorised, their name can be checked against a list of permitted insurers produced annually by the DTI.

Definition of a supply of insurance

5.6 There is no definition of insurance itself but there are clear guidelines as to when a particular supply is of insurance rather than part of a composite supply of other goods or services which takes it out of the exemption, Customs relying on those arising from the decision in *Medical Defence Union v Department of Trade* [*1979*] *2 All ER 421*:

- there must be a right to receive money or money's worth as a result of a contract when a specific event occurs;
- the contract must provide that the insured will become entitled to something on the occurrence of some event;
- the event must involve some element of uncertainty;
- the insured must have an insurable interest in the subject matter of the contract.

The exemption is confined to supplies made within the UK.

Insurance provided to anybody who belongs in a place outside the EC other than the Isle of Man or to a taxable business belonging in another member state which uses the cover for business purposes is outside the scope of VAT. This means that no VAT is charged by the insurer but input tax is still recoverable on associated expenditure, so such supplies have the same effect as they would if they were zero-rated.

5.7 The main types of insurance covered by the exemption are as follows:

- insurance in the everyday sense of the word
- assurance (almost synonymous with 'insurance' but usually used in connection with people's lives)
- reinsurance (cover supplied to providers of insurance against their exposure to risks)
- marine, aviation and transport insurance (MAT)
- export insurance
- engineering insurance (but that part of premiums which relates to the cost of annual inspection and maintenance is not exempt but standard-rated)
- warranties (although tax avoidance in this area, especially as regards mechanical breakdown insurance on cars, has led to a new anti-avoidance measure whereby Insurance Premium Tax is charged at 17.5% rather than at the normal rate)
- self insurance schemes.

Customs Leaflet 701/36 on insurance provides in-depth guidelines as regards the treatment of various types of insurance including MAT supplies by the Export Credits Guarantee Department and engineering insurance.

Reinsurance

5.8 This is exempt if supplied in the UK by a permitted insurer or, under 5.3(2) above, supplied in the UK by a person who belongs outside the UK under Item 2. Consequently, input tax on associated expenditure would normally be non-reclaimable. Where the supply of reinsurance takes place outside the UK and is outside the scope of UK VAT, there is scope for recovery of VAT on associated expenditure (see 12.26–12.39 on international services especially 12.36).

MAT insurance

5.9 As this type of insurance deals with transport, often across international boundaries, there used to be a problem deciding where the supply took place because the risk related to particular journeys. Since 1 January 1993 when the basis of the Single European Market was established, the liability has been determined according to where the insured belongs. Thus exemption applies where the insured belongs in the EC. The place where a business belongs is explained at 12.27.

Export insurance

5.10 This means insurance directly related to an export of goods from a place within to a place outside the EC. Although the insured may be a freight forwarder belonging in the EC, there is provision for input VAT incurred by the insurer in connection with such a supply to be recovered.

The specific exemption for supplies of insurance or reinsurance by the Export Credits Guarantee Department is only included to avoid distortions of competition. Without this item, supplies by the Department would be standard-rated because it is not a permitted insurer.

It can sometimes be difficult to determine whether or not a particular supply of insurance is 'directly' connected to an export of goods. Clearly, the supply must cover the risks of the person exporting them or arranging their export but Customs themselves admit to a number of 'grey areas' so it is best to obtain their opinion in cases of doubt.

Engineering insurance

5.11 This is not listed under the relevant Schedule of the *Insurance Companies Act 1982* but still qualifies for exemption including fees for inspection services for the benefit of the insurer, not the insured, as part of an engineering insurance contract.

Warranties

5.12 Two types of warranty are included:

(*a*) where a supplier of goods to a customer agrees to meet the cost of repairs and parts over a given period of time if the goods are faulty; and

(*b*) a contract of insurance supplied to the customer by a third party (not the supplier of the goods) which provides cover in case the goods prove faulty over a given period of time.

Type (*a*) can only be exempt if the supplier is a permitted insurer under the relevant legislation. Even if the supplier of the goods himself has insurance cover for the goods which he recharges to customers, he would not normally be regarded as providing insurance intermediary services at 5.3(4) above, those charges having the same liability as the goods themselves.

Example 36
A retailer sells a fridge freezer to a customer for £400 + £70 VAT and also recharges the £20 insurance premium he has paid to a permitted insurer. The charge to the retailer from the permitted insurer is exempt but the recharge to the customer is standard-rated. Therefore, unless the retailer is willing to absorb some of the costs himself, he would charge £493.50, being £470 for the goods and £23.50 for the insurance.

5.13 For the warranty to be exempt, there must be a separate, optional contract between the third party permitted insurer and the customer and, even then, Insurance Premium Tax is 17.5% to prevent artificially loading the warranty element of the contract.

Self insurance schemes

5.14 Certain businesses may offer their customers 'insurance' or a 'warranty' without themselves insuring their products with a permitted insurer. The customers' premiums are used to cover any costs incurred by the supplier but the supplier only takes out a policy to protect himself against excess costs.

The amounts paid to the supplier by customers are not exempt unless they relate to a contract of insurance with a permitted insurer.

Services of intermediaries including brokers and agents

5.15 Item 4 at 5.3(4) clarifies the extent to which services of brokers and agents may be exempt.

The term 'services of an intermediary' means services of an insurance broker or agent in carrying out the following:

- bringing together seekers and providers of insurance or reinsurance with a view to a supply being effected;
- preparatory work prior to the conclusion of contracts of insurance or reinsurance;
- providing assistance in the administration and performance of these contracts including claims handling;
- collecting premiums.

An insurance broker or agent is acting in this way if he is the intermediary or one of the intermediaries between an insurer or reinsurer making supplies under Items 1 to 3, and a person who is *or may be* seeking such a supply *or is already an insured person.*

Other rules and exceptions for intermediaries

5.16 If a supplier is making positive rated supplies (17.5% or 5%) of goods or services to a customer and a transaction is entered into which will or could lead to the provision of insurance on those goods or services, then any services related to that provision of insurance made by the supplier of the goods or services or somebody connected with him who deals directly with the customer are not exempt under Item 4 at 5.3(4) unless certain other conditions are fulfilled.

The conditions are:

- a document containing details of the premium and any other amounts payable under the transaction by the customer, and any obligations on the part of any of the parties to the transaction, must be prepared;
- the contents of the document must be disclosed to the customer in full either before or when the transaction is effected; and
- the supplier must comply with the rules set out in a current Customs public notice or leaflet concerning:
  - (*a*) the preparation and form of the document,
  - (*b*) how the content should be disclosed to the customer,
  - (*c*) the delivery of a copy of the document to the customer.

These obligations along with the requirement to pay Insurance Premium Tax at 17.5% reduce significantly the likelihood of tax avoidance in this area.

The definition of a 'connected person' is that in *ICTA 1988, s 839.*

Exclusions

5.17 The exemption under Item 4 at 5.3(4) for intermediary services does not include:

- the supply of any market research, product design, advertising, promotional or similar services;
- the collection, collation and provision of information for use in connection with the services listed in the first indent;
- the supply of any valuation or inspection services;

- the services of loss adjusters, average adjusters, motor assessors, surveyors or other experts except where:
  - (*a*) the services are of claims handling under a contract of insurance or reinsurance,
  - (*b*) the business handling the claim is authorised to act on behalf of the insurer or reinsurer when providing the service, and
  - (*c*) that authority includes written permission to accept or reject the claim and to settle any amount accepted;
- the supply of any services in pursuance of any contract of insurance or reinsurance or any associated arrangements and which are so supplied either:
  - (i) instead of the payment of all or any part of any indemnity for which the contract provides, or
  - (ii) for the purpose, in any other manner, of satisfying any claim under that contract, whether in full or in part.

The last main indent means that if services are supplied instead of financial restitution in a given situation, the services cannot be exempt under Item 4 at 5.3(4) and are usually standard-rated.

Example 37
A private individual takes out an insurance policy on his house. Under its terms, the insurer agrees to send somebody out free of charge if the central heating system breaks down. Even though the insurer pays the repairer's bill, the latter's services cannot be treated as exempt.

In Business Brief 3/2001, 20 February 2001, Customs confirmed that following the Court of Appeal Decision in *Century Life plc* [*2001*] *STC 38*, pension review services are exempt insurance related services by insurance agents. They stress, however, that not all services outsourced by insurers to brokers or agents are necessarily exempt. Each case must be treated on its merits.

Group 3 — Postal services

5.18 Delivery services and any services in connection therewith by the Post Office are exempt.

See 3.53 for the position where a supplier provides a delivery service to his customer through the Post Office.

Group 4 — Betting, gaming and lotteries

5.19 The provision of facilities for placing bets, playing games of chance or the right to take part in any lottery is exempt.

There are certain exclusions:

- admission to premises;
- the grant of a right to take part in a game in return for a charge under *section 14* of the *Gaming Act 1968* or the Northern Irish equivalent, *Article 76* of the *Betting, Gaming, Lotteries and Amusements (Northern Ireland) Order 1985 (SI 1985/1204)*;
- the provision of these facilities by a club to its members within the normal subscription;
- the provision of a gaming machine.

5.20 Customs' Leaflet 701/26 'Betting and Gaming' clarifies these exclusions further by stating that session and participation charges levied at premises which are licensed or by clubs which are registered under *Part II* of the *Gaming Act 1968* are also excluded.

Standard-rating applies to the exclusions.

It stresses that *Part III* of that Act only refers to gaming machines so if the premises or club is only registered under *Part III*, session or participation charges do qualify for exemption.

5.21 A 'game of chance' for VAT purposes has the same meaning as in the gaming legislation (including roulette, black jack etc. but also games which include an element of skill as well e.g. whist or bridge) and a 'gaming machine' must fulfil the following conditions:

- it must be built or adapted for playing games of chance;
- there must be a charge to play e.g. by coin or token unless a free go is awarded for initial success;
- the machine produces an element of chance.

The value of exempt supplies under this category is the amount paid to take part less money paid as prizes, or if the prizes are in the form of goods, the cost of them to the supplier. The value cannot be reduced by duties such as betting duty.

> *Example 38*
>
> (i) In the quarter to 31 October 2001, the Fortune Casino receives £20,000 in participation charges for games of Black Jack and Roulette but has to pay out £4,000 in prize money. The value of its exempt income for period 10/01 is £16,000.
>
> (ii) From 1 November 2001, it changes its structure and offers goods as prizes instead of cash. In the period to 31 January 2002, it receives £19,000 in participation charges and gives away watches and other items of jewellery as prizes which cost £5,000 + £875 VAT to buy. The value of its exempt income for period 01/02 is £13,125 (£19,000 – £5,875) because the VAT on the purchase of the prizes relates to an exempt supply and cannot be reclaimed.

Casino card room games

5.22 Sometimes casinos hold special competitions in addition to making available the normal gambling games. VAT is due on the gross entry fees unless the competition is run exactly in accordance with guidelines agreed between Customs and the British Casino Association, in which case the income is outside the scope of VAT.

Bingo

5.23 In accordance with the main conditions, the following charges are exempt:

- session and participation charges for playing

  (*a*) prize bingo,

  (*b*) cash bingo at premises not licensed or clubs not registered under *Part II* of the *Gaming Act* (Chapter III of the Northern Ireland Order referred to heretofore).

The main difference between prize bingo and cash bingo concerns the treatment of prizes and is explained in full in Customs Leaflet 701/27. In prize bingo, the cost to the promoter of the goods given as prizes is deducted from the participation charges to calculate the exempt value, whereas if goods are given as prizes at all in cash bingo, they are treated as gifts and VAT is payable by the promoter on their cost if it exceeds the *de minimis* level of £50 (see 3.57).

Value of exempt supply — prize bingo

5.24 The value is calculated as follows:

Total gross session and participation charges including any prize vouchers used to pay for further games of bingo (without deduction of any bingo duty payable) less:

- the tax inclusive cost of goods and the value of vouchers given as prizes (if vouchers are given as prizes and redeemed for goods, only the tax-inclusive cost of the goods is included, and not the face value of the vouchers);
- any cash prizes given (any participation charges used as additional prize money is excluded); *and*
- payments made to retailers who redeem prize vouchers for goods on the promoter's behalf.

No VAT is due on the goods given as prizes but no input tax can be deducted either (subject to the normal rules) because it relates to an exempt supply.

Value of exempt supply — cash bingo

5.25 The exempt value is the gross session and participation charges (without deduction of any bingo duty payable) less stake money returned to players as prizes (excluding participation charges used as additional prize money).

The normal rules for gifts apply to goods given as extra prizes in cash bingo.

Lotteries

5.26 The right to take part in a lottery for a charge and the service of selling lottery tickets is exempt but lottery management services are standard-rated. Full details are provided in Customs Leaflet 701/28 'Lotteries'. The provisions also cover the National Lottery.

Value of exempt supply — lotteries

5.27 The exempt value is the gross proceeds from ticket sales less either the amount of cash prizes or the VAT-inclusive cost of prizes in the form of goods.

Prizes — goods

5.28 If the lottery is free to enter, prizes are treated as gifts. Input tax is recoverable on them subject to the normal rules and output tax is payable on the cost to the promoter if its value exceeds £50 (see 3.57).

There are two notable exceptions to this rule:

(*a*) when cars are given as prizes no output VAT is due because the input tax cannot be recovered; and

(*b*) input tax incurred on holidays given as prizes cannot be reclaimed under the business entertainment provisions.

Prizes — services

5.29 No VAT is due on services provided as a prize.

Group 5 — Finance

5.30 Most services supplied in connection with finance either directly or through the making of arrangements by agents are exempt. This Group is divided into ten items including dealings in money, credit finance, dealings in stocks and shares, the services of banks and the services of agents bringing together providers of the main services and those seeking them.

As these services are normally the main or sole activity of the business providing them, there tends to be a severe restriction on recovery of input tax under the partial exemption rules (see Chapter 7) and difficulty in calculating exactly how much can be recovered because of the complexity of the legislation. Certain trade bodies have reached administrative agreements with Customs in order to produce consistency of treatment amongst their members and these are published in Leaflet 701/57 'VAT: Administrative Agreements Entered into with Trade Bodies'. The Leaflet covering the Items within Group 5 is 701/29 'Finance'.

Supplies of coins or bank notes as collectors' items or investment articles are excluded from the exemption and are normally standard-rated.

The exemption does apply to income received for operating credit card, charge card or payment card services for any business which agrees to accept the card as payment for goods or services supplied by them. Thus, the exempt service is from the provider of the card (e.g. Visa/Mastercard) to the outlet which accepts the card from the cardholder as payment (e.g. restaurants, shops etc.).

5.31 In their Business Brief 17/98 issued on 7 August 1998, Customs clarified the treatment of charges made to customers paying by credit card. If the business that supplies the goods or services that the customer is buying also makes a charge for paying by credit card, the normal liability of the goods or services also applies to the charge for using the card. For example, if a football fan books tickets for a match by telephone using his credit card and pays an extra £1 for each ticket, the whole charge is standard-rated. However, if an agent of the business supplying the main goods or services makes the charge, the agent is supplying an exempt financial service under this Group. Customs cite the example of a travel agent acting on behalf of a tour operator.

The exempt items are at 5.32 to 5.42.

Item 1

5.32 Issues, transfers, receipts of money, any security for or dealings in money or any note or order for the payment of money.

Item 2

5.33 The making of an advance or the granting of any credit, including the supply of credit by a business in connection with other goods or services it supplies, provided that there is a separate charge made for the credit element which is disclosed to the customer. The main area of finance to which this item relates is loans.

Item 3

5.34 The provision of finance where the terms require payment by instalments. The most common examples are HP, conditional sale and credit sale agreements such as lease purchase where the credit charge is separately made and disclosed to the customer.

Example 39

A computer supplier also provides hire-purchase facilities directly to his customers. A customer buys a PC and accessories for £2,000 + VAT under an HP agreement over three years. The interest over the three years will be £300. So long as the documentation given to the customer shows the £300 as a separate charge, the total payments made will be £2,000 + £350 VAT for the goods and £300 exempt credit.

5.35 Where the finance terms are separately supplied by a finance company, the supplier of the goods (or services) first sells them to the finance company, which must then follow the disclosure rules in its contract with the final customer for the credit element to be exempt.

Item 4

5.36 The provision of administrative arrangements and documentation and the transfer of title to the goods in connection with the type of supply described in Item 3 at 5.34, provided that the amount paid for the service is specified in the agreement and does not exceed £10.

Items 5 and 5A

5.37 The *Value Added Tax (Finance) Order 1999 (SI 1999/594)* introduced a new Item 5, replacing exemption for the 'making of arrangements' for other financial services with an exemption for 'intermediary services'. The Order came into force on 10 March 1999.

In practice, this means that the exemption no longer applies to credit management and certain outsourced financial services such as:

- credit checking
- valuation
- authorisation services
- taking decisions in relation to a grant of or application for credit
- record-keeping for a credit provider in relation to a grant of or application for credit
- monitoring payments or dealing with overdue payments.

Also excluded are:

- market research, product design, advertising promotional and similar services
- preparatory services in connection with transactions in money, securities for money or notes or orders for the payment of money.

The new Order clarified that for an intermediary service to be exempt, the intermediary must take an active part in assisting two or more parties to conclude an agreement unless that activity constitutes credit management services. The following would be accepted as exempt services:

- assisting with completion of forms
- checking completed forms
- forwarding completed forms to the provider of the financial service

- making representations to one party on behalf of the other involved in an actual or proposed financial transaction.

The Order also introduced a new Item 5A making the underwriting of an issue within Item 1 or Item 6 exempt. There is considerable opposition to the changes as they affect outsourced services as the reason for outsourcing is not 'VAT-driven' but for other commercial reasons. As a result of the changes, it is envisaged that many providers of financial services will bring in-house those activities that are currently outsourced.

The main case on outsourcing is *C&E Commrs v FDR Ltd* — Court of Appeal (Civil Decision), judgment delivered 13 July 2000. FDR provides data processing and management services to banks relating to their credit card operations. Customs considered that these services did not fall within the exemption but FDR claimed that UK law was out of line with EC law, relying on Article 13B(d)(3) of the Sixth Directive. The Tribunal and the Court of Appeal agreed with FDR.

In Business Brief 10/2000, 8 August 2000, Customs announced that they had sought leave to appeal the decision to the House of Lords and that businesses providing identical services could exempt them. Protective assessments would be issued but not enforced pending a final decision.

Business Brief 10/2001, 16 July 2001, announces that Customs were refused leave to appeal to the House of Lords. Those that have treated identical supplies as standard-rated may now make retrospective claims subject to the three-year cap. All taxpayers that consider they are affected by the decision should write to their local VAT office. After a consultation process involving relevant trade bodies, UK law will be changed to align it with the Sixth Directive.

Item 6

5.38 Any dealings in securities or secondary securities including issues, transfers and receipts. Again, definitions are crucial, so the item is further broken down into five sections listing the full coverage of 'securities' and 'secondary securities'. These are:

(*a*) shares, stocks, bonds, notes (excluding promissory notes), debentures, debenture stock or shares in an oil royalty;

(*b*) any document relating to money, in any currency, deposited with the issuer or another person giving the obligation to pay the stated amount to the bearer or to order, with or without interest, and by the delivery of which, with or without endorsement, the right to receive the stated amount is transferable, with or without interest;

(*c*) any bill, note or other obligation of the Treasury or any foreign government, which is a document by the delivery of which, with or without endorsement, title is transferable (note that the obligation must not be or have been legal tender in any part of the world);

(*d*) any letter of allotment or rights, any warrant conferring an option to acquire a security included in this item, any renounceable or scrip certificates, rights coupons, coupons representing dividends or interest on such a security, bond mandates or other documents conferring or containing evidence of title to or rights in respect of such a security; or

(*e*) units or other documents which confer rights under any trust set up for, or having the effect of providing for, people with funds available for investment, facilities for them to use as beneficiaries of the trust any profits or income arising from the acquisition, holding, management or disposal of any property whatsoever.

Note that Item 1 at 5.32 does not include anything listed in Item 6.

Item 7

5.39 The services of an agent in making arrangements for any supply listed under Item 6 and the underwriting of any transaction. These services include the bringing together of a person or business effecting transactions in any of the securities or secondary securities listed in Item 6 with anyone wishing to acquire or dispose of them.

Item 8

5.40 The operation of a current, deposit or savings account. This type of service is normally provided by banks or the former mutual building societies which have now converted to banks.

Item 9

5.41 The management by its operator of an authorised unit trust or trust based scheme.

The Tribunal in *Prudential Corporation plc VTD 17030* considered whether sub-contracted investment management services provided to the operator of an Authorised Unit Trust were exempt. It found that the services were standard-rated under UK law but EC law was unambiguous in making them exempt. Customs have appealed the decision to the Court of Session. Until the matter is resolved, taxpayers providing the same services may file refund claims and Customs will issue protective assessments but neither will be enforced (see Business Brief 6/2001, 18 April 2001).

Item 10

5.42 The services of an authorised corporate director of an open-ended investment company ('OEIC') to the extent that they relate to the management of the scheme's property.

A person is an 'authorised corporate director' of an OEIC if he is currently a director of that company and not only has responsibility for managing its property but is also actually fulfilling that responsibility.

The property of an OEIC is that subject to the collective investment scheme constituted by that company and the term 'director' includes anyone effectively occupying the position of a director no matter what they are called.

The terms 'OEIC', 'collective investment scheme', 'authorised unit trust scheme', 'operator' and 'trust based scheme' used in the VAT legislation have the same meaning as they are given in the *Financial Services Act 1986* in accordance with Notes (6) and (10) to the Group.

Financial services excluded from exemption

5.43 Inevitably, there are certain services most would regard as financial services but which are excluded from exemption and normally standard-rated. These are listed at paragraph 20 of Leaflet 701/29 which is reproduced below.

> **'CUSTOMS LEAFLET 701/29 PARA 20**
>
> The following supplies, which may be connected with financial services, are not covered by any of the exemption provisions:
>
> - debt collection, credit control and sales ledger accounting services,
> - equipment leasing,
> - executor and trustee services and the administration of estates,
> - investment, finance and taxation advice,
> - management consultancy,
> - management of trust funds,
> - merger and takeover advice,
> - portfolio management,
> - registrar services,
> - safe custody and safe transportation services,

- service companies' activities, e.g. administration, payment of salaries and wages.'

Group 6 — Education

5.44 It is important to distinguish between education supplied by an eligible body in return for a fee (which is a business supply and usually exempt) and education supplied free of charge, which is outside the scope of VAT because it is not supplied in the course or furtherance of business. Examples of each are given at 5.45 and 5.46.

Training courses normally provided by businesses not falling within the definition of an 'eligible body' (see 5.51 and below) are standard-rated.

5.45

Examples of establishments providing exempt education

Independent fee paying schools

Universities including former polytechnics that have become universities

Institutions teaching English as a foreign language.

5.46

Examples of establishments outside the scope of VAT

Local authority schools ('state' schools)

Voluntary aided schools

Grant-maintained schools.

5.47 Although supplies of education to pupils and students under either category do not carry VAT, the difference is that the partial exemption rules might apply to the former but not to the latter category (see Chapter 7 on partial exemption). Also, exempt education is a business activity and the establishments listed at 5.46 are not regarded as being businesses. Therefore, the establishments listed at 5.45 cannot usually obtain zero-rated construction services in the course of construction of buildings for a 'relevant charitable purpose' (see 8.7(4)) whereas those listed at 5.46 can. See also 5.59.

5.48 Where sixth form colleges, tertiary colleges and colleges of further education normally require a fee from overseas students or those under 19 years old when they are admitted while other types of student receive their education free, any charge is exempt.

5.49 The deciding factor for exemption is not the content of courses and whether or not they are supplied for profit, but whether the educational establishment is an 'eligible body', thus removing any doubt where a course might be regarded as for vocational or recreational purposes.

5.50 The Group is split into six items with five explanatory notes. Customs give detailed clarification as to their interpretation of the Group in their Leaflet 701/30 'Education'. The exempt items are dealt with at 5.51 to 5.58.

Item 1

5.51 This general item exempts the provision by an 'eligible body' of:

- education,
- research (where supplied to an eligible body), or
- vocational training.

Although the item itself is fairly self-explanatory, application would not be so clear without the accompanying Note (1) which is effectively an exhaustive list of eligible bodies. Note (1) is reproduced below.

> **'ELIGIBLE BODIES PROVIDING EXEMPT EDUCATION**
>
> (1) For the purposes of this Group an "eligible body" is—
>
> (a) a school within the meaning of the Education Act 1996, the Education (Scotland) Act 1980, the Education and Libraries (Northern Ireland) Order 1986 or the Education Reform (Northern Ireland) Order 1989, which is—
>
> (i) provisionally or finally registered or deemed to be registered as a school within the meaning of the aforesaid legislation in a register of independent schools; or
>
> (ii) a school in respect of which grants are made by the Secretary of State to the proprietor or managers; or
>
> (iii) a county school, voluntary school or maintained special school (other than one established in a hospital) within the meaning of the Education Act 1996 or a maintained school within the meaning of the Education and Libraries (Northern Ireland) Order 1986; or
>
> (iv) a public school within the meaning of section 135(1) of the Education (Scotland) Act 1980; or
>
> (v) a grant-maintained school within the meaning of the Education Act 1996; or

(vi) a self-governing school within the meaning of section 1(3) of the Self-Governing Schools (Scotland) Act 1989; or

(vii) a grant-maintained special school within the meaning of the Education Act 1996; or

(viii) a grant-maintained integrated school within the meaning of Article 65 of the Education Reform (Northern Ireland) Order 1989;

(b) a United Kingdom university, and any college, institution, school or hall of such a university;

(c) an institution—

(i) falling within section 91(3)(a) or (b) or section 91(5)(b) or (c) of the Further and Higher Education Act 1992; or

(ii) which is a designated institution as defined in section 44(2) of the Further and Higher Education (Scotland) Act 1992; or

(iii) managed by a board of management as defined in section 36(1) of the Further and Higher Education (Scotland) Act 1992; or

(iv) to which grants are paid by the Department of Education for Northern Ireland under Article 66(2) of the Education and Libraries (Northern Ireland) Order 1986;

(d) a public body of a description in Note (5) to Group 7 below;

(e) a body which—

(i) is precluded from distributing and does not distribute any profit it makes; and

(ii) applies any profits made from supplies of a description within this Group to the continuance or improvement of such supplies;

(f) a body not falling within paragraphs (a) to (e) above which provides the teaching of English as a foreign language.'

The final category of eligible body at (f) of the Note above is helpful in that establishments offering English as a foreign language do not have to fall within one of the types of body covered by (a) to (e) for exemption to apply. Legislative Note (2) to Item 1 ensures that exemption would only apply to their supplies of English as a foreign language, not to any other education they offer.

Legislative Note (3) to Item 1 defines 'vocational training' as training, re-training or the provision of work experience for any trade, profession or employment, or any voluntary work connected with education, health, safety, welfare, or the carrying out of activities of a charitable nature.

Item 2

5.52 The supply of private tuition in a subject normally taught in a school or university by an individual teacher acting independently of an employer is exempt. Teachers can still provide exempt supplies of private tuition even if they teach a particular method of education and have materials provided for them so long as they are self-employed. In practice, it may not matter because even if the tuition was standard-rated, the total income per annum received by one teacher would rarely exceed the registration threshold (currently £54,000 per annum).

Item 3

5.53 Certain examination services in connection with education are exempt. They must be provided by or to an eligible body or to a person receiving education or vocational training which is itself exempt under Item 1 or 2 at 5.51 and 5.52 or Item 5 at 5.57, or which is provided otherwise than in the course or furtherance of business. In other words, if a business provides examination services, charges are only exempt if the services are to an institution covered by Legislative Note (1) (see 5.51) or to someone receiving education or vocational training which is either free or exempt if charged for.

Definition of examination services

5.54 There is no legal definition but the term includes the setting of exams and educational or training standards, the marking of exams, the making of assessments and other services aimed towards ensuring educational and training standards are maintained. Notable examples are services in connection with GCSE exams, National Curriculum tests and NVQ assessments.

Item 4

5.55 This item is drafted in a way which is open to different interpretations. Therefore, official clarification may be required before the exemption can be applied. The supply of *any* goods or services (except examination services) *closely related* to an exempt service covered by Item 1 at 5.51 is exempt provided that it is made by or to the eligible body supplying the education, research or vocational training.

5.56 *Exemptions*

The service covered by Item 1 is known as the 'principal supply' and the term is used in the two other conditions which must be met before the exemption can apply. These are:

(*a*) the goods or services are for the direct use of the pupil, student or trainee receiving the principal supply; and

(*b*) if the supply is to the eligible body making the principal supply, it must be made by another eligible body.

Customs have given their interpretation of the meaning of 'closely related' in Leaflet 701/30. Apart from the direct use condition stipulated in the law, they also state in paragraph 27 that the associated goods or services must be necessary for delivering the education to the pupil, student or trainee which includes accommodation, catering, transport and school trips.

Example 40
If an independent fee-paying school makes separate charges for boarding accommodation, those charges are also exempt because the provision of accommodation is closely related to the exempt education. (The meaning of 'closely related' has been challenged by Customs and may change.) Compare this with a state school which sells standard-rated exercise books to pupils. The charges are not 'closely related' to exempt education because the education is free and outside the scope of VAT. However, Customs allow such supplies to be treated as non-business and VAT free provided that they would otherwise be closely related to the education the pupils receive and charges are at or below cost. Any goods or services provided which are not closely related to the principal supply are standard-rated unless relief can be obtained under another heading, e.g. zero-rated text books.

5.56 If an eligible body supplies associated goods or services to another educational establishment, that establishment must be an eligible body supplying exempt education to its pupils, students or trainees for the charge between the two institutions to be exempt as well. If the recipient provides free education, the goods or services it receives carry their normal VAT liability.

Example 41

(i) A university sells works of English literature to a fee-paying school for use by its pupils. These supplies are exempt as both bodies are eligible and provide exempt education.

(ii) The same university supplies works of English literature to a state comprehensive school. The latter provides free education to its pupils, therefore the books carry their normal zero-rated VAT liability.

Note that commercial teachers of English as a foreign language may not also exempt closely related goods or services (see 5.51).

Item 5

5.57 The provision of vocational training and associated goods and services essential to that supply when made by the provider of the training are exempt to the extent that payment due is ultimately a charge to funds under arrangements covered by the *Employment Training Act 1973*, the *Employment and Training (Northern Ireland) Act 1950* or the *Enterprise and New Towns (Scotland) Act 1990*.

This item is simply a broadening of the exemption for vocational training which otherwise would not have been covered by Item 1. Associated goods and services are 'essential' if made direct to the trainee.

Item 6

5.58 The item exempts the provision of facilities by a youth club or association of youth clubs to its members or by an association of youth clubs to members of a youth club which is a member of that association.

For a youth club to qualify under this heading, it must be established to promote the social, physical, educational or spiritual development of its members, at least 51% of whom must be aged 20 or younger. The club must be a non-profit-making organisation fulfilling the conditions of Note (1)(e) at 5.51 above. Customs Leaflet 701/35 covers youth clubs and paragraph 5 lists charges which would not qualify for exemption. These are:

- fund-raising events where tickets are sold to the public although these may still be exempt under Group 12 (see 5.79)
- sales of food and drink
- overnight accommodation

- recreational holidays (those providing spiritual welfare may be exempt under Group 7 — see 5.60)
- supplies not made to members.

Educational institutions and the construction of new buildings

5.59 Many, but not all, educational institutions have charitable status.

Zero-rating is available for the construction of new buildings intended for use solely for non-business charity purposes.

Non-business use for educational institutions means use to provide services free of charge.

Therefore, if a state school has a new teaching block built, the construction services are zero-rated subject to the normal rules, whereas if an independent fee-paying school has a similar block built, zero-rating is not available because the block will be used for a business activity i.e. the provision of exempt education.

The normal rules for zero-rating and the subject of land, property and construction are covered in detail in Chapter 8.

Group 7 — Health and welfare

5.60 Most services in the health sector are exempt so long as they are provided by properly registered practitioners. The relief also extends to services closely related to those of the practitioners themselves. Included within the Group are the services of registered doctors and dentists; suppliers of false teeth and other dental prostheses such as bridges and crowns; ophthalmic and dispensing opticians; qualified nurses, midwives and health visitors; hearing aid dispensers; pharmaceutical chemists; care, medical and surgical providers in hospitals; locums and those who transport sick and injured people in vehicles specially adapted for that purpose, e.g. ambulances (note that international transport is still zero-rated — see 4.34 *et seq.* — *Schedule 8 Group 8* 'Transport').

The Group is widely drawn and also covers the supply of human blood, products for therapeutic purposes derived from human blood and human (including foetal) organs or tissue for diagnostic purposes, therapeutic purposes or medical research.

Welfare services and goods in connection therewith are included if provided by a charity or public body otherwise than for profit. So are goods and services incidental to the provision of spiritual welfare by a religious community to its resident members in return for any payment made as a condition of their membership (usually subscriptions).

The Group comprises eleven items dealt with at 5.61 to 5.70:

Item 1

5.61 This provides for exemption of five types of health service although the stress is on the provider being registered or enrolled in a recognised register covered by the relevant legislation. The five categories of registration are:

- medical practitioners or those with limited registration
- ophthalmic and dispensing opticians (note that the supply of spectacles is taxable; essentially the exemption covers the eye test)
- the *Professions Supplementary to Medicine Act 1960* (e.g. chiropodists, occupational therapists, physiotherapists, remedial gymnasts)
- nurses, midwives and health visitors
- hearing aid dispensers or employers of hearing aid dispensers.

The exemption does not extend to the letting on hire of goods except where it is in connection with the supply of other services covered by the item.

The first four categories include the services of people who are not registered under the relevant Acts but are operating under the supervision of somebody who is.

Item 2

5.62 The provision of treatment and the supply of dental prostheses by a dentist, dental auxiliary or dental technician is exempt. Again, the requirement exists to be registered under the appropriate Act but services provided by those who are not registered are still exempt if under the supervision of somebody who is.

The above references to exempt services by those registered under the relevant Acts only apply to the services for which they are registered. Thus, a registered doctor can only provide the services of a doctor exempt from VAT.

If he were to sell fitness equipment as well, income received therefrom would be chargeable to VAT.

5.63 *Exemptions*

If a visiting EC practitioner handles an urgent case under *section 18(3)* of the *Medical Act 1983* and is not registered under the appropriate Act which would exempt his services, he can still exempt them if he would be entitled to register.

Item 3

5.63 The services of pharmaceutical chemists registered under the appropriate Act of Parliament are exempt. Legislative Note (2A) to the Group took effect from 1 January 1997, extending coverage to services of a non-registered person where the services are wholly performed or directly supervised by somebody who is so registered.

The item does not include the letting on hire of goods.

Item 4

5.64 Care, medical or surgical treatment provided in recognised hospitals or other institutions which are approved, licensed, registered or exempted from registration by the Government under certain Acts is exempt.

The supply of goods in connection with the treatment is also exempt.

Recent Governments have changed the way care is provided and have encouraged its provision to individuals in their own homes under the Care in the Community programme. The exemption can be extended to this type of care under strict detailed conditions laid down by Customs including development and oversight of the care programme by a qualified person (see 5.61).

Item 5

5.65 This item exempts doctors' deputising services and the services of locums where provided for fully registered doctors or those with limited registration.

Items 6 to 8

5.66 These items exempt human blood, products derived from it and organs etc. as described in the general introduction to this Group.

Item 11

5.67 This has been taken out of order because it exempts services associated with health, being the transportation of sick or injured people in vehicles specially adapted for that purpose.

Zero-rating is still available should the journey constitute international transport (see 4.34 *et seq.*).

Ambulance services take various forms all of which are included in this category, notably air and waterborne ambulances.

Restrictions to exemptions for services relating to health

5.68 The services supplied by medically registered individuals include the provision of expert evidence in courts of law and lecturing to audiences about their own or their families' health.

Other lectures, e.g. to factory managements about their staff, to medical students, first-aid staff and the police, are not exempt but standard-rated.

Sometimes practitioners may have to assign copyright for their material, grant licences or appear on radio or television. These services are liable to VAT.

Also liable to VAT are the services of health related outlets such as health farms and health clubs (although it may be possible to run a non-profit-making health club the subscriptions to which are exempt under Group 10 — see 5.76).

Customs' interpretation of the legislation on health is in Leaflet 701/31.

Items 9 and 10

5.69 These two items are dedicated to welfare services.

Since they are often supplied by charities, the zero rate can often apply under Groups 12 'Drugs, Medicines, Aids for the Handicapped etc.' and 15 'Charities' of *Schedule 8* (see Chapter 4).

Those welfare services not within zero-rating, and thus within the exemption are set out below.

The supply by a charity or public body of welfare services and goods supplied in connection therewith otherwise than for profit is exempt. A 'public body' is:

- a government department as defined in *section 41(6)*;
- a local authority; or
- any body established under law for public purposes and not to generate profit and which carries out activities similar to those of government departments and local authorities.

'Welfare services' means services which are directly connected with:

- the provision of care, treatment or instruction designed to promote the physical or mental welfare of elderly, sick, distressed or disabled people;
- the protection of children and young people; or
- the provision of spiritual welfare by a religious institution as part of a course of instruction or a retreat which is not designed primarily for recreational or holiday purposes, e.g. a teaching weekend for members of a church or a religious convention.

Item 9 does not include accommodation or catering except where it is part of the provision of care treatment, or instruction.

Item 10 covers the provision of goods and services by religious communities to their members and which are incidental to the provision of spiritual welfare.

'Otherwise than for profit' means that the particular service is not planned to make a profit but if a surplus is inadvertently made and is ploughed back into the same activity, the service is still exempt.

'Care' in this context means some form of continuing personal contact in looking after, helping or supervising somebody.

5.70 In certain circumstances, charities or other non-profit-making bodies supply welfare services which are not regarded as business activities. The two examples mentioned by Customs in their Leaflet 701/1 'Charities' are as follows:

- Supplies of services and related goods made consistently below cost by charities to distressed people for the relief of their distress.

  'Consistently below cost' means that the charity must contribute at least 15% of the cost of providing the service from its own funds or, in other words, the recipient of the welfare services can pay a maximum of 85% of the cost.

- meals on wheels services provided by a charity as agent of a local authority which constitute part of the non-business activities of the local authority.

The importance of this is that the value of the services is not reckoned in calculating the allowable input tax under the partial exemption rules (see Chapter 7).

Group 8 — Burial and cremation

5.71 Disposal of the remains of the dead and associated services are exempt. Principally, this covers the services of funeral directors and undertakers. The exemption covers all the expected services such as embalming, provision of the coffin and accessories, transport of mourners to and from the graveyard, crematorium etc. and graveyard services. The exemption still applies if the undertaker does not supply the coffin for whatever reason, e.g. the undertaker comes from the place where the deceased lived but the death happened somewhere else and an undertaker there was instructed to provide the coffin only.

If goods or services other than embalming and work on the grave are provided but that person does not also conduct the funeral itself, those supplies are standard-rated, e.g. provision of the coffin only or supplying additional limousines to another undertaker.

Certain other items may be supplied by the undertaker, e.g. wreaths, announcement cards, orders of service. These are standard-rated.

Services of monumental masons

5.72 Where a monumental mason is hired to remove or refix a headstone as part of a funeral, his services are exempt but if he is required to perform any other service such as engraving the headstone, those services are standard-rated.

Removal of corpses

5.73 Where a corpse is transported as part of a funeral, the charge is exempt but other removals such as coroner's removals from the scene of an accident to a mortuary are standard-rated. The international transportation of a corpse may be zero-rated under the rules in *Schedule 8 Group 8* covered at 4.34 *et seq.*

Exhumation

5.74 Any charge for exhumation is standard-rated but any subsequent reburial is exempt.

Further details can be found in Customs Leaflet 701/32 'Burial, Cremation and the Commemoration of the Dead'.

Group 9 — Subscriptions to trade unions, professional and other public interest bodies

5.75 The supply of services and associated goods by certain non-profit-making organisations are exempt. Those services must be referable only to the aims of the organisation and available without payment other than a membership subscription. The organisations covered are:

(*a*) trade unions or other organisations of persons having as their main object the negotiation on behalf of their members of the terms and conditions of their employment;

(*b*) professional associations, membership of which is wholly or mainly restricted to individuals who have or are seeking a qualification appropriate to the practice of the profession concerned;

(*c*) associations, the primary purpose of which is the advancement of a particular branch of knowledge, or the fostering of professional expertise, connected with the past or present professions or employments of their members;

(*d*) associations, the primary purpose of which is to make representations to the government on legislation and other public matters which affect the business or professional interests of their members;

(*e*) bodies which have objects which are in the public domain and are of a political, religious, patriotic, philosophical, philanthropic or civic nature.

The term 'non-profit-making' is explained at 5.69. 'Wholly or mainly' in paragraph (*b*), according to Customs in their Leaflet 701/33, means that at least 75% of the membership must be seeking the appropriate qualification.

The legislation includes notes for clarification. The exemption does not apply to the right of admission to any premises, event or performance if non-members are admitted for a charge but it covers organisations and associations the membership of which consists wholly or mainly of constituent or affiliated associations which on their own would be covered. Therefore, the reference to 'member' includes these affiliated associations and 'membership subscription' includes an affiliation fee or similar.

For paragraph (*c*) to apply, the association must restrict its membership wholly or mainly to individuals whose present or previous professions or employments are directly connected with the purposes of the association.

For paragraph (*d*) to apply, the association must restrict its membership wholly or mainly to individuals or corporate bodies (usually companies) whose business or professional interests are directly connected with the purposes of the association.

The description of Group 9 was changed to 'Subscriptions to trade unions, professional and other public interest bodies' from 'Trade unions and professional bodies' by *SI 1999/2834, art 4(a)*, operative from 1 December 1999.

Indent (*e*) was also added by the same statutory instrument and means that from 1 December 1999, subscriptions to such bodies have been exempt rather than outside the scope of VAT as they were previously under *VATA 1994, s 94(3)*. Now these bodies may benefit from the partial exemption provisions (see Chapter 7) and apportion subscriptions to allow for the zero-rated element relating to publications provided for members. Thus, they will be able to recover a proportion of their input tax.

Group 10 — Sport, sports competitions and physical education

5.76 Where someone has to pay to enter a sports or physical recreation competition, the payment is exempt from VAT if the money is put towards a prize or prizes for that competition. Also exempt is the grant, by a non-profit-making body established for the purposes of sport or physical recreation, of a right to enter a competition in the activity the body represents.

The difference between the two categories of exemption is that if the organisation holding the competition is not a non-profit-making body, all money paid as entry fees must be put towards prizes, whereas all entry fees received by non-profit-making bodies are exempt unless they give the competitor the right to use facilities for which a charge is normally made, in which case the entry fees would be standard-rated.

If a sports club holds a competition on its premises for which non-members have to pay for admission but members do not, entry fees charged to non-members are standard-rated. For events to be exempt, they must include some form of physical activity, so sports such as football, cricket and golf are included as are less strenuous sports such as snooker or darts but payments to participate in games like chess, cards and dominoes are standard-rated because they are not considered to constitute physical recreation.

If goods are given as prizes, they are treated as gifts. Input tax is deductible on their purchase but output tax is due on the cost to the organiser if the value exceeds £50 (see 3.57). If services are given as prizes, no VAT is due because there is no supply under VAT law and cash prizes are also outside the scope of VAT.

Further details can be found in Customs Leaflet 701/34 'Competitions in Sport and Physical Recreation'.

Non-profit-making members clubs

5.77 This Group also exempts the supply by a non-profit-making body to an individual of services closely linked with and essential to sport and physical education in which the individual is taking part, although where the body operates a membership scheme, services to non-members are not exempt.

Ever since this part of the Group was introduced, there have been disputes as to what constitutes a 'non-profit-making body' and services 'closely linked with and essential to sport and physical education'. The notes specifically state that residential accommodation, catering and transport services are not exempt and that an individual in a membership scheme is only a member if he is granted membership for a period of at least three months. A 'non-profit-making body' in this case excludes:

- a local authority;
- a government department as defined in *s 41(6)* (see comments on Group 7 Items 9 and 10 above);
- a non-departmental public body which is listed in the 1993 edition of the publication prepared by the Office of Public Service and Science and entitled 'Public Bodies'.

Many proprietary clubs, notably golf and health clubs restructured their affairs in order to create a non-profit-making body and make subscriptions exempt whether or not they planned to pass the VAT benefit on to their members. For some of these, Customs argue that the overall intention was still to make a profit because any surpluses made by the new non-profit-making body were transferred over by whatever means to another legal entity set up, for example, to manage the club or to hold property and rent it without VAT to the club. Customs lost a Tribunal case on the subject (*Chobham Golf Club LON/96/833, No 14867*), only for the law to be changed, the *Value Added Tax (Sport, Sports Competitions and Physical Education) Order 1999 (SI 1999/1994)* coming into effect on 1 January 2000.

The following supplies are exempt under the revised Group 10:

1. The grant of a right to enter a competition in sport or physical recreation where the consideration for the grant consists in money which is to be allocated wholly towards the provision of a prize or prizes awarded in that competition.

2. The grant, by an eligible body established for the purposes of sport or physical recreation, of a right to enter a competition in such an activity.

3. The supply by an eligible body to an individual, except, where the body operates a membership scheme, an individual who is not a member, of services closely linked with and essential to sport or physical education in which the individual is taking part.

The 17 notes which follow in the legislation provide detailed clarification of the type of arrangement that would be acceptable for an 'eligible body' to exist. The new Group effectively prevents the schemes that had been set up to distribute profits to the business owners through, for example, management charges or variable rents payable to separate legal entities.

The notes also define key terms and relevant supplies for the avoidance of doubt.

The actual exemption only applies to charges for participating in the activity concerned, not to social charges. For example, charges to play golf would be covered but social membership subscriptions would be standard-rated.

Customs Leaflet 701/45 provides more guidance on this issue, paragraph 18 of which is a table of services included and excluded from the exemption. Now that the changes to Group 10 have been implemented, a revised version of this leaflet is expected.

Group 11 — Works of art etc.

5.78 The following four disposals are exempt:

(1) an object which is relieved from the one time charge to estate duty;

(2) an object which is relieved from inheritance tax;

(3) property which is relieved from inheritance tax;

(4) where any gain accruing is relieved from capital gains tax.

Group 12 — Fund-raising events by charities and other qualifying bodies

5.79 Prior to 1 April 2000, charities and certain similar non-profit-making bodies could exempt all the income they received from 'one-off' fund-raising events. Conditions and criteria were strict and clearly laid out in Group 12.

From that date, the exemption has been greatly extended.

The following can benefit from the new provisions:

- charities, including a body corporate wholly owned by a charity which has agreed in writing to transfer its profits, from whatever source, to a charity;
- non-profit-making bodies with aims of a political, religious, philanthropic, philosophical or patriotic nature;
- trade unions, professional associations, learned societies and pressure groups;
- non-profit-making bodies established for the principal purpose of providing facilities for participating in sport or physical education; and
- non-public cultural bodies which qualify for exemption of admission charges to cultural facilities.

Under the old rules, a qualifying fund-raising event was described as a fête, ball, bazaar, gala show, performance or similar event which does not form part of a series of similar events.

The new rules define an exempt fund-raising event as an event, including those accessible through electronic communication, which is both organised and promoted primarily for the purpose of raising money. During a financial year (pro-rata if not 12 months) each charity or qualifying body can now conduct up to 15 qualifying events of any one kind held in any one location. Small scale events of any one kind, such as coffee mornings, are not subject to this restriction provided gross takings do not exceed £1,000 in any one week.

Events where accommodation is provided for more than two nights are not exempt but standard-rated unless they qualify under any other relief. The exemption also does not apply in cases where doing so is likely to create distortion of competition with VAT registered commercial providers.

These new provisions also apply to direct tax relief for fund-raising events by charities and their wholly owned trading companies but they do not affect the charity law position which charities must consider when deciding if such events should be undertaken through a wholly-owned trading company.

> *Example 42*
>
> A children's welfare charity organises three concerts of classical music each year to raise funds. The event falls within the new acceptable definition of a qualifying event for exemption from VAT. Therefore, all income generated from the events is exempt although much of it e.g. admission charges and sponsorship would normally be standard-rated.
>
> The disadvantage is that the VAT on the standard-rated costs of running the event (e.g. orchestra fees, catering company charges) would normally be irrecoverable under the partial exemption rules (see Chapter 7).

Group 13 — Cultural services etc.

5.80 This group has two items and was introduced from 1 June 1996 to align UK with EC law.

Item 1

5.81 The supply by a public body of a right of admission to a museum, gallery, art exhibition, zoo, or a theatrical, musical or choreographic performance of a cultural nature is exempt.

Therefore, certain bodies have been able to revise their admission charges since the introduction of the exemption, although they will also have taken into account lost input tax which now relates to exempt outputs.

A public body is any of the three categories of organisation listed above as the exclusions to non-profit-making bodies under Group 10 (see 5.77).

Item 1 does not include any supply which would cause distortions of competition if the exemption were applied thus putting commercial providers of the same at a disadvantage.

Item 2

5.82 Item 2 exempts the supply by an eligible body of a right of admission to the same venues and events described at Item 1 above.

An 'eligible body' means any body other than a public body which is a non-profit-making body, applies any profits it does make from these admission charges to the continuance or improvement of the facilities to which the admission charges were made, and is managed and administered on a voluntary basis by people who have no direct or indirect financial interest in its activities.

The right of admission to performances in Item 1 (rather than places of interest) is only exempt if provided exclusively by one or more public bodies, one or more eligible bodies or any combination of the two.

Customs Leaflet on the subject is 701/47 'Culture'. As the law does not explain how to discern whether there would be distortion of competition if public bodies were to apply the exemption, Customs have taken the initiative by requiring those proposing to exempt their supplies to identify all local suppliers of similar services and notify those suppliers of their intention, giving them a period of time to object in writing (usually 30 days). If no objections are received, the exemption may start from the end of the period allowed, but if objections are received and the public body disagrees, the matter should be referred to Customs for a ruling. Copies of all relevant correspondence and documentation should be sent to Customs. One comprehensive enquiry by the public body is sufficient so that if the exemption is allowed, later objections from third parties will have no effect.

The disqualification for bodies which pay staff only applies if they are paid for managerial or administrative functions.

Note also that Customs currently still allow qualifying bodies to standard rate their admission charges if they so wish so that even if it applies, the exemption is not compulsory. This matter is under review.

Although UK law states that eligible bodies must be managed and administered on a voluntary basis, Customs do not currently disqualify such bodies where they employ staff to fulfil those functions and pay an annual salary of up to £11,300. However, this is a temporary concession pending the answers to questions put to the ECJ by the court in *C&E Commrs v Zoological Society of London CJEC Case C-267/00*. Should Customs' original insistence that such bodies be managed and administered on a voluntary basis be proven correct, organisations that have employed staff and treated admissions as exempt will have to treat them as standard-rated. Customs will also assess retrospectively.

Group 14 — Supplies of goods where input tax cannot be recovered

5.83 This group applies to UK law following the decision in the *Italian Republic* case (see 9.38) and was inserted by *SI 1999/2833* effective from 1 March 2000.

Essentially, the onward supply of goods where the original input tax was non-deductible is now exempt. The relevant items involved are not those on which input tax recovery is denied because of partial exemption but because they are 'blocked' items, notably:

- motor cars
- business entertainment
- certain building materials incorporated in a building or its site.

The exemption does not apply where the onward supply is one that would have been exempt under Group 1 of *Schedule 9* but for an election to waive exemption under *Schedule 10, paragraph 2* (see 5.2 and 8.40 *et seq.*).

Customs' policy is to produce a list of qualifying items on 1 January each year. The items are not considered to be collectors' items eligible for the margin scheme.

Other provisions associated with the change such as an option to tax for producers and refiners of investment gold will be introduced after a consultation exercise. It is not expected that these changes will affect the zero-rate available for transactions in gold in the limited circumstances described at 4.46.

Group 15 — Investment gold

5.84 This new group became effective from 1 January 2000 as a result of *Finance Act 1999, s 13, SI 1999/3115* and *SI 1999/3116*. From that date the following supplies are exempt:

Item 1 — The supply of investment gold

Item 2 — The grant, assignment or surrender of any right, interest, or claim in, over or to investment gold if the right, interest or claim is or confers a right to the transfer of the possession of investment gold

Item 3 — The supply by a person acting as an agent for a disclosed principal, of services consisting of

- arranging a supply within the first two items made by or to his principal, or
- attempting to arrange such a supply but which, for whatever reason, falls through.

Note (1) to the new group defines 'investment gold' as:

- gold in the form of a bar or wafer of a purity of 995 thousandths or greater and of a weight accepted by the bullion markets;
- gold coins which:
  - — are of a purity of 900 thousandths or greater;
  - — are minted after 1800;
  - — are or have been legal tender; and
  - — are of a description of coin that is normally sold at a price that does not exceed 180% of the open market value of the gold contained in the coin; or
- a gold coin of a description specified in a notice that has been published by the Commissioners for the purposes of this Group and has not been withdrawn.

SI 1999/3116, reg 3 provides for an election to waive exemption similar to that available for commercial property as described in 8.40 *et seq.* The election relates to supplies made under Items 1 and 2 above and where the supplier has elected, his agent making supplies under Item 3 may also elect.

An election to waive exemption is irrevocable. However, where Customs have allowed a person to elect, they may change their minds if it appears necessary to do so for the protection of the revenue.

Where an election is in place, the customer accounts for the VAT direct to Customs rather than the supplier in accordance with *section 55(1)* to *(4)*. For example, if the charge by the supplier were £5,000 + £875 VAT, the supplier would issue a tax invoice in the normal way but indicate on the invoice that the purchaser is to pay the output VAT to Customs. The purchaser then pays the supplier the net amount, declares the VAT on his next return and claims the same amount back as input tax subject to the normal rules.

Chapter 6

VAT on Expenditure

Introduction

6.1 Every individual, business or organisation pays VAT on positive rated expenditure. The benefit to the Treasury is where the VAT paid on expenditure cannot be reclaimed. Examples are expenditure incurred by:

- the general public (mainly through shops);
- exempt businesses;
- organisations with non-business activities; and
- where VAT on business expenditure is irrecoverable e.g. most new cars and business entertainment.

6.2 If an amount of VAT charged by a supplier of goods or services can be reclaimed, the government does not benefit because the one business pays it and the other reclaims it (*s 24*).

Example 43

J F Smith Electrical Goods Limited sells 20 CD players to G K Jones Electrical Store for £4,000 + £700 VAT. Both businesses are registered for VAT. J F Smith accounts for £700 output tax on his next return and GK Jones claims the whole amount back on his return.

G K Jones sells each CD player to members of the public for £350 each including VAT. He accounts for output tax of £52.12 on each sale (£350 × 7/47) on the appropriate return, but the customer, who is not VAT registered, cannot reclaim the VAT he has paid.

6.3 This chapter covers the treatment of VAT on expenditure incurred by VAT registered businesses, referred to as 'input tax'. For compliance purposes, it is essential to understand the definition of input tax, when it can be reclaimed, the conditions and time limits for recovery, and special circumstances covered by the law.

Definition of input tax

6.4 Input tax is usually the VAT charged on goods or services bought in for business purposes, but for those involved in international trade, there can be up to four other sets of circumstances creating input tax:

- on goods imported into the UK from a country outside the EC ('imports' – see Chapter 12);
- on goods imported into the UK from another EC country ('EC acquisitions' – see Chapter 11);
- on goods removed from a warehouse (see Chapter 12);
- on services received from another country (see Chapter 12).

6.5 In the four categories at 6.4, the UK business paying the VAT does not settle it within the amount due to its supplier. Goods or services acquired from abroad are usually invoiced in the currency of the supplier's country without VAT. The recipient in the UK then converts the value into sterling at the exchange rate approved by Customs, calculates VAT due, includes it as if it were output tax on the next VAT return and claims back such of it as he is able as input tax. So the VAT is not 'charged' by the supplier but 'levied' on the buyer as if he had made the sale to himself. The reason for this practice is to avoid the complicated alternatives which could involve overseas businesses having to register in the UK or the establishment of a system to balance payments of VAT between countries where businesses claim foreign VAT on their domestic returns.

Example 44

(1) Jack Davies has a chain of bicycle shops and wishes to expand into France. He has identified suitable properties in France and engages the services of a French solicitor who charges FF20,000. The invoice does not show VAT. Davies converts the value to sterling, say £2,000, adds £350 VAT at 17.5%, then on his next return pays £350 output tax and claims £350 input tax (see 12.40 *et seq*).

(2) Jenkins Machine Tools Ltd imports parts from the Netherlands. The latest assignment was for NLG 12,000 without VAT. The company converts this to sterling, say £4,000, adds £700 VAT, and includes this as payable in Box 2 of its next return (i.e. the £700 is added to other output tax in Box 1). It then claims back the same amount as input tax (see 11.3 *et seq*).

6.6 For input tax to be recovered the expenditure must have been incurred for the purposes of any business carried on or to be carried on by the VAT registered entity (*s 26*) and the goods or services purchased must have been used to make taxable supplies (at the 17.5%, 5% or zero rate).

Example 45

(*a*) VAT could not be recovered by a company where one of the directors has a loft conversion on his house for use as an extra bedroom which is occasionally used as an office.

(*b*) Input tax is recoverable on petrol used for business purposes. As it is almost impossible to quantify business mileage only unless detailed records of business journeys are kept, the fuel scale charge system exists which gives a flat rate of VAT deemed attributable to private motoring to be added to output tax on each return.

6.7 Input tax may also relate to a business 'to be carried on'. As explained in Chapter 2 on registration, a business may register before it starts receiving income from taxable activities so long as it can demonstrate to Customs an intention to do so. Therefore, it is often advantageous to register as soon as expenditure is incurred on setting up a business because the VAT involved may then be recovered immediately; there is no obligation to wait until sales are made so long as the future activities generate taxable, not exempt income.

Example 46

John Cooper sets up in business as a house builder. His plan is simply to buy land, build houses and sell them. He cannot start the business until he has worked his notice at his current employment. Before he leaves, he incurs the following set-up costs:

- Tools £5,000 + £875 VAT
- Solicitors fees £800 + £140 VAT
- Accountants fees £1,000 + £175 VAT

He may register immediately and reclaim the £1,190 input tax on his first return. He would probably complete returns monthly because all of his outputs (sales of houses) would be zero-rated and he would always be claiming a refund from Customs (see 6.34 *et seq*).

6.8 There is an onus on the business incurring the input tax to ensure the right amount is recovered even if there is an error on the invoice itself.

6.9 Irrecoverable VAT incurred by partly exempt businesses is known as 'exempt input tax'. For accounting purposes, it increases the particular expenditure to which it relates (see Chapter 7).

How input tax is recovered

6.10 VAT registered businesses complete periodic returns (*Regulation 25* of *VAT Regulations 1995, SI 1995/2518*) showing the amount of output VAT due on their taxable activities less the amount of input tax which they are entitled to reclaim. The difference could either be a payment due to Customs or a repayment due from them although the latter is only likely if there has been significant abnormal expenditure in the period (e.g. the purchase of a capital item) or because most sales are zero-rated (e.g. exports) (*VATA 1994, s 25*).

The input VAT which may be deducted is all that shown on purchase invoices in the VAT return period with a tax point falling therein provided the expenditure related to taxable business activities, unless the cash accounting scheme is used, in which case the deductible amount is the VAT on invoices paid during the period (see 6.16).

Input tax is shown in Box 4 of the return form and is explained further at 15.16–15.19.

Circumstances in which input tax is recoverable

6.11 Most recoverable input tax is from purchases made in the UK on which VAT has been charged at either 17.5% or 5% by businesses whose activities in the UK generate income subject to VAT at the 17.5%, 5% or zero rate. Where businesses have exempt or non-business activities as well as taxable ones, they must attribute the VAT on expenditure to the relevant activity first to determine whether or not it is recoverable.

Example 47
A property investor may from time to time sell properties in his portfolio. Some sales might be exempt from VAT, e.g. houses, and some might be taxable, e.g. commercial properties less than three years old. VAT on legal fees in connection with the sale of a house would be irrecoverable because it is directly attributable to an exempt supply, but the costs in connection with the sale of a commercial property would be recoverable in full because they are directly attributable to a taxable supply.

6.12 VAT on overheads is not directly attributable to any particular activity so an apportionment is necessary for those with a mixture of taxable and exempt activities (either using a partial exemption method as explained in Chapter 7 or normally in the ratio of taxable sales to total sales for the period for those with a mixture of business and non-business activities).

Example 48

The property investor at *Example 47* buys some new office furniture. The VAT charged is not directly attributable to exempt sales of houses or taxable sales of commercial properties so an apportionment is necessary.

Recoverable input tax — special circumstances

6.13 There are two further situations where input tax is recoverable:

- where it relates to sales made outside the UK which would have been taxable supplies if made in the UK (*s 26(2)(1)*); and
- where it relates to supplies of services to anyone who belongs outside the EC or to supplies of services directly linked to an export of goods to a place outside the EC and the making of arrangements for such supplies so long as those arrangements would have been exempt under any item in *Schedule 9 Group 2* or Items 1 to 8 of *Schedule 9 Group 5* (see Chapter 5) if made within the UK.

Late claims

6.14 Input tax can be claimed in the period in which the tax point falls or in a later period if, for some reason, the taxpayer fails to claim it at the earliest opportunity but there is a three-year time limit on such claims. It is important for partly exempt traders to attribute input tax to the correct tax period to ensure their apportionment calculations are accurate (see 6.12 and Chapter 7).

Example 49

Humphries runs a clothing shop and is VAT registered, completing returns to the end of March, June, September and December. He bought a computer for £2,000 + £350 VAT on 30 June 1997. He also had some shop repairs carried out. The invoice was for £3,000 + £525 VAT and dated 30 December 1998. He failed to claim the input tax on either at the time.

When completing his September 2001 return, he realises the error. He can still reclaim the £525 on this return but the £350 cannot be claimed because the supply took place more than three years ago.

Input tax recoverable on research and development costs

6.15 Since the object of research and development is to produce something which can be sold if the work is successful, and because in almost all cases that product would be a taxable supply, VAT on associated costs can be provisionally reclaimed as input tax. The claim is provisional until taxable supplies are made or the research and development activities cease because they are unsuccessful because, until then, there is a possibility that the first supply will be exempt necessitating a clawback of input tax previously claimed.

Example 50
Both ABC Ltd and DEF Ltd start research into an aids vaccine on 30 September 1999 and register for VAT as intending traders. On 31 December 2001, ABC launches its new successful product and starts making taxable supplies. However, DEF is unsuccessful and the research stops on 30 September 2001. Neither has made exempt supplies so all input tax reclaimed prior to making taxable supplies/ceasing research will not be disturbed and will not be clawed back by Customs.

The cash accounting scheme and input tax

6.16 Businesses with annual taxable turnover of less than £600,000 (from 1 April 2001, previously £350,000) may use the cash accounting scheme whereby output tax is accounted for according to the date payment is received, not the tax point as shown on sales invoices. On the other hand, input tax is recoverable only when purchases and expenses are paid for, not according to the date of the purchase invoice (*Regulation 65(2)* of the *VAT Regulations 1995 (SI 1995/2518)* and 15.27–15.35).

Non-deductible input tax (VAT (Input Tax) Order 1992, SI 1992/3222)

6.17 Some input tax cannot be recovered even though the cost is attributable to a taxable activity, viz.:

- new cars (except when bought by businesses dealing in cars, private hire firms, driving schools and self-drive hire firms or where they are to be used 100% for business activities — see 6.18)
- business entertainment
- goods purchased under one of the second-hand schemes (in which case a tax invoice should not be received anyway — see Chapter 9)

- certain goods installed by builders in new buildings (see Chapter 8)
- purchases of goods and services by businesses operating the tour operators' margin scheme (see Chapter 10)
- purchases for private or non-business purposes
- purchases of goods and services used to make exempt supplies
- residential accommodation provided by a company for use by any of its directors or members of their families.

Cars — rules from 1 August 1995

6.18 Since 1 August 1995, businesses have been able to recover VAT on the purchase of a new car but only if it is to be used wholly and exclusively for business purposes. This change particularly affects leasing companies that buy cars specifically to lease out. Other businesses are unlikely to satisfy the condition because there is private use as soon as the car is taken away from the business premises (say, to the user's home). Genuine pool cars, demonstrators and courtesy cars can qualify but only if they are never kept overnight at the user's home, so the input tax on most cars purchased by businesses is still not deductible.

Cars — accessories and modifications

6.19 The input tax restrictions on the purchase of cars also apply to accessories and modifications supplied or carried out at the time of supply even if invoiced separately. Input tax is recoverable under normal rules if accessories are supplied or modifications made at a later date.

Cars — repairs and maintenance

6.20 The normal input tax rules apply, so a business which only has taxable activities may recover input tax on all repairs and maintenance costs if the car is used at all for business purposes. There is no restriction for private use.

Leased cars

6.21 The advantage of leasing companies being able from 1 August 1995 to recover input tax on new cars has been somewhat offset by lessees now being able to recover only 50% of it unless there is no private use whatsoever.

All cars with an 'L' registration or earlier are treated under the old rules and all cars with an 'N' registration or later are treated under the new rules unless the leasing company states otherwise (there are certain circumstances where they paid for 'N' registered cars before 1 August 1995 and thus the old rules still apply). The leasing company should have indicated the status of 'M' registered cars so the lessee knew whether or not to restrict his input tax claim.

Cars bought which are immediately sold and then leased back qualify under the exclusive business use test so long as there is no private use in the interim.

Cars that are subject to the 50% input tax restriction are known as 'qualifying' cars. Motor dealers and lessors must indicate on their invoices if the car is a qualifying car in accordance with the *VAT (Input Tax) Order 1992 (SI 1992/3222), art 7(2)*.

Cars — rebates of rentals

6.22 If a rebate is received from the leasing company at the end of the term, only 50% of the VAT on the credit note need be accounted for by the lessee if he was only claiming 50% of the VAT on the rentals paid. Where agreements are terminated early, the lessor can decide whether to treat additional payments due or rebates as taxable supplies or outside the scope of VAT. If he chooses the former option and a payment is due, the lessee need not apply the 50% input tax restriction but if he receives a credit note because the rebate is higher than the termination payment, he need only account for 50% of the VAT if that has applied on the main rental payments.

Example 51
Carter Deliveries Ltd leases a small fleet of cars from a leasing company that chooses to treat payments or rebates for early terminations as taxable supplies. All cars are subject to the 50% input tax restriction. Carter terminates two agreements early. One requires an additional payment of £500 + £87.50 VAT which Carter can recover in full as input tax, i.e. there is no 50% restriction. The other is a net rebate (after allowing for the termination payment) of £400 but Carter only pays £35 VAT (rather than £70) on the amount received because the 50% restriction applied to the original rentals.

Short-term car hire

6.23 Cars hired for business purposes for a period of less than five days are not subject to the 50% restriction on input tax but if a car is hired for five days or more, there is a restriction unless an exclusive business use can be demonstrated through maintenance of detailed records made available to Customs.

Business entertainment

6.24 This has caused many disputes, since whilst input tax incurred on entertaining is not recoverable, it is sometimes difficult to establish when a business is undertaking a promotional exercise to raise its own profile and when it is simply entertaining others, even though the purpose may be to maintain a good relationship and win new or further business from them.

According to Customs Leaflet 700/65, paragraph 1, business entertainment is entertainment or hospitality of any kind provided for business purposes to anyone who is not an employee and includes the expenses of staff acting as hosts. It also includes:

- provision of meals and drinks
- provision of accommodation or facilities for sport or recreation
- visits to theatres, nightclubs etc.
- capital goods such as yachts, power boats, private aircraft used wholly or partly for entertaining.

The expenditure must be distinguished from that of subsistence expenses when working away from the main place of work, which are deductible.

Example 52

(1) The staff of an accountancy firm stay in a hotel whilst on audit a long way from their office. VAT on accommodation, meals etc. is deductible because the main reason for incurring the cost is to perform the audit.

(2) Compare the situation where the same staff could stay away from home to take part in a golf day put on for clients and contacts. In this case, the main reason for being away is business entertainment so the VAT on expenditure would not be recoverable.

Staff parties

6.25 There have been a number of disputes concerning staff parties and to what extent the VAT on costs should be treated as non-deductible business entertainment. The typical scenario involved cases where a business would put on a party to which staff could invite their spouse or partner. Traditionally, Customs disallowed the whole amount relating to the partners and deemed 50% of the amount relating to the staff themselves as business entertainment, leaving, on average, 25% of all the VAT to be recovered. Decisions in appeal cases have resulted in Customs now accepting that the whole cost relating to the staff is recoverable, their now normally accepting a 50% recovery of the total input tax involved. However, future cases may result in further changes.

6.26 Further details on the treatment of specific types of entertainment are in Leaflet 700/65.

Tribunal appeals in cases involving luxuries, amusements and entertainment

6.27 If a business appeals against a decision by Customs to disallow input tax relating to luxuries, amusements or entertainment, a Tribunal can only decide in the appellant's favour if it considers Customs' decision was unreasonable. This is difficult to prove. Typical disputes in this category could involve the acquisition of yachts, racehorses and personalised number plates for cars. Further details are in Leaflet 700/55 'VAT Input Tax Appeals: Luxuries, Amusements and Entertainment'. This restriction on the Tribunal stresses the importance of claiming the right amount of input tax so if there is any doubt, Customs should be consulted in advance of a claim.

Transfers of businesses as going concerns

6.28 Within certain conditions, the sale or transfer of a business or part of a business as a going concern is not a supply for VAT purposes which means VAT must not be charged on any of the standard-rated elements of the sale by the vendor. Consequently, there is no input tax to be claimed by the purchaser (*VAT (Special Provisions) Order 1995 (SI 1995/1268), art 5*).

The conditions are as follows:

- the effect of the transfer must be to put the purchaser or transferee in possession of a business which can be operated as such;
- the business must be a going concern at the time of the transfer;
- the assets included in the transfer must be intended for use by the transferee in operating the same kind of business (special rules apply where commercial property is involved which are explained in Chapter 8);
- there must be no significant break in trading before or after the transfer;

- if part of a business is being transferred, that part must be capable of separate operation even if the transferee does not actually operate it separately;
- there must not be a series of immediately consecutive transfers of the business and, perhaps most importantly, by whatever means, the transferee must be VAT registered from the date the transfer is completed.

Input tax incurred in arranging a business transfer

6.29 If the assets acquired by the transferee are used solely to make taxable supplies, the input tax incurred on the cost of acquiring them can be reclaimed in full but if they are used solely to make exempt supplies, none of the input tax can be reclaimed. If they are used to make both taxable and exempt supplies, the input tax must be apportioned using a suitable partial exemption method (see Chapter 7). Any input tax on costs incurred by a partly exempt transferor must be apportioned using his agreed method.

Example 53

(1) A partly exempt housing association takes over the business of another association and incurs legal fees of £6,000 + £1,050 VAT in arranging the transfer. At the time of purchase, the buyer can recover 10% of its input tax, so it would reclaim £105 of the VAT on the legal fees.

(2) An engineering company takes over the business of another and incurs the same legal costs in arranging the transfer. The buyer is fully taxable and can therefore reclaim all the £1,050 as input tax.

Customs have announced minor changes to the rules regarding a transferor's entitlement to deduct from 1 August 2001 as a result of the ECJ case *Abbey National plc (C-408/98)* decided on 22 February 2001 (Business Brief 8/2001, 2 July 2001). The court confirmed that there is a direct and immediate link between the VAT on the costs of a going concern transfer and the business activities of a transferor. Where that transferor makes both taxable and exempt supplies, that VAT is a general overhead and should be apportioned (see Chapter 7) but if it is clear that the VAT was directly attributable to its taxable activities only, all of it is deductible. Customs will apply the changes from 1 August 2001 but taxpayers that have already suffered restrictions may make a retrospective claim subject to the three-year cap.

Holding companies

Holding companies not carrying on a separate business

6.30 A pure holding company (one which only holds the shares in its subsidiaries) does not get involved in the day-to-day management of its subsidiaries and since it is not regarded as making taxable supplies, it cannot register for VAT and reclaim input tax on positive rated expenditure.

A holding company is not regarded as having taxable business activities if its activities only comprise the following:

- the acquisition of shares in subsidiaries
- the receipt of dividends arising from the shareholdings
- defending itself and its subsidiaries against takeovers
- disposing of shares in its subsidiaries.

When a holding company is a business and can be VAT registered

6.31 In order to be registered for VAT, the holding company must make or intend to make taxable supplies, normally meaning the provision of management services to subsidiaries in return for a management charge. Some holding companies also have trading activities of their own, but if not, they may still be registered as part of a VAT group registration provided that the subsidiary companies make taxable supplies to customers which are not part of the group.

Input tax recovery by VAT registered holding companies

6.32 If a holding company is registered for VAT in its own right because it makes or intends to make taxable supplies, it can recover as input tax all the VAT incurred in managing its subsidiaries *including* that which relates to any of the activities listed at 6.30 which would otherwise not qualify it for registration.

Where a holding company receives both taxable and exempt income, input tax on overheads must be apportioned using a fair and reasonable partial exemption apportionment method (see Chapter 7).

Farmhouses

6.33 Customs accept that VAT incurred on farmhouses should be treated differently from normal domestic accommodation. In the case of repairs and maintenance to a working farmhouse where the business is a full-time activity carried on by a sole proprietor or partnership, 70% of the VAT is usually allowed as input tax in accordance with an agreement between Customs and the National Farmers' Union.

If the house is only used as living accommodation or farming is only a part-time activity, a fair and reasonable apportionment should be agreed with Customs based on actual business use. Customs' view is that such business use does not normally exceed 40%.

If the farming business is a company, VAT on farmhouse expenditure cannot normally be reclaimed if it is occupied by a director or somebody connected with a director, but if the occupant is an employee, input tax is allowable to the extent that the provision of the accommodation is to benefit the business. Any charge made to the employee for occupation is exempt and so associated input tax is normally restricted anyway under the partial exemption provisions (see Chapter 7).

When a farmhouse is constructed, VAT must be applied to the main contractor's service to the extent that it relates to the part for business use, e.g. the office. Input tax is deductible on this element.

VAT on expenditure incurred before registration and after deregistration

6.34 Special rules allow VAT registered businesses to claim certain input tax incurred prior to registration and after deregistration which related to the period when they were registered. Each provision has conditions attached.

VAT on expenditure incurred prior to registration

6.35 There are slightly different rules governing the treatment of goods and services received before registration. In both cases, the relevant supplies must have been received by the business which becomes registered for VAT and be for the purposes of that business. A separate record of all goods or services received showing appropriate dates must be kept.

The differences are as follows:

- On the date of registration for VAT the goods purchased must still be in the business or have been used to make something still in the business. There is a three-year time limit (e.g. if the effective date of registration is 1 January 2002, the VAT shown on goods purchased before 1 January 1999 cannot be recovered even if they fulfil the other conditions);
- Services acquired must have been for the purposes of establishing the business (e.g. solicitors' and accountants' fees, but not charges

for repairs to machinery which is sold before the registration date). In that case there is a six-month time limit.

If the expenditure is attributable to future exempt supplies, the VAT is irrecoverable.

If a proportion of it is attributable to a mixture of future taxable and exempt supplies, the amount attributable to future taxable supplies may be recovered. The VAT on pre-registration expenditure is strictly not input tax so the minimum limits below which partly exempt businesses can recover all exempt input tax cannot and do not apply (see Chapter 7). Evidence of the expenditure incurred must be kept and made available to Customs for inspection on request.

The onus is on the business reclaiming the VAT to demonstrate to Customs that all the conditions have been met, so full documentary evidence should be kept if goods purchased have been made into something else still in the business on registration date.

It is even possible for companies to claim back VAT on certain costs incurred before incorporation. The conditions are as follows:

(*a*) the normal rules would have applied if the goods or services had been supplied to the person who is now registered for VAT;

(*b*) the goods or services were obtained or imported by a person who became a member, officer or employee of the company;

(*c*) the person was reimbursed for the full cost; and

(*d*) the person was not a taxable person at the time of the supply or importation.

Further special rules apply for input tax incurred prior to registration which has taken place only because the business involved has opted to tax commercial properties which it owns. These are explained in Chapter 8.

VAT on expenditure incurred after deregistration

6.36 Deregistered businesses may use Form VAT 427 to make a reclaim after the effective date of deregistration. There are two types of situation in which a refund is allowed:

(1) on services received after deregistration but which relate to taxable supplies the business made whilst it was registered (the obvious examples are solicitors' and accountants' bills); and

(2) on goods and services with a tax point falling within the period of registration but which the business failed to claim on its final return.

There is a three-year time limit for making such claims which must be supported by the evidence necessary to prove entitlement. For businesses which deregistered after 30 April 1997 the three years is calculated from the tax point of the supply concerned.

Example 54
Atkinson Pressings Ltd deregisters on 30 October 2001. It receives an invoice for accountants' fees dated 30 November 2001. The company has three years from 30 November 2001, i.e. until 30 November 2004, to reclaim the VAT on the accountants' invoice using Form VAT 427.

For businesses which deregistered on or before 30 April 1997 the three-year time limit applies if the supplies had a tax point later than that date.

In paragraph 7 of Customs' Leaflet on cancelling registrations, they stress the importance of punctual claims because delays can occur when the business bank account into which the repayment would be paid has been closed.

When an Insolvency Practitioner has been appointed to handle the affairs of an insolvent business, he can still make post-deregistration claims for the business, but on Form VAT 426. The specific rules applicable to insolvency situations are explained in Customs Leaflet 700/56 'VAT: Insolvency'.

Input tax used for business and non-business activities

6.37 The special rules for determining how much input tax is recoverable when it is incurred for both taxable and exempt activities are explained fully in Chapter 7 on Partial Exemption. There are similar rules for the treatment of input tax attributable to both taxable and non-business activities (see Public Notice 700 Appendix F).

Businesses may use one of two methods to calculate the recoverable element. They may either apportion the total in the ratio of taxable outputs to total outputs for the period concerned or claim all the input tax and account to Customs for a calculated amount of output tax on the non-business element.

Example 55
Children of Today is a small charity dealing with specific aspects of child welfare. In its VAT return period 08/01 it buys a new computer system for £3,000 + £525 VAT. It has £1,000 taxable income and £4,000 grants and donations (i.e. non-business income) in that period. It can either apportion the £525 in the ratio of taxable to total income i.e. 1,000/5,000 = 20% and claim £105 input tax on the 08/01 return, or it can reclaim the £525 in full as input tax and pay 80% of it (£420) as output tax.

The second method is often known as the 'Lennartz' method, named after a German businessman whose case was decided by the European Court of Justice and established this treatment. It cannot be used for purchases of services for mixed use or for purchases on which input tax is blocked under UK law anyway, e.g. cars and business entertainment.

Where input tax on goods or services is reclaimed because they are to be used for business purposes but later there is a change so that they are to be used permanently for non-business purposes, there is a clawback by means of an output tax calculation based on the original cost or taking depreciation into account.

Documentary evidence required to support input tax claims

6.38 From time to time, Customs make selective checks to confirm the accuracy of VAT returns submitted by registered businesses. This is usually done by a visit to the principal place of business where activities are discussed and the officer checks the books and records which must be kept (see Chapter 14). The visit is not a full audit but because the tax is self-assessing, the officer must be satisfied that input tax claimed is accurate.

Acceptable forms of evidence

6.39 The basic form of evidence is the tax invoice (*Regulations 13* and *29* of the *VAT Regulations 1995, SI 1995/2518*) although in certain circumstances, less detailed invoices (where the gross value is £100 or less), self-billed invoices and authenticated receipts in the construction industry (see Chapter 8) are acceptable. Paragraphs 3.25–3.37 explain the information needed on an invoice for it to be acceptable as a tax invoice.

Customs explain their requirements for valid input tax claims at paragraph 8.6 of Public Notice 700 'The VAT Guide'. They stress that invoices must be kept for both standard and zero-rated supplies received for business purposes (this must also include invoices for supplies at the reduced rate of 5% even though there is no specific reference). The way they are kept must make it easy for visiting officers to cross-check input tax claims to the relevant invoice.

Self-billed invoices

6.40 If a business intends to claim input tax by issuing self-billed invoices, prior authorisation is required and all the conditions of that authorisation must be met (see 3.32).

Pro-forma invoices

6.41 These are not tax invoices and cannot be used as evidence to support an input tax claim. The recipient must wait until a supply has actually been made and a valid tax invoice has been issued (see 3.31).

Imports from outside the EC

6.42 Importers of goods from outside the EC cannot use the supplier's invoice or the import agent's commission invoice as evidence for input tax claims. The correct evidence is the monthly VAT certificate C79 issued by Customs and showing the date input tax may be claimed alongside each entry. See Chapter 12 for further details on the treatment of imports.

Acquisitions from other EC countries

6.43 Businesses acquiring goods from suppliers in other EC member states should hold an invoice from them showing the supplier's VAT registration number and their own, preceded by the relevant two-letter country of origin prefix. The acquirer is thus obliged to pay UK output tax on the sterling value and is entitled to reclaim the same amount as input tax if the acquisition is attributable to his taxable activities. For further details on EC acquisitions, see Chapter 11.

Services acquired from abroad

6.44 The place where a supply of services is made dictates in which country any VAT due is payable and by whom. Therefore, if a UK business buys in services from abroad, it should ensure it obtains an invoice from the supplier providing a full description of the services performed. If the service requires the UK recipient to account for output tax using the reverse charge mechanism, he will also be entitled to recover the same amount as input tax if the services are attributable to his taxable activities. Further details on international services and the reverse charge are in Chapter 12.

Cash and carry invoices

6.45 Many cash and carry businesses now have modern equipment enabling them to produce full tax invoices with a full description of each item and its appropriate VAT rate. Where they only provide a till roll with codes for each item, the purchaser must obtain and keep with the till roll receipts an up-to-date code list so that visiting Customs officers can check input tax claims (see 3.30).

Input tax reclaims without supporting tax invoices

6.46 Input tax may be reclaimed without a supporting tax invoice on the following:

- supplies through coin-operated machines;
- car parking charges (this applies to designated car parks as charges through on-street meters are not subject to VAT); and
- calls from public or private telephones,

provided that the total charge including VAT does not exceed £25.

Alternative evidence

6.47 In certain circumstances, Customs will accept alternative evidence to support input tax claims such as photocopies (so long as they are endorsed by a responsible person as a true copy of the original), copies on microfiche etc. but the original should be available for inspection on request. Officers are more likely to accept alternative evidence once they have checked that the output tax has been paid by the supplier through an internal referencing system and if the claimant has a good compliance history.

On occasions, Customs may even be prepared to accept input tax claims on taxable purchases from suppliers who should be registered but (for some reason) are not. There is no automatic entitlement so it should not be presumed that all claims will be allowed, but because a taxable supply has been made in such circumstances, input tax should normally be allowed even if there is no valid tax invoice and Customs may not be able to recover the output tax from the supplier.

VAT refund scheme for national museums and galleries

6.48 Prior to 1 April 2001, museums and galleries that do not charge for admission could not normally deduct VAT on their expenditure because they were not in business and consequently not VAT registered. From that date certain such museums and galleries will become eligible for a refund. HM Treasury will decide which museums and galleries qualify and the new provision will be enacted by means of a new section added to *VATA 1994*. The measure will come into effect no later than 1 September 2001 but eligible bodies will be able to claim the VAT they have incurred since 1 April 2001.

Chapter 7

Partial Exemption and the Capital Goods Scheme

Introduction to partial exemption

7.1 Exemption implies a more favourable position than if tax were applied.

On the contrary, the more outputs which are exempt from VAT, the higher the proportion of input tax which is irrecoverable.

Thus either the business must absorb the VAT cost in its overheads or increase its price to the detriment of the customers.

7.2 A business is *wholly exempt* if all of its activities in the course or furtherance of business generate exempt income. The converse is a *fully taxable* business which generates income at the standard rate, the zero rate or the reduced rate of 5%.

Example 56

A small insurance brokerage has exempt commission turnover of £60,000 and standard-rated expenditure of £30,000 + £5,250 VAT. It is not registered for VAT and therefore the cost of its standard-rated purchases is £35,250. This business is wholly exempt.

A small engineering company has taxable turnover of £60,000 and is VAT registered. It has charged its customers £60,000 + £10,500 VAT which they have paid. Its expenditure is £30,000 + £5,250 VAT. It pays £10,500 output tax and recovers £5,250 input tax from Customs. This company is fully taxable.

A *partly exempt business* is one whose activities generate both taxable and exempt income, although in certain circumstances special rules enable the business to be treated as fully taxable. Partly exempt businesses can only claim a proportion of their input tax to reflect the extent to which costs have been incurred for their taxable activities. The way this is done is explained below.

Example 57
An insurance brokerage has exempt commission turnover in excess of £200,000 and taxable fee turnover of £50,000. Therefore, the taxable turnover is 20% of the total turnover (50,000/50,000 + 200,000). The company would normally be able to recover 20% of the VAT on its overheads.

7.3 *Exempt input tax* is the term applied to the amount of VAT incurred on expenditure in any tax period which is either directly attributable to exempt activities or is deemed irrecoverable after an apportionment calculation as explained below.

All businesses pay VAT on positive rated goods and services provided by their suppliers but can only recover it from Customs as input tax to the extent it has been used to generate taxable outputs.

European law

7.4 By signing the Treaty of Rome in 1972 and joining the EC on 1 April 1973, the UK committed itself to adopting the provisions of European legislation on VAT, including provisions on the right to deduct input VAT and when it should be restricted.

Directive 77/388 on harmonisation of VAT laws within the member states, known as the Sixth Directive, was published on 17 May 1977 and clarified existing rules. Article 17(5) in particular sets the ground rules for input tax deduction but the UK would appear to give partly exempt businesses more rein than other member states as regards methods of apportionment. This may be relevant to partly exempt businesses that are required to register for VAT in other member states in that their overall input tax recovery percentage may not be as high as in the UK.

The Sixth Directive states that partly exempt businesses must determine the reason why a particular item of expenditure has been incurred. If it has been incurred solely to generate taxable activities and income, any VAT charged may be recovered as input tax if not restricted under other rules such as new cars and business entertainment; but if it has been incurred solely to generate exempt activities and income, any VAT charged cannot be recovered at all.

Any VAT on expenditure that cannot be attributed solely to specific activities must be apportioned. 'Non-attributable' input tax would normally be recoverable in the ratio of taxable supplies to total supplies in the relevant period.

The Sixth Directive allows member states to apply different methods of apportionment where they consider it necessary and to permit full recovery of input tax where the amount calculated as irrecoverable is insignificant.

UK law

7.5 The primary UK legislation concerning the recovery of input tax is *VATA 1994, s 26* which enables Customs to make further regulations on the subject. They have done so in *Regulations 99-110* of the *Value Added Tax Regulations 1995 (SI 1995/2518)*, although the regulations have been amended from 10 March 1999 to simplify the rules and prevent them being misused (see 7.14 and 7.15). (All subsequent references to regulations in this chapter are to *SI 1995/2518* unless stated.)

In general, the regulations appear to provide scope for UK businesses to negotiate a wider range of apportionment methods than permissible under the Sixth Directive which specifically refers only to methods based on sectors of a business or use of relevant goods and services.

7.6 *Exempt supplies* are covered in detail in Chapter 5 but, for ease of reference, supplies within the scope of *Sch 9* are exempt under the following numbered groups:

1. — Land
2. — Insurance
3. — Postal Services
4. — Betting, Gaming and Lotteries
5. — Finance
6. — Education
7. — Health and Welfare
8. — Burial and Cremation
9. — Trade Unions and Professional Bodies
10. — Sport, Sports Competitions and Physical Education
11. — Works of Art etc.
12. — Fund-Raising Events by Charities and Other Qualifying Bodies
13. — Cultural Services

14. — Supplies of Goods where Input Tax cannot be Recovered

15. — Investment Gold

The mechanics and consequences of partial exemption

7.7 Partial exemption calculations are made on a provisional basis according to the VAT return periods and then adjusted by reference to a longer period, which is usually twelve months. The twelve months to the annual adjustment date is defined as the 'tax year' in *Reg 99*, but is referred to hereafter as the VAT year. Since input VAT may only be recovered from Customs to the extent it has been incurred or is deemed to be incurred in generating taxable supplies, with partly exempt businesses not usually able to recover all the VAT they incur on purchases and expenses, many partly exempt businesses examine their structures carefully to ensure they keep irrecoverable VAT to a minimum.

Direct attribution

7.8 Direct attribution was introduced in 1987 to bring UK law more into line with the Sixth Directive (*Reg 101*).

This means that all input VAT must be attributed wherever possible to the supply or output it is used to generate. Consequently, if VAT is incurred to generate standard-rated outputs, it is recoverable in full, whereas if it is used for an exempt activity, no recovery is allowed.

Example 58

A property company incurs VAT on professional fees provided when building new houses for sale. This is directly attributable to a taxable supply (the zero-rated sale of the completed houses) and so can be recovered in full.

The company also incurs VAT on refurbishing existing houses it buys for subsequent letting. The rents will be exempt so this input VAT is directly attributable to an exempt supply and irrecoverable, subject to the *de minimis* limits described below.

Apportionment

7.9 It will only be possible to attribute certain standard-rated costs directly to taxable or exempt supplies.

Other costs, in particular the general overheads of a business, cannot be so attributed because they are indirectly used to generate both taxable and exempt supplies.

The input VAT on these costs must be apportioned using an approved method to produce an amount deemed attributable to taxable supplies.

The standard method of apportionment

7.10 Normal procedure is first to identify all input VAT directly attributable to taxable supplies, which is recoverable in full; then input tax directly attributable to exempt supplies which is wholly irrecoverable.

The remainder is usually known as 'residual input tax' or the 'pot' and is apportioned in the same ratio as the value of taxable outputs to total outputs for the same tax period (*Reg 101(2)(d)*).

Example 59

A chain of funeral directors has £2,000,000 exempt income. The VAT on directly attributable costs is £87,500 which is irrecoverable. The chain has taxable income of £500,000 (from flower shops, limousine hire etc.). The VAT on directly attributable costs is £22,000 which is recoverable in full. The VAT on office and administrative overheads is £6,500, which will be apportioned in the ratio of taxable to total income, i.e. 500,000 : 2,500,000 = 20%. Total recoverable input tax would be £22,000 + £1,300 (£6,500 × 20%) = £23,300.

This method of apportionment became standard in 1992 as a result of the last significant overhaul of the partial exemption provisions.

The previous standard method was to apportion non-attributable input VAT in the ratio of input VAT directly attributable to taxable supplies to total input VAT. This can still be used as an alternative special method subject to prior written approval from Customs.

Example 60

A partly exempt business receives £2,000,000 taxable income excluding VAT and £1,000,000 exempt income in period 08/01. Total input VAT for the quarter is £150,000 of which £60,000 is directly attributable to taxable supplies, £50,000 is directly attributable to exempt supplies and £40,000 is non-attributable.

The non-attributable input VAT is apportioned as follows:

$$40{,}000 \times \frac{2{,}000{,}000 \text{ (value of taxable supplies)}}{2{,}000{,}000 + 1{,}000{,}000 \text{ (value of total supplies)}}$$

The ratio must be expressed as a percentage rounded up to the next whole number (in this case 66.66% rounded up to 67%) so here the recoverable amount is:

40,000 × 67% = £26,800.

Total VAT recoverable for the period is therefore £60,000 (direct attribution) + £26,800 (partial exemption calculation) = £86,800.

If the previous standard method had been used, the apportionment would have been as follows:

$$40{,}000 \times \frac{60{,}000 \text{ (input tax directly attributable to taxable supplies)}}{150{,}000 \text{ (total input tax)}}$$

40,000 × 40% = 16,000.

Clearly, on this occasion, the outputs based method gives a better result.

Example 61

For the VAT year ended 31 May 2001 Mr V A Terry had the following transactions:

	£
General sales (standard rate VAT)	120,000
General sales (zero rate VAT)	10,000
Plant sold to UK trader	5,000
Plant sold to a trader in New Zealand and exported to him	5,000
Exempt supplies made	100,000
Wages to employees	75,000
New motor car purchased April 2001 for use by salesman (petrol only provided for business use)	12,000
(None of the above amounts include VAT)	

Input tax:	
Attributable to taxable supplies	10,000
exempt supplies	6,000
overheads	4,000
purchase of car	2,100

The total amount of output tax for which Terry is required to account and his deductible input tax for the year ended 31 May 2001 is as follows:

Output tax and input tax for year ended 31 May 2001

	£	£	£
Outputs chargeable at standard rate:			
Sales	120,000		
Plant sold to UK trader	5,000	125,000	
Outputs chargeable at zero rate:			
Sales	10,000		
Plant sold to New Zealand trader	5,000	15,000	
Total taxable outputs		140,000	
Exempt outputs		100,000	
Total outputs		240,000	
Output tax on taxable outputs of £125,000 at 17.5%			21,875
Input tax attributable to taxable supplies		10,000	
Input tax attributable to overheads	4,000		
Allowable proportion:			
$\frac{130,000}{230,000}$ = 57% × £4,000		2,280	12,280
Net payment to Customs for year			9,595

The sales of capital items, i.e. the plant sold to UK and New Zealand traders, are distortive and left out of the fraction — see 7.13.

The irrecoverable input tax of £7,720 (6,000 + (4,000 – 2,280) = 1,720) will be treated as an allowable expense in computing Mr Terry's profit for income tax purposes.

The input tax on the purchase of the car is also irrecoverable and will count as part of the cost of the car for capital allowances purposes.

Further examples can be found in Customs & Excise Public Notice 706 on partial exemption.

Certain businesses make supplies outside the UK that would be taxable if made in the UK. Following the Court of Appeal case involving the *Liverpool School for Performing Arts*, it is not now possible to include the value of such supplies in the numerator of a partial exemption standard method of apportionment calculation. This is because the deduction of input tax relating to these supplies is provided for separately and is determined on the basis of use. Customs & Excise Business Brief 8/99 dated 31 March 1999 refers.

Special methods (Reg 102)

7.11 Businesses may normally use the standard method without prior approval but if by doing so less input tax is recoverable than is considered attributable to taxable activities, an alternative or 'special' method of apportionment may be sought requiring written authorisation from Customs before it can be used. Customs will authorise methods that they consider 'fair and reasonable'. This means they agree that the method gives a result that accurately reflects the use of taxable purchases and expenses in making taxable supplies.

The best approach for the partly exempt business is to try out a selection of methods including the standard method and if a special method produces the optimum result, propose its use in writing.

A proposal for a special method should include a request to round up the recovery percentage to the nearest whole number, because there is no automatic entitlement as with the standard method (see *Example 60* at 7.10 above).

Customs will also normally accept a request to use the previous year's recovery percentage as the provisional rate for all quarters of the current year with just one adjustment calculation at the end of the VAT year.

This may cause a cash flow problem if the adjustment is significant.

Whatever is agreed with Customs must be kept under review because significant changes in the mix of taxable and exempt income could mean the agreed method is no longer fair and reasonable.

Customs have the power to direct use of a particular apportionment method or to cancel approval for use of a special method at any time but will normally only do so if they cannot agree a fair and reasonable method with the taxpayer.

7.12 The most effective special methods are those which remove the effect of high values in the denominator of the apportionment fraction.

Thus, if a partly exempt business has low value taxable transactions and high value exempt transactions over a typical year, it is more likely to benefit from a special method.

Example 62

In his VAT year, a property dealer buys and sells 50 existing quality homes (exempt) for a total of £7,500,000 and sells 4 small flats he has built himself (zero-rated) for £80,000. The standard method would allow a recovery of:

$$\frac{80,000}{7,580,000} \times 100 = 1.05\% \text{ rounded to } 2\%.$$

A method based on numbers of transactions would allow a recovery of:

$$\frac{4}{54} \times 100 = 7.4\%.$$

Customs themselves list a number of special methods in Public Notice 706 including:

- the number of taxable transactions as a percentage of the total transactions in the period;
- taxable floor space area as a percentage of the total floor space area.

However, they stress that any method must be fair and reasonable as explained at 7.11.

Decisions by Customs officers should be objective but the term 'fair and reasonable' inevitably contains an element of subjectivity. Consequently, many disputes concern whether or not a particular method is fair and reasonable.

The inherent problem has been partly addressed in that Customs have entered into agreements with certain trade bodies concerning special methods. These have been published in VAT Leaflet 700/57. The trade bodies include the Association of British Insurers, the Finance Houses Association, the Society of Motor Manufacturers and Traders, and opticians' professional bodies. Strict conditions apply.

Other special methods which have proven cost-effective include using cost centres and a hybrid method using different calculations for each sector of the business.

Example 63 showing comparison of methods

A housing association has 15 sources of income. The 12 exempt sources produce £2,300,000 turnover and the 3 taxable sources generate £500,000 turnover.

	£
Total input tax	400,000
Input tax directly attributable to taxable supplies (recoverable)	(30,000)
Input tax directly attributable to exempt supplies (irrecoverable)	(310,000)
Input tax to be apportioned	60,000

Consider the following 3 methods of apportionment:

(*a*) Pre-April 1992 standard method (inputs based) – still available with Customs' permission.

$$£60,000 \times \frac{£30,000}{£400,000} = £4,500$$

(*b*) Standard method (from 1 April 1992 and outputs based)

$$£60,000 \times \frac{£500,000}{£2,800,000} = 17.8\% \text{ rounded up to } 18\% = £10,800$$

(*c*) Method based on numbers of activities

$$£60,000 \times \frac{\text{3 taxable activities}}{\text{15 total activities}} = £12,000$$

Method (*c*) is clearly favourable, subject to Customs agreeing that it is fair and reasonable.

Apportionment calculations — excluded and incidental items

7.13 Certain items which would otherwise distort the calculation should be omitted from apportionment calculations, in particular:

- sales of capital items used in the business;
- incidental land and property transactions including those where the option to tax has been exercised;

- incidental financial transactions falling under *Sch 9 Group 5*;
- self-supplies.

7.14 For all partial exemption VAT years up to and including 31 March, 30 April or 31 May 1999, where exempt input tax was incurred in the following areas, it was treated as if it were attributable to taxable supplies which means the VAT charged was normally recoverable:

- any deposit of money;
- the grant of any lease or tenancy of land, or any licence to occupy land provided that the exempt input tax relating to all such supplies in any tax year was less than £1,000 and the business incurred no exempt input tax other than relating to the supplies in this list;
- making arrangements for the provision of insurance or mortgages;
- making arrangements for any hire-purchase, credit sale or conditional sale transaction;
- the assignment of any debt in respect of a supply of goods or services by the assignor.

If exempt input tax attributable to one of the five supplies listed above was made by a business in the list below, that exempt input tax could not be disregarded. However, if a business carried on one or more of the activities listed below and incurred exempt input tax in making one of the five supplies listed above but in the course of a different business activity (i.e. not one of the 18 listed below), it could still disregard that exempt input tax. The 18 types of business were as follows:

- banks
- accepting houses
- insurance companies, agents or brokers
- investment trusts or unit trusts
- investment companies
- Stock Exchange brokers/dealers or share dealing companies
- trustees of pension funds
- unit trust management companies
- building societies
- discount houses
- finance houses
- friendly societies
- money lenders

- money brokers
- mortgage brokers
- pawnbrokers
- debt factors
- credit card or charge card companies.

7.15 Paragraph 7.14 relates to *Regulation 105* which was withdrawn on 10 March 1999. This means that from partial exemption VAT years starting after 10 March 1999, businesses could no longer ignore exempt input tax relating to the activities listed in 7.14.

The de minimis limits (Reg 106)

7.16 If exempt input tax is below certain limits, all input VAT can be treated as if it were directly attributable to taxable supplies and is recoverable in full. Exempt input tax can only be calculated in the first place by a provisional apportionment calculation and adding any deemed exempt input tax to the amount already identified as attributable to exempt supplies. When the provisional amount to be disallowed is known (input tax directly attributable to exempt supplies plus the irrecoverable amount from the apportionment calculation), the *de minimis* limits can then be applied.

Currently, there are two *de minimis* limits.

If exempt input tax is less than £625 per month on average **and** less than 50% of all input tax, there is no restriction in the relevant period.

Example 64

Total input tax for quarter August 2001 is £4,000. Input tax directly attributable to exempt supplies is £1,200 and the amount deemed attributable to exempt supplies from the provisional apportionment calculation is £600. The total potentially irrecoverable is £1,800 (£1,200 + £600) but as this is less than £625 per month on average (i.e. £1,875 for the quarter) and 50% of the total input tax, the whole £4,000 may be recovered.

If, however, the apportionment calculation produced further exempt input tax of £700 rather than £600, the total exempt input tax would be £1,200 + £700 = £1,900. This is still below 50% of all input tax but exceeds £1,875 (£625 per month on average). Therefore, in this case, only £2,100 input tax would be recoverable (£4,000 – £1,900).

Annual adjustments (Reg 107)

7.17 Partial exemption calculations for each tax period produce only provisional results. This is because the mix of taxable and exempt supplies in other periods may vary, so the extent to which standard-rated purchases are used to make taxable supplies may not be accurately reflected in the recovery percentage for the tax period in which they were made.

Therefore, in order to reflect fluctuations in the proportion of taxable supplies, an annual adjustment calculation is usually required at the end of each VAT year (normally 31 March, 30 April or 31 May depending on which VAT return stagger is used). Customs may agree to dispense with the requirement but this is more usual with special methods.

The adjustment consists of one calculation for the whole VAT year using the same formula as for each period. The deductible proportion of non-attributable input tax for the year is compared with the aggregate claimed during the year and any difference is then paid to or claimed from Customs on the first return after the VAT year-end (the period ending 30 April for monthly returns, or 30 June, 31 July or 31 August for quarterly returns).

If the total resultant exempt input tax is below the *de minimis* limits, any input tax blocked in previous periods can be recovered. However, the converse is also true in that if the business was deemed fully taxable in certain earlier periods but exempt input tax is above the *de minimis* limits as a result of the annual adjustment, a payment to Customs is required.

Example 65

Amount of non-attributable input tax claimed in each tax period within a VAT year is as follows:

Period 06/01 –	£28,800
Period 09/01 –	£29,300
Period 12/01 –	£33,425
Period 03/02 –	£23,750
Total	£115,275

Total non-attributable input tax for the four quarters 06/01 – 03/02 =	£175,000
Total taxable income 06/01 – 03/02 =	£1,000,000
Total exempt income 06/01 – 03/02 =	£500,000
Therefore, total income 06/01 – 03/02 =	£1,500,000

Calculation is as follows:

% recovery: $\frac{1,000,000}{1,500,000} \times 100 = 66.66\%$ rounded up to 67%

£175,000 × 67% = £117,250

Total recovered to date = £115,275

Therefore, £117,250 – £115,275 = £1,975 can be reclaimed in Box 4 with other input tax in period 06/02. (NB If the adjustment showed an amount owing to Customs, this would be included in Boxes 1 and 3 of the return for period 06/02.)

7.18 If a business *first incurs exempt input tax during a particular VAT year*, its first annual adjustment will be from the beginning of the tax period in which it first incurs exempt input tax until the end of the VAT year. But if it incurred exempt input tax in the preceding VAT year or in its 'registration period' (see 7.19), the annual adjustment period is the whole VAT year. This is applicable even if exempt input tax in the preceding year or in the 'registration period' was covered by the rules for businesses which can ignore exempt input tax (for VAT years ended up to 31 May 1999 – see 7.14 and 7.15) or was within the *de minimis* limits. If a business first incurs exempt input tax in the last tax period of the VAT year, it does not have to carry out an annual adjustment.

The 'registration period' (Reg 99)

7.19 For newly registered businesses, the period starting on the effective date of registration and ending on the day before the start of its first full VAT year is known as the 'registration period'. If it incurs exempt input tax in the registration period, the annual adjustment period will begin on the day it first incurs exempt input tax and end on the last day of the registration period.

Example 66

A partly exempt business registers on 1 October 2001 and will complete quarterly VAT returns to 31 December etc., so that its VAT year will be to 31 March. Its registration period runs from 1 October 2001 to 31 March 2002.

If retrospective registration applies, the first VAT return may cover a period longer than a VAT year. In such cases, the business must break down the whole period into its registration period and subsequent VAT years and carry out separate annual adjustments accordingly.

Example 67

A partly exempt business is late in notifying its requirement to register, doing so on 1 October 2001. It will complete quarterly VAT returns to 31 December etc. and its VAT year will end on 31 March. It should have registered on 1 July 1999 so its first return (period 12/01) covers 30 months. For partial exemption purposes, it must break down the period into the registration period 1 July 1999 to 31 March 2000; the VAT year 1 April 2000 to 31 March 2001, and then the period 1 April 2001 to 31 December 2001. A further annual adjustment will follow the 03/02 return and any adjustment will be applied to the 06/02 return.

Change of use or intended use (Regs 108 and 109)

7.20 If a partly exempt business attributes an amount of input VAT directly to taxable supplies or has residual input tax and within a period of six years from the first day of the accounting period in which the attribution was made, the goods or services are used for non-attributable or wholly exempt purposes respectively, or the intended use changes, an adjustment must be made in Customs' favour on the VAT return for the period in which the change was identified.

Conversely, if the input VAT is attributed wholly to exempt supplies or to residual input tax and the actual use or intention changes within the six-year period, an adjustment is made on the relevant return in the taxpayer's favour.

7.21 Customs clarified their policy as to how the three-year cap affects partial exemption in their Business Brief 8/99 dated 31 March 1999. They stated that the cap does not affect businesses operating partial exemption correctly and those that correct errors they find within three years. Therefore, it does affect those that underclaim or overclaim input tax and fail to correct this within the three years. The Brief added that if businesses fail to make an initial deduction and the error relates to a period more than three years' old, the annual adjustment cannot be used to correct the mistake, even if the adjustment itself is not capped. However, Customs then added that the annual adjustment should be based on the true amounts of input tax and output tax.

The following examples are taken from the Brief and help clarify the position:

(i) A partly exempt business (which makes both exempt and taxable supplies) fails to use a partial exemption method and does not claim any input tax for a number of years. After an audit, the business submits a refund claim, in which the first quarter of the third tax year is 'capped' (i.e. more than three years' old) but the annual adjustment period itself is not 'capped' (it falls within the three-year period). Can the input tax in that period be recovered in the annual adjustment?

No – The trader, by failing to recover input tax in the relevant period, has failed to exercise the right to deduct. The trader is not able to claim this 'capped' amount in the annual adjustment.

(ii) A partly exempt business calculates deductible input tax in accordance with his partial exemption method. In the first two quarters he fails the *de minimis* limits and so correctly restricts his exempt input tax. In the second two quarters he is able to benefit from the *de minimis* limits and so correctly recovers all his input tax in those quarters. At the end of the year he is able to benefit from the *de minimis* rules for the year as a whole but does not apply them. If he discovers this mistake within three years from the last day of the annual adjustment quarter is he able to correct it?

Yes – The partly exempt trader has correctly applied the *de minimis* rules to each quarter. Since it is at the time of the annual adjustment that the *de minimis* rules are applied to all the input tax incurred in the previous four quarters, it is at that time that any exempt input tax previously restricted may be recovered.

However, where a trader was entitled to apply the *de minimis* rules to a particular period but did not do so, and that period was 'capped', any affected input tax falling in that period may not be recovered in the final *de minimis* calculation at the time of the annual adjustment (which itself is not 'capped'). This is because the trader failed to exercise the right to deduct within the three-year period.

(iii) A business with an agreed partial exemption method mistakenly treats taxable input tax as exempt. Can this input tax be recovered at the time of the annual adjustment if the input tax is proper to a period which is 'capped' (but the annual adjustment is not 'capped')?

No – We would not allow the trader to recover the exempt input tax at the time of the annual adjustment. The trader has mistakenly treated taxable input tax as exempt, and so he has failed to recover it.

Similarly, if the trader had incorrectly claimed exempt input tax and the input tax was proper to a period which was 'capped', we would be unable to recover it under the assessment provisions in that period or the period of the annual adjustment (even if it was not 'capped').

Introduction to the capital goods scheme (Regs 112 to 116)

7.22 The partial exemption adjustment system enables businesses to recover non-attributable input VAT according to the recovery percentage established in the VAT year of purchase. Input VAT may be recovered only to the extent it is 'used' in making taxable supplies, but most capital items are not used only in the year of purchase, so the restriction determined by that year's annual adjustment may advantage or disadvantage the business. The capital goods scheme enables further annual adjustments for specific capital items over their useful lives.

7.23 Article 20 of the Sixth Directive provides for annual adjustments of capital items over five years although the adjustment period for immovable property may be extended up to 20 years.

Member states are permitted to include or exclude certain items as appropriate and the UK has implemented these provisions for selected items only, namely a five-year adjustment for individual items of computer hardware costing £50,000 or more excluding VAT, and a ten-year adjustment for standard-rated land and property acquisitions costing £250,000 or more excluding VAT (*Reg 113*).

How the capital goods scheme works – overview

7.24 In the year of purchase the input VAT is apportioned using the normal partial exemption method but at the end of each subsequent VAT year or 'interval', an adjustment is made (*Regs 114 and 115*).

If the amount claimed in the year of purchase was, say, 50% and the partial exemption recovery percentage in year 2 increased to 55%, the adjustment calculation is as follows:

$$\frac{\text{The total input tax on the purchase of the item}}{\text{5 or 10 (number of years)}} \times 5\%\ (55\% - 50\%)\ \text{'the adjustment percentage'}$$

The difference is claimed from Customs (or paid to them if the adjustment percentage is negative) on the second return after the tax year-end (the period ending 31 May for monthly returns, or 30 September, 31 October or 30 November for quarterly returns).

7.25 If the item is sold during the five or ten-year term, it is deemed to be used wholly to make taxable or exempt supplies according to the liability of the sale, thus linking the input tax recovery with the output tax position on the sale. This can have a detrimental effect on the business if property is sold without the option to tax. Fully taxable businesses should be aware that the scheme can apply to them if they acquire standard-rated property and sell it within the ten-year period without the option to tax.

7.26 Where a business is transferred as a going concern incorporating an item to which the scheme applies, all documentation should be passed to the transferee to enable him to perform the remaining adjustments.

7.27 Sales of computer hardware are always standard-rated, so that the input tax is deemed to relate to a standard-rated supply as indicated in 7.25.

Mechanics of the capital goods scheme in detail

7.28 An item falls within the scope of the scheme if it is used in the relevant business, usually determined by inclusion in the business accounts.

As well as the minimum cost limits for each type of item (see 7.23) there are other conditions which must be considered.

Computers

7.29 Apart from individual items of hardware costing less than £50,000 excluding VAT not being included, the scheme does not cover:

- items acquired before 1 April 1990;
- items acquired for resale or sold before used;
- software;
- hardware not acquired but made by the business itself;
- computerised equipment.

Land and property

7.30 Clearly, the scheme can only apply to acquisitions where VAT has been charged. The following are included where the tax exclusive value is £250,000 or more:

- freehold purchases for own occupation or leasing;
- extensions, annexes, alterations to a building in which an interest is held increasing the floor area by at least 10%;
- premiums on leasehold acquisitions;
- buildings constructed by a business;

- refurbishments to relevant buildings.

Excluded are:

- acquisitions below the monetary threshold;
- buildings acquired for resale or sold before used;
- freehold purchases of bare land for possible development and not used before any development or sale.

How to determine value

7.31 Normally the invoice value applies (or if applicable the import value of computer hardware). If invoiced at the same time, installation and delivery charges for hardware are included.

As regards buildings, the value is the interest in the land (if standard-rated) plus any standard-rated costs subsequently incurred in making the building available for occupation.

Adjustment periods

7.32 These are technically known as 'intervals' because they do not always cover one year. Notably, the first interval runs from the date of acquisition to the end of the VAT year.

The ten-year adjustment period for property is reduced to five years where a lease has less than ten years to run.

Date of acquisition

7.33 The invoice date usually applies but the date of import can apply where applicable, as can the date of first use or the date a building is first leased.

Further issues concerning adjustment calculations

7.34 The normal principles of partial exemption still apply in that if the item is used all the time for taxable purposes, 100% of the input tax relevant to that period is recoverable but if it is used all the time for exempt purposes, the converse is true. If it is used for both taxable and exempt activities (as buildings and computer hardware normally would be), the overall partial exemption recovery percentage for that year applies.

The option to tax leased property clearly affects capital goods scheme adjustments. Prior to an option being taken, a property might have been used 100% for exempt purposes so that no input tax on the acquisition will have been recovered.

After the option to tax has been taken, the property will be used 100% for taxable purposes, enabling an appropriate part of the input tax on the acquisition to be recovered in subsequent adjustment periods. A fully taxable business will have reclaimed input tax in full at the time of acquisition. No capital goods scheme adjustment will have been necessary because of the 100% taxable use. If that business disposes of the property after the three-year period (during which time freehold sales are always subject to VAT), but within the ten-year adjustment period, it must exercise its option to tax in order to retain the 100% recovery of VAT which it has made. If the option is not exercised on disposal of that property, a single adjustment is performed in that adjustment period and it is deemed that the building would have been used 100% for exempt purposes by the vendor in all remaining adjustment periods if he had not sold it, with an appropriate payment to Customs of part of the VAT originally recovered.

Example 68

An engineering company bought a new factory on 1 July 1997 for £2,000,000 + £350,000 VAT which it recovers in full because it is fully taxable. By 1 July 2001 the company has outgrown the factory and wants to sell it. An insurance company agrees to buy it to turn into offices but insists that the vendor does not opt to tax the sale because of the input tax restrictions. The engineering company agrees and sells for £2,400,000 + no VAT. The factory is a capital item even though for four years, the engineering company used it 100% for taxable purposes. It is now deemed that the company has 'used' the factory for the last six of the ten intervals for 100% exempt purposes. Therefore, it would have to repay 60% of the input tax (£210,000).

If a business deregisters before an adjustment period has ended, a final adjustment is necessary and a property on which the option to tax has not been taken would be deemed 100% for exempt use.

The use of a capital item may change during the course of an interval. If, for example, a building is used 45% for taxable use for 120 days of the year and 90% for the remaining 245 days, the percentage taxable use would be calculated as follows:

$$\frac{(45\% \times 120) + (90\% \times 245)}{365} = \frac{54 + 220.5}{365} = \frac{274}{365} \times 100 = 75.06\%$$

SI 1995/2518, Reg 115 was amended by *SI 1999/599* for intervals beginning on or after 10 March 1999. Businesses must now compare the use of the capital item in the interval concerned with the use or intended use that gave rise to the original input tax claim. This provision closes a previous loophole that could create avoidance.

Responsibility for adjustments and record-keeping

7.35 In most cases, the owner of the capital item is responsible for adjustments although in a VAT group registration, the representative member is responsible. In a transfer of a going concern, the transferee must carry on the scheme. Therefore, he must know the date the item was acquired; the number of intervals left; the total VAT charged on the original acquisition and the percentage claimed at the end of the first interval.

Records must normally be kept for a maximum of six years but as capital goods scheme adjustments are over ten years for relevant land and property, appropriate records should be kept for that length of time.

Example 69

Input tax on capital goods

Independent Advisors are a firm specialising in the provision of financial advice (including taxation advice) and the selling of pensions, insurance and other pooled investments. They are VAT registered and their VAT year ends on 30 April.

A. Set out the value added tax implications of the following transactions, stating the VAT return in which any adjustment should be made.

(*a*) On 20 July 1996 Independent Advisors took possession of a new office block. The purchase price was £1,000,000 plus VAT of £175,000. On the same day a mainframe computer was installed in the offices at a cost of £200,000 plus VAT of £35,000.

The offices and computer are both used by all aspects of the business and the agreed exempt proportion as at 20 July 1996 is 60%. Subsequently the 1997 annual partial exemption adjustment revised the exempt proportion to 65%.

(*b*) The 1998 annual partial exemption adjustment revises the exempt proportion to 75%.

(*c*) Due to expansion, on 1 January 1999 the business divides its activities into two parts. The taxation advice remains in the office block acquired in July 1996, and the sales of insurance etc. are administered wholly from premises owned prior to July 1996. The computer remains in the new building and from that date is only used for taxation matters. The 1999 annual partial exemption adjustment gives an exempt proportion of 67%.

(*d*) In January 1999 the firm received an offer from Westshire Building Society to purchase its new office building, including the computer, for £2,000,000 for the building plus £1,000 for the computer, both figures exclusive of any VAT.

B. Contrast the VAT treatment of the offer from the Westshire Building Society in A with an offer from Brown Green & Co, Chartered Accountants, in January 2000, of £1,950,000 for the building plus £50,000 for the computer, both figures exclusive of any VAT.

A. **Independent Advisors — purchase and sale of office building and computer**

(*a*) **20 July 1996 — VAT input tax recoverable**

	£	£
Building — input tax Adjustment period — 10 intervals i.e. to 30.4.06	175,000	
Computer — input tax Adjustment period — 5 intervals i.e. to 30.4.01	35,000	
Recovery percentage (100 – 60) 40% ×	210,000	£84,000

This claim should be included in the quarterly VAT return to 31.7.96.

1997 annual partial exemption adjustment

	£
Revised recovery percentage (100 – 65) 35% × 210,000	73,500
Original recovery	84,000
Payable on quarterly VAT return to 31.7.97	(10,500)

(*b*) **1998 annual capital goods scheme adjustment**

First year recovery percentage (as adjusted)	35%
1998 recovery percentage (100 – 75)	25%
Adjustment percentage	– 10%

	£
Buildings $\frac{175{,}000}{10 \text{ years}} \times (10\%)$	(1,750)
Computer $\frac{35{,}000}{5 \text{ years}} \times (10\%)$	(700)
Payable on quarterly VAT return to 31.10.98	(2,450)

(*c*) **1999 annual capital goods scheme adjustment**

Building and computer are in 33% taxable use from 1.5.98 to 31.12.98 = 245 days, and in 100% taxable use from 1.1.99 to 30.4.99 = 120 days. The percentage of taxable use for the year as a whole is therefore:

$\frac{(33\% \times 245) + (100\% \times 120)}{365} =$	55.03%
First year recovery percentage	35%
Adjustment percentage	+ 20.03%

Buildings $\frac{175{,}000}{10 \text{ years}} \times 20.03\%$	3,505
Computer $\frac{35{,}000}{5 \text{ years}} \times 20.03\%$	1,402
Amount to be recovered on quarterly VAT return to 31.10.99	£4,907

(*d*) **Offer from Westshire Building Society**

Building — 100% taxable use in 2000 to date of sale.

— sale more than three years after completion therefore exempt.

— remaining complete years of adjustment period 1.5.2000 to 30.4.06 = 6 years.

Adjustment percentage up to sale (100 – 35)%	+ 65%
Adjustment percentage for remainder of adjustment period (Nil – 35)%	– 35%
	£
For 2000 $\frac{175,000}{10} \times 65\%$	11,375
On sale $\frac{175,000}{10} \times (35\%) \times 6$ years	(36,750)
Computer — 100% taxable use in 2000 to date of sale.	
— sale taxable.	
— remaining complete years of adjustment period 1.5.2000 to 30.4.01 = 1 year.	
Adjustment percentage is (100 – 35)% = 65% both for 2000 and for the remaining year of the adjustment period.	
For 2000 $\frac{35,000}{5} \times 65\%$	4,550
On sale, as above but restricted to output tax payable of 1,000 × 17.5%	175
Amount *payable* on quarterly VAT return to 31.10.2000	(20,650)
Output VAT on sale:	
Building (exempt)	–
Computer 1,000 at 17.5%	175
Payable on quarterly VAT return to 31.1.2000	£175

B. **Offer from Brown Green & Co, Chartered Accountants** (assuming option to tax exercised on sale of building)

Building — sale more than three years after first occupied would be exempt but option to tax taken.

— remaining complete years of adjustment period 1.5.2000 to 30.4.06 = 6 years.

Adjustment percentage up to sale as in A(*d*)	+ 65%
Adjustment percentage for remainder of adjustment period (100 – 35)%	+ 65%

	£
For 2000 $\frac{175,000}{10} \times 65\%$	11,375
On sale $\frac{175,000}{10} \times 65\% \times 6$ years	68,250
Computer	
Adjustment percentages as in A(*d*)	
For 2000	4,550
On sale (output tax on sale 50,000 × 17.5% = £8,750 therefore no restriction)	4,550
Amount repayable on quarterly VAT return to 31.10.2000	88,725
Output VAT on sale:	
Building 1,950,000 at 17.5%	341,250
Computer 50,000 at 17.5%	8,750
Payable on quarterly VAT return to 31.1.2000	£350,000

When considering the effect of disposing of capital goods scheme assets, it is important to review the VAT liability. In part A of this example the Westshire Building Society has offered a total of £2,001,000 exclusive of any VAT, but the sale will result in a VAT payment of £20,650 under the capital goods scheme, leaving Independent Advisors with net proceeds of £1,980,350.

In part B, Brown Green & Co, Chartered Accountants, have offered £2,000,000 exclusive of VAT. With the option to tax taken in respect of the building there will be a recovery of £88,725 VAT under the capital goods scheme, giving net proceeds of £2,088,725, an increase of £108,375 compared with the sale to Westshire Building Society.

The actual consideration will be £2,001,175 from the building society, out of which output tax of £175 is payable, or £2,350,000 from Brown Green & Co, with output tax payable of £350,000.

As a VAT exempt business, the building society would probably not be prepared to purchase the building if the option to tax was taken, because they would not be able to recover the VAT, whereas Brown Green & Co would not be disadvantaged if VAT was charged.

Chapter 8

Land, Property and Construction

Introduction

8.1 Most businesses are at some time or other affected by this area, either because they buy or rent, or have work done on property, or because they sell or let their own property.

8.2 Some property transactions appear especially complicated because of the lengthy legal documents and large sums involved, but the VAT treatment can be understood more easily by applying the basic principles and asking oneself the fundamental question: who is supplying what, to whom and for how much?

8.3 The supply may be of goods or services which often have different liabilities; there are differences in the treatment of residential and commercial property; and additional rules may apply if the transaction value is above certain monetary limits.

All aspects are dealt with in this chapter. The main legislation is *VATA 1994, Schedule 7A Group 6* — Residential Conversions and *Group 7* — Renovation and Alteration of Dwellings (from 1 November 2001); *Schedule 8 Group 5* — Construction of Buildings, etc. and *Group 6* — Protected Buildings; *Schedule 9 Group 1* — Land and *Schedule 10* — Buildings and Land (*Schedule 10* covers the option to tax).

The capital goods scheme

8.4 Businesses that acquire commercial property or in certain cases extend it or refurbish it, must apply the capital goods scheme in each of up to ten years from acquisition if the initial transaction value is at least £250,000 excluding VAT and an input tax restriction is applied because of partial exemption.

8.5 This means that the original amount of input tax recovered is adjusted in subsequent years to reflect changes in the percentage of input tax recoverable in later years because of the partial exemption rules.

8.6 The capital goods scheme also applies to individual items of computer hardware costing £50,000 or more excluding VAT. The scheme is covered in paragraphs 7.22 *et seq.*

Definition of commonly used terms

8.7 The VAT treatment of transactions involving land, property and construction services requires a full understanding of certain terms used by buyers, sellers, agents and solicitors, as set out below.

(1) A '*dwelling*' is a house or flat used as a private residence or which could be so used if it is currently empty. The term also includes a garage which is constructed at the same time and is used together with the residence.

Certain reliefs are available in respect of dwellings, and those reliefs also apply to buildings:

- designed as a dwelling or a number of dwellings;
- intended for use *solely* for a relevant residential purpose (see (2)–(3) below);
- intended for use *solely* for a relevant charitable purpose (see (4) below);
- which are protected and designed to remain or become residential buildings after substantial reconstruction (see (5) below).

(2) A building designed for a '*relevant residential purpose*' is a building which cannot be described as a house or flat but is used as the principal private residence of the people living in it, the legislation listing the types of building *within the definition* as follows:

- a residential children's home;
- armed forces accommodation;
- student accommodation and school boarding houses;
- a monastery, nunnery or similar establishment;
- a residential home providing care for persons who are aged, disabled, with past or present dependence on alcohol or drugs or with past or present mental disorders;
- a hospice;
- any institution which is the sole or main residence of at least 90% of its residents.

Where a number of buildings are constructed at the same time or under the same contract on a particular site and collectively they will be used for one of the above purposes, the whole site qualifies as constructed for a relevant residential purpose even though one of the buildings taken alone might not otherwise have qualified.

(3) The following are specifically *excluded* from the definition of *relevant residential purpose*:

- NHS and private hospitals;
- all forms of penal institution, notably prisons; and
- hotels, inns or similar establishments.

(4) A building designed for a '*relevant charitable purpose*' is one which is intended for use by a recognised charity otherwise than in the course or furtherance of business activities, for example, a church.

It would not include charity shops because goods sold therefrom are in the course of business, being either standard or zero-rated, so the condition is not fulfilled.

The definition extends to buildings that are used for business or non-business purposes by a charity, for example, as a village hall or similarly in providing social or recreational facilities for a local community, so that if an organisation with charitable status were to commission the construction of a community centre, the definition would normally apply.

In the remainder of this chapter when the term 'qualifying building' is used, it refers to dwellings, relevant residential and relevant charitable buildings.

(5) A '*protected building*' is a listed building but the term also applies to scheduled monuments. Listed buildings usually require special written consent before alterations can be made affecting the external 'character'.

Special VAT reliefs apply to approved alterations to listed buildings to be used for a qualifying purpose and which require and have obtained listed building consent as well as planning permission.

Reliefs also apply to certain disposals of listed buildings that have been substantially reconstructed. The details of reliefs for listed buildings are explained at 8.35 *et seq.*

(6) Buildings that are not defined above and which are not 'qualifying buildings' will be called 'commercial buildings' in this chapter.

(7) The 'option to tax' is a facility available to suppliers of certain land and commercial buildings. Without the option being exercised, the relevant supplies are exempt (see 8.40 *et seq.*).

From 12 May 2001, the reduced rate of 5% applies to certain renovations and alterations of dwellings and residential conversions. The provisions involve a number of new terms, the definitions of which are at 8.52 *et seq.*

8.8 The *key factors* in deciding the correct VAT treatment of a particular land transaction are:

(*a*) Is the property a 'qualifying building', or is it a commercial property?

(*b*) If a commercial property, is it within the definition of new, being up to three years from the earlier of first use or issue of certificate of practical completion?

(*c*) Who is constructing the property? (This means the legal entity responsible for the construction work, commissioning or financing the construction.)

(*d*) Is the transaction part of a transfer of a going concern (and therefore not a supply subject to VAT)?

(*e*) If the supply of bare land or a commercial property would ordinarily have been exempt (*Sch 9 Group 1* — Land), has the option to tax been taken, thus overriding the exemption? (see 8.40).

(*f*) In the case of a sale of a commercial property on which the option to tax has been taken, will the purchaser also opt to tax on completion thus ensuring that the sale is treated as a going concern transfer and not subject to VAT? (see 8.40 *et seq.*).

(*g*) What is the nature of the transaction, e.g. a major interest (namely a freehold sale or a lease for more than 21 years), a lease, an option to purchase, an inducement, a surrender, an assignment of a lease, a reverse assignment, a reverse surrender etc.? (see 8.24 *et seq.* and 8.29 *et seq.*).

(*h*) Is the property a listed qualifying building, and if so and alteration work is to be carried out on it, is listed building consent required and obtained? (see 8.35 *et seq.*).

(*j*) Is the property inside or outside the UK?

(*k*) Is the land or property to be acquired for £250,000 or more plus VAT, if so invoking the implications of the capital goods scheme? (see 8.4 to 8.6 and Chapter 7).

(*l*) Is the transaction between members of the same VAT group and thus ignored for VAT purposes?

(*m*) Is the property for use as holiday accommodation?

(*n*) Does the planned transaction fall within the definition of a renovation or alteration of a dwelling, or a residential conversion qualifying for the reduced rate (see 8.52)?

VAT liability of typical land, property and construction transactions

8.9 The main types of transaction are detailed in the annex at the end of this chapter. The following paragraphs explain the correct VAT treatment in special circumstances.

Further comment regarding construction services

General

8.10 The contents of the table in the Annex may be summarised by saying that all construction and building work is standard-rated except for the construction of new qualifying buildings (8.8(*a*)); approved alterations to listed buildings designed to remain or become qualifying buildings after the work has been done (8.36); certain conversion services such as those provided to registered housing associations in the course of converting commercial buildings into residential property (Annex Note (5)) and those falling within the new provisions from 12 May 2001 (see 8.52), and certain renovation and alteration services from 12 May 2001 (see 8.52). The exceptions are all zero-rated subject to the rules regarding issue of certificates explained at Annex Note (1) (see *Schedule 8 Group 5* Items 2–4) except those introduced from 12 May 2001, which are at 5%.

Extent of zero-rating

8.11 Zero-rating for the construction of new qualifying buildings extends to all physical work by the main contractor. Associated professional services such as those of architects, chartered surveyors, quantity surveyors and solicitors are standard-rated. However, under design and build contracts, the VAT charged on professional services to the main contractor is recovered by him and his overall supply becomes one of zero-rated new construction services. This reduces the cost to customers who may only intend to use the completed buildings to generate exempt income (e.g. from residential lettings).

How to decide whether or not a qualifying building is new is covered at 8.15.

Zero-rating for the construction of new dwellings includes necessary associated civil engineering works such as the construction of new roads and the provision of mains water, sewerage, gas and electricity up to the nearest point of connection. These works must be either within the curtilage of the dwelling or within the development site. 'Curtilage' means a reasonable amount of land surrounding a building and could include other buildings. 'Reasonable' will differ according to the type of building and its setting.

Construction services in the course of construction of a new garage built at the same time as a new dwelling and for use with it are also zero-rated.

Granny flats and annexes built after the main dwelling to which they are attached are almost always standard-rated even though they are independent of the main accommodation and may even be physically separate and just located in the grounds of the house.

Annexes constructed for a relevant charitable purpose etc.

8.12 When a builder constructs an annex onto an existing building, his services are zero-rated if the annex:

- is intended for use solely for a relevant charitable purpose;
- is capable of functioning independently from the existing building;
- has its own main entrance;
- does not provide the main entrance to the existing building; and
- is covered by the proper certificate.

According to Public Notice 708, the intention of this relief is to treat a charity annex connected by a door or corridor to another building in the same way as a fully independent structure separate from an existing building. Customs consider that the new annex must be capable of fulfilling the function for which it was designed if the connection or corridor were to be closed.

This relief does not mean that an enlargement or extension to an existing charity building is zero-rated.

It does not matter if there is more than one means of access, provided:

- the main access to the annex is not via the existing building, and
- the main access to the existing building is not via the annex.

Apart from the main zero-rated services described above, the following are also zero-rated:

- the enlargement or extension of a building to create an additional new dwelling, the separate disposal of which is not prevented by any planning or similar consent;
- the incorporation of certain goods into a building by a builder whose services are zero-rated.

Exclusions from zero-rating

8.13 New construction services do not include the conversion (except for the special relief already explained), reconstruction, alteration and enlargement of existing buildings.

Construction of a new house on the end of a terrace or in the middle of a terrace, or a new semi-detached house still qualifies for zero-rating.

The normal deciding factor as to whether or not a new building is being constructed is the existence of internal access. Where there is internal access between an existing building and new work, the services are usually standard-rated.

Repair and maintenance work to any building including listed buildings is always standard-rated. Therefore, especially in the case of work on qualifying listed buildings, where there is a mixture of alterations and repairs and maintenance, a suitable apportionment must be made.

Example 70

Dobson Builders Ltd is instructed to carry out work on a Grade II listed manor house. The work consists of roof repairs and alterations to the stone porch for the main entrance. Listed building consent was required and obtained for the porch. Dobson's quote of £3,000 + VAT has been agreed. To ensure zero-rating for the approved alteration to the porch, Dobson splits his invoice as follows:

Roof repairs – £1,000 + £175 VAT

Porch alterations – £2,000 (zero-rated)

Total – £3,175.

For further information on approved alterations to qualifying listed buildings, see 8.36.

Mixed standard and zero-rated services — apportionment

8.14 Occasionally, only part of a new building will be used for a qualifying purpose.

Where the main contractor can demonstrate through plans and certificates that a clearly defined part of the finished work will be used for qualifying purposes, he may apportion his invoice accordingly.

An apportionment is not normally allowed if a part of the building is only used for a qualifying purpose part of the time. If that is the case, the whole supply of construction services should be standard-rated.

However, non-qualifying use is ignored if the building will be used for qualifying purposes more than 90% of the total time it is available for use, and in the case of non-business charitable educational establishments such as grant-maintained sixth form colleges, if the number of fee paying students is less than 10% of total students calculated on a full-time equivalent basis.

Until recently, by concession, Customs has ignored up to 10% use of relevant buildings by charities for non-qualifying purposes and still deemed the construction 'solely' for a relevant charitable purpose thus ensuring the construction services remained zero-rated. However, a measurement by reference to use was not appropriate for all charity buildings so in Business Brief 8/2000 dated 31 May 2000, Customs announced that this concession would be extended so that the 10% can be measured by reference to:

- time,
- floor space, or
- the number of people using the building.

How to decide if a building is new

8.15 This issue has been the subject of many disputes between Customs and businesses in that the statutory guidelines have to be applied to each situation. In Customs' opinion, the following construction services constitute 'new' work and are thus zero-rated (Customs Public Notice 708, paragraph 6.1 referring):

- The construction of a dwelling or qualifying building making use of the foundations of an existing building, where the whole of the former building has been demolished to ground level (for this purpose ground level may include the 'slab' of the ground floor of the former building).
- The construction of a dwelling or qualifying building making use of what remains of a pre-existing building where, before construction starts, this is no more than the foundations and a single facade, or double facade on a corner site, but only where the facade has been retained to comply with statutory planning consent.
- The building on to an existing house of another house to form two semi-detached houses without internal access to the existing building, and where planning permission, etc. does not prevent its separate use or disposal (most small additional living accommodation either built on to an existing house or constructed adjacent to

an existing house — commonly known as 'granny annexes' — will fail the internal access or disposal test and their construction will therefore be standard-rated).

- The building of a new house within an existing terrace of houses on the site of a house that has been totally demolished ('infilling'), or totally demolished except for the front facade, where that facade has been retained because of the conditions of the planning consent.
- The construction of a new, self-contained flat which enlarges or extends an existing building and there is no prohibition on the separate use or disposal of the flat under the terms of the statutory planning consent or similar provision. This does not include the extension or enlargement of any existing dwelling, or part of a dwelling, even if the result of the work is an additional dwelling.

Services ancillary to construction services

8.16 Certain services associated with construction services are zero-rated if the construction services themselves are zero-rated whilst others are standard-rated. These are listed succinctly in paragraphs 9.1 and 9.2 of Public Notice 708, the relevant sections of which are summarised below:

> 'Zero-rated supplies:
>
> - demolition work carried out as part of a single project for the construction of dwellings or qualifying buildings
> - site clearance
> - earth moving
> - necessary civil engineering works done in the course of the construction of dwellings or qualifying buildings (this does not include tennis courts, outdoor swimming pools or similar works)
> - laying of foundations
> - bricklaying, plastering, carpentry, roofing and plumbing services
> - mechanical and electrical services (including central heating)
> - plant hire provided with an operator (other than a machine minder)
> - erection and dismantling (but not hire) of scaffolding, formwork or falsework (further information is in paragraph 11.5 of the same notes)
> - incorporation of "building materials" (see paragraph 9.3 of the same notes)

- fitting of kitchen units and worktops, and domestic appliances (but not the appliances themselves which are standard-rated, except for those listed in paragraph 9.4 of the same notes)
- fitting of carpets (but not the carpets themselves — see paragraph 9.5 of the same notes)
- internal and external cleaning ("builders' cleans")
- first time decoration
- office partitioning (for non-business charity use)
- construction of vehicle crossings
- remedial or repair work carried out while a dwelling or qualifying building is under construction, and
- site restoration (but not landscaping or ornamental work).

The following services are always standard-rated:

- site investigations (before the letting of any building contract)
- temporary fencing around a site
- concrete testing
- site security
- catering
- cleaning of site offices, huts etc.
- temporary lighting
- transport and haulage to and from the site
- plant hire without operator
- professional services of architects, engineers, surveyors, solicitors, estate agents, valuers, consultants and other persons supplying supervisory services
- construction management services, and
- landscaping, including the planting of trees, flowers, shrubs and the provision of ornamental works, etc.'

With reference to landscaping, Customs used to allow zero-rating only for the laying of turf within a house plot on a new development. However, following the *Rialto Homes plc* [*1999*] *VATDR 477 (VTD 16340)* case, Customs now accept that other types of soft landscaping can be zero-rated. 'Soft landscaping' means the 'planting of trees, shrubs, grass etc., as opposed to the construction of fencing, paths, driveways etc.' (Business Brief 7/2000, 18 May 2000).

Soft landscaping may now be zero-rated when supplied in the course of construction, which means:

— it must be done at the same time as, or immediately after the construction, and

— it must be connected with the construction work.

Customs accept that the second condition is met for all planting carried out within the new dwelling plot if detailed on a landscaping scheme approved by a planning authority under the terms of a planning consent condition.

The additional paragraph references from Public Notice 708 help a fuller understanding of the correct treatment.

Building materials

8.17 Normally, 'building materials' included in a building under construction may be zero-rated if the construction services themselves are zero-rated. The term means goods which are ordinarily installed in the type of building under construction or on its site and includes normal builders' hardware and sanitary ware. The incorporation of such goods includes their installation as fittings. There are, however, certain exceptions to the rule, the following being standard-rated even if supplied as part of a zero-rated construction service:

- finished or prefabricated furniture and materials for the construction of fitted furniture (excluding fitted kitchen furniture and materials)
- gas or electrical appliances except those listed at 8.18
- carpets, carpeting materials, underlay and carpet tiles even when stuck to the floor
- goods incorporated as part of a standard-rated construction service
- goods not ordinarily installed in the type of building under construction
- goods not incorporated into the building under construction
- goods supplied on their own and not as part of an associated service
- deemed supplies.

8.18 Despite the items listed at 8.17 above, the following electrical appliances can be zero-rated when supplied with zero-rated construction services so long as the goods are supplied before the building is completed:

- space or water heaters, ventilators, appliances providing air cooling, air purification or dust extraction
- door entry systems, waste disposal units, waste compacting machines and similar items used in buildings designed as a number of dwellings (e.g. blocks of flats)
- burglar alarms, fire alarms, fire safety equipment and devices for summoning aid in an emergency excluding telephones
- lifts and hoists
- fixed amplification equipment in churches.

When VAT on construction services should be paid

8.19 For construction services completed on or after 9 June 1999, VAT is due on completion of the construction service in certain circumstances, i.e. where the supplier of the service, or the person financing the transaction, has an intention or expectation that the land to which the construction services relate is, or will, become 'exempt land'. Where more than 80% of the supplies made using a building are taxable supplies, this does not normally apply (compare 8.45).

In other circumstances, construction companies only have to account for VAT on receipt of a payment or issue of a tax invoice, which was the position prior to December 1997.

Between December 1997 and June 1999, the tax point was no later than 18 months after the certificate of practical completion had been issued or the building was first occupied, whichever was the earlier.

Subcontractors

8.20 Essentially, services provided by sub-contractors are standard-rated because a certificate confirming eligibility for zero-rating can only be given to a main contractor. Subcontractors may, however, zero rate their services when constructing a new dwelling or assisting with a zero-rated approved alteration to a listed building.

Authenticated receipts

8.21 Unlike normal services, there is no basic tax point when a construction contract is completed unless it is a single payment contract. VAT is due when payment is received or on completion, whichever is the earlier.

The authenticated receipt procedure is unique to the construction industry and allows the supplier to issue a receipt instead of a normal tax invoice at the time of each stage payment. The authenticated receipt must contain all the information normally shown on a tax invoice and no tax invoice can be issued as well.

The receipt is actually prepared by the customer and is sent to the supplier with payment. The receipt becomes valid when authenticated by the supplier. Both parties must agree to the procedure before it can be adopted. This system means that the tax point is only triggered by the payment accompanying the receipt because the receipt itself is not a tax invoice.

Customers are allowed to recover input tax in the tax period they make the payment even if the receipt is not returned authenticated until a later period.

All authenticated receipts must be kept and made available for inspection by Customs.

If a supplier persistently fails to authenticate receipts, the customer (after the third occasion it has happened) may contact his local VAT office who may accept alternative evidence to support an input tax claim. On the supplier's part, failure to issue an authenticated receipt is a regulatory offence.

Change of use

Disposal or letting

8.22 If, within ten years of obtaining zero-rating for a residential or charitable building, a business grants any interest in or licence to occupy the building so that it is no longer used for purposes which would have qualified for the relief, it will have to charge VAT on the value of the grant.

Example 71

The Friendly Neighbourhood Housing Association (FNHA) had two small old people's homes built. Work was completed on 31 March 1996. The building work cost £800,000 on each and was zero-rated as the buildings were designed solely for a relevant residential purpose. On 30 June 2001, one of the homes was closed and sold for £1,000,000 to a firm of solicitors for use as offices. FNHA must add £175,000 VAT to the sale price.

Change of use by occupier

8.23 If, within ten years of obtaining zero-rating for a residential or charitable building, a business changes its use so that it is no longer used for the purposes which qualified for the relief, the business will have to pay an amount of tax equal to the tax that would have been chargeable at the construction stage had it not qualified for zero-rating at the time.

Example 72
FNHA in *Example 71* above closed the second home on 30 September 2001 and began using the building as its own administrative offices. The change of use took place within 10 years of obtaining zero-rating, so FNHA must pay £140,000 VAT (VAT that would have been due at the construction stage) when the change occurred.

Property sales

General

8.24 Whatever VAT is chargeable on property sales normally depends on three key factors:

- whether the property is new (see definitions at 8.15);
- whether it is qualifying or non-qualifying (see 8.7(1) to (5)); and
- who is making the sale.

Qualifying buildings

8.25 The first freehold sale of a qualifying building by the person or legal entity that has constructed it is zero-rated subject to the rules regarding certificates at Annex Note (1) (*Schedule 8 Group 5* Item 1). All subsequent freehold sales are exempt, as are first sales if made by a person or business other than the one that constructed the building or buildings. The option to tax (see 8.40) is not available for qualifying buildings, which means that VAT on costs incurred after the first freehold sale is normally irrecoverable.

The 'person who has constructed' a qualifying building is the legal entity that physically constructed, financed the construction or commissioned the construction and subsequently granted a major interest in it.

Commercial buildings

8.26 Sales of new commercial buildings are compulsorily standard-rated. Commercial buildings are regarded as new up to three years from completion so there could be a number of compulsory standard-rated sales during this time. As soon as a commercial building is over three years old, it becomes an 'existing building' the sale of which is exempt, albeit the option to tax the sale being available (see 8.40).

Listed buildings (Schedule 8 Group 6)

8.27 The treatment of listed buildings is covered separately below (8.35).

Zero-rating applies to freehold sales of substantially reconstructed listed buildings which are for qualifying use and subject to the normal certificate requirements (see Annex Note (1)).

A listed building is substantially reconstructed if at least 60% of the work carried out on it consists of approved alterations or if it has been gutted and rebuilt retaining only the shell.

No specific reliefs apply to commercial listed buildings.

Converted buildings

8.28 The final relief for freehold sales of buildings applies to sales of buildings which have been converted from commercial to residential use. Sales of converted buildings by the person or business converting them are zero-rated. This applies to dwellings and buildings designed solely for a relevant residential purpose. It does not apply to buildings designed in any way for charitable purposes. Where a building will be used for a relevant residential purpose, a certificate is required from the purchaser.

Conversion services supplied to the person making the sale are still standard-rated or reduced-rated from 12 May 2001 (see 8.52 *et seq.*) but this can be recovered as input tax subject to the normal rules.

The relief also applies to buildings which may have originally been for residential purposes but have not been used as such since 1 April 1973 (the date VAT was introduced). Derelict buildings could thus fall within the scope of the relief.

Some charitable organisations cannot benefit from this relief because they are legally prevented from selling the converted property but, by concession, charities in this category may apply for a refund to VAT Construction Branch, HM Customs & Excise, New Kings Beam House,

22 Upper Ground, London SE1 9PJ. For registered housing associations and individuals who have such buildings converted for their own use, the conversion services themselves are zero-rated rather than the subsequent sale.

The 5% rate applies to certain renovation, alteration and conversion services from 12 May 2001 (not to sales of those properties) (see 8.52). From 1 August 2001, the zero rate applies to the sale of renovated houses that have been empty for at least 10 years.

Leases

General

8.29 The VAT treatment of leases applies equally to formal and informal agreements, written or oral under the legal term 'a licence to occupy land'. This must be compared with the grant of a right to use facilities such as the contents of or equipment within a building, which is compulsorily standard-rated. The most usual form of income from leases is rent but several other types of income can be received as a result of a lease, such as service charges, money paid to a tenant to surrender a lease, money paid to a landlord to be released from obligations under a lease, money paid to a tenant to enter into a lease, tenants agreeing to meet fitting-out costs in return for rent-free periods. These should all be considered carefully and the correct treatment confirmed through Customs where there is any doubt.

For example, in the Tribunal case involving Mirror Group Plc, it was decided that part of the £12m the Mirror Group received from Olympia & York Canary Wharf Limited as an inducement to take several floors of a Docklands building was subject to VAT. The reason was that when the Mirror Group received payment it was not in a position to grant an exempt interest in property. Customs have appealed to the High Court against the exemption from VAT on that part of the amount received that was considered payment for a lease.

Rental income

8.30 Rental income is basically exempt from VAT under *Schedule 9 Group 1* Item 1.

There are exceptions, as follows:

- rent from commercial lettings is standard-rated where the lessor has exercised the option to tax (*Sch 10 para 2*) (see 8.40);
- the first payment of rent or the premium payment from a new qualifying building let for a term exceeding 21 years by the person

who constructed it is zero-rated although all subsequent rent payments are compulsorily exempt; the effect of this is that the lessor may recover VAT on all positive rated costs incurred before the first payment but not on any later costs (subject to the partial exemption rules) because they would be attributable to exempt supplies (*Sch 8 Group 5* Item 1);

- the first payment of rent or the premium payment from a substantially reconstructed listed building for qualifying use after the reconstruction let for a term exceeding 21 years by the person who reconstructed it is zero-rated although all subsequent rent payments are compulsorily exempt (*Sch 8 Group 6* Item 1);
- the first payment of rent or the premium payment from a building converted from commercial to residential use let for a term exceeding 21 years by the person who converted it is zero-rated although all subsequent rent payments are compulsorily exempt (*Sch 8 Group 5* Item 1).

Example 73

A builder constructs new houses to hold as investments and rent out to tenants on 25-year leases. On his first house, professional fees (architects, surveyors and solicitors) are £4,000 + £700. He grants a 25-year lease and receives a down payment of £2,000. Subsequent rent is £750 per month. Six months after he has let the house, there is a major electrical problem requiring specialist repairs costing him £2,000 + £350 VAT.

The down payment is zero-rated so the £700 input tax on professional fees is fully recoverable. The subsequent rent is exempt so the £350 input tax on repairs is normally irrecoverable, subject to the partial exemption rules (see Chapter 7).

Service charges

8.31 These are often levied on tenants in blocks of flats or in multi-tenanted commercial buildings.

The normal rule is that if the charge is for the general upkeep of the structure and common areas, the VAT liability follows that of the rent.

Thus, if the service charge is for maintenance of lifts, cleaning of stairs and landings, landscaping etc., the charge is exempt if the rent is exempt, e.g. to tenants of blocks of flats.

On the other hand, the charge would be standard-rated if the property were commercial and the landlord had opted to tax.

If the charge is for a supply direct to a tenant's individual unit, it carries its normal VAT liability unless only the exact cost is passed on to the tenant and conditions for treating it as a disbursement are met (see 3.75). In that case, the charge is outside the scope of VAT.

Lease variations

8.32 Guidelines have been agreed between the Law Society and Customs following many disputes in this extremely complicated area relating to commercial property.

(*a*) If money is received by a lessor from a lessee, this is usually the grant of a new lease which is exempt from VAT, with the option to tax available even if the lessor is effectively accepting the surrender of an onerous lease (a 'reverse surrender').

(*b*) If money is received by a lessee from a lessor, this is usually in respect of a surrender. This is exempt but with the option to tax available. Customs might look at the terms of the new lease to make sure they are not considerably more favourable than should be expected for a lessee with no existing lease to surrender. In this case, the taxable value could be partly the money paid and partly the grant of the new lease.

Where no money changes hands, Customs now agree there is not a surrender of an old lease for non-monetary consideration when the new lease is for:

- the same building or part of a building but for an extended term;
- a larger part of the same building but for the same or an extended term; or
- the same land but for an extended term.

The above three situations do not apply where a lease is granted on condition that the lessee will carry out development work. These leases are known as 'new for old' ground leases or 'building leases'. In such situations, Customs expect the new lease to be more favourable than the old. Therefore, there would be a surrender of the old lease, the consideration for which is the grant of the new lease on favourable terms. The value of the surrender is the open market value.

As there are so many different types of variation, each should be considered carefully and the correct VAT treatment specifically agreed with Customs.

Civil engineering works

8.33 Civil engineering works are normally standard-rated unless they constitute part of a zero-rated contract for the construction of new qualifying buildings or numbers of qualifying buildings (*Sch 8 Group 5* Item 2).

Civil engineering works are zero-rated when the main construction services are zero-rated to the extent that they are necessary and within the curtilage of the development site. For example, services providing mains water, sewerage, gas and electricity up to the nearest point of connection would be included in the zero-rating but tennis courts, swimming pools and similar would be standard-rated.

Where a development includes a mixture of standard-rated and zero-rated work, e.g. the construction of an estate including houses and shops, the civil engineering work may be apportioned in a fair and reasonable way. If the value is not apportioned, the whole work is standard-rated.

The sale of a new or partly completed civil engineering work is standard-rated but leases are exempt with the option to tax (see 8.40). As with commercial buildings, civil engineering works are regarded as new until they are three years old, so sales of older works are exempt with the option to tax.

Land (Sch 9 Group 1 Item 1)

8.34 'Land' includes buildings.

Grants of interests in and rights over bare land including sales of and licences to occupy land are exempt from VAT although the person or business making the grant has the right to waive exemption and opt to tax subject to the conditions explained below.

There are a number of exceptions to the basic rule.

They are as follows:

(*a*) Zero-rating of certain major interests (freehold sales or leases exceeding 21 years) in qualifying buildings (see 8.25 and 8.30).

(*b*) In cases where property forms part of the transfer of a business as part of a going concern providing the normal conditions are met (see 8.40), in which case the supply is outside the scope of VAT.

(*c*) The following are standard-rated:

(i) the grant of the non-exclusive use of an area or site such as:

- allowing the general public to tip rubbish on land,
- storing another person's goods in a warehouse without allocating any specific area for them,
- sharing the same parts of business premises,
- allowing the general public admission to premises or events.

(Note that there is a specific exemption applicable to certain fund-raising events by charities which can include admission charges.);

(ii) supplies of non-qualifying buildings or civil engineering works which are either:

- the freehold interest in a new building, or
- the freehold interest, lease, tenancy or licence of new holiday accommodation for which payment is made in the form of a premium, or
- subject to an election to waive exemption (see 8.40), or
- subject to a developmental tenancy, lease or licence, or
- specifically excluded from exemption as further listed;

(iii) supplies which are not actually the grant or assignment of an interest in, right over or licence to occupy land (e.g. licences to use land);

(iv) any grant of land clearly incidental to the use of facilities on it such as:

- granting the right to use machinery in a factory,
- hiring out safes for storage of valuables,
- granting the right to use facilities in a hairdressing salon;

(v) the grant of any interest, right or licence to take game or fish, other than the freehold sale of land which includes the sporting or fishing rights;

(vi) the provision of pitches for tents or of camping facilities, including caravan pitches on seasonal sites;

(vii) the grant of facilities for parking a vehicle;

(viii) the grant of any right to fell and remove standing timber. This must be a separate and specific grant. Where exempt land is sold which contains standing timber which the buyer can cut down once the land has been bought, the whole supply will be exempt with the option to tax;

(ix) the grant of mooring and storage facilities for aircraft, ships, boats and other vessels. (Note that some supplies of these facilities may qualify for zero-rating if they are supplied in a port or Customs airport. Special rules also apply to the mooring of some houseboats.);

(x) the grant of any viewing facilities and accommodation including boxes at a sports ground, theatre, concert hall or other place of entertainment. This applies whether or not an event is in progress when the facilities are in use. If the whole venue is hired out, the supply is normally exempt with the option to tax;

(xi) the grant of facilities for playing any sport or participation in any physical recreation, unless the grant is for a continuous period of use exceeding 24 hours or for a series of 10 or more periods, whether or not exceeding 24 hours in total providing the following conditions are met:

- each period is in respect of the same activity carried on at the same place;
- the interval between each period is not less than one day and not more than 14 days;
- payment is by reference to the whole series and is evidenced by written agreement;
- the grantee has exclusive use of the facilities; and
- the grantee is a school, a club, an association or an organisation representing affiliated clubs or constituent associations.

Listed buildings (Sch 8 Group 6)

Introduction

8.35 There are two key terms used in the VAT relief provisions applicable to listed buildings: 'approved alteration' and 'substantial reconstruction'.

The following qualify as listed buildings:

In England and Wales, Grade I, Grade II* and Grade II buildings.

In Scotland, Grade A, Grade B and Grade C(S).

Unlisted buildings in conservation areas, buildings included in a local authority's non-statutory list of buildings of local interest, previously known as Grade III buildings, and Grade C buildings in Scotland are not listed buildings for the purposes of VAT reliefs.

Approved alterations

8.36 Certain works of alteration to listed buildings are zero-rated for VAT purposes if certain conditions are fulfilled:

- the building must be for a qualifying purpose;
- the work must be to a listed building and to the 'fabric' of such a building (defined in this paragraph);
- the work must both require and be granted listed building consent by the proper authority or be eligible for ecclesiastical exemption (see 8.37 below);
- the person having the work done must give the main contractor a certificate if the building is to be used for a relevant residential or relevant charitable purpose.

Works of repair and maintenance and incidental alterations to the fabric of a listed building carried out as part of a work of repair or maintenance, are not zero-rated.

If the building is repaired or maintained but in that process is incidentally altered, the work is standard-rated.

Mixed work may be apportioned between the qualifying zero-rated alterations and the standard-rated elements so long as the alteration work is more than incidental.

'Fabric' has its ordinary dictionary definition, i.e. a structure, frame or the basic structure of a building. Therefore the fabric of the building includes its walls, roofs, internal surfaces, floors, stairs, landings and all its doors and windows.

'Incidental' must be given its everyday use and meaning, i.e. happening or likely to happen in connection with or subordinate to something more important.

8.37 Certain types of Church in England and Wales are afforded ecclesiastical exemption under planning legislation. All alterations for these churches are therefore approved and zero-rated as they are for all listed ecclesiastical buildings in Scotland and Northern Ireland. The denominations covered in England and Wales are:

- the Church of England
- the Church in Wales
- the Roman Catholic Church
- the Methodist Church

- the Baptist Union of Great Britain and the Baptist Union of Wales
- the United Reformed Church.

8.38 In general terms, certain buildings such as those on Crown or Duchy land are exempt from the requirement for listed building consent. In such cases, where alteration work would normally have required listed building consent, zero-rating still applies.

Major interests in substantially reconstructed listed buildings

8.39 The sale or long lease (over 21 years) of a substantially reconstructed listed building which is for qualifying use subsequently is zero-rated if the supply is made by the person or business substantially reconstructing the building.

There are two basic definitions of 'substantial reconstruction':

- no more of the original building than an external wall or walls, or external walls together with other external features of architectural interest can be retained (i.e. the building must be gutted); or
- 60 per cent or more of the total cost of the works must be attributable to approved alterations.

The sale or long lease of a qualifying building which has only been extended cannot be zero-rated, but the extension itself can be an approved alteration, so if there are other approved alterations carried out on the existing building at the same time and the approved alteration aggregate cost is at least 60% of the total cost of the work, the sale or long lease of the final product can be zero-rated.

If a listed building is substantially reconstructed and only part will be used for a qualifying purpose, that part may be zero-rated provided both the above tests apply to the qualifying part.

Example 74

Jackson, a speculative builder and VAT registered, buys a derelict Grade II listed house that he intends to 'do up' and sell. He plans to add two extensions, completely change the front elevation and replace the roof using a different type of slate. The structure of the inside will be unchanged but obviously brought up to habitable standards. All work except to the interior constitutes alterations that have required and obtained listed building consent.

The costs are as follows:

Approved alterations — £200,000 (zero-rated)

Interior work — £100,000 + £17,500 VAT

The cost of the approved alterations is more than 60% of the total so Jackson's sale of the finished house will be zero-rated as the substantial reconstruction of a qualifying building. Jackson can recover the £17,500 charged to him on the interior work as input tax because his sale is taxable, albeit at the zero rate.

The election to waive exemption (the 'option to tax') (Sch 10 paras 2 to 3A)

Introduction

8.40 The option to tax enables those who would receive exempt income from supplies in connection with land and property under *Sch 9 Group 1* to choose to standard rate that income. The main benefit of so doing is the entitlement to recover input tax on associated costs.

The option to tax applies to:

- any building other than a qualifying building (see 8.8(*a*)) although it does apply to a charity building used as an office;
- any land except land granted to a registered housing association for residential development or to an individual for construction of a dwelling to be used by him;
- agricultural land in which the electing person has an interest (excluding farmhouses and other such dwellings).

The option relates to single buildings. A single building normally includes buildings linked internally or by covered walkways, parades, precincts and complexes divided into individual units, although Customs sometimes approve separate options where, for example, buildings on an industrial estate have been built at different times or where buildings on a site are used for different purposes such as an office block, a factory and a garage.

As regards agricultural land, from 1 March 1995 it has been possible to opt on discrete parcels of land without affecting adjoining land.

How the option to tax works

8.41 A person or business exercising an option to tax does so in respect of all grants of interests in the building or land concerned which would otherwise have been exempt. Therefore, if a landlord of commercial property opts to tax, he not only charges VAT on rents but must also charge VAT if he eventually sells the property unless the transfer of going concern rules apply.

Example 75
Mr Hale buys a small factory as an investment, paying £200,000 + £35,000 VAT. He registers for VAT, opts to tax the building from completion date and recovers the £35,000 VAT. He charges £10,000 pa rent + £1,750 VAT. After four years he sells the building to the tenant for £300,000 and must add £52,500 VAT to the sale price. If he sold to a third party buyer and the same tenants remained in place, the sale would be the transfer of a property letting business as a going concern if the buyer opted to tax on the date of purchase. In that case, VAT would not be added to the selling price.

The option must be notified in writing to Customs within 30 days of the date it is intended to take effect and can be revoked within three months or not until 20 years later.

VAT is added to rents on opted property unless the lease agreement specifically states otherwise, e.g. 'rent shall be deemed inclusive of any VAT due' which would mean that if annual rent were £5,000, VAT would be £744.68 (£5,000 × 7/47) rather than £875.00 (£5,000 × 17.5%). This particularly helps partly exempt tenants who cannot reclaim all input tax on their overheads, but means that the landlord loses part of the rent to Customs.

Example 76
Mr Pace owns an office and lets it to a charity that has input tax restrictions. The monthly rent is agreed at £1,000 including VAT. Each month, Pace will receive £851.06 rent + £148.94 VAT = £1,000 (not £1,000 + £175 VAT = £1,175).

Opting prior to the creation of a lease which makes no specific mention of VAT means that rent will be VAT-inclusive.

Effect of the option to tax and permission options

8.42 Apart from standard-rating all income in respect of the opted building, the option ensures the building owner can claim input tax now attributable to taxable rather than exempt supplies.

Where exempt income has been received in respect of a building, the owner must obtain written permission to opt to tax before he can actually do so. Permission is not normally granted until the owner has proposed an apportionment of input tax incurred on the building to date but not recovered.

Buildings which were acquired with an addition for VAT and which cost more than £250,000 excluding VAT are subject to the capital goods scheme and input tax is adjusted over ten years (see Chapter 7). It follows that if a building is outside the capital goods scheme provisions (e.g. because it cost less than £250,000 excluding VAT), Customs consider the apportionment of input tax should also be based on a ten-year period even if it is quite clear that the useful life of the building is longer.

Where, under a permission option, some of the invoices for standard-rated services are dated more than six months before the option date, Customs usually allow a deduction by concession because there is no automatic right (see 6.35).

Example 77

The following would normally be regarded as a fair apportionment and permission to opt would be given:

Input tax incurred to date but not recovered — £5,000

Months let to date (exempt rents) — 12

Proposed apportionment: recoverable amount of input tax =

$$£5,000 \times \frac{108 \text{ months taxable}}{120 \text{ months (total)}}$$

Assuming Customs allow the option, the building will only have been used for 12 months out of 120 for receiving exempt rents, i.e. 90% of the input tax should relate to the 9 years of taxable use after the option took effect.

Customs agree the input tax allowable *before* permission is granted; the option is not backdated and no input tax can be claimed until the option has been exercised. Once Customs give written permission, the business must still formally exercise the option in writing for it to be valid.

Notification of the option to tax

8.43 Although it is possible to notify in respect of all properties under current ownership or even which will be owned, it is normal and sensible to name each building or plot of land individually, adding the specific name and address if appropriate.

Customs are not obliged to acknowledge the notification in writing but they can be asked to do so.

All options to tax must be notified to Customs. Where a lessor opts to charge tax but fails to notify Customs, charges his tenant VAT, issues tax invoices and declares output tax, with the tenant claiming input tax accordingly, Customs may ignore the failure to notify and deem it to have been made because there is no loss to the revenue.

Businesses receiving this treatment must then formally notify Customs in writing.

Transfers of going concerns

8.44 One of the conditions for the transfer of a going concern to be outside the scope of VAT is that the business or part of a business being transferred must be for use by the transferee in operating the same kind of business. Where a landlord of opted property sells it with sitting tenants, the sale price would normally be subject to VAT, but if the purchaser opts to tax with immediate effect i.e. from completion date, this is regarded as the transfer of the same kind of business and VAT must not be charged on the sale price. The option by the purchaser clearly means that he must register for VAT simultaneously if not already registered.

When the option to tax is not available

8.45 The option to tax is not available where:

(*a*) the land or building is subject to the capital goods scheme in the hands of the business that could otherwise opt to tax;

(*b*) a relevant supply in connection with the land or building was made during the period for adjustment of input tax under the capital goods scheme;

(*c*) at the time of that relevant supply the person making it, or a person funding that person, intended or expected that the property would be occupied, or continue to be occupied, by any of:

 (i) the person making the grant,

(ii) a person funding that person, or

(iii) a person connected with either of them

other than mainly for taxable business purposes.

The term 'other than mainly for taxable purposes' was previously defined as where the relevant business could not claim 80% or more of its input tax, but there is no clear definition now although the same interpretation is expected. This restriction on the option does not apply to supplies arising from grants made before 26 November 1996, or from grants made before 30 November 1999 on terms agreed in writing before 26 November 1996. The following examples are taken from an amendment to Public Notice 742 'Land and Property':

'Example 1

Eastham Ltd is a bank which only recovers ten per cent of the VAT which it incurs. It has a fully-owned subsidiary, Dobing Ltd, which is also partly exempt and also has a input tax recovery rate of ten per cent. Today Eastham Ltd plans to purchase a building costing £750,000 and then lease the building to Dobing Ltd.

Any election which Eastham Ltd might make is disapplied because:

(1) the building is within the capital goods scheme (it cost not less than £250,000 after 31 March 1990);

(2) the grant is made during an adjustment period for the capital goods scheme;

(3) it is intended that the building will be occupied by a connected person other than mainly for taxable business purposes.

Example 2

Eastham Ltd changes its plan and proposes that today Conroy Ltd, an unconnected person, will:

(1) purchase the building;

(2) elect to waive exemption; and

(3) then lease it to Dobing Ltd.

The purchase of the building will be funded by a loan from Eastham Ltd.

Conroy Ltd's election is disapplied. Although it is unconnected with either Dobing Ltd or Eastham Ltd, the person funding the person making the grant (i.e. Eastham Ltd) intends that the building will be occupied by a connected person other than mainly for taxable business purposes.'

Further anti-avoidance legislation was enacted in the *Value Added Tax (Buildings and Land) Order 1999 (SI 1999/593)*. It came into force on 10 March 1999. The above restriction now also applies to land and buildings that will or are intended to become subject to the capital goods scheme but are not at the time of a relevant grant.

Persons bound by the option to tax

8.46 It is important to understand who is bound by an option to tax with respect to VAT group registrations and joint ownerships.

VAT groups — all supplies in connection with a property are standard-rated through the representative member if any member of the group has opted to tax it whether before or after joining the group. If a company leaves the group but retains an interest in a property on which the group would have charged tax, that company must also charge tax on any supplies of that property subsequently made.

Example 78

Hill Properties Ltd owns an industrial estate which it has opted to tax. It receives £100,000 pa rent + £17,500 VAT. It subsequently joins the group registration of Schumacher Holdings Ltd, which must continue to charge VAT on the rents. Schumacher Holdings Ltd has also been accounting for £8,750 VAT on the £50,000 pa rent received from an estate owned by Irvine Properties Ltd, which subsequently leaves the group registration because there is a relationship breakdown between the directors of Hill and Irvine. The latter must continue to charge VAT on rents after it has left the group.

Example 79

Hakkinen Ltd and Coulthard Ltd agree to buy a large office block together. They opt to tax and register for VAT as a single taxable person calling themselves The McLaren Partnership.

Joint owners — where property is owned jointly by two or more legal entities, it is likely that the only supply that can be made of the property is by all the parties together. This applies even if each party has been allocated a designated part of the property. A supply can only be made standard-rated if all parties together opt to tax the property. The taxable supply of the property is then made by all the parties as one person. To account for output tax and to be able to recover input tax, all the parties should register for VAT together to create a single taxable person. This is a deemed partnership even if there is no partnership for any other purpose.

Miscellaneous issues concerning the option to tax

8.47 The normal tax point rules apply in respect of rents received on properties where the option to tax has been exercised.

8.48 A VAT registered vendor of commercial property, where there is no option to tax in place on a particular property, may normally opt to tax that property if it is going to be converted by the purchaser into residential property provided that both vendor and purchaser agree that the sale should be taxable. (The purchaser may then reclaim the VAT if he sells it or grants a lease for over 21 years, but not if he occupies it for himself.)

Following the recent Tribunal case of *SEH Holdings Limited (VTD 16771)*, Customs have reviewed their policy. Where the immediate purchaser of a building does not intend to use it himself as a dwelling or to convert it into dwellings for sale or rent, and the vendor has opted to tax the building, the latter must charge VAT on the sale. Customs admit that their previous policy was unclear and so do not require affected taxpayers to make retrospective adjustments. However, all transactions from 1 August 2001 are subject to the new policy.

Where the immediate purchaser does intend to use the building as a dwelling or convert it into dwellings for sale or rent, the previous policy remains whereby both vendor and purchaser must agree for the sale to be taxable rather than exempt.

8.49 Where the legal title or ownership in land is held by a nominee for a named beneficial owner, Customs can and usually will allow the beneficial owner to be treated as the transferee in a going concern situation.

8.50 Commercial property is often owned by pension funds and rented to an associated company. These pension funds may opt to tax commercial properties held by them, register for VAT and function as if they were a normal business for VAT purposes. However, in certain circumstances, especially where the main trading company is partly exempt, the restrictions at 8.45 may apply.

8.51 Customs are committed to reviewing the option to tax on a regular basis, the last review being in 1999. No changes have been introduced as yet as a result of this latest review (see Business Brief 16/99 dated 20 July 1999).

Example 80

Steven owns a small complex which embraces the following, from all of which he either already receives rent or will do so when the appropriate work on that part is complete:

- a public house
- an office block
- a retail shop
- a car sales area
- several buildings used for storage
- a former office block which is being converted into several flats for residential occupation, and
- two small rooms which are to be let commercially.

The option to tax the office block was taken several years ago and the input tax recovered. The option to tax has not been taken in respect of any of the other commercial buildings nor in respect of the car sales area.

Steven asks whether the VAT on the conversion costs of the former office block to flats can be recovered, and if so how; what his VAT position would be were he to sell the complex, and how his general VAT position could be improved.

If Steven sells the complex without taking the option to tax the commercial buildings (except the office block) and car sales area, he must split the proceeds between each unit and add VAT to the amount relating to the office block. Assuming the conversion work is completed prior to the sale of the whole complex, the amount relating to the former office block (now flats) is zero-rated (see below). The remainder of the sale price is exempt. Note that the sale of the opted office block is compulsorily standard-rated because the option can only be revoked after 20 years and the provision has only existed since 1989. If Steven opts to tax other buildings within the complex prior to selling the whole, he must add VAT to the part of the proceeds attributable to those buildings as well as the office block.

Steven would pay VAT on the costs of arranging the sale such as professional fees. He needs to establish what proportion of this input VAT is attributable to the exempt part of the sale (probably by reference to the split of proceeds). Thereafter, he would apply the partial exemption *de minimis* limits (see 7.16) to the input VAT attributable to the exempt part of the sale along with any other exempt input tax (see 7.3) he may have incurred in the tax period in which the sale was made.

If Steven sells the former office block once it has been converted into flats, his supply is zero-rated under *Sch 8 Group 5* Item 1(b). The same applies if he grants a lease exceeding 21 years in the building although only the premium or first payment of rent is zero-rated, subsequent rents being exempt. This applies if he sells or leases the building as a whole or each flat individually.

Steven could improve his VAT position by considering the option to tax the public house, the retail shop, the car sales area, the storage buildings and the two rooms (unless those rooms are to be let for residential or non-business charitable purposes in which case rents are always exempt). *Sch 10 para 3(3)* states that the option to tax must be taken for whole buildings. Buildings linked by a covered walkway, linked internally or consisting of a complex of units grouped around a fully enclosed concourse might be treated as one building for the purposes of the option (see 8.40). Therefore, if the restriction applies here, Steven cannot opt for each commercial building individually because one option covers all the buildings of the complex.

However, as these buildings were probably built at different times and are almost certainly not enclosed, Steven could opt separately for each building. He may wish to clarify the issue with Customs first to ensure they agree the complex is not subject to one option for the whole. In any case, Steven must obtain Customs' prior written approval to opt to tax buildings from which he has already received exempt rent. Approval will be granted provided that Steven proposes a fair and reasonable apportionment of the input VAT he has incurred on those buildings prior to the required option date (see 8.42).

Although Steven does not have to consult his tenants before opting, it may be sensible to do so to ensure a sound commercial relationship. He may choose not to take the option where tenants are partly exempt or not VAT registered because these tenants would not be able to recover some or all of the VAT charged on rents. However, as tenants are normally responsible for repairs and maintenance, Steven's exempt input tax would not be significant in relation to the buildings he has not opted to tax.

New reduced rate for conversion, renovation and alteration of dwellings

8.52 From 12 May 2001, the reduced rate of 5% has been introduced for certain services connected with the conversion, renovation and alteration of dwellings, the main reason being the Government's desire to support and encourage urban regeneration projects. An overview of the new provisions follows but further detail is available in VAT Information Sheet 4/01 (May 2001) available from local VAT offices and Customs website.

For residential conversions, as stressed at 8.7, it is important to understand the definition of new terms in deciding whether or not specific services qualify for the 5% rate.

Residential conversions — definition of terms

8.53 There are three types of services within this category:

— 'change in number conversions' — these are conversions which create a number of single household dwellings different from the number, if any, that existed before the work started. A 'single household dwelling' ('SHD') logically means a dwelling that is designed for occupation by a single household. This category includes the conversion of non-residential buildings into one or more SHDs. It is assumed that should the converted property be sold, the vendor may still zero rate the sale and that registered housing associations may have the conversion work zero-rated in the first place (see 8.28).

— 'house in multiple occupation conversions' — these are conversions of buildings containing one or more SHDs to create one or more houses in multiple occupation. This category excludes conversion into a building to be used for a relevant residential purpose (see 8.7(2) but also third indent below). A 'house in multiple occupation' ('HMO') is a multiple occupancy dwelling designed for occupation by more than a single household.

— 'special residential conversions' — these are conversions of buildings containing SHDs or HMOs into buildings for use solely for a relevant residential purpose. The definition of 'relevant residential purpose' ('RRP') is at 8.7(2). The recipient of the services must give the main contractor a certificate to confirm eligibility for zero-rating (see Note (1) to the Annex below).

The reduced rate applies to the supply of the conversion services and related goods. The legislation was introduced at *VATA 1994, Schedule A1 para 1(6)* but constitutes the new *Group 6* to *Schedule 7A* from 1 November 2001.

Renovation and alteration of dwellings

8.54 The services of renovating or altering (including extending) dwellings and the supply of related goods is also subject to the 5% rate from 12 May 2001 where the dwelling is an SHD that has been unoccupied for at least three years.

A dwelling qualifies under this heading if:

(1) it has not been lived in for the whole three years ending on the day the work starts; or

(2) (a) there has been at least three years that it has not been lived in, and

(*b*) a person, whose occupation of the building ended the period that the dwelling was not lived in, acquired it before starting to live there and at a time when it had not been lived in for three years, and

(*c*) there were no works of renovation or alteration during the three years ending with the acquisition, and

(*d*) the supply is actually made to the person whose occupation brought the period when it was not occupied to an end and who also acquired it in the way explained above, and

(*e*) the works are carried out no later than one year after its acquisition.

The legislation was introduced at *VATA 1994, Schedule A1 para 1(6)* but constitutes the new *Group 7* to *Schedule 7A* from 1 November 2001.

The supply of related goods (building materials)

8.55 The rules regarding the supply of materials that can be included in the supply at 5% are as described at 8.17. The supply of non-qualifying materials is standard-rated as is the service of fitting or installing them.

Miscellaneous issues

8.56 As is normal for any type of construction project, certain services are always standard-rated, such as supplies by architects, surveyors and any person acting in a supervisory capacity; the hiring out of goods and work on outbuildings that remain outbuildings. However, work on a garage may be reduced-rated if carried out at the same time as the main conversion work and it is intended for use with the SHD, HMO or RRP. In such circumstances, the garage can be built from new or converted from a non-residential building.

8.57 Where a particular project involves a mixture of services subject to the standard and reduced rate, a suitable apportionment should be made.

8.58 Sub-contractors may also apply the reduced rate for the above unless the work constitutes:

— a conversion into an RRP building;

— the renovation of an empty SHD where the owner is in residence. (This is the exact wording used at para 3.5 of Information Sheet 4/01. The exact meaning is unclear although Customs have indicated that it is a cross-reference to the conditions at 2(a)–(e) in paragraph 8.54.)

Transitional rules

8.59 The normal principles regarding changes of rate apply here. If a supplier of one of the above services has not issued an invoice or received payment, his services will all be subject to VAT at 5%. However, if he had to account for VAT at the old rate and the services were completed after the change, the total charge can be split between the two rates. If the requirement to account for VAT at the old rate was only because of the issue of an earlier VAT invoice, he must issue a credit note in accordance with the VAT Guide (Notice 700) Appendix C, paragraph 7 (see Information Sheet 4/01 para 4.1).

New zero rate for sales of renovated houses

8.60 From 1 August 2001, the sale of renovated houses that have been empty for 10 years or more is zero-rated. Therefore, those having such houses renovated for sale may now benefit from the 5% rate on the renovation services and the zero rate on the subsequent sale. This change is introduced into law by way of an amendment to Note (7) to *Group 5* of *Schedule 8*.

Annex

TYPE OF TRANSACTION	Refer to note hereafter	Standard-rated	Zero-rated	Reduced-rated (5%)	Exempt	Exempt but the option to tax may be exercised
Construction						
Construction services – new commercial buildings		✓				
Construction services – new qualifying buildings (see 8.8(*a*))	(1)		✓			
Approved alterations to listed buildings	(1)	✓	✓			
Conversion of non-residential buildings into dwellings or relevant residential property	(5)	✓				
Change in number conversions	(8)			✓		
House in multiple occupations conversions	(8)			✓		
Special residential conversions	(1) and (8)			✓		
Renovations or alterations of dwellings unoccupied for at least 3 years	(8)			✓		
Self-supply of construction services		✓				
All other types of refurbishments not previously mentioned	(5)	✓				

TYPE OF TRANSACTION	Refer to note hereafter	Standard-rated	Zero-rated	Reduced-rated (5%)	Exempt	Exempt but the option to tax may be exercised
Freehold sales						
New commercial buildings		✓				
Existing commercial buildings (3 years +)						✓
Listed commercial buildings						✓
Qualifying buildings sold by person constructing (see 8.8(*a*))			✓			
Qualifying buildings sold by other persons					✓	
Listed buildings designed to remain or become qualifying buildings after substantial reconstruction by person reconstructing			✓			
Buildings converted from commercial use to residential use by person converting			✓			
Renovated houses that have been empty for 10 years or more	(7)		✓			

TYPE OF TRANSACTION	Refer to note hereafter	Standard-rated	Zero-rated	Reduced-rated (5%)	Exempt	Exempt but the option to tax may be exercised
Leases						
Most commercial leases	(6)					✓
New qualifying buildings let by person constructing for a term exceeding 21 years	(1) and (2)		✓		✓	
Listed dwelling, property, relevant charitable purpose substantially reconstructed by owner and let for a term exceeding 21 years	(1) and (2)		✓		✓	
Buildings converted from commercial to residential use — term exceeding 21 years	(1) and (2)		✓		✓	
Other types of leases by other persons, involving dwellings, relevant residential properties, relevant charitable purposes					✓	
Civil engineering works						
New construction and demolition	(3)	✓	✓			
Sale of freehold land including new or partly completed civil engineering works		✓				

TYPE OF TRANSACTION	Refer to note hereafter	Standard-rated	Zero-rated	Reduced-rated (5%)	Exempt	Exempt but the option to tax may be exercised
Sale of freehold land with existing civil engineering works (3 years old +)	(6)					✓
Land						
Most freehold sales	(6)					✓
Most leases	(6)					✓
Surrenders						
Most surrenders	(4)					✓

Notes:

(1) Except for dwellings where the purpose of the construction or conversion is normally clear, the recipient of the supply must give the supplier a certificate if the supply is for a qualifying purpose (see 8.8(*a*) above). This is so that the supplier of construction services can know whether or not his supply is zero-rated or reduced-rated.

It is only the recipient of construction or conversion services or purchaser of a new building who can confirm if the work or sale relates to a property to be used for a relevant residential purpose or relevant charitable purpose, hence the requirement for a certificate. There is no set format for the certificate, but recommended wording is provided by Customs in their Public Notice 708. Certificates for relevant residential purpose or relevant charitable purpose can only be issued if the relevant building is intended for use *solely* for the qualifying purpose, although Customs may agree to ignore nominal or incidental non-qualifying use.

There are nine principal types of transaction requiring the recipient of services to issue the supplier with a certificate in order to qualify for zero-rating:

(i) The first disposal, sale or long lease, of a building (or part of a building) intended for use solely for a qualifying residential purpose by the person constructing the building.

(ii) The first disposal, sale or long lease, of a building (or part of a building) intended for use solely for a qualifying charitable purpose by the person constructing the building.

(iii) The first disposal, sale or long lease, of a building (or part of a building) intended for use solely for a qualifying residential purpose by the person converting it. Relief is not available for conversion services, or the first disposal, sale or long lease, of a converted building (or part of a building) which can only be used for a qualifying charitable purpose.

(iv) The supply of goods and services in the course of construction of a new building intended solely for a qualifying residential purpose. The building must be complete and not an extension of an existing building.

(v) The supply of goods and services in the course of construction of a new building intended for use solely for a qualifying charitable purpose.

(vi) The supply of goods and services in the course of construction of a connected annex intended for use solely for a qualifying charitable purpose. The conditions on what constitutes a connected annex are explained below.

(vii) The supply of goods and services in the course of an approved alteration to a protected or listed building intended for use solely for a qualifying residential purpose. Repairs are always standard-rated even if included in the listed building consent (8.35 refers).

(viii) The supply of goods and services in the course of an approved alteration to a protected or listed building intended for use solely for a qualifying charitable purpose. Repairs are always standard-rated even if included in the listed building consent (8.35 refers).

(ix) The supply to a relevant housing association of goods and services in the course of conversion of a non-residential building (or a non-residential part of a building) into a building (or part of a building) intended for use solely for a relevant residential purpose. The housing association must also confirm in writing that it is registered as such.

A certificate must also be given to the main contractor by the recipient of special residential conversion services in order to qualify for the reduced rate of 5% from 12 May 2001.

(2) Zero-rating only applies to the premium, or the first payment of rent if there is no premium. Subsequent rent is exempt.

(3) Such civil engineering works can still be zero-rated if they are part of a development contract which is itself zero-rated. The supply of any civil engineering work necessary for the development of a permanent park for residential caravans is also zero-rated.

(4) The vires of standard-rating surrenders was tested by the *Lubbock Fine* case (*Lubbock Fine & Co, LON/90/1657, No 6242*) which the London Tribunal referred to the ECJ. The final decision was in favour of the taxpayer in that surrenders should be exempt with the option to tax.

(5) Zero-rated from 21 July 1994 when supplied to registered housing associations. This is because, by their nature, housing associations can rarely grant major interests (freehold sales or leases exceeding 21 years) in such property so unless they were granted this special relief, costs would be standard-rated, income would be exempt and input tax would be irrecoverable.

Generally, the grant of a major interest in a building converted from commercial to residential status is now zero-rated. The basic relief (applicable to all types of business except housing associations) does not apply to construction services supplied in the course of such conversions, nor to sales of non-residential buildings converted into buildings for use for a qualifying charitable purpose. Representations have succeeded in extending application to buildings designed for a relevant residential purpose.

(6) The option to tax cannot be taken in certain circumstances (see 8.45).

(7) Zero-rated from 1 August 2001 (see 8.60).

(8) The reduced rate of 5% applies to certain services connected with the conversion, renovation or alteration of dwellings from 12 May 2001. Further details are at 8.52–8.54 above.

Chapter 9

Margin Schemes for Second-hand Goods

Introduction

9.1 The fundamental principle of margin schemes is the calculation of output VAT only on the difference between the selling and buying price of included items, with input tax not being recovered on the original purchase (*VATA 1994, s 50A*).

Example 81
Cost price of relevant item — £1,000 including VAT
Selling price of relevant item — £1,400 including VAT
Profit margin = £400 including VAT
No input tax is claimed. Output tax is £400 × 7/47 = £59.57.

9.2 Since 1 January 1995, it has been possible to operate a margin scheme for almost all dealings in second-hand goods but essentially there are three areas to consider:

- second-hand goods, works of art, antiques and collectors' items;
- global accounting;
- a special scheme for auctioneers.

Strict conditions apply but providing they are met, schemes can be of particular benefit to businesses buying second-hand goods from those who are not registered for VAT.

> *Example 82*
>
> Class Jewellers buys a diamond ring from Mrs Jones (a private individual not registered for VAT). The agreed price is £500. Class sells the ring for £600 and pays VAT on the £100 profit (100 × 7/47 = £14.89). If the scheme were not available, there would still be no input tax, but VAT would be due on the full selling price i.e. £600 × 7/47 = £89.36.

9.3 The scheme is available in respect of tangible movable property that is suitable for further use in its present condition or after repair, works of art, collectors' items or antiques, other than precious metals or precious stones.

9.4 Works of art, collectors' items and antiques are defined by Customs as follows:

'*Works of Art*

Pictures, collages and similar decorative plaques, paintings and drawings executed by hand by the artist, other than plans and drawings for architectural, engineering, industrial, commercial, topographical or similar purposes, hand decorated manufactured articles, theatrical scenery, studio back cloths or the like of painted canvas.

Original engravings, prints, lithographs, being impressions produced in limited numbers directly in black and white or in colour of one or of several plates executed entirely by hand by the artist, irrespective of the process or of the material employed by him, but not including any mechanical or photomechanical process.

Original sculptures and statuary in any material, provided that they are executed entirely by the artist; sculpture casts the production of which is limited to eight copies (or for statuary casts produced before 1 January 1989, such greater number as Customs allow).

Tapestries and wall textiles made by hand from original designs provided by artists, provided that there are not more than eight copies of each.

Individual pieces of ceramics executed entirely by the artist and signed by him.

Enamels on copper, executed entirely by hand, limited to eight numbered copies bearing the signature of the artist or the studio, excluding articles of jewellery and goldsmiths' and silversmiths' wares.

Photographs taken by the artist, printed by him or under his supervision, signed and numbered and limited to 30 copies, all sizes and mounts included.

Collectors' Items

Postage or revenue stamps, postmarks, first day covers, pre-stamped stationery and the like, franked or if unfranked not being of legal tender and not being intended for use as legal tender.

Collections and collectors' pieces of zoological, botanical, mineralogical, anatomical, historical, archaeological, palaeontological, ethnographic or numismatic interest.

Antiques

Antiques means objects other than works of art or collectors' items which are more than 100 years old.'

9.5 A special type of margin scheme applies to cars which is covered separately at 9.35 to 9.43, but commercial vehicles may be included under the general rules for second-hand goods.

9.6 Certain basic conditions must be fulfilled to operate a scheme:

(1) the operator must be registered for VAT;

(2) purchase invoices for included goods must not show VAT separately (although there are some exceptions for second-hand cars — see 9.35 *et seq.*);

(3) the operator must not issue a VAT invoice or other invoice which shows VAT separately for the sale of the goods; and

(4) the operator must meet all the record-keeping, accounting and invoicing requirements.

Record-keeping requirements

9.7 Correct operation of margin schemes is centred around purchase and copy sales invoices showing key information and a stock book.

Section II of VAT Public Notice 718 has statutory authority and lists the following as compulsory information in the stock book:

- a stock number in numerical sequence
- the date of purchase
- the purchase invoice number

- the seller's name
- any unique identification number for the item
- a description of the item or items
- the date of the sale
- the sales invoice number
- the buyer's name
- the purchase price
- the selling price or method of disposal
- margin on sale
- the VAT due.

See how to calculate VAT due at 9.12 below.

Purchases and purchase invoices

9.8 If the seller to the scheme operator is a dealer, the former prepares the purchase invoice but if the seller is a private individual, the operator prepares it. In either case, the seller must certify in writing that he or she has sold the item to the operator at the price shown on the invoice. The certification need not be on the invoice itself but cross-referencing must be clear if a separate document is used. It is the operator's responsibility to ensure the goods are eligible for the scheme in the first place.

The operator must then show the agreed purchase price in his stock book. If items are bought as a job lot, a fair allocation must be made in the stock book.

9.9 The purchase invoice itself differs from 'normal' invoices in that it must include:

- a stock book number in numerical sequence and a day book number or similar reference to the business accounts;
- a unique identification number if possible accompanying the description of the goods;
- a declaration signed by VAT registered suppliers that input tax has not and will not be claimed by them on the goods sold and that they have been sold at the price shown.

Sales and sales invoices

9.10 When an operator sells eligible goods, he must:

- make out a sales invoice;
- sign and date it and add the same declaration as required from purchasers explained at 9.9 concerning input tax recovery;
- get his customer to sign and date the invoice and declare that he is the buyer of the goods concerned at the stated price;
- enter the sales invoice details in the stock book and keep a copy of the sales invoice.

9.11 The sales invoice itself differs from 'normal' invoices in that it must include:

- a stock book and day book number or similar reference;
- a description of the goods, including any unique identification (e.g. registration number, hallmark etc.);
- the declaration set out at 9.9 on input tax recovery.

9.12 *The margin* between the buying and selling price is inclusive of VAT so output tax is calculated by applying the relevant VAT fraction (17.5/117.5 or 7/47 when the rate is 17.5%).

If the selling price is the same as or less than the purchase price, no output tax is due.

9.13 Items bought from VAT registered suppliers can be excluded from the scheme, leaving input tax to be reclaimed (assuming a valid purchase invoice) and output tax being due on the full selling price, not just on the margin.

9.14 Input tax can be claimed in full on overhead costs and items such as repair and maintenance costs, but the purchase price shown in the stock book (for the calculation of the margin) cannot be increased by such costs.

Use of a margin scheme by agents

9.15 Agents who act in their own name may use a margin scheme for eligible goods because the goods are treated as sold to and by them. The gross amount given by the agent to the owner of the goods constitutes the purchase price to be entered in the stock book and the amount received from the ultimate buyer, including incidental expenses and commission charged, is the selling price. Associated costs such as packing, transport and insurance may be left out of the selling price for the scheme calculation but VAT must be charged specifically on the full value of these supplies at the appropriate rate.

Example 83

Hall acts as agent for Wise (the seller) and Morris (the buyer).

Wise receives £1,000 gross which Hall enters as the purchase price in his stock book.

Hall receives £1,500 from Morris made up as follows:

Goods — £1,000

Commission — £100

Out of pocket expenses — £100

Packing and insurance — £300

The packing and insurance are dealt with outside the scheme, so Hall's selling price for the scheme is £1,200 and his margin is £200. He pays £200 × 7/47 output VAT = £29.78.

9.16 *A hire-purchase sale* by a business operating a margin scheme is a sale to the finance company. Where the interest element is shown separately, it is left out in making the scheme calculation. Thus the selling price to be entered in the stock book will equal the deposit paid whether in cash or by part exchange plus the amount borrowed.

The hire-purchase invoice must contain all the details required on margin scheme sales invoices.

9.17 It is quite normal for eligible goods to be sold in part exchange for other goods. Where this happens, the selling price will equal the cash paid plus the part-exchange allowance. If the item taken in part exchange is itself eligible for inclusion in the scheme, the allowance given constitutes the purchase price to be entered in the stock book for the item taken in.

Example 84
Honest Cars Ltd operates the second-hand margin scheme for cars. It sells a Vectra and receives £3,000 in cash and gives a £2,000 allowance on a Polo. The selling price of the Vectra under the scheme is £5,000 and the Polo is entered in the stock book with a purchase price of £2,000.

Global accounting

9.18 Under the global accounting provisions, businesses selling second-hand goods through a margin scheme need not maintain records for each transaction, but instead account for VAT on the margin between total eligible sales and total eligible purchases in a tax period.

The provisions apply if businesses deal in high volume, low value transactions.

Unlike a normal margin scheme, the calculation effectively embraces a VAT credit at the point of purchase and offsetting of losses against profits. However, as with the main scheme, VAT must not be shown on purchase invoices.

Only goods below a certain value are included and there are also specific other exclusions.

Where eligible goods are sold to customers in other EC Member States, the VAT under this scheme is accounted for in the UK under the scheme, not by the purchaser in the other member state. The scheme operator then excludes such sales from his EC Sales Lists (see 11.26–11.30).

Eligible goods

9.19 Global accounting only applies to goods costing £500 or less but always excludes the following whatever the price:

- aircraft
- boats and outboard motors
- caravans and motor caravans
- horses and ponies
- motor vehicles including motorcycles (except certain vehicles broken up for scrap).

Bulk purchases where each individual item costs less than £500 may be included. If a bulk purchase includes an item costing over £500, that item can be removed and accounted for under the basic margin scheme or under normal VAT accounting rules.

The scheme operator may remove items from bulk purchases, recording them separately and selling them as individual items or with other groups of items.

Record-keeping requirements

9.20 Except for the following, these are similar to those for basic margin schemes:

- purchase invoices must be endorsed 'global accounting invoice';
- purchases must be recorded in a special global accounting purchase section of a stock book;
- sales invoices must be endorsed 'global accounting invoice';
- sales must be recorded in a special global accounting sales section of a stock book;
- so long as the essential information is available, the sales and purchase records need not be kept in any specific way.

Calculating output tax due under global accounting

9.21 At the end of each tax period, VAT is paid on the difference between total sales and total purchases in the global accounting record for the period. If the net result is negative, no VAT is due and the deficit can be carried forward and offset against ensuing surpluses.

Scheme purchases in any period will exclude at a fair and reasonable value any item which the scheme operator wishes to deal with outside the bulk purchase.

Example 85

Hopkins Records Ltd sells second-hand records. Its margin scheme activities over the VAT periods 05/01 and 08/01 are as follows:

Period 05/01

Aggregate purchase prices—	£10,000
Aggregate selling prices—	£9,500
Net loss—	(£500)

Period 08/01

Aggregate purchase prices—	£11,200
Aggregate selling prices—	£13,100
Net profit—	£1,900

No output VAT is due in period 05/01 under the scheme because of the net loss. Output tax due in period 08/01 is £1,400 (£1,900 – £500) × 7/47 = £208.51.

Starting to use global accounting

9.22 If eligible goods are held in stock when an operator wishes to start using global accounting, he may apply a fair and reasonable valuation to these items and enter them in the purchase section of the global accounting records. The normal way of doing this is from purchase invoices but if this is not possible, other means may be used so long as they are fair and reasonable and agreed by Customs.

The auctioneers' scheme

9.23 The scheme is available to auctioneers who sell eligible goods on behalf of a seller and operates in a similar way to the basic margin scheme. It is optional and can be agreed on a transaction by transaction basis between the auctioneer and his principal. The auctioneer's services in return for a commission and any buyer's premium charged are not dealt with separately but are taken into account in calculating the margin.

Conditions for operating the scheme

9.24 An auctioneer can use the scheme if the seller of the eligible goods is:

- not VAT registered (see below);
- VAT registered and using a margin scheme or global accounting;
- an insurance company selling goods acquired from a claim provided they are sold through an auction in the same state;
- a finance house selling repossessed eligible goods in the same state through an auction.

In Business Brief 23/98 dated 17 November 1998, Customs announced the extension of the auctioneers' scheme to make eligible all goods grown, made or produced (including bloodstock or livestock reared from birth) by non-registered persons. Therefore, auctioneers selling such goods now only pay VAT on their services, not on the goods themselves. The non-registered vendors are required to certify their status and confirm their name, address and a description of the goods. The change is by Extra Statutory Class Concession.

Calculating output tax due

9.25 The auctioneer's commission charge is not declared separately but accounted for within purchase and selling prices as explained below.

(1) The purchase price is the hammer price less commission and all other charges made to the seller for services connected to the sale of the goods.

It is thus the amount that the seller would expect to get from the auctioneer.

(2) The selling price is the hammer price plus the buyer's premium or other commission including any other incidental expenses relating to the sale and recharged to the buyer.

(3) The margin is obviously the difference between (1) and (2) above and effectively represents the buyer's premium, commission and incidental expenses.

(4) Packing, transport, insurance and similar costs are charged outside the scheme.

Example 86

Squeaky Clean Auctions handles the following transaction:

1. Hammer price — £5,000
2. Commission charged to vendor — £500
3. Miscellaneous costs charged to vendor — £100
4. Net amount paid to vendor (1 – 2 – 3) = £4,400
5. Buyer's premium — £300
6. Costs recharged to buyer — £150.

The scheme purchase price is 1 – 2 – 3 = £4,400

The scheme selling price is 1 + 5 + 6 = £5,450

Therefore, the margin is £5,450 – £4,400 = £1,050

Squeaky Clean's output tax due on this transaction is £1,050 × 7/47 = £156.38.

Purchase invoices

9.26 The only differences from the normal requirements for margin scheme invoices are:

- the hammer price must be shown, plus
- the commission due from the seller, plus
- the net amount due to the seller.

Sales invoices

9.27 The only differences from the normal requirements for margin scheme invoices are:

- the hammer price must be shown, plus
- any other charges made, plus
- the amount due from the buyer.

The declaration that no input tax has been or will be claimed is still applicable.

Where invoices cover a mixture of scheme and non-scheme items, there must be a clear differentiation enabling Customs to understand the transaction.

A description of the goods is not obligatory, but if it is omitted there must be a clear cross-reference to another document containing a description.

The reference to commission cannot show VAT separately but wording can be included to avoid room for doubt. For example, if commission were 20%, the wording could be: 'VAT-inclusive commission at 23.5%' or 'commission at 20% plus VAT at 17.5%'. If this wording is included, an additional statement is required as follows: 'this amount includes VAT which must not be shown separately or reclaimed as input tax'.

Auctioneers' scheme calculations — charges to be included or excluded

9.28 Charges which depend on the sale of the goods, such as the commission, must be included in scheme calculations and so must incidental charges passed on to the client. Certain expenses are excluded:

- disbursements — if the normal rules for not treating them as a supply are met (see 3.75);

- exempt supplies — e.g. insurance supplies from a permitted insurer to a buyer or seller;
- overseas sellers — advisory services such as consultancy services, valuation services etc. to sellers that are businesses established in another EC country or to any type of seller based outside the EC are normally subject to VAT in the seller's country and the seller pays it under the reverse charge mechanism (see 12.40).

  Therefore, the value should be excluded from scheme calculations (note that if the services are not in this category and subject to UK VAT, the value is included);
- other charges not directly related to the sale of goods.

Zero-rated goods

9.29 Where the seller's goods are zero-rated, the auctioneer's margin under the scheme is also zero-rated.

Margin schemes and international trade

General

9.30 For a full understanding of how margin schemes interact with international trade, this section should be read in conjunction with Chapters 11 and 12.

Purchases from EC countries

9.31 If eligible goods are bought from a supplier based in another EC country, entitlement to use the scheme depends on the supplier's status:

- if the seller is a private individual — the margin scheme or global accounting can be applied;
- if the seller is VAT registered in another member state but not using a scheme and sells the goods on a VAT invoice — the scheme cannot be used;
- if the seller is VAT registered in another member state and sells the goods using the scheme — the scheme can be used.

Sales to buyers in EC countries

9.32 All sales of eligible goods within a scheme to buyers in other EC countries are subject to VAT on the margin. The seller pays the VAT in the UK, which contrasts with the normal treatment for sales to VAT registered customers in other member states (see Chapter 11).

Imports of goods from outside the EC

9.33 VAT is usually due on standard-rated imported goods at 17.5% but a special reduced rate can apply to works of art, antiques and collectors' items (see 12.5). A special rule also applies to imported cars (see 9.35). The margin schemes can be used for these items when imported but cannot be used for any other imported goods.

Exports

9.34 VAT is not due on goods which are exported to a destination outside the EC provided documentary proof of export is held. If a buyer intends to use goods in the UK before they are taken outside the EC, VAT must be paid on their sale (see 12.15–12.25 for further details on exports).

Second-hand cars

9.35 The margin scheme for sales of second-hand cars works in a similar way to the basic margin schemes with some additional special rules. Cars are only eligible if they have actually been used on the road for business or pleasure or been appropriated by a dealer for use in his business before being sold. Registration and delivery mileage are not enough for a car to qualify as used.

If a business buys a car from an unconnected person who has personally imported it as new, it can sell it under the margin scheme but if the import is channelled through an employee, agent or other connected person, the scheme cannot be used.

The basic principle of all margin schemes applies in that the scheme cannot be used for the purchase of a car on which input tax was recovered.

The accounting and record-keeping requirements are essentially the same as for basic margin schemes.

Example 87

A garage owner who uses the margin scheme for second-hand car sales and meets all the required conditions for the scheme has the following transactions in motor vehicles during the quarter ended 31 January 2001 (all the amounts being stated inclusive of VAT where appropriate):

		Purchase Price	Repair Costs	Selling Price
		£	£	£
Second-hand car	(i)	900	112	805
Second-hand car	(ii)	4,250	140	5,895
Second-hand car	(iii)	6,900	853	7,370
Second-hand van	(iv)	2,961	1,000	3,760
Second-hand van	(v)	4,230	480	5,875
New car	(vi)	17,860	–	19,975
New car	(vii)	11,750	–	–*
			2,585	

The second-hand vans were purchased on tax invoices from registered traders. The cars were taken in part exchange from private customers.

* Used by garage owner personally — list selling price £14,995.

The VAT implications of the above transactions are as follows:

Second-hand car margin scheme	**Cost**	**Selling Price**	**Margin**		
	£	£	£		£
(i)	900	805	(Loss)		
(ii)	4,250	5,895	1,645		
(iii)	6,900	7,370	470		
		14,070	2,115	× 7/47 =	315
Other outputs:			£		
(iv) Van			3,760		
(v) Van			5,875		
(vi) New car			19,975		
(vii) Self-supply new car			11,750		
			41,360	× 7/47 =	6,160
				cf	6,475

Inputs	**£**	bf 6,475
Repair costs	2,585	
Second-hand cars		
(i) (ii) and (iii)	–	
Vans (iv)	2,961	
(v)	4,230	
New cars (vi)	17,860	
(vii)	11,750	
	39,386	× 7/47 = (5,866)
VAT payable		609

Incomplete records

9.36 Where a trader cannot meet all the record-keeping, invoicing and accounting requirements of the scheme but has the necessary records for either the purchase or the sale of a car, and his mark-up does not exceed 100%, he may be allowed to account for VAT on either the price he paid for the car or half of his selling price. In *Example 87* above, on the 50% of selling price basis, his liability would be 50% × 14,070 (the aggregate selling prices of the three second-hand cars) × 7/47 = £1,048.

If, in the absence of records, Customs did not agree the concessionary treatment, the liability of the garage owner on the second-hand cars in *Example 87* would have been:

£(805 + 5,895 + 7,370) = 14,070 × $\frac{7}{47}$ =	2,095
In place of above calculation of	315
Increase in liability	1,780
plus computed liability	609
Total payment due	2,389

Road fund licences

9.37 If road fund licences are surrendered, the refund is outside the scope of VAT.

Where a car is bought under the scheme and the licence is subsequently surrendered, the stock book purchase price is not reduced by the amount of the refund.

If cars are sold with a valid licence or a licence is offered with the car as part of the agreed sales price, the price agreed for the car plus the value of the licence constitutes the sale price for margin calculation purposes.

It is, however, possible for the dealer to buy the licence on behalf of the purchaser, show it separately on the sales invoice and exclude the amount for margin calculation purposes.

Demonstration cars

9.38 Until the European Court of Justice decision against the Italian republic, car dealers were unable to recover VAT paid on the purchase of cars to be used as demonstrators. They entered the VAT-inclusive amount in their second-hand margin scheme stock book as the purchase price and declared VAT on any profit made when the cars were eventually sold.

The decision confirms that where input tax is blocked on items such as cars, their onward sale should be exempt from VAT. Many car dealers have reclaimed output VAT paid under the margin scheme in error.

The case *EC Commission v Italian Republic (Case C-45/95)* resulted in the following changes to UK law affecting cars, introduced in two stages (C&E Business Brief 24/99, 25 November 1999 and Information Sheet 12/99 refer):

On 1 December 1999:

- stock-in-trade cars of motor dealers and manufacturers were removed from the list of cars on which input tax is blocked;
- the self-supply provisions were amended to ensure that a self-supply is not triggered by private use of a stock-in-trade car;
- the self-supply legislation has also been tidied up and changes made to ensure that it operates correctly when cars have been sold as part of a transfer of a going concern;
- other changes are made to the definition of a motor car for VAT purposes to reflect developments in the industry.

On 1 March 2000:

- a new VAT exemption was introduced applicable to sales of goods on which input tax was blocked, or was wholly irrecoverable because of exempt use;
- the input tax margin schemes for cars (and goods used for business entertainment) were abolished. These schemes used to apply where the seller paid VAT on the full price when purchasing the goods, and that VAT was blocked in full. Sales of such goods are now exempt under the new arrangements. The input tax margin schemes described here should not be confused with the output tax margin scheme used by second-hand car dealers and described earlier in the chapter.

Businesses able to recover input tax on new cars

9.39 Certain types of business, such as private taxi firms, driving schools and self-drive hire firms may recover input VAT on purchases of cars. Therefore, when they sell these cars, VAT is due on the full selling price but the sales invoice should show varying information according to the status of the next purchaser.

If the next purchaser can recover the input VAT, the seller should issue a normal sales invoice showing VAT separately but if that purchaser cannot recover input VAT, the sales invoice should not show VAT separately so that the purchaser can operate the margin scheme.

Private taxi firms, driving schools and self-drive hire firms trading at auctions

9.40 These businesses may recover input VAT on auction purchases provided input VAT was recovered on the previous purchase of the relevant car, it is bought from another qualifying trader and a proper VAT invoice is received. The business must tell the auctioneer it qualifies under these rules.

If a relevant business sells through an auction, it must, for correct invoicing purposes, inform the auctioneer that input VAT has been recovered.

Imports

9.41 Businesses unable to recover VAT charged on imported cars may sell them under the scheme using the import value plus the VAT itself as the purchase price. The import entry or VAT certificate must be kept as evidence (see 12.8).

Cars other than those classified as 'new means of transport' bought from private individuals or from registered margin scheme users in other EC Member States are eligible for the scheme. Also, if a car is bought from a registered supplier in another member state but outside the scheme, the UK buyer can still use the scheme for the onward sale if he is unable to recover the acquisition VAT as input tax (see Chapter 11). The purchase price is the acquisition value plus the VAT paid.

Exports

9.42 Provided that satisfactory evidence of export is kept, exports of second-hand cars are zero-rated.

Mechanical breakdown insurance (MBI) and warranties

9.43 Under certain circumstances, these can be exempt from VAT and therefore should not be taken into account when calculating the standard-rated margin on which output VAT is due. Until recently, this procedure was significantly abused in that exempt values were often overstated resulting in a reduction in the standard-rated margin and less output VAT being paid.

This tax avoidance was effectively blocked by an increase in the rate of insurance premium tax (IPT) to 17.5% on such supplies of insurance.

Further details on the treatment of MBI insurance and warranties is at paragraph 73 of Public Notice 718.

Horses and ponies

9.44 A margin scheme may also be operated for sales of horses and ponies. The basic conditions are the same but certain special rules are contained in Section VIII and Annex 4 of Public Notice 718.

Chapter 10

The Tour Operators Margin Scheme

Introduction

10.1 The Tour Operators Margins Scheme is abbreviated to TOMS.

EC VAT law includes a special scheme for tour operators which is similar to the margin schemes described in Chapter 9 in that no input tax is claimed on standard-rated purchases and output tax is only paid on the difference between the buying and selling price of relevant services.

The scheme is under Article 26 of the Sixth Directive and entitled 'special scheme for travel agents' although in practice in the UK, it is used by businesses selling packages as principals rather than as pure agents (*VATA 1994, s 53* and *SI 1987/1806* as amended). The reason for its existence is that without it many tour operators would have to register in several member states of the EC because of the rules for the place of supply of services. The scheme requires registration only in the country in which the operator has a fixed establishment from which the services are arranged.

With the exception of the items at 10.17–10.20, TOMS is compulsory for businesses that buy in and resell travel, hotel, holiday and similar services as principal.

The services must be for the direct benefit of a traveller.

The term 'tour operator' and 'traveller' have wider application than their normal definitions.

In principle, supplies or packages sold under the scheme that are enjoyed inside the EC are standard-rated and those enjoyed outside the EC are zero-rated.

Mechanics of TOMS

10.2 The scheme applies to 'designated travel services' or 'margin scheme supplies' sold individually or as a package. Where a package is sold which includes margin scheme supplies and other services, margin scheme supplies are identified and VAT calculated on the margin, together with VAT on the full selling price of other supplies.

10.3 Certain supplies are excluded as follows:

- services supplied as an agent or intermediary provided commission earned can be clearly identified;
- services supplied from the business's own resources, i.e. not bought-in (these are known as 'in-house' supplies);
- wholesale supplies, i.e. services to other businesses for subsequent resale by them.

It is possible, however, to include these supplies within the scheme provided authorisation from Customs is obtained.

Calculations under TOMS

10.4 Input tax is not deductible on the purchase of relevant services bought in for resale under the scheme, but it can be recovered on the purchase of non-margin scheme services, on all overheads and on costs relating to the provision of 'in-house supplies' (see 10.3).

10.5 When a business first uses the scheme, it must estimate its margin on margin scheme supplies, identify the ratio of margin scheme supplies to total supplies, then declare a provisional amount of output tax. This is explained further at 10.21 to 10.24.

10.6 Thereafter, an annual calculation is made giving an actual figure for the preceding year with an adjustment of output tax already paid. This split of standard and zero-rated margin scheme supplies, other supplies and in-house supplies is then used on a provisional basis for the tax periods of the next year until the year-end when another actual calculation is performed, and so on.

Place where margin scheme supplies are provided

10.7 This is straightforward if the supplier of margin scheme supplies only operates in one EC Member State but, if it has branches in more than one country, VAT is due in the country where the branch that arranged the supply is located if that country is a member state of the EC.

If the supply is arranged from a branch in a non-EC country, say, Switzerland, the TOMS does not apply.

Example 88

A UK tour operator may buy in hotel accommodation from hotels in France, Germany and Austria for a European tour. The hotels would pay French, German and Austrian VAT respectively to their national authorities.

The UK supplier claims no input tax, converts the accommodation costs (including VAT) into sterling for the purchase value of its package and uses the formula to calculate UK output tax on the margin.

10.8 The margin scheme still applies to supplies enjoyed totally within the UK and totally outside the EC (even though the latter services are zero-rated).

10.9 The normal VAT rules for determining the place of supply apply to in-house supplies. Thus, passenger transport is supplied where it takes place, accommodation is supplied where it is physically located and live entertainment is supplied where it is performed. This could entail having to register in other countries.

VAT registration

10.10 The registration threshold applies to the aggregate of margin values on margin scheme supplies and full values of all other outputs.

Group registration

10.11 A business making margin scheme supplies cannot be part of a VAT group if any of the other group members:

- has a place of business abroad;
- makes taxable supplies abroad which would be subject to any rate of tax if made in the UK (including the zero rate); and
- supplies goods and services which will become, or are intended to become, margin scheme supplies.

Tax points

10.12 The normal tax point rules do not apply to the margin scheme.

Instead, the tax point is the first of:

(1) the earlier of the date of departure or of occupation of any accommodation supplied; and

(2) the date on which a minimum amount of the total payment is received.

10.13 Clearly, if the whole payment for a package is received at the same time, output tax is due at that time on the whole amount.

Payment is received by the operator when a payment is made to an agent.

10.14 The minimum amount at 10.12(2) is 20% of the total package price. A tax point is created every time a part payment of 20% or more of the total price is received and every time a smaller payment is received which, when added to earlier payments received, takes the total received over 20%.

10.15 If any payment is outstanding at the first of the trigger points at 10.12, VAT is due immediately on that amount.

VAT invoices

10.16 Normal tax invoices cannot be issued under TOMS because the exact information required is not known until the end of year calculation.

However, under certain circumstances and with Customs' approval, supplies may be accounted for outside the scheme (i.e. VAT would be paid on the full selling price) where the customer needs or is able to recover the input tax (see 10.17 *et seq.*).

Specific exclusions from TOMS

10.17 Sometimes, margin scheme supplies to business customers are excluded from the scheme. The treatment depends on the intended use by the business customer.

Wholesale supplies

10.18 These are margin scheme supplies to business customers that intend to resell them. Normally, VAT must be accounted for on the full selling price but if the supplier prefers to use the margin scheme for these, he may submit a written request to Customs who will approve it provided that the supplier includes all wholesale supplies under TOMS and that the records facilitate the checking process by visiting officers.

The VAT authorities in other member states may not recognise this concession with the result that UK suppliers may still have to register abroad.

Margin scheme supplies used by business customers

10.19 The basic rule is that these should be accounted for under TOMS but may be excluded under certain circumstances as set out below.

- *Margin scheme supplies enjoyed in the UK* — the supplies must be to business customers and used by them in the UK for business purposes. Customs' written permission is required, after which all such supplies can be dealt with outside the scheme, tax invoices can be issued and the customer can recover input tax.
- *Margin scheme supplies enjoyed outside the UK* — the supplies must be to business customers and used by them for business purposes. If they are enjoyed in another EC Member State, the supplier must provide evidence to demonstrate that he is registered there and has paid output tax to the appropriate VAT authorities. The concession also applies to supplies enjoyed outside the EC.
- *Transitional arrangements* — where input tax has been claimed on relevant purchases before 1 January 1998 and the tax point is after that date, output tax is due on the full selling price, not under TOMS but if input tax has not been claimed, output tax is accounted for under TOMS. Where a package is sold where input tax has been claimed on some of the relevant purchases, TOMS applies to the element on which input tax has not been claimed, although the concession for supplies enjoyed by business customers in the UK described above could apply.

Nominal margin scheme supplies that can be ignored

10.20 TOMS need not be used if:

- the supplier does not buy in any supplies of accommodation or passenger transport, and
- other margin scheme supplies are bought in, and
- turnover from these supplies is not expected to exceed 1% of total annual turnover.

Record-keeping requirements

10.21 In order that the calculation can be made and verified by Customs, it is crucial to keep a record of the total selling price of margin scheme supplies and packages; costs of margin scheme supplies at all rates; costs of in-house supplies at all rates; and standard-rated and other agency supplies where commission cannot be easily identified.

How to determine the total selling price in an annual calculation

10.22 The selling price in the calculation must include:

- the total VAT-inclusive selling price of all margin scheme supplies and in-house supplies made together with margin scheme supplies;
- Air Passenger Duty payable by the customer;
- surcharges;
- the full customer payment, i.e. no deduction for agents' commission should be made;
- amounts received which relate to any supplies provided with margin scheme supplies arranged as an agent but where the commission received is not easily identifiable.

10.23 Sales are reduced by refunds made to dissatisfied customers.

The following are excluded from the selling price in the margin scheme calculation:

- all packages containing no margin scheme supplies;
- forfeited deposits and cancellation fees from customers, but monies received from customers who just fail to appear are included; and
- identifiable commission from agency services supplied.

How to determine the purchase price in an annual calculation

10.24 The purchases included in the annual calculation must only be those which relate to the supplies included at Step 1 of the formula at 10.35.

The purchase price includes:

- discounts or price reductions received from suppliers to the business operating TOMS even if they are received after the main package is supplied to the ultimate customer;
- Air Passenger Duty payable.

The purchase price excludes:

- costs relating to packages without margin scheme supplies;

- indirect costs such as brochures, own office expenses, professional services, commission paid to agents.

Costs charged in a foreign currency

10.25 All such costs must be converted into sterling using one of the following methods:

- the exchange rate shown in the Financial Times using the Federation of Tour Operators' base rate current when costing is carried out by the supplier;
- the commercial exchange rate applicable when brochure supplies were costed;
- the FT rate on the date of payment;
- the exchange rate that applied to the purchase of foreign currency bought to pay for the supplies;
- Customs' published period exchange rate applicable when the supplies are paid for.

The chosen method must be used for a complete financial year.

Holiday and travel insurance

10.26 Where a business operating TOMS obtains insurance for the traveller from a permitted insurer, the premium passed to the insurer is omitted from the scheme calculation, as is any easily identifiable commission received. If the commission cannot be identified, it is included in the calculation.

On rare occasions, tour operators enter into agreements with insurers whereby the operator is reimbursed for any claims made by travellers but is legally the insured person. The cost is indirect and omitted from the scheme calculation but any charge passed on to the traveller is included in the selling price at Step 1 of the calculation at 10.35.

Air passenger duty (APD)

10.27 Air transport bought in for resale includes APD which should be included in margin scheme costs. Where it is supplied in-house, APD is a direct cost. If the APD is passed on to the traveller, it is included in the selling price at Step 1 of the calculation at 10.35.

Bad debt relief

10.28 This relief is still available but is restricted to a maximum of the VAT fraction on the profit margin. It can be claimed at the later of six months after the payment is due and six months from when the supply is made. Where the debtor is a taxable business, it should be informed of the claim in writing.

> *Example 89*
>
> Medgolf organises a golf holiday for 10 people on the Algarve. It completes VAT returns for the quarters ending 31 March, 30 June etc. The total cost of the package to Medgolf is £7,000 and the total selling price is £10,000. Full payment is due by 31 March 2001 and the holiday ends on 31 May 2001. Payment is not received so bad debt relief can be claimed on the 12/01 VAT return (i.e. the return that includes 30 November which is six months from the later of the date payment is due and when the supply is made). The margin is £3,000 so bad debt relief is £3,000 × 7/47 = £446.80.

Representatives and guides

10.29 The services of representatives are not in-house supplies but indirect costs which should be omitted from scheme calculations. The services of guides are supplies in their own right. If they are made from the tour operator's own resources, the VAT treatment will depend on where they are supplied from and the exact description of the service provided.

Extra costs

10.30 Sometimes circumstances change resulting in extra costs. These are margin scheme costs unless somebody else pays, in which case they should be omitted, or they relate to in-house supplies, in which case they are direct costs for calculation purposes.

How to calculate VAT due under TOMS

10.31 The TOMS formula firstly calculates the total margin in the relevant period, then apportions that margin between different types of supply, e.g. margin scheme supplies, in-house supplies and other supplies. It also apportions the margin between supplies at different rates, e.g. standard-rated supplies enjoyed within the EC and zero-rated supplies enjoyed outside the EC. Finally, it calculates the value of in-house supplies on which VAT is due and the output tax on margin scheme supplies.

The formula covers every possible type of supply so certain steps are not applicable to every supplier. It also assumes the same uplift on cost on elements of a package. A simplified calculation formula exists if all margin scheme packages are subject to VAT at the same rate in that it does not require the supplier to work out the costs on his in-house supplies. The formulae are set out below at 10.33 and 10.35.

10.32 The annual adjustment must be applied to the first VAT return ending after the end of the business's financial year whether or not financial statements have been audited and finalised. If the audit highlights differences, the calculation must be reworked and the differences disclosed as errors in the normal way (see 16.44).

The calculation also provides the basis for a provisional output tax calculation for the tax periods of the business's next financial year which becomes actual when the next annual adjustment is performed.

Calculating the provisional value

10.33 The provisional percentage is calculated as follows:

1. The VAT-inclusive amount of standard-rated margin scheme supplies and packages for the business's preceding financial year is calculated by adding the totals from 4., 12. and 14. at 10.35 below.
2. The VAT-inclusive standard-rated percentage of the total selling price of all margin scheme supplies and packages for the business's preceding financial year is calculated as follows:

$$\frac{\text{Total at 1. above}}{\text{Total at 1. in main calculation}} \times 100$$

The VAT return figures are calculated as follows:

3. Take the total VAT-inclusive selling prices of margin scheme supplies and packages supplied during the tax period.
4. Calculate the provisional VAT-inclusive amount of standard-rated margin scheme supplies and packages made during the period by multiplying the total at 3. by the percentage obtained at 2. above.
5. Calculate the output tax due for the period by multiplying 4. by the VAT fraction.

The simplified formula

10.34 This is effectively the same as the main calculation at 10.35 but confined to the margin scheme supplies elements, whereas the main calculation allows for all types of supply made including margin scheme supplies. The VAT-inclusive purchase prices of margin scheme supplies are deducted from the VAT-inclusive selling prices of the same and the VAT fraction is applied for output tax due. This actual amount is then compared with provisional output tax declared during the course of the year and the adjustment made as described above.

10.35 The following process is taken from Customs' Leaflet 709/5 on the scheme and covers the calculation for a financial year:

1. **To work out the total sales of margin scheme packages**, take the total VAT-inclusive selling prices of margin scheme supplies and packages sold during the financial year.
2. **To work out purchase prices of margin scheme supplies**, take the total VAT-inclusive purchase prices of standard-rated margin scheme supplies included in 1., then
3. take the total VAT-inclusive purchase prices of zero-rated margin scheme supplies included in 1.
4. **To work out the direct cost of in-house supplies** (i.e. supplies from one's own resources rather than bought in), take the total VAT-inclusive cost of standard-rated in-house supplies included in 1. and add an amount equivalent to the standard rate of VAT (currently 17.5%), then
5. take the total VAT-exclusive direct costs of zero-rated in-house supplies included in 1. (note that the costs of making the zero-rated supply may not themselves be zero-rated), then
6. take the total VAT-inclusive direct costs of exempt in-house supplies included in 1. but deduct any input tax recoverable on these costs, then
7. take the total direct costs of in-house supplies included in 1. that are supplied outside the UK, excluding any recoverable input tax on the costs but adding an uplift percentage equivalent to the VAT rate applicable to each category of supply so long as output VAT has been paid to the VAT authorities in other member states in which supplies have been made.
8. **To work out the cost of agency supplies**, take the total VAT-inclusive amounts paid to principals in respect of agency supplies included in 1. where the money received by the supplier is standard-rated, then
9. take the total VAT-inclusive amounts paid to principals in respect of agency supplies included in 1. where the money received by the supplier is not standard-rated.

10. **To work out the total margin**, add the total costs from 2. to 9. above, then

11. calculate the total margin for all supplies in 1. by deducting the total at 10. from the total at 1.

12. **To apportion the margin**, use the totals at 2. to 11. as follows:

    the margin for standard-rated margin scheme supplies is:

    $$\frac{2}{10} \times 11$$

13. The margin for zero-rated margin scheme supplies is:

    $$\frac{3}{10} \times 11$$

14. The margin for standard-rated in-house supplies is:

    $$\frac{4}{10} \times 11$$

15. The margin for zero-rated in-house supplies is:

    $$\frac{5}{10} \times 11$$

16. The margin for exempt in-house supplies is:

    $$\frac{6}{10} \times 11$$

17. The margin for supplies made outside the UK is:

    $$\frac{7}{10} \times 11$$

18. The money received for standard-rated agency supplies is:

    $$\frac{8}{10} \times 11$$

19. The money received for non-standard-rated agency supplies is:

    $$\frac{9}{10} \times 11$$

20. **To work out output tax**, relevant totals above are multiplied by the VAT fraction (currently 7/47 for VAT at 17.5%). Output tax on margin scheme supplies is: 12 × VAT fraction.

21. Output tax on standard-rated in-house supplies is: 4 + 14 × VAT fraction.

22. Output tax on standard-rated agency supplies is: 18 × VAT fraction.

23. **To work out sales values**, certain totals above are deducted from or added to others. The VAT-exclusive value of margin scheme supplies is: 12 – 20.
24. The VAT-exclusive value of standard-rated in-house supplies is: 4 + 14 – 21.
25. The value of zero-rated in-house supplies is: 5 + 15.
26. The value of exempt in-house supplies is: 6 + 16.
27. The value of supplies outside the UK is: 7 + 17.
28. **To work out the annual adjustment**, take the total output tax due on margin scheme supplies and packages which is: 20 + 22, then
29. take the total provisional output tax declared during the course of the financial year on supplies included in 1. then
30. deduct 29. from 28. and declare the result on the appropriate VAT return. An amount due to Customs goes in Boxes 1 and 3, and a refund goes in Box 4.

European case law

10.36 Following the European Court of Justice (ECJ) decision in *Madgett & Anor (t/a Howden Court Hotel) (Joined Cases C-308/96 and C-94/97)*, Customs clarified their policy in Business Brief 10/99 issued on 22 April 1999.

The ECJ addressed two issues:

(i) whether businesses not normally regarded as tour operators (such as hoteliers) should be required to operate TOMS if they made supplies covered by the scheme, and

(ii) whether Article 26 of the Sixth Directive (covering the scheme) required an apportionment of the total amount received by a tour operator by reference to the cost of the components (in other words, whether the relationship between the cost of in-house and margin scheme supplies should be applied to income to determine VAT payable).

The ECJ decided that any business making margin scheme supplies must operate the scheme unless the supplies constitute a nominal proportion of all supplies made. However, they decided that only supplies bought in from third parties were covered by Article 26. Therefore, the in-house element of total supplies cannot be calculated by reference to the actual cost.

Customs believe that this case was about simplification of TOMS rather than about the amount tour operators pay under the scheme. However, they instigated a consultation process with the industry and affected parties to see how the case can be used to simplify the scheme further.

10.37 Customs have not made any changes as yet as a result of the *Madgett* case, but part of their review concerned the interaction between TOMS and EFL (English as a foreign language) courses. In Business Brief 27/99, 21 December 1999, Customs confirmed that TOMS no longer applies to EFL providers that fall within the education exemption (see 5.51).

Affected EFL providers may make adjustments to VAT returns where appropriate. Claims are subject to the three-year cap and unjust enrichment provisions.

Chapter 11

Trading in Goods within the EC

Introduction

11.1 The VAT treatment of trading in goods within the EC changed radically when the 'Single Market' was introduced on 1 January 1993. The intention was to create an environment where goods and people could move freely within the member states of the EC without the need for strict Customs controls.

The impact on VAT was significant in that sales of goods to customers in other member states were no longer called 'exports' but 'EC sales' and purchases of goods from suppliers in other member states were no longer called 'imports' but 'EC acquisitions'. The treatment of EC sales and acquisitions is different from that of exports and imports in a number of ways explained in this chapter.

Further additional rules and compliance requirements were introduced, such as the concept of distance selling (sales of goods to non-registered customers in other member states where the supplier arranges delivery), EC Sales Lists (a summary of all EC sales within a calendar quarter) and additional monthly declarations showing movements of goods from the UK into other member states or from other member states into the UK if the annual value of those movements exceeds a minimum monetary limit. These statistics are gathered by a different section within Customs known as the Tariff and Statistical Office under the Intrastat regime.

The Intrastat declarations are not strictly linked to VAT but are a method of identifying movements of goods within the EC now that there is no longer any need for Customs declarations at the point of entry. The general term used for them is 'supplementary statistical declarations' ('SSDs') or 'supplementary declarations' ('SDs'). Declarations of goods leaving the UK are called 'dispatches' (Customs' spelling) declarations and declarations of goods entering the UK are called 'arrivals' declarations. In theory, they identify where any goods are at any given time.

This chapter covers EC trade in goods in general, distance selling, EC Sales Lists and Intrastat declarations.

EC trade in goods — general

EC sales

11.2 Goods sold to customers in other member states of the EC are zero-rated if:

- the customer is registered for VAT in another member state and gives the UK supplier his VAT registration number;
- the supplier shows his own and his customer's VAT registration number on the sales invoice, both prefixed by the two-letter country code;
- the goods are physically removed from the UK to a destination in another member state; and
- within three months of the sale, the supplier obtains and keeps documentary evidence to prove the goods have been removed to another member state.

The two-letter country codes are as follows:

Austria — AT

Belgium — BE

Denmark — DK

Finland — FI

France — FR

Germany — DE

Greece — EL

Ireland — IE

Italy — IT

Luxembourg — LU

Netherlands — NL

Portugal — PT

Spain — ES

Sweden — SE

United Kingdom — GB

The inclusion of the customer's VAT registration number and country code prefix are essential to safeguard zero-rating. Normally, where the customer is not VAT registered in another member state or is registered but fails to produce his registration number, the UK supplier must add UK VAT unless the goods are zero-rated anyway. There is clearly a danger that numbers provided by customers may be invalid so suppliers may ask their local VAT office to verify that the number received is valid and belongs to the business that supplied it.

Example 90

International Castings Ltd (ICL) receives an order from ABCD Amsterdam BV in the Netherlands. ICL arranges delivery. ABCD signs the delivery note which is returned to ICL promptly. ICL's VAT registration number is 812 1111 08 and ABCD's is 123456789B01. For the supply to be zero-rated, the invoice should include the following with the usual information:

GB 812 1111 08

NL 123456789B01

ABCD would then convert the invoice value into Dutch guilders; add Dutch VAT and pay it as output tax on its Dutch VAT return at the same time recovering the same or a restricted amount of input tax.

Distance sales

Where goods are supplied to non-registered suppliers in other member states and the supplier arranges delivery, the supplier should consider his responsibilities under the distance selling provisions (see 11.13).

Exciseable goods

If the UK seller is dealing in goods liable to Excise duty, there are special rules if the buyer is not VAT registered in another member state and makes the purchase for non-private purposes. When the goods are transported, they must carry an accompanying administrative document (AAD), but before they are despatched the customer must make a declaration to the tax authorities in the country to which the goods are being sent and guarantee that Excise duty will be paid before they are despatched. If the goods are bought for a non-private purpose by a non-registered customer, the sale can still be zero-rated provided the customer or his representative arranges for the goods to be removed to another member state and the supplier obtains and keeps copy 1 and a receipted copy 3 of the AAD certified by the consignee or the fiscal authorities in the destination member state within 15 days of the end of the month in which the goods were sent. The movement of the goods must be completed and the receipt issued within four months of the date of supply. The customer is responsible for paying any Excise duty and VAT due in the destination country and where the non-private purpose condition is not met, the supplier must observe the distance selling provisions.

Tax points

The tax point rules are slightly different for EC sales, in that for VAT return, EC Sales List and Intrastat purposes, the declaration is made on the 15th day of the month following the despatch or the date an invoice is issued, whichever is the earlier. This is principally for recording purposes because no actual tax is due on a zero-rated supply. If the customer is not registered and UK VAT is charged, the normal tax point rules apply.

Entries on VAT returns

The total EC sales for a tax period (including those on which VAT is added because the customer is not registered or does not supply a number) are entered in Box 8 of the return form and annual totals are used by the Tariff & Statistical Office ('T&SO') to determine whether monthly dispatches SSDs should also be completed.

EC acquisitions (VATA 1994, ss 10–14)

11.3 When goods are purchased from a supplier in another member state, the UK purchaser should give the supplier his VAT registration number, which should then appear on the sales invoice prefixed by GB. The supplier's number should also appear prefixed by his country code. The supply is then zero-rated in the country of origin but the purchaser must convert the value into sterling, add VAT at the appropriate rate (currently 17.5% for standard-rated goods) and enter acquisition VAT for each return period in Box 2 of the return form. This is then added to output tax in Box 1 to give total output tax in Box 3.

The acquisition VAT is also recoverable as input tax in Box 4 of the return form subject to the normal rules.

If goods acquired are normally zero-rated in the UK, no acquisition VAT is due.

Example 91

ICL (see *Example 90* above) buys parts for its machines from BFT GmBH based in Munich. ICL completes VAT returns for the calendar quarters and receives a delivery from Germany accompanied by an invoice on 30 June 2001. The value is DM 2,500 and the invoice contains all the correct information for BFT to zero rate its supply.

ICL converts the value to sterling (say, £800), adds 17.5% VAT (£140). ICL includes this in Box 2 and Box 4 of its 06/01 return so effectively, the VAT is paid and reclaimed at the same time.

Tax points

The time acquisition VAT is due is the earlier of the 15th day of the month following the acquisition and the date of the invoice. There is no tax point for part payments made as there is for UK only transactions.

> *Example 92*
>
> ICL (see *Examples 90* and *91*) receives its next order from Germany on 15 September 2001 but BFT does not send an invoice until 10 January 2002. ICL must account for the VAT in its records on 15 October (the fifteenth day of the month following the one in which the goods were despatched). Therefore, the VAT will actually get paid on ICL's 12/01 return, which includes October 2001.

Entries on VAT returns

Total net acquisitions in any tax period are entered in Box 9 of the return form. Annual Box 9 totals are then used by the T&SO to determine whether monthly arrivals SSDs should also be completed.

Values on which acquisition VAT is calculated

11.4 The amount to which VAT is added is normally the price paid for the goods plus packing, transport and insurance costs where the customer meets them on behalf of the supplier. Where discounts are offered, the value is the discounted amount if the purchaser pays the discounted amount. If the discount is conditional, the value is the full amount paid but can be reduced and the VAT adjusted later if the discount is actually earned.

If payment is partly in money and partly in other goods or services, the value is the amount that would have been paid if the whole payment were in money.

> *Example 93*
>
> The value of the order received by ICL (see *Examples 90* to *92*) on 15 September 2001 (see *Example 92* above) was DM 5,250 with a discount to DM 5,000 for payment within 10 working days of the invoice which ICL earns. ICL pays additional packing, transport and insurance costs of DM 750. The acquisition value is DM 5,750 (DM 5,000 + DM 750), which ICL would convert to sterling (say, £1,900) and add VAT.

Invoices in a foreign currency

If invoices received from suppliers are in a foreign currency, they must be converted into sterling using either the UK market selling rate at the time of acquisition (usually published in daily newspapers) or the Customs' period rate of exchange available from the local VAT office. The second option can be used for all acquisitions or just certain types of acquisition but the method used should be clearly noted in records. Any change to the method used must first be approved by Customs, preferably in writing.

If an acquirer wishes to adopt any other method, a written application should be made to Customs and approval will be granted if it meets their normal criteria.

Transferring own goods to another EC country

11.5 When a UK registered business transfers its own goods to another member state, it makes a 'deemed' or 'fictitious' EC sale. If there is an intention to sell the goods in the other member state, there is normally a need to register there and pay VAT on the deemed acquisition and again on the actual sale of the goods to the customer. The value of the fictitious supply is the price the business would have to pay at the time of the acquisition or, if that is not known, the amount it would cost to produce the goods. Therefore, the business would normally issue an invoice to itself in the other country showing its UK and other member state VAT numbers plus prefixes, pay no VAT in the UK, convert the value (if in sterling) to the currency of the other country, pay acquisition VAT there and claim the same amount as input tax subject to that country's rules.

Example 94

A sales team from Top Laptops Ltd is sent into France to develop a market for its laptop computers. The team takes 100 computers with it, and starts trading from a Paris address having registered for French VAT (TVA). The computers are valued at £1,500 each.

Although no money would necessarily change hands, Top Laptops Ltd would issue an invoice to itself in France showing its UK and French VAT numbers preceded by GB and FR respectively. The invoice would be for a value of £150,000 without VAT. However, Top Laptops Ltd would convert the value into French francs (say FF 1,500,000) and treat the fictitious supply as an acquisition in France, paying and reclaiming the French VAT on its appropriate French VAT return.

In Business Brief 22/99, 12 October 1999, Customs announced that following the *Centrax Limited* tribunal case (*LON/98/218, No 15743*), they will exceptionally allow zero-rating for the transfer of a VAT registered person's own goods to another member state where that person is not VAT registered in the other member state. The movement must be for a supply of installed or assembled goods or for repair services and the owner of the goods must provide written confirmation from the relevant tax authorities in the destination member state that retrospective VAT registrations are not allowed there.

Goods sent to other EC countries for repairs and processing

11.6 Repairs and processing are supplies of services, not goods, so the intra-EC movements of goods rules are not applicable. The value of the goods does not therefore go on the owner's VAT return but output tax is declared by the owner on the value of the service provided to him under the reverse charge mechanism when the goods are returned (see Chapter 12). The owner shows the value of the goods when sent away for the work on his dispatches SSD and the enhanced value on his arrivals SSD when they are returned (see 11.31).

Goods supplied and installed by businesses in other EC countries

11.7 On occasions, suppliers of goods in one member state to customers based in another also install or assemble them. The goods are usually items of plant, machinery or technical equipment. The basic place of supply rules state that the goods are supplied where they are installed, which means the supplier would be making taxable supplies in the customer's country and may have to register for VAT there. However, to avoid unnecessary numbers of foreign registrations in each member state, a simplified rule exists whereby, provided certain conditions are fulfilled, the customer can pay the VAT and treat the supply as an acquisition.

The simplified rule should be available in most countries where UK businesses are installing goods and is available for foreign businesses installing goods in the UK. Where the supply and installation takes place in the UK, the foreign supplier must endorse his invoice with the words 'Section 8D2 VATA invoice' and issue it within 15 days of the normal UK tax point rules. This could include receipt of a part payment. The supplier must then inform Customs in writing that the simplified arrangement has been adopted. The letter must be sent to Aberdeen VAT Office at Custom House, 28 Guild Street, Aberdeen AB9 2DY and include the supplier's name, address and VAT registration number; the name, address and VAT registration number of the customer and the date the installation began or will begin. The customer must receive a copy of this letter which should not be sent later than the date of issue of the first invoice. One notification is required for each customer to which this procedure applies.

Once the customer has received notification from the supplier that the simplified procedure is to be used, he will be required to account for acquisition VAT each time an invoice is received.

> *Example 95*
>
> Machines Internationales SA from France (MI) supplies and installs a large item of plant for a customer in Birmingham. The first payment of 30% of the total price is payable with order. On the due date for this payment, MI sends its customer an invoice endorsed 'Section 8D2 VATA invoice' along with a copy of the letter it sends to Aberdeen VAT Office the same day containing the required information. No VAT is added to the invoice, the value of which the customer converts into sterling and treats as an EC acquisition in the normal way.

Consignment and 'call-off' stocks

11.8 The UK distinguishes between the treatment of consignment and 'call-off' stocks although since not all other member states do so it should not be assumed that the following explanation applies everywhere.

Consignment stocks are those which have been transferred to another member state under the control of the owner and are held there for subsequent sale by the owner. The movement from the UK to the other member state is treated as a deemed or fictitious supply as described at 11.5 above. Where goods are brought into the UK on this basis, the deemed supply takes place the other end and the owner pays VAT on the acquisition here and reclaims the same amount as input tax when they are brought in. The owner then pays VAT again on the ultimate sale (usually on a higher value if he makes a profit).

Call-off stocks are goods provided to a customer in another member state but held in a place there where the customer can 'call off' the goods when he needs them. Payment is usually made for the goods as they are called off. The supply in the UK is treated in the same way as normal intra-EC movements so the goods are normally zero-rated when they leave the UK. Where UK businesses acquire such goods here and call them off at a later date, the acquisition VAT is payable when they are acquired, not when they are called off. If a supplier from another member state supplies goods at the same time for call-off by more than one customer, they can be treated as consignment stocks. Call-off stocks put into storage facilities operated by the supplier can also be treated as consignment stocks unless the customer is aware of the details of deliveries into storage.

> *Example 96*
>
> Midlands Widgets Ltd (MWL) based in Leicester buys products from Spain for resale. It makes an order on 31 March 2001 consisting of goods it will pay for in stages as and when it has found a buyer although it will hold the stock in Leicester. Its next VAT return covers the quarter to 30 April 2001. On that return MWL will account for this transaction as an EC acquisition having converted the invoice value into sterling and added VAT at 17.5%. MWL will reclaim the same amount of VAT as input tax.
>
> If MWL were to enter into similar agreements with its own customers in other EC member states, it should check the VAT rules in the relevant country first.

Goods sold on sale or return or approval

11.9 A UK business selling such goods to customers in other member states makes a deemed supply and acquisition as described at 11.5 above, then a further supply within the customer's country when the latter decides he wants to keep the goods.

Affected businesses must check the registration rules in each relevant member state.

When a business established in another member state supplies goods on these terms to a UK customer, he must first sort out VAT registration and pay acquisition VAT if applicable, then pay VAT on subsequent sales of the goods when the customer indicates he wishes to keep them (assuming they are not zero-rated). If the customer has not adopted the goods within 12 months, the supplier must pay VAT at that point.

> *Example 97*
>
> On 31 October 2001, a Portuguese supplier of PCs supplies 20 on a sale or return basis to a UK customer. The value of the goods is ESC 5,000,000, converted to £20,000. The supplier registers in the UK and accounts for £3,500 VAT on the fictitious EC supply and acquisition. He reclaims the same amount as input tax. If the UK customer wishes to keep the goods, the supplier will charge £1,200 + VAT for each PC (thus making a profit of £200 on each).
>
> On 31 July 2002, the customer indicates he wishes to keep 10 of the PCs. The Portuguese supplier then invoices him for £12,000 (10 × £1,200) + VAT (£2,100) on that day and accounts for the output tax

through his UK VAT registration. By 31 October 2002 (12 months from the original supply), the UK customer has not indicated a desire to keep the other 10 PCs so the Portuguese supplier then accounts for the remaining output tax on his next return.

Triangulation

Introduction

11.10 A simplified procedure exists where goods are sold between businesses based in three different member states. The procedure applies if goods are sold by company X in member state A to a customer Y in member state B who in turn sells them on to a customer Z in member state C but the goods are delivered direct from country A to country C. The procedure is known as 'triangulation' and would normally require Y to register in either A or C.

The procedure without simplification

11.11

Example 98

Without the simplified rules, the situation at 11.10 would work as follows.

Y could be registered either in A or C. If he were registered in A, X would charge that country's VAT to Y who would then make an EC sale to Z at the zero rate. Z would pay acquisition VAT in country C. If he were registered in C, X would make an EC sale to Y who would pay acquisition VAT in C then charge C's domestic rate of VAT to Z. This assumes that all three parties are VAT registered in their respective countries and the goods are not zero-rated.

The simplified procedure

11.12 In *Example 98*, company Y would not have to register in either of country A or C and the only VAT payment would be by Z on its acquisition in country C.

The simplified procedure works by Y issuing its VAT number to X and thus acquiring the goods at the zero rate. However, Y can also zero rate its onward supply to Z by issuing an invoice to Z showing all the normal details (e.g. both VAT numbers and country code prefixes) but also containing the additional wording: 'VAT: EC Article 28 Simplification invoice'. Y shows the supply on its EC Sales List but identifies it as a simplified triangular transaction by using the figure 2 in the indicator box (see 11.26 below), and treats the supply as a normal EC sale. Details of these simplified transactions are not shown on Intrastat declarations (see 11.31 below) which just identify the actual movement of the goods.

If Y were a business based in another member state and wished to use the simplified procedure to avoid UK registration, it can do so following the above rules but it must also notify the Aberdeen VAT Office at the address shown at 11.7 above giving its own VAT registration details, those of its customer (Z in the example) and the date of delivery or intended delivery. As with supply and installation contracts, separate notifications are required for each customer and a copy must be sent to the customer by the date of the first invoice.

Any UK customer in receipt of a notification from an overseas supplier must account for acquisition VAT in the normal way.

The final customer, Z in the example, that accounts for acquisition VAT must record the arrival of the goods on its arrivals SSD declaration if the aggregate value of arrivals exceeds the national threshold (see Intrastat at 11.31 below).

Example 99

Relojes Clásicos SA (RC) in Madrid sells 500 watches to Classical Watches of London (CW) which sells them on immediately to Montres Classiques in Paris (MC). The watches are delivered direct from Madrid to Paris.

CW gives RC its UK VAT number and receives a zero-rated invoice from RC. CW then issues a further zero-rated invoice to MC endorsed 'VAT: EC Article 28 Simplification invoice'. CW includes the transaction on its EC Sales List using the indicator '2' for triangular transactions. However, CW excludes the transaction from its arrivals and dispatches Intrastat declarations because the goods have never come into the UK.

MC accounts for acquisition VAT on its French VAT return.

Distance selling (SI 1995/2518, Reg 98)

General

11.13 The standard rate of VAT within the member states of the EC ranges from 15% to 25%. Where a supplier in one member state supplies goods to a non-registered customer in another, the supplier must charge the applicable rate of VAT in its own country. Where the supplier arranges delivery of the goods, notably under a mail order arrangement, there would be distortion of competition and an incentive for suppliers to base themselves in countries with a low standard rate such as Germany, Luxembourg or Spain unless special rules applied.

How distance selling works

11.14 The distance selling provisions require suppliers arranging delivery to non-registered customers in other member states to charge their own rate of VAT until aggregate turnover to a particular member state in a calendar year exceeds that country's distance selling threshold. Thereafter, the supplier must register in that other country and charge its appropriate VAT rate.

Member states may choose one of two distance selling thresholds, i.e. either 35,000 ECU or 100,000 ECU. The ECU limits are converted into the national currency and there is an even split between the member states that have chosen the higher and lower limits.

Example 100
Classical Watches of London (see *Example 99* at 11.12 above) sells watches to non-business customers in France by mail order. The French distance selling threshold is, say, FF 700,000. From January to June 2001, sales to France are £10,000 (FF 100,000) so CW adds UK VAT at 17.5% to all sales to 30 June 2001. Sales in July are £11,000 (FF 110,000). UK VAT is added in July but at the end of the month the French distance selling threshold has been exceeded, so CW immediately registers in France and thereafter charges 19.6% French VAT (TVA) to mail order customers.

Voluntary registration under distance selling

11.15 Businesses making distance sales may opt to register in relevant other member states before they have reached the turnover threshold. Where UK businesses choose to register in this way, they must notify Customs in writing at least 30 days before the first sale which follows the option. The notification should state clearly the countries involved. Also, the same supplier must provide Customs with clear documentary evidence that the relevant tax authorities have been notified of the intention to pay tax in their country within 30 days of the first sale after the option.

Once the option is in place, it cannot be cancelled for at least two calendar years. After that date, if the business chooses to cancel the option, Customs must be notified not less than 30 days before the first intended sale after the decision to cancel.

Distance sales and exciseable goods

11.16 Registration is always required in other member states where the supplier makes distance sales of exciseable goods to non-registered customers there because such goods are always subject to Excise duty and VAT in the destination country. The rules are different for non-distance sales, i.e. where the customer arranges delivery of the goods or collects them (see 11.2 above), in that the seller charges his own country's VAT all the time because the customer cannot provide a VAT registration number to guarantee zero-rating.

Distance sales and group registrations

11.17 Each member of a VAT group must apply the distance selling rules to its own sales. If compulsory foreign registration applies, the whole group must register in the relevant country.

New means of transport (VATA 1994, ss 40 and 95; SI 1995/2518, Regs 146 to 155)

Definitions

11.18 Since the introduction of the Single Market, special rules have applied to the purchase of new means of transport (NMT) whereby VAT is payable in the member state to which the NMT is being taken.

To qualify as a means of transport, the item must be for transportation of passengers or goods and fall within one of the following categories:

(*a*) ships more than 7.5 metres long;

(*b*) aircraft with take-off weight of more than 1,550kg;

(*c*) motorised land vehicles which

- (i) have an engine with a displacement or cylinder capacity of more than 48cc, or
- (ii) are constructed or adapted for electrical propulsion using more than 7.2kw (c. 9.65 horsepower).

A means of transport is an NMT unless:

(*a*) it is more than three months since it was first entered into service; and

(*b*) since its first entry into service, it has travelled under its own power for more than

- (i) 100 hours for ships,
- (ii) 40 hours for aircraft,
- (iii) 3,000km for motorised land vehicles.

Date of first entry into service

11.19 These are identified as follows:

(1) *Ships and aircraft*

- the date of delivery from manufacturer to first purchaser or owner; or
- the date it was first made available to the first purchaser or owner, whichever is the earlier.

(2) *Motorised land vehicles*

- the date of first registration for road use in the EC country of manufacture; or
- the date it was first liable for registration for road use in the EC country of manufacture, whichever is the earlier.

(3) *Motorised land vehicles not liable for registration for road use in the EC country of manufacture*

- the date it was taken away by the first purchaser or owner;
- the date of delivery to the first purchaser or owner; or
- the date it was first made available to the first purchaser or owner, whichever is the earlier; or
- the date it was taken into use as a demonstration vehicle by the manufacturer.

Where the date cannot be established clearly from the above, the date of the invoice for its first supply is used.

Sales of an NMT in the UK for removal to other member states

11.20 The customer is responsible for paying the VAT on an NMT acquired in the UK for removal to another member state provided certain conditions are fulfilled. The requirements concerning official Customs documentation to be completed are slightly different where the customer is registered for VAT in the destination member state or is not registered for VAT. These rules are explained below but there are also common conditions:

- the means of transport must be new;
- the NMT must be transported or despatched to the destination member state within two months of the invoice date (for registered customers) or just the date of supply (for non-registered customers);
- the supplier must keep documentary evidence to prove the NMT has left the UK.

The sale by the UK supplier is zero-rated but if the customer is VAT registered, the normal invoicing requirements apply concerning the showing of both registration numbers and country code prefixes.

Where the customer is VAT registered and the NMT is a motorised land vehicle intended for use in the UK before it is taken to the customer's country, it must be licensed and registered. This is achieved by the purchaser completing Form VAT 411A available from the local VAT office. The supplier must then make the completed form available to a Vehicle Registration Office or VRO which allocates a special registration mark showing that the vehicle will be removed to another member state and has been supplied free of VAT.

There are currently 12 VROs listed at paragraph 7.11 of Public Notice 725.

If the customer is not VAT registered, both supplier and customer must complete Form VAT 411 and ensure the vehicle has 'type approval' if the customer wants to license and register the vehicle in the UK. Form VAT 411, available from the local VAT office, must be completed in full. The form consists of the original and three carbon copies. The original must be sent to:

HM Customs & Excise
Central Processing Unit
Postal Depot
Charlton Green
Dover
Kent CT16 1EH

within six weeks of the end of the calendar quarter in which the relevant sale was made. The carbon copies are used as follows:

- first copy — to the customer
- second copy — kept by the supplier
- third copy — needed when registering the vehicle.

Type approval

11.21 A vehicle with 'type approval' has met certain international safety standards. A vehicle cannot be licensed or registered in the UK unless it is type approved or specifically exempted from type approval. If a UK supplier sells a vehicle which is not type approved and the customer intends to take it to another member state but fails to do so and keeps it in the UK, it may not be licensed and registered in the UK. Details on type approval can be obtained from:

The Vehicle Certification Agency
1 The Eastgate Office Centre
Eastgate Road
Bristol BS5 6XX
Tel: 0117 951 5151

Using new vehicles in the UK before they are taken abroad

11.22 New vehicles must be licensed and registered in the UK if they are to be used in the UK before being taken abroad. This is achieved by sending an application for registration to a VRO with the third carbon copy of Form VAT 411. The VRO then allocates the special registration number indicating VAT free status. The special number must be entered on the original and other two copies of Form VAT 411 before they are sent to the relevant recipients.

UK VAT registered businesses bringing NMTs into the UK from other member states

11.23 Under these provisions, the supplier in the other member state will normally zero rate the sale. Therefore, the UK buyer accounts for the VAT on his VAT return as normal. Clearly, new vehicles must be licensed and registered in the UK before they can be used.

Tax representatives (VATA 1994, s 48; SI 1995/2518, Reg 10)

11.24 Overseas businesses that have taxable business in the UK but do not have a physical business establishment in the UK from which they operate may choose to appoint a person or business established in the UK to act as their tax representative. Until 31 December 2001, Customs may exercise their power to direct that a tax representative be appointed. However, from 1 January 2002 Customs can no longer have the power to make such a direction where the non-established taxable person is from a country that organises mutual assistance under EC or similar arrangements. The power is removed by an amendment to *VATA 1994, s 48*. After that date, Customs can still insist on the appointment of a representative if the non-established taxable person is from a country that does not offer mutual assistance under one of the recognised arrangements.

Tax representatives in the UK may act for more than one overseas principal but must register for VAT separately for each one. Forms VAT 1 and VAT 1TR must be completed and sent to the local VAT office for the representative along with evidence of the appointment within 30 days of the appointment. Where the representative or the overseas principal is a partnership, Form VAT 2 must also be completed.

The representative is jointly and severally liable for the debts of his principal so, normally, some sort of legal indemnity is preferred. It is also permissible, unless Customs direct otherwise, for the overseas principal to appoint a UK agent where joint and several liability does not apply. In such cases, Customs require a letter of authority from the principal before they approach the agent.

If the arrangement with the principal comes to an end, Customs must be notified in writing within 30 days of the cessation and the period of representation is normally deemed to end on the date of the notification or the date the new representative is appointed, whichever is the earlier.

The representative or agent must keep all the normal books and records required of a UK VAT registered business and is responsible for completing returns and arranging for any net payments to be made to Customs. Where thresholds have been exceeded, the representative or agent must also complete and submit SSDs.

Where UK businesses have taxable business in other member states, they must observe the registration and tax representative rules there. In certain countries, the appointment of a tax representative might be compulsory.

Record-keeping and reporting requirements for trading in goods within the EC

11.25 The normal record-keeping requirements apply equally to intra-EC trade but additional documents must be kept as follows:

- copies of sales invoices received from suppliers in other member states;
- copies of EC Sales Lists and SSDs (see 11.26 and 11.31 below);
- supporting documentation in connection with EC acquisitions;
- supporting documentation in connection with EC sales (including proof that the goods have left the UK and been sent to the customer's member state).

If a UK business moves goods temporarily into another member state or brings goods from another member state temporarily into the UK, a special register must be kept. This must include the following information:

(1) *Goods despatched to other member states from the UK:*

- materials sent for processing work;
- goods sent for repair or alteration;
- goods moved for use in connection with a supply of services to be performed in another member state;
- goods sent under what would be Temporary Import relief conditions if the goods were imported from a country outside the EC.

The register should show the date the goods were moved from the UK to the other member state; the date they were returned; a description of the goods; the reason they were moved and the payment due as a result of the movement if applicable.

(2) *Goods brought into the UK from another member state:*

- goods received for processing.

The register should show the date the goods arrived; the date they are sent back; a description of the goods; the reason why they were brought into the UK and the payment due as a result of the movement if applicable.

EC Sales Lists (VATA 1994, Sch 11 para 2(3) and SI 1995/2518, Regs 21 to 23)

Introduction

11.26 Businesses registered for VAT in the UK that make sales to VAT registered customers in other member states must also complete quarterly EC Sales Lists ('ECSL'). These are a summary of each EC sale made within a calendar quarter so businesses that complete quarterly VAT returns to the end of January or February should be aware that there will be an overlap.

EC transactions are included on the ECSL if they are:

(*a*) normal EC sales,

(*b*) transfers of one's own goods to another member state, or

(*c*) sales by the intermediary in a triangular arrangement.

Where customers are not VAT registered in their member state and UK VAT is charged, the sales are not EC sales and are therefore excluded from the ECSL. Distance sales are also excluded.

How ECSLs work

11.27 The basic entry on the ECSL (Form VAT 101) consists of the two-letter country code prefix, the customer's VAT registration number, the total value of supplies to that customer within the calendar quarter and an indicator for the type of transaction. The quarters are called Q1, Q2, Q3 and Q4 corresponding to January to March, April to June etc. Continuation sheets are called Form VAT 101A and correction sheets Form VAT 101B.

Businesses may wish to complete ECSLs monthly but they must obtain Customs' permission first. Businesses that complete annual returns may apply to complete annual ECSLs if total annual taxable turnover does not exceed £145,000, the annual value of supplies to other EC Member States is less than £11,000 and those supplies do not include any NMTs.

If annual ECSLs are approved, there must be an agreement between the business and Customs as to when it will be submitted.

Sometimes it is possible to complete just an annual ECSL showing no more information than the registration numbers of customers in other member states. Businesses may apply for this method if:

(*a*) their annual taxable turnover does not exceed £72,500;

(*b*) the annual value of supplies to other EC Member States is less than £11,000; and

(*c*) those supplies do not include any NMTs.

Businesses that use non-standard tax periods for VAT returns may do the same with ECSLs but they must relate to calendar quarters e.g. in 2001 these could be 25 March, 24 June, 23 September and 30 December.

The ECSL must be sent in no later than six weeks after the end of the calendar quarter to which it relates but if no EC sales are made in a particular quarter, the form need not be submitted.

Methods of submitting ECSLs

11.28 Essentially, ECSLs can be submitted in one of three ways:

(i) on Form 101;

(ii) by electronic data interchange (EDI) (via a Value Added Network or Port Community) including magnetic tape or diskette — this can be arranged by contacting the following address:

HM Customs and Excise
Intrastat Compliance (Trades Management)
Tariff and Statistical Office
Helpdesk
27 Victoria Avenue
Southend-on-Sea
SS2 6AL
Tel: 01702 367248;

(iii) on plain paper, although if this method is used it must be approved by Customs, who apply strict conditions as to format because of the way ECSLs are processed.

Errors

11.29 Minor errors need not be disclosed but the following should always be disclosed using Form VAT 101B:

- errors exceeding the greater of £100 and 2% of the declared value of supplies to a particular customer;
- incorrect customer registration numbers;
- incorrect nature of transaction indicators.

Example 101

European Electronics makes the following mistakes on its EC Sales List for quarter 3/01 (July to September 2001):

1. Sales to Dutch customer — registration number recorded NL 123456789B01, should be NL 123456987B01.
2. Triangular transactions to a French customer — indicator 1 instead of 2 recorded.
3. Sales to a Portuguese customer — recorded total — £20,000. Should be £20,300.

Form VAT 101B should be used to disclose errors 1 and 2 but not 3 as the error at 3 is not more than the greater of £100 and 2% of the declared value (the error is £300 which is 1.5% of the declared value).

VAT groups and branches

11.30 Individual members of a VAT group and branches of a company may complete separate ECSLs on written request. Each company or branch must be allocated a three-digit identifying number. In the case of members of a VAT group, this normally is the same number as the company identifier under the group registration. Separately registered divisions of a company must submit separate declarations.

Intrastat and supplementary statistical declarations (SSDs) (SI 1992/2790)

Introduction

11.31 Intrastat is the regime whereby statistics showing the movement of goods between member states of the EC are gathered. Each member state sets thresholds for EC sales and acquisitions applicable to a calendar year and if a business exceeds its national thresholds, it must record the movements of goods to other member states, from other member states or both on supplementary statistical declarations or SSDs. It must be stressed that the system is for statistical purposes only and so most movements of goods must be recorded, not just sales and purchases.

In the UK, the threshold from 1 January 2000 for both EC sales and acquisitions is £233,000 but this is normally increased annually (although there was no increase on 1 January 2001). Therefore, if the Box 8 value of EC sales on VAT returns covering a calendar year exceeds £233,000, the business must start submitting 'dispatches' declarations and if Box 9 values of EC acquisitions on the returns covering a calendar year exceed the limit, the business must start submitting 'arrivals' declarations. The words 'dispatches' (*sic*) and 'arrivals' are used because they cover all movements, not just sales and purchases.

SSDs in detail

11.32 Dispatches and arrivals declarations are recorded on Forms C1500 and C1501. They record movements of goods within the EC only. Services are excluded as are movements to a place or from a place outside the member states.

Although the Tariff & Statistical Office monitor Box 8 and 9 figures on VAT returns and inform businesses when they must start completing SSDs, it is the responsibility of the business to ensure all declarations are made at the correct time and contain all the correct information. Failure to comply with Intrastat rules is strictly an offence and could be subject to criminal proceedings, albeit Customs prefer to accept financial offers out of court.

In practice, major problems with Intrastat compliance are rare, but Customs are adopting a stricter approach than when Intrastat was first introduced.

Frequency of SSDs

11.33 Declarations are made monthly and must be submitted within ten working days of the end of the month to which they relate. Customs may allow different month ends to apply where businesses use non-standard tax periods for VAT purposes. Also, if it is administratively preferable for a business to complete declarations more often than monthly, Customs will normally grant permission on request.

Responsibility for submitting declarations

11.34 Normally, the business responsible for making declarations is the one that concluded the contract for the removal of goods to another member state in the case of dispatches and the contract resulting in the delivery in the case of arrivals.

However, where that person is not established in the relevant country, the business that dispatches the goods or takes possession of them must make the declaration.

Agents may make declarations on behalf of their principals but ultimate liability remains with the principal. As with ECSLs, businesses can apply for individual members of a VAT group or branches to complete separate declarations, although separately registered divisions of a company must submit separate declarations.

When a movement must be recorded on an SSD

11.35 Although the fundamental rule in the EC is that a transaction must be recorded when goods are dispatched, in the UK the recording date is the earlier of:

- the date the supplier issues an invoice, and
- the 15th of the month following that in which the supply took place.

Customs also say that where a supply of goods is invoiced more than one month before delivery, the date the goods are received or delivered becomes the recording date. If a payment on account is received, an invoice must be issued immediately, thus creating a requirement to record the transaction for Intrastat purposes at the same time. If goods are supplied under a contract of sale, the recording is not required until the customer indicates his desire to keep the goods.

Information required on SSDs

11.36 Declarations show goods:

- bought and sold;
- transferred within the same business;
- subject to repair or processing terms;
- supplied as part of a contract for services;
- for installation, assembly or used in construction;
- supplied free of charge;
- on long term hire, loan or operational lease.

The following are excluded:

- certain temporary movements provided the goods will be returned to the original member state within two years without change of ownership;
- movements not by way of trade;
- certain samples free of charge — goods in transit in the UK should also be excluded.

Each type of goods moved between member states must be classified according to the Intrastat Classification Nomenclature (ICN), a copy of which is provided free of charge by Customs when a business starts completing SSDs. The codes are consistent throughout the EC so each product should have the same code when it appears on a dispatch declaration in one member state and an arrivals declaration in another. As interpretation concerning the nature of a product may vary, the same goods are not always allocated the same code. Additional copies of the ICN are available for a small charge.

SSD header information

11.37 The header of an SSD contains all details identifying the business responsible for the declaration including:

- name, address, VAT registration number and three-digit branch identifier (where applicable) of the declarer;

- the same information for the declarer's agent where applicable;
- the heading 'ARRIVALS' or 'DISPATCHES';
- the period identifier e.g. 0601 for June 2001;
- the number of lines completed — Customs prefer not more than 14 continuation sheets in addition to the front sheet in any one batch, so if more than 177 lines are necessary, more than one batch should be sent.

Item information

11.38 The main body of the declaration contains 11 boxes of which 9, 10 and 11 are not compulsory but assist Customs when checking accuracy. The information required in each box is as follows:

Box 1 — commodity code from the ICN. Help to identify the correct code is available from Customs Classification Liaison Officers.

Box 2 — the sterling value calculated in the same way as for VAT purposes and to the nearest pound. Freight and insurance charges are included when part of the invoice or contract price.

Box 3 — delivery terms. Three-letter codes are used as follows:

- EXW — ex works
- FOB — free on board at port of departure
- CIF — cost/insurance/freight at port of arrival
- DDU or DDP (either acceptable) — delivered domicile
- XXX — other.

Box 4 — nature of transaction. This is a two-digit code where each digit has its own meaning as follows:

(*a*) first digit:

- 1 — all transactions involving actual or intended change of ownership for a price other than those covered by 2, 7 and 8 below i.e. normally a sale
- 2 — returned and replacement goods
- 3 — free of charge transactions involving change of ownership
- 4 — goods for processing or repair other than 7 below
- 5 — goods returned after process or repair

- 6 — movements without change of ownership for hire, operational leasing and other temporary use but not process or repair
- 7 — joint defence projects or other joint international governmental production programmes such as the airbus project
- 8 —supplies of building materials and equipment where they form part of a general construction or engineering contract
- 9 — other transactions.

Item 1 includes stock moved within the same business and financial leasing.

Where the first digit is 8, the value of the goods is entered in Box 2, not the total contract value.

(*b*) second digit:

- 0 — all cases unless 6, 7 or 8 below apply
- 6 — credit notes
- 7 — transactions included on the SSD but not required in Box 8 or 9 of the VAT return form
- 8 — transactions included in Box 8 or 9 of the VAT return form but not included on the SSD form.

The use of 6, 7 and 8 as the second digit is not compulsory.

Box 5 — net mass in whole kilograms rounded up.

Box 6 — supplementary units. Only required where a second quantity is shown in the ICN.

Box 7 — country of consignment or destination of the goods. This is the two-letter code as used for invoices except for: Greece — GR instead of EL, and Belgium and Luxembourg, which are combined as BL rather than having their own separate codes.

Box 8 — mode of transport. Identified by a single digit as follows:

- 1 — sea (including road freight crossing by sea)
- 2 — rail (including by Channel Tunnel)
- 3 — land (crossing Irish land boundary only)
- 4 — air
- 5 — post
- 6 — not allocated

- 7 — fixed installations
- 8 — inland waterway
- 9 — own propulsion.

The code entered should be the one applicable to the method of transport used at the frontier and the presumed mode should be entered where there is any doubt.

Box 9 — country of origin. Applicable to arrivals only and optional. The two-letter codes apply but some countries use a three-digit code.

Box 10 — number of consignments. Only needed where consignments have been aggregated (see 11.39 below).

Box 11 — trader's reference. The business completing the declaration may include its own reference number, usually the invoice number, to facilitate the response to queries.

Low value consignments

11.39 Transactions with a value of £80 or less may be aggregated and given the Box 1 commodity code of 9950 0000. Where the declaration is submitted by manuscript or typescript, only the value need be shown and the country of consignment for arrivals and country of destination for dispatches.

Those submitting declarations by EDI must show full line details.

Where aggregation takes place, Customs prefer Box 10 to be completed.

Nil returns

11.40 Customs encourage the submission of declarations for periods where there has been no movement of goods in the relevant direction so that they do not raise unnecessary queries with the declarer.

Correcting errors and omissions

11.41 If a declarer omits transactions from a period, he must submit an additional SSD and indicate the period to which the omitted transaction related. This declaration should be clearly headed 'ADDITIONAL' in red ink.

Where errors are discovered on previous declarations, a copy of the declaration should be sent to the T&SO headed 'SD Error Correction' in red ink. Each line containing an error should be crossed out and the correct information inserted above it in red ink.

The address to which error correction forms should be sent is:

HM Customs & Excise
Tariff & Statistical Office
Sort Section
Portcullis House
27 Victoria Avenue
Southend-on-Sea SS2 6AL

A covering letter is not necessary so long as Customs can clearly identify the declarer's name, address, VAT registration number and the period to which the errors relate. Declarers using EDI should contact the above address first to discuss the method they can use for error correction.

Visits by Customs to check SSDs

11.42 For statistical information to be reliable, it must be punctual and accurate so Customs will check SSDs submitted by businesses from time to time. This is normally done during the routine VAT visit by the same officer.

In order that Customs can satisfy themselves as to the accuracy of SSDs, the declarer must keep copies of all declarations and any supporting documentation, paperwork, calculations etc. for six years. The visiting officer will attempt to reconcile VAT returns with SSDs so it is advisable to include all optional information on SSDs as well as compulsory information.

Where a declarer uses somebody else such as an agent to complete SSDs, he must ensure he obtains copies of all declarations and relevant paperwork because the Customs visit is made to the declarer, not the agent.

Intrastat Simplification

11.43 From 1 January 2001, Customs have reduced the amount of data required on Intrastat declarations and extended the amount of time allowed to file declarations. From that date, the following are no longer required:

- mode of transport;
- country of origin;
- number of consignments.

The boxes for the above information have been removed from paper versions of the SSD.

11.44 Businesses exceeding the £233,000 threshold for either arrivals or dispatches must still complete declarations, but with the reduced information. Those whose trade is below £12,500,000 in 2001 for arrivals or dispatches also no longer have to supply delivery terms for whichever aspect of trade is below that threshold. Both thresholds will be reviewed annually. Exceeding the higher 'delivery terms threshold' during a year does not require the terms to be included immediately, unlike the normal threshold. The requirement starts from the beginning of the year following the one in which the threshold was exceeded. Businesses may continue to supply delivery terms on a voluntary basis if they so wish.

11.45 From 1 January 2001, businesses that file SSDs by EDI or the Internet now have until the end of the month following the reference period to file them (extended from 10 working days). However, those that file paper declarations must still file them within 10 working days until January 2002 when they also will have until the end of the month. Customs have indicated that this staggered change is to ensure that data can definitely be sent to Eurostat on time.

11.46 The SSD forms have been re-designed and must be used for all periods from May 2001. The old forms could be used for the first four months of the simplified regime.

Chapter 12

Imports, Exports and International Services

Introduction

12.1 Especially with international trade, it is essential to understand the difference between supplies of goods and services. A supply of goods is the transfer of the right to dispose of tangible movable property as owner in the course or furtherance of business. In other words, this normally means the sale of physical items to somebody else as a business activity.

Anything done in the course of business in return for 'consideration' which is not a supply of goods is a supply of services.

'Consideration' usually means payment in the form of money but it can also include payment with other goods or services, or the provision of some benefit to the supplier of the service.

Example 102
Watson buys a new motorbike for his courier business priced at £8,000 plus VAT. He receives an allowance of £1,000 plus VAT for his old motorbike and pays £7,000 plus VAT. The 'consideration' for the new motorbike is £9,400 (£8,000 + £1,400 VAT) i.e. the allowance for the old motorbike is included in calculating the purchase price.

The VAT treatment of international supplies of goods and international services can be significantly different. For example, if a certain sale were treated as goods, VAT may be payable in one country, whereas if it were services, the VAT would be due in another country.

This chapter covers:

- the treatment of imports (goods purchased from a supplier based outside the EC and brought into the UK);

- exports (goods sold to and sent by a UK supplier to a customer based outside the EC);
- the provision of international services by UK businesses to customers based in other EC countries and outside the EC; and
- imported services (services bought in by UK businesses from suppliers based outside the UK).

Imports

General

12.2 The basic rule is that VAT is payable by the importer of goods into the UK when they are cleared into free circulation. That is, when all Customs formalities have been completed and any duties paid. No import VAT is due if the goods are zero-rated in the UK, e.g. books, most food items.

Example 103
Collins imports 1,000 widgets at £10 each. The goods reach Felixstowe on 30 March and Customs' formalities are completed on 31 March, Collins paying an extra £1,000 in duty. VAT is due on £11,000 (£10,000 goods + £1,000 duty) on 31 March.

Special rules apply for determining the value on which import VAT is calculated; the time it is due; the identity of the importer and the supporting documentation to be maintained.

Value of imports

12.3 The value of imported goods for VAT purposes is their Customs value (explained in full in Customs Notice 252 and normally the price charged) plus:

- all associated expenses such as commission, packing, transport and insurance charges up to the first place of destination;
- all further associated expenses if they relate to transport to an onward destination in another EC Member State if that destination is known when the goods are first imported into the UK;
- any Customs duties, levies payable on importation;

- any Excise duties payable,

provided these additional charges are not included in the basic price.

Example 104
Robinson imports 1,000 widgets into the UK for onward transport to Germany. The widgets cost £10 each; commission, packing and transport costs to Robinson's factory are £1,000 and further transport costs to Germany are £500. Duty is £1,000. The import value to which VAT is added is the aggregate of all the above, i.e. £12,500.

Transport costs include handling, loading and storage charges but additional costs such as royalties and licence fees should be excluded because they are subject to VAT using the reverse charge mechanism (see 12.40 below).

Where the exporter from outside the EC and UK importer are related, the import value must not be artificially reduced.

The importer declares the goods to be imported on a Single Administrative Document (SAD or C88). The Customs Handling Import Export Freight (CHIEF) computer calculates the VAT due automatically from information provided but, where certain costs are not recorded, other boxes on the SAD make provision for adjustments so that the correct amount of import VAT is paid.

Customs normally accept Form C105 (Valuation declaration) or 109 (General Valuation Statement) as the value for VAT purposes on imports where Customs duty is payable. However, where no duty is payable, Customs only require a declaration if the value exceeds £4,000 and the importer is not registered for VAT, or the importer is VAT-registered but the goods are for non-business use or non-deductible for input tax purposes or if the value is not being calculated using the normal method. The supplier's invoice is also normally required as evidence of value (copies are acceptable).

Other methods of valuation where the basic price is inappropriate

12.4 Sometimes, it may be inappropriate to use the basic valuation rules. In such cases, the following bases are used in the order listed until a suitable value is found:

(*a*) the price paid or payable by a buyer for delivery of goods into the EC;

(*b*) the value of identical goods produced by the same business or by another business if identical goods from the same business cannot be valued. If there is more than one example of identical goods, the lowest available value applies;

(*c*) the value of similar goods produced in the same country for the same purpose;

(*d*) the 'deductive method', i.e. three further methods taken in turn:

(i) the unit price at which the imported goods or identical or similar imported goods are sold to unrelated third parties using the largest aggregate quantity sale made around the time when the relevant goods are imported,

(ii) the price of imported goods or identical or similar goods imported at the earliest date after the date of importation of the relevant goods, although these goods must be imported within 90 days of the relevant goods,

(iii) at the importer's request, he may use the price at which the imported goods are sold to unrelated third parties after further processing;

(*e*) the computed value method where the value is the sum of:

(i) material and fabrication costs in addition to processing costs employed in producing the relevant goods,

(ii) an element to cover profit and other expenses usually reflected in the sales of similar goods made by producers in the consignor's country of export to the EC,

(iii) transport, insurance, loading and handling charges to the place of importation of the relevant goods into the EC,

(iv) the cost of containers and packing, and

(v) an element of the costs involved in engineering, development, artwork and design work to the extent that these are charged by the consignor;

(*f*) the 'fall back' method which is only a last resort based on criteria consistent with the underlying principles of General Agreement on Tariffs and Trade (GATT). The goods may not be valued according to these bases:

(i) the selling price in the EC of goods produced in the EC,

(ii) a system allowing for the higher of two alternatives to be accepted for Customs purposes,

(iii) the price of goods on the domestic market of the country of exportation,

(iv) the cost of production, other than that allowed under the computed value method,

(v) prices for export to a country outside the EC,

(vi) minimum Customs values, or

(vii) fictitious values.

Under the first four options (*a*) to (*d*) above, a deduction from price is allowed for commissions; the profit element and general expenses such as marketing costs; transport, insurance and associated costs incurred within EC boundaries; EC Customs duties and any internal taxes payable in the country of importation and, applicable to the third option only, the value added by processing.

Imported works of art, antiques and collectors' items

12.5 A special reduced value applies to imported and reimported works of art, antiques and collectors' items. The normal Customs value including the additional costs listed above is multiplied by 28.58%. The VAT is then added at 17.5%. In effect, this means that the VAT rate on imports of these items is 5%. Prior to 27 July 1999, the effective rate was 2.5% meaning relevant costs were multiplied by 14.29%.

The time VAT is payable on imports

12.6 VAT is payable by the importer on imported goods whether or not he is VAT registered.

VAT registered importers may, subject to the normal rules, reclaim as input tax, in the tax period in which the import was made, the VAT which they have paid. The input tax is included with all other input tax in Box 4 of the return form and not accounted for in the same way as EC acquisitions (see 11.3 *et seq.*).

VAT becomes due when Customs legally accept an entry. The time an entry is required depends on the mode of transport used as follows:

- sea — when the ship comes within the UK port limits;
- air — when the plane lands or the goods are unloaded in the UK, whichever is the earlier;
- land (only applicable to crossing the boundary between the Republic of Ireland and Northern Ireland) — when the goods cross the boundary;
- pipeline — when the goods are brought within the limits of a UK port or when they cross the Irish land border.

Goods are not released into free circulation until all relevant duties are paid but there are circumstances when payment of such duties is not required immediately:

- when the goods are put into a warehouse;
- when the goods are put into a designated free zone;
- when the importer is approved to use the duty deferment system.

In the first two cases, the duties and VAT are payable when the goods are taken out of the warehouse or free zone. These facilities are discussed further at 12.14 below. The duty deferment system allows importers to delay payment of duty and VAT until the 15th day of the month following the importation providing certain conditions are fulfilled.

Deferring duty and VAT

12.7 Normally, import VAT is payable immediately by cash, cheque or banker's draft.

However, many importers choose to opt for the duty and VAT deferment system, paying by direct debit on the 15th day of the month following the importation.

Example 105
A consignment of dustbins ordered from Taiwan by Total Rubbish Ltd arrives on 20 April 2001. The company's next VAT return is for the quarter to 30 April 2001. It has a duty deferment facility so the goods are cleared by Customs immediately and VAT on the import is not due until 15 May 2001 (by direct debit). The company will actually account for it on its VAT return for the quarter to 31 July 2001.

The facility is granted by Customs on application from the importer but in order to use the scheme, the importer must pay Customs a guarantee normally equal to twice their estimated value of monthly imports. A supplementary guarantee may also be required to cover periods of greater import activity.

The importer usually obtains the guarantee through a bank but this usually reduces available borrowing facilities, so an alternative is to arrange it through an insurance company even though it may be more expensive in terms of interest payable.

When the facility is approved, the importer is given a Trader's Unique Reference Number (TURN) which he should provide along with his VAT registration number in order to clear goods through Customs without depositing the duty and VAT due. Where importing is fairly infrequent and values are insignificant, an importer should consider using an agent to carry out the administrative obligations. Agents usually have their own duty deferment numbers which they can quote to release the goods. They then issue their own invoice to the importer showing duty and VAT paid on the importer's behalf plus their commission charges. Importers often mistakenly use these invoices as evidence to support input tax claims although only a monthly certificate issued by Customs (C79) is acceptable.

Evidence for input tax claims

12.8 Although all documents relating to the import of goods should be kept, such as suppliers invoices, SADs, shipping documents and agents' invoices, none of these are acceptable as evidence to support input tax claims. The correct evidence is the monthly summary of imports issued to the importer by Customs on Form C79.

The person or business that imports the goods may not be the person or business for whom the goods are destined. The importer may be responsible for paying the import VAT but the ultimate consignee only may recover the input tax if he is VAT registered and the goods are going to be used by him for the purposes of his taxable activities.

Overseas businesses importing goods into the UK

12.9 It is possible for businesses not established in the UK and not registrable here to import goods into the UK, usually through an agent. Where this is the case, they may reclaim the VAT paid from the UK Customs using the 8th Directive provisions if they are a VAT registered business in another EC Member State, or the 13th Directive if from a non-EC country. Chapter 13 deals with the recovery of foreign VAT by UK businesses and UK VAT by foreign businesses.

Postal imports

12.10 Goods (other than Datapost packets) brought into the UK that do not exceed £2,000 in value are treated in a similar way to EC acquisitions. If the importer is VAT registered and imports the goods for business purposes, has completed a Customs declaration showing his VAT registration number and a description of the goods including their quantity and value, he need not pay the VAT immediately but includes it as output tax in Box 1 of his next return. The same amount is then recovered as input tax subject to the normal rules.

Example 106
On 1 October 2001, O'Brien imports 50 electrical components by post that cost £30 each. He is VAT registered and completes the relevant Customs declaration. His next VAT return covers the quarter to 31 December 2001. The goods are cleared on 1 October without payment of VAT but on his return for period 12/01, O'Brien includes £262.50 (50 × £30 × 17.5%) output tax in Box 1 and reclaims the same amount in Box 4.

Import VAT cannot be deferred on Datapost packages not exceeding £2,000 in value so the importer must pay the VAT immediately on request by the Post Office. The importer should keep the charge label as evidence for input tax.

For all postal imports exceeding £2,000 the importer must make a proper entry on the form which he will receive by post. The VAT is either paid immediately or deferred if the importer has approval to use the duty deferment system.

The time VAT is payable on postal imports depends on the type. If there has been a full entry, it is due when the declaration is delivered to Customs but if there is no entry, it is due when duty and VAT are assessed by a Customs officer after declaration or, when there is no assessment to duty or tax, when the Post Office delivers the goods.

Bulked entries

12.11 There are special provisions for a person making one entry on behalf of several importers (e.g. an agent acting for several principals) or a single importer making an entry of goods from one ship or aircraft from several suppliers. A person making the entry on behalf of several importers must obtain prior permission from the Customs Collector based at the port of entry, although this is not necessary for single importers making one entry from several suppliers.

The agent under the first category must either pay the VAT immediately or use his own deferment number to delay payment. Only his principals can claim the VAT as input tax but as they each need a valid C79, the agent must complete the relevant part of Box 44 on the entry document as follows:

- for single consignees — 'RC = 5' followed by the consignee's TURN (see 12.7 above)
- for multiple consignees — 'MC' followed by the TURN of each consignee.

Import VAT repayments on second-hand cars for subsequent export

12.12 Under certain circumstances, import VAT on second-hand cars could be reclaimed. The conditions were that the car was imported before 1 August 1995, it is to be re-exported unused and has not been registered and licensed for UK use. The local Collector's office should be contacted.

Registered businesses that import second-hand cars exclusively for business use after 1 August 1995 may recover the VAT paid as input tax.

Relief from VAT on certain permanent and temporary imports

12.13 Certain goods are relieved from import VAT when imported permanently as follows:

- Imports of certain goods by charities
- Donated medical equipment
- Museum and gallery exhibits
- World Health Organisation sample reference substances
- Decorations and awards
- Animals for laboratory research
- Biological and chemical substances for research
- Blood grouping, tissue typing and certain therapeutic substances
- United Nations visual and auditory materials
- Goods for blind and other handicapped persons
- Goods for testing.

These are also listed at paragraph 5.1 of VAT Public Notice 702 on imports with cross-references to other Customs' notices explaining the conditions for the reliefs.

Certain goods brought into the UK by registered businesses on a temporary basis may be subject to reliefs although the importer may choose to treat them as normal imports. Partly exempt businesses are the principal beneficiaries of temporary importation reliefs because they would otherwise suffer input tax restrictions.

Free zones and warehouses

12.14 There are certain areas in the UK which are not considered part of the UK for Customs' purposes. This means that goods can be imported into these areas and duty and VAT is not payable. There are currently eight free zones at:

- Birmingham
- Liverpool
- Prestwick
- Southampton
- Tilbury
- Sheerness
- Stoneferry
- Ronaldsway (Isle of Man).

Free zones work in a similar way to Customs' warehouses in that duty and VAT is not payable until the goods kept there are released into free circulation or are consumed within the zone. Where goods are sold whilst still in a free zone, VAT is due as normal, unlike a Customs' warehouse where such transactions are ignored. If goods are sold in a free zone to a non-registered customer, VAT is paid when the goods are removed from the zone but reduced by the amount of tax already paid on the sale.

Exports

General

12.15 Exports are sales of goods to businesses established outside the member states of the EC where the goods physically leave the EC. The emphasis in UK legislation is on Customs being satisfied that the export has actually taken place. They must be satisfied that the exporter has physically exported the goods to a destination outside the member states or 'has shipped them for use as stores on a voyage or flight to an eventual destination outside the United Kingdom, or as merchandise for sale by retail to persons carried on such a voyage or flight in a ship or aircraft' (*s 30(6)(b)*).

Customs may set further regulations as they see fit to ensure controls are in place. Clearly, they must guard against businesses labelling goods as for export to obtain zero-rating and then selling them to a UK customer or putting them to some other home use.

It is important to appreciate that sales of goods to customers in the Isle of Man are regarded for VAT purposes as within the UK. Therefore, these sales are not exports and VAT is due unless the goods themselves are zero-rated. However, the Channel Islands are not part of the EC for VAT purposes so sales to customers based there are exports provided the goods are actually sent to the Channel Islands, although simplified rules apply to procedures and evidence of export required by Customs.

This section covers the various different types of export which exist, the time limits as to when goods must leave the UK and the EC for zero-rating to apply, and the types of evidence required to support zero-rating including the time limits by which the evidence must be obtained.

Types of export

12.16 The three main types of export are direct exports, indirect exports and retail exports.

(1) *Direct exports* are those where the owner or supplier is in control of the movement of the goods. Control is not lost if the owner or supplier arranges the movement through an agent, although the owner or supplier should always ensure that the agent makes the correct evidence of export available within three months of the time of supply (see 12.22).

(2) *Indirect exports* are those which relate to goods exported outside the EC by a person or business other than the owner or supplier, such as an overseas business or a freight forwarder acting on their behalf. The goods must be exported within three months of the time of supply and the correct evidence obtained within three months of the export (see 12.22).

(3) *Retail exports* under the retail export scheme which entitles UK retailers to zero rate sales of eligible goods to eligible customers where those goods are being taken outside the EC. The three-month rule applies for obtaining evidence of export but retailers usually take a deposit of the VAT so they can pay it to Customs if the customers fails to send back the necessary evidence (see 12.22).

The SAD described at 12.3 above also applies to exports and this should always show the exporter's TURN (see 12.7). Accompanying transport documentation should show a full description of the goods, their quantity, value and weight.

Direct exports

12.17 Customs consider that the exporter controls the movement of the goods if they transport them in their own baggage; in their own transport; by rail, post or courier service; or through a shipping line, airline, freight forwarder or other type of agent employed by the exporter.

Deliveries of aircraft, vehicles and boats for export outside the EC under their own power are also direct exports.

Indirect exports

12.18 These are supplies to overseas businesses which take control of the goods in the UK and then make all the arrangements themselves for removal to a place outside the EC. Customs define an overseas person as:

(*a*) a person not resident in the UK;

(*b*) a business that has no establishment in the UK from which it makes taxable supplies; or

(*c*) an overseas authority.

Zero-rating can still be applied where the sale to an overseas person involves carriage by them in baggage, in an accompanied vehicle or as freight, provided the goods are exported within three months of the time of supply and evidence of export is obtained within three months of the export. The supplier would normally consider taking a deposit of the VAT he would have to pay if the customer fails to send back the evidence on time. Records must clearly identify such transactions and the goods must not be used for their normal purpose before they are transported outside the EC.

Retail exports

12.19 The retail export scheme can be used by retailers selling goods for export to overseas visitors, entitled EC residents and crews of ships and aircraft. An overseas visitor is somebody who has not been in the EC for more than 365 days in the two years immediately preceding the purchase of the goods and will be leaving the EC within three months of the date of purchase. An EC resident is somebody who has lived in the EC for more than 365 days in the two years immediately preceding the purchase and is leaving the EC for a continuous period of more than one year. To qualify for the scheme, crew members of ships and aircraft cannot have been in the EC for more than 365 days in the two years immediately preceding the purchase and must be leaving for a destination outside the EC. This definition of an 'overseas visitor' is in *SI 1995/2518, Reg 130* as clarified by *SI 1999/438, Reg 12*, effective from 1 April 1999.

All standard-rated goods can be sold under the scheme except the following:

- new motor vehicles for personal export;
- used motor vehicles for export;
- boats sold to visitors who intend to sail them to a destination outside the EC;
- goods over £600 in value exported for the customer's business purposes;
- goods for consumption in the EC;
- goods requiring an export licence (but antiques can be sold under the scheme even if they require an export licence);
- unmounted gemstones;
- bullion (over 125g (2.75 troy ounces or 10 Tolas)).

VAT must be charged on retail exports until the valid evidence is received from the customer to prove the goods have left the EC, hence the preferred procedure of taking a deposit equal to the VAT from the customer.

Other types of export — export houses

12.20 It is possible for goods to change hands more than once before they are finally exported. The basic VAT provisions state that only the final transaction, the physical export itself, may be zero-rated.

Export houses are charged VAT in the same way as businesses that take delivery of goods before their subsequent export.

Other types of export — supplies to overseas businesses for export after consolidation, processing or incorporation

12.21 It may be that goods are supplied to an overseas business for export but first they are delivered to a third party in the UK who is also intending to make a zero-rated sale to the same overseas business. The supplier can still zero rate his sale if:

(*a*) the third party is not buying the goods, just taking delivery;

(*b*) the goods are only used for processing or incorporation into other goods or consolidation with other goods for export;

(*c*) the goods are exported within six months of the time of supply (note more time allowed than normal) and valid evidence is obtained within one month of export (see 12.22);

(*d*) the supplier's records include the name and address of the overseas business; the invoice number and date; the description, quantity and value of the goods; the name and address of the third party taking delivery; the dates by which the export must be made and valid evidence obtained and the date the goods were actually exported.

Time limits for zero-rating of exports

12.22 As time limits are based on the time of supply (not strictly a tax point if the supply is zero-rated), it is important to clarify the time of supply for exports before explaining the time limits for zero-rating.

The time of supply is normally the earlier of the date the goods are sent to the customer or the customer takes them away and the date full payment is received.

Example 107
Plants and Machinery Ltd receives a 20% deposit from a South African customer for a consignment of hedge trimmers on 28 September 2001 and the balance on 15 October 2001. The goods are despatched on 17 October 2001. The time of supply is 15 October 2001.

The time of supply is still the date full payment is received even if a deposit or progress payments are received.

These time of supply rules are different from those applying to EC sales (see Chapter 11).

The time limits for zero-rating are as follows.

- *Direct exports* — the goods must be exported and valid evidence obtained within three months of the time of supply. If the goods have not been exported within three months, they cannot be zero-rated but if they are subsequently exported and valid evidence is obtained, zero-rating is allowed and the VAT account may be adjusted for the tax period in which valid evidence was obtained.
- *Indirect exports* — the goods must be exported within three months (one month prior to 1 September 2000) of the time of supply and valid evidence of export obtained within three months of the date of export. If the goods are not exported or valid evidence is not obtained within the time limits, zero-rating is not allowed but if the goods are exported later and valid evidence is obtained, zero-rating is allowed and the VAT account may be adjusted for the tax period in which valid evidence was obtained.

Example 108

If, in the above example, the company uses a freight forwarder to deal with the export but no proof of export was forthcoming by 20 January 2002, the company must take VAT out of the amount received and account for it to Customs on its next VAT return. If this return were for the quarter ending 31 January 2002, the VAT would be accounted for as output tax in Box 1. If, then, the freight forwarder exported the goods and provided evidence on 8 February 2002, the company could reclaim the output tax previously paid on its return for the quarter ending 30 April 2002.

The bringing into line of time limits for the export of goods and production of appropriate evidence was announced by Customs in Information Sheet 2/00, issued on 1 September 2000. This also clarified the types of documentation that Customs will accept as proof of export.

Summary of exporters' obligations

12.23 The obligations of UK VAT-registered businesses exporting goods to a final destination outside the EC can be summarised as follows. For zero-rating to apply, they must:

(*a*) ensure that the goods are exported from the UK within the time limits;

(*b*) obtain and keep valid evidence of export within the time limits;

(*c*) not deliver or post the goods to a UK customer's address in the UK even if it is claimed they are for subsequent export;

(*d*) not allow the goods to be collected by or on behalf of a UK customer even if it is claimed they are for subsequent export (although they may deliver the goods to an independent freight forwarder, shipping line or airline for immediate export on behalf of a non-VAT registered UK customer), or on behalf of an export house (until 31 March 1999), provided that valid evidence of export is obtained from the carrier;

(*e*) keep records of export transactions which must be made available for inspection by visiting officers; and

(*f*) comply with the law and the conditions of VAT Public Notice 703 (which includes the requirement to keep adequate books and records as described in VAT Public Notice 700 Section 8).

Acceptable evidence of export

12.24 The most obvious document to be used to support zero-rating for exports is the SAD (C88). This is known as 'official evidence' but other forms of evidence known as 'commercial evidence' can be equally acceptable. Whether official or commercial evidence is used, other documentation relating to the export should be kept as follows:

- customer orders
- sales contracts
- inter-company correspondence
- copies of export invoices
- advice notes
- consignment notes
- packing lists
- insurance and freight charges
- evidence of payment
- evidence that the goods have been received abroad.

There are two types of commercial evidence: primary and secondary. Primary evidence consists of authenticated sea waybills, air waybills, PIM/PIEX International Consignment Notes for individual consignments, vehicles and containers, and Master air waybills or bills of lading in connection with individual or groupage shipments. Secondary evidence consists of documentation issued by freight forwarders and other carriers for a number of exporters by sea, air, road or rail. In practice, the freight forwarders get the primary evidence and pass on secondary evidence to the actual exporter (their principal). Authenticated house air or sea waybills, CMR notes for goods carried by road, or certificates of shipment based on primary evidence are the main forms of secondary evidence.

Any evidence of export must contain the full particulars of the exporter, the customer, a full description of the goods, an accurate value and the destination of the goods. Any additional information which assists the visiting Customs officer in confirming the validity of an export is always helpful.

If the supplier or overseas customer wishes to export goods in baggage or in a private vehicle, copies 2 and 3 of the SAD must be submitted to the Merchandise In Baggage (MIB) officer at the point of export. He will certify the export on the back of copy 3 and then give it back to the supplier or overseas customer to keep. If the overseas customer is arranging the export, the supplier should give him a completed SAD showing his name and VAT number so that the customer does not include the consignment with others thus preventing him from obtaining a certified copy 3 only relating to the one supplier.

Special evidence requirements for less common types of export are covered under Sections 5 and 6 of VAT Public Notice 703.

Photocopied and duplicated evidence is not acceptable unless authenticated. Other evidence not mentioned above may be accepted if it clearly proves that an export has actually taken place.

Accounting issues concerning exports

12.25 If an exporter fails to observe the three-month time limit for direct or indirect exports, he should treat any payment received for the sale as VAT-inclusive in the month the limit expires and where VAT is at 17.5%, calculate and show VAT due as 7/47 of the amount received. A VAT account adjustment can be made in the month in which valid evidence is received. See *Example 108* at 12.22 above.

If a business exports more than it sells in the UK, its input tax may regularly exceed its output tax. It may, therefore, apply to complete monthly VAT returns so that net refunds can be received more quickly.

Some larger concerns prefer to set up a separate export company which receives goods at the standard rate from the main company and then handles all the exports and completes monthly returns for cash flow purposes. Customs do not normally object to such structures.

Example 109

Universal Products Ltd (UP) manufactures office furniture for sale to UK customers and for export. UP completes VAT returns for the quarters March, June, September and December. However, all of its sales are standard-rated because it sells goods for export to its export company, Universal Exports Ltd (UE). Sales for period 09/01 are as follows:

July 2001 — £120,000 + £21,000 VAT (including £80,000 + £14,000 VAT to UE)

August 2001 — £160,000 + £28,000 VAT (including £100,000 + £17,500 VAT to UE)

September 2001 — £140,000 + £24,500 VAT (including £96,000 + £16,800 VAT to UE)

UP pays £73,500 output VAT when it files its 09/01 return by 31 October 2001. However, UE completes monthly returns and reclaims £14,000 input tax on its 07/01 return, £17,500 on its 08/01 return and £16,800 on its 09/01 return. These could be filed as early as 1 August, 1 September and 1 October respectively. The cash flow advantage is clear.

International services

12.26 Before one can hope to understand the basics of VAT applicable to international services, it is necessary to have a fundamental appreciation of the difference between supplies of goods and services. This immediately causes a problem in that not all EC Member States interpret European VAT law in the same way.

The Sixth Directive states that anything which is not a supply of goods is a supply of services. The purpose of the directive is to harmonise the treatment of turnover taxes in each member country but it has achieved only partial success. For example, some countries treat certain types of computer software as goods, others as services. The effective result can be the threat of double taxation or no taxation at all.

This section endeavours to define and compare different types of services and examine their treatment for VAT purposes. It will also review the simplifications to the basic rules on imported services applied in the UK. Finer points of detail are in VAT Public Notice 741 on the subject of place of supply.

This section principally covers three areas:

(1) the treatment of services supplied by businesses in the UK to customers in other member states of the EC;

(2) the treatment of services supplied by businesses in the UK to customers outside the EC;

(3) the treatment of services 'imported' into the UK.

The place of supply

12.27 The treatment of an international service for VAT purposes is determined by the law stipulating where it is deemed to have taken place. The provisions dictate in which country, if at all, VAT is payable and whether the provider or the recipient of the service is responsible for paying the tax to the fiscal authorities.

The basic rule is that a supply of services is deemed to take place where the supplier 'belongs'. However, it is essential to understand the meaning of belonging and how the UK has implemented the overriding principles of EC Law. These issues are covered below.

The law

12.28 The EC Sixth VAT Directive (Directive 77/388), Article 6 defines a supply of services as any transaction which is not a supply of goods as previously described in Article 5. So the definition is broad and can include types of transactions one would not immediately consider as services.

The Article makes specific mention of certain transactions which are supplies of services, such as assignments of intangible property, obligations to refrain from or tolerate an act or situation, and services performed under a legal or public authority order.

It also stresses that a supply of services takes place when business assets are put to private use by a taxable business or its staff where the VAT on the original purchase has been recovered, or when the taxable business performs services free of charge for its own private use or that of its staff.

It should now be clear that the first hurdle to overcome is discerning whether one is supplying goods or services because the treatment can be vastly different. Only when services are confirmed can the question of place of supply be addressed.

Historically, the whole matter has caused confusion, misunderstanding and disputes, perhaps to a greater extent than the other major problem areas of partial exemption and land and property, but recent efforts to simplify legislation have helped.

Basic rule in the UK

12.29 Article 9 of the Sixth Directive contains the principal place of supply rules which have been incorporated into UK law. In the UK, the basic place of supply is where the supplier belongs, but Customs can make exceptions where necessary (*s 7(10) and (11)*). A business belongs where it is physically established. This normally means at least the presence of human and technical resources. If a business belongs in more than one place, e.g. international branches, the establishment most closely connected with the relevant supply is used to determine the VAT treatment.

Exceptions to the place of supply rules (SI 1992/3121)

General

12.30 It makes sense for legislation to make specific reference only to exceptions. Therefore, if a particular international service supplied by a business belonging in the UK is not listed under one of the exception categories, it is most likely that the place of supply is the UK and any VAT due is payable by the supplier.

The four main exceptions to the basic rule are:

(1) services directly connected with land and property;

(2) transport services and hire of means of transport;

(3) cultural, artistic, sporting, scientific, educational and entertainment services;

(4) certain intangible, intellectual services including most professional services.

Exception (1) — Services relating to land

12.31 The supply of any interest in, right over or licence to occupy land or property; any work of construction, demolition, conversion, reconstruction, alteration, enlargement, repair or maintenance and, most significantly, associated services such as those provided by estate agents, auctioneers, architects and surveyors, are supplied where the land is situated.

Example 110

(*a*) A private individual from London who has acquired a significant inheritance asks a local architect to design a villa on the Costa del Sol.

Although both the architect and his client belong in the UK, the land is in Spain so, unless a special arrangement applies, the fees are not subject to UK VAT. However, the architect is making a supply of services in Spain so he should check the Spanish registration requirements and charge Spanish VAT if necessary.

(*b*) A private individual from Madrid has also acquired an inheritance and wants to use some of it to build a cottage in England. He travels to London and instructs the same architect to design the cottage for him.

UK VAT should be added to the architect's fee even though the client belongs in Spain, because the land is situated in the UK.

Services indirectly connected with land are not included within this category, such as the installation of machinery in buildings but not as fixtures. This is a supply of goods.

Exception (2) — Transport services and hire of means of transport — passenger transport

12.32 Essentially, the supply of passenger transport services takes place in the country in which it is provided. Therefore, international passenger transport starting in the UK is supplied partly in the UK and partly elsewhere depending on the destination. This means that there may be a requirement to account for VAT to fiscal authorities in other member states of the EC (but see also 'The reverse charge for imported services' at 12.40 below).

At present, passenger transport in the UK is zero-rated unless the means of transport is designed to carry less than 12 passengers, in which case it is standard-rated. This relief is, however, under threat because unless EC legislation is rewritten, the UK may have to introduce a positive rate of VAT to such services although no decision regarding a change has yet been taken.

Exception (2) — Transport services and hire of means of transport — freight transport

12.33 The transport of goods from the UK to a destination outside the EC or to a place in the EC for subsequent export outside the EC is zero-rated even if the journey involves passing through other member states. Documentary evidence should always be kept to show the purpose of a journey and the ultimate destination of the goods.

Intra-community freight transport

The intra-community transport of goods is treated differently.

The place of supply of intra-community freight transport is where the goods start their journey, albeit if the transport is provided from the UK and the customer is registered for VAT in another member state and gives the supplier that number, the customer accounts for VAT under the reverse charge system according to the rules in that country (see 12.40).

Example 111

(*a*) A UK transport company is instructed by a French entrepreneur to move a crate of widgets from Birmingham to Lyons. The entrepreneur has not yet informed the French VAT authorities of his planned business activities and consequently has no registration number.

The UK company should charge UK VAT on its sales invoice and account for output tax on its next VAT return because the movement of goods begins in the UK.

(*b*) A French haulage company receives a large contract from a Spanish company to transport car parts from Sunderland to Barcelona. The total contract is worth FF600,000 (around £60,000).

If the Spanish company gives its Spanish VAT registration number to the haulier, the place of supply becomes Spain and the Spanish company accounts for VAT under the reverse charge system. If for some reason the number was not made available, the haulier has made a supply in the UK (where the goods movement begins) and should consider UK registration because the contract value exceeds the registration limit.

Although freight transport services in the UK are usually standard-rated, it may be possible to zero-rate certain services under *Schedule 8 Group 8* (see 4.34 *et seq.*).

Exception (2) — Hire of means of transport

12.34 Normally, the hire of means of transport takes place where the supplier belongs but there are two notable exceptions:

(1) If a supplier belonging in the UK hires out a means of transport for use exclusively outside the EC, no VAT is due.

(2) If the supplier belongs outside the EC but the transport is used by a UK VAT-registered business in the UK, the supply takes place in the UK and the recipient must account for VAT under the reverse charge (see 12.40).

Under (1), the means of transport must be exported outside the EC by the supplier or must be already outside the EC when hired out. Under (2), certain types of transport hire may be zero-rated in accordance with *Schedule 8 Group 8* (see 4.34 *et seq.*) but when the transport is supplied with a driver, pilot, crew or operator, the supply will be transport services rather than hire of means of transport.

Exception (3) — Cultural, artistic and similar services

12.35 Services specifically listed in this category are supplied where they are physically performed, and the output VAT is paid in the country of performance by the supplier unless simplified rules apply (see last two paragraphs after *Example 112* below). Included are:

- cultural, artistic, sporting, scientific, educational and entertainment services
- services relating to exhibitions, conferences and meetings
- services ancillary to the above
- the valuation of, or work carried out on, goods
- ancillary transport services.

Example 112	
(*a*)	A production company based in London asks a British actor to star in a play at a theatre in Madrid. The place of supply is Spain.
(*b*)	A German car company uses a British paint-spraying machine on the assembly line of its plant in the Netherlands but it has broken down. Engineers are sent to the Netherlands from the UK to repair it. The place of supply is the Netherlands.

Technically, it does not matter where the customer belongs.

However, the general attitude prevailing in the EC is a reluctance to register large numbers of foreign businesses.

Some member states, including the UK, allow the recipient of any international service to account for VAT using the reverse charge where the place of supply is their own country (see 12.40 below) but if such services are performed abroad, it is always advisable to check whether registration is required.

Exception (4) — Intangible, intellectual, professional services etc.

12.36 This category generally causes the most difficulty.

The place of supply of services under this heading is usually the place where the recipient belongs and the VAT itself is usually paid by the recipient using the reverse charge described at 12.37 and 12.40. Therefore, compliance becomes even more difficult because in order to establish whether VAT is payable, where, and by whom, it is necessary first to identify where the supplier and the recipient belong. The types of service under this heading are as follows (taken directly from *Schedule 5*):

'(1) Transfers and assignments of copyright, patents, licences, trademarks and similar rights.

(2) Advertising services.

(3) Services of consultants, engineers, consultancy bureaux, lawyers, accountants and other similar services; data processing and provision of information (but excluding from this head any services relating to land).

(4) Acceptance of any obligation to refrain from pursuing or exercising, in whole or part, any business activity or any such rights as are referred to in paragraph 1 above.

(5) Banking, financial and insurance services (including reinsurance, but not including the provision of safe deposit facilities).

(6) The supply of staff.

(7) The letting on hire of goods other than means of transport.

(7A) Telecommunications services, that is to say services relating to the transmission, emission or reception of signals, writing, images and sounds or information of any nature by wire, radio, optical or other electromagnetic systems, including the transfer or assignment of the right to use capacity for such transmission, emission or reception.

(8) The services rendered by one person to another in procuring for the other any of the services mentioned in paragraphs 1 to 7A above.

(9) Any services not of a description specified in paragraphs 1 to 8 above when supplied to a recipient who is registered under this Act.'

Paragraph 8 essentially covers the services of agents in arranging any of the main services.

The most common services in the list are advertising services; the services of professionals including consultants, lawyers and accountants; certain financial services and the supply of staff (see examples below).

There are two sets of circumstances under which these services are supplied where received:

(i) if they are performed for someone in business who belongs in a different EC Member State from the supplier, or

(ii) if they are performed for anybody, in their business or private capacity, who belongs outside the EC.

Example 113
(*a*) A UK based accountancy firm provides international tax advice to a French company considering expansion. The client company receives the service in a business capacity in a different member state from that in which the supplier belongs, therefore the place of supply is France and the French company would normally account for French VAT using the reverse charge (see 12.37). (*b*) A UK based accountancy firm provides personal tax services to a German businessman who has taken early retirement and plans to move to the UK. It can be argued that the client does not receive the service in a business capacity, therefore the service falls outside this category. If so, the supplier must charge and account for UK VAT.

If a supplier or customer has more than one business establishment, the one most closely associated with the service provided determines the place of supply (see 12.29).

Example 114
ABC Advertising has offices in London, Paris and Munich. A client company with offices in France, Germany and Spain has its headquarters in Lisbon from where ABC's London office receives instructions regarding proposed activities in the UK. The supply is effectively made from the UK to Portugal so the place of supply is Portugal.

Accounting for VAT on intangible, intellectual, professional services etc.

12.37 The recipient must account for VAT where he belongs if he is registered for VAT elsewhere in the EC using the reverse charge system (see 12.40). In *Example 113* above, the UK firm would invoice its French client without VAT and the client would convert the sterling value into French francs and pay French VAT on its own return, claiming the same amount back as input VAT subject to the normal rules.

Example 115
UK fee is £10,000 + no VAT

> The French client declares TVA on around FF100,000 at 20.6% (the current standard rate in France) and claims the same amount back as input VAT unless it is partly exempt.

Evidence of business status

12.38 Supplies of these services to business customers in other EC member states are not subject to UK VAT provided that evidence of business status can be made available to Customs.

The most obvious and acceptable evidence is the customer's VAT registration number which can be shown on the invoice, but if no number is provided alternative documentary evidence is usually accepted. Business status rather than VAT registration is the key to supplies being VAT free in the UK so it is possible to provide a service under this heading to a non-registered business customer in another EC country so long as alternative evidence of their status is kept.

No such evidence is required for customers belonging outside the EC because all services under this heading to those customers are free of UK VAT.

Services of a Schedule 5 type (intangible services etc.) supplied in connection with land

12.39 Professional services are often supplied in connection with land and property, such as those of architects, surveyors and lawyers. Where the services performed are directly connected with land and property, the first exception to the basic place of supply rule (see 12.31) overrides this exception for professional services etc. In such cases, the place of supply is where the land is physically situated and responsibility for paying VAT rests with the supplier, subject to national registration provisions and the extent to which the reverse charge is extended to services outside *Schedule 5* (see 12.40 below).

The reverse charge for imported services (s 8)

12.40 Until now, this section has concentrated on supplies of services provided by UK suppliers to customers belonging abroad. However, it is also important to consider the treatment of services bought in from foreign suppliers by UK customers. These are normally subject to the 'reverse charge' or 'tax shift' mechanism whereby the customer converts the purchase invoice into sterling (if not already in sterling), adds VAT and pays it as output tax on the appropriate return, then claims it back as input tax on the same return subject to the normal deduction rules.

The reverse charge applies to all services 'imported' into the UK where the place of supply is the UK.

Example 116
A UK VAT-registered client receiving services relating to land in France from a French solicitor would not account for UK VAT using the reverse charge. Instead, the French solicitor would account for French VAT in France and the UK customer would have to recover it using the international recovery procedure as described in Chapter 13. If the land were in the UK, the basic rule states that the French solicitor would be making a taxable supply here and have to register if his total taxable UK turnover exceeded the registration thresholds. However, Customs would normally allow the UK client to account for the VAT using the reverse charge mechanism.

If a UK business imports services which are zero-rated or exempt from VAT, the reverse charge does not apply.

All taxable services imported (positive or zero-rated) must be aggregated with other taxable turnover for the purposes of determining when to register (see Chapter 2). It is possible for a business to have to register as a result of the value of its imported services only, i.e. it may not make other taxable supplies in the UK but still be liable to register.

Foreign businesses applying the EC place of supply rules may identify a requirement for UK registration but the extended use of the reverse charge by Customs ensures the majority of UK VAT is paid by UK registered businesses, thus keeping a tighter rein on revenue control.

The time of supply of an imported service is the date payment is made or the last day of the tax period in which the services were performed if payment is not in money.

Other member states have also adopted this common sense approach but as has been stated, national legislation should always be checked for certainty.

Special treatment of telecommunications services

12.41 UK suppliers of telecommunications services may zero rate their services when supplied to a customer belonging outside the EC or to a business customer based in another EC member state. Supplies received by UK businesses from suppliers without a business establishment in the UK or not registered here are treated as within the UK and the recipient pays VAT using the reverse charge.

Where these rules are applied and it seems the supply is outside the UK, it is treated as inside the UK if the service is effectively used and enjoyed here. The converse also applies, i.e. if the rules suggest the supply is in the UK but use and enjoyment is outside the UK, no VAT is due. This means that where supplies are made by non-EC suppliers to final consumers (usually non-registered businesses or private individuals) in the UK, the supplier must register here and account for UK VAT.

The above provisions are covered by *para 7A* of *Schedule 5* to *VATA 1994* (see 12.36 above). The treatment of telecommunications services, which includes certain Internet services (see 12.42 below), has been the subject of continued debate at EC level.

Internet services

12.42 The rules at 12.41 do not affect services that are merely delivered via the Internet. It is the nature of those services that determines their VAT treatment, not their means of delivery. Also, the straightforward supply of Internet access, e-mail addresses and chatlines is a telecommunications service under *Schedule 5 para 7A*. The difficulty concerns the supply of more involved Internet packages. Typically, these packages could involve some or all of the following:

- access to the Internet and World Wide Web (www);
- one or more e-mail addresses;
- access to chatline facilities;
- web space to create one's own web-site or 'home page';
- access to specially prepared information pages such as those provided by AOL;
- access to on-line shopping;
- home banking facilities;
- games.

Sometimes the above are supplied for an all-inclusive price. This would still fall within *para 7A* of *Schedule 5*. However, it is possible for each part to be sold separately, in which case each part takes its normal VAT liability, e.g. weather and travel information would fall within *para 3* of *Schedule 5*. Although it appears that the effective VAT treatment of services falling within *paras 3* and *7A* of *Schedule 5* is the same, this is not so because of the special 'use and enjoyment' test applicable solely to telecommunications services as described in 12.41 above. Therefore, Customs have ruled that the use and enjoyment test does not apply to these Internet services.

Consequently, the treatment of these supplies by UK established Internet Service Providers (ISPs) is as follows:

- to UK customers — standard-rated
- to non-business customers in other EC member states — standard-rated
- to business customers in other EC member states — no VAT (ISPs should obtain proof of intended business use)
- to non-EC customers — no VAT

UK established business customers should apply the following principles:

Where a UK established business receives a package of these services and the ISP is not established in the UK, the former must pay the VAT using the reverse charge mechanism (see 12.40). Input tax is then recoverable subject to the normal rules.

The Sixth Directive, effective from 1977, does not allow for the considerable technological advances since then, so debate continues as to the correct and most effective way of taxing telecommunications, Internet transactions and E-commerce.

Chapter 13

Recovery of Foreign VAT

Introduction

13.1 From time to time, UK businesses incur VAT on expenditure in other member states of the EC, or even in countries outside the EC that have a VAT system, although they are not required to register there. Conversely, foreign businesses may incur VAT in the UK without being required to register here.

Under EC law (the EC Eighth and Thirteenth Directives), a system exists whereby this foreign VAT incurred may be recovered subject to certain conditions. This chapter covers the rules in general governing claims by UK businesses abroad and by foreign businesses in the UK and also examines specific rules relating to individual member states (*s 39* and *SI 1995/2518, Regs 185 to 197*).

The fundamental rule is that the claimant must not be registered, registrable or entitled to be registered for VAT in the country in which he is making the claim. Also, he must not have a place of business or other residence there and he cannot be making any supplies there apart from transport services in connection with the international carriage of goods or goods and services on which the VAT is payable by the recipient.

Each claim is made on a form available in all the official languages of the EC and, most importantly, must be completed in block capitals in the language of the country in which the claim is being made. The claim form is accompanied by a certificate of taxable status stamped by the VAT authorities in the claimant's country as proof to the authorities in the country from which he is claiming that he is VAT-registered. At one time, the originals of all invoices included in the claim had to be sent with the forms but, as a result of a court case, it has been decided that foreign businesses should be treated in the same way as nationals, meaning that as alternative evidence (such as authenticated copy purchase invoices) is accepted to support domestic input tax claims, it should also be accepted from foreign businesses.

How the claim procedure works

UK businesses claiming from other EC countries — general

13.2 The claimant must first ensure that he is not making taxable supplies in the country in which the expenditure has been incurred. He must then ensure Form VAT 65 or the relevant country's equivalent is completed in that country's accepted official language and currency. The form must be accompanied by the certificate of taxable status (Form VAT 66 in the UK) stamped by the local VAT office (if a UK registered business claiming abroad). Certificates are valid for 12 months but need only be sent with the first claim for that year.

The claim should be accompanied by the original purchase invoices and submitted within the specified time limits. The claimant should also ensure the type of expenditure is deductible in the first place and that the supplier has charged VAT correctly. Customs can normally confirm whether a foreign VAT number is valid and has been allocated to the business using it on the relevant invoice.

Non-deductible items

13.3 Foreign VAT can never be recovered on dispatches of goods but these are normally zero-rated anyway (see Chapter 11), or on designated travel services under the tour operators' margin scheme (see Chapter 10). The finer points of detail on what is deductible varies between member states and is covered below. There is also a minimum amount to be claimed which varies from country to country.

Time limits

13.4 The key deadline for all reclaims by UK businesses from other EC countries is 30 June each year, because all claims relate to calendar years and must be made within six months of the end of the year. Claims must normally be for at least three months but for no more than the full calendar year. However, the claim can be for less than three months if less than three months of the calendar year remains. The claims can be made by the claimant or by an agent, although a letter of authority from the claimant is normally required by the authorities before they accept agents' claims. In the UK, many professional firms act in this capacity and some businesses are established purely to provide this service. Agents' commissions are often calculated as a percentage of the refund obtained.

When refunds are received

13.5 Clearly, claims relating to a particular year can be submitted before the six-month time limit and usually are. Claimants normally benefit from submitting claims as early as possible because the tax authorities to whom they are made must make refunds within six months of receiving satisfactory evidence.

The method of refund is usually credit transfer in the currency of the authorities making the refund although some member states use payable order. If errors are found, the foreign authorities will usually seek recovery, often by offsetting the amount involved against future claims.

Foreign authorities can refuse claims but they must provide an explanation as to why. If the claimant disagrees, he may use the appeals process in the country in which he is claiming but cannot ask UK Customs to help him.

New anti-avoidance measure

13.6 A new anti-avoidance measure was introduced on 21 March 2000. Prior to that date, certain businesses not established for VAT in the UK recovered VAT on the purchase of capital assets in the UK through an Eighth or Thirteenth Directive reclaim. Thereafter, they sold them in the UK without having to register for VAT because such sales are ignored when determining whether the VAT registration threshold has been exceeded.

From 21 March 2000, such persons must register for VAT in the UK if they have claimed back VAT on relevant goods under the Eighth or Thirteenth Directive or intend to do so. The measure equally applies to VAT paid on imported goods and to goods supplied to the person claiming the refund as part of the transfer of a going concern. Where there is no intention to make such a claim, these new measures do not apply.

The requirement to register must be notified to Aberdeen VAT office on Form VAT 1C. Thereafter, the business must account for VAT on all taxable supplies it makes in the UK. If it ceases to make relevant supplies, it can deregister so long as it is not registrable under any other provision of UK VAT law. It may have to pay output tax on stocks and assets held at deregistration.

A new *Schedule 3A* to *VATA 1994* incorporates the new measures and *Schedule 4, paragraph 5* is extended to ensure free supplies of goods are covered if the supplier originally recovered input VAT through the Eighth or Thirteenth Directive. *VATA 1994, s 69* is extended to cover penalties for non-compliance with these measures.

Specific rules for each member state

General

13.7 The following paragraphs provide an outline as to procedures, minimum claims, non-deductible items and methods of repayment in each member state of the EC applicable to UK VAT-registered businesses making claims there. As Customs state in their Public Notice 723 on the subject, these are only guidelines so that claimants should check specifics with the relevant tax authorities.

Austria

13.8

Claim Form: U5

Authorities Address: Finanzamt Graz-Stadt, Referat für ausländische Unternehmer, Conrad von Hotzendorfstrasse 14-18, 8018 Graz, Austria, Tel: +43-316 88 10 34, Fax: +43-316 81 76 08.

Language: German.

Additional Non-Deductible Items: entertainment expenses, car hire, petrol.

Minimum Claim: AS500 for a whole calendar year or for the last period of a year, AS5,000 for a quarter or other period less than a year.

Time Limits: always observed.

Agents: must be authorised by claimant.

Method of Payment: credit transfer.

Appeals: within one month of refusal. The German for the appeal is 'Berufung'.

Belgium

13.9

Claim Form: available from the address below.

Authorities Address:

Dutch — Centraal BTW-kantoor voor buitenlandse belasting-plichitgen, Terruggaven Zaveltoren-25ste verdieping Stevensstraat, 7, 1000 Brussel, Tel: +32-2 5525977/5525982, Fax: + 32-2 5525542.

French — Bureau Central de TVA pour assujettis etrangers, Remboursement Tour Sablon-25ème étage Rue Stevens, 7, 1000 Bruxelles, Tel and Fax as Dutch.

Language: Dutch or French (in triplicate).

Additional Non-Deductible Items: entertainment expenses; manufactured tobacco; alcoholic drinks unless meant for resale or for provision as part of a supply of services; accommodation and food and drink for on the spot consumption unless the cost is incurred by staff supplying goods or services away from business premises or by a taxable person who supplies it on for a charge in money or kind; 50% of VAT incurred on a motor vehicle used in any way for passenger transport and on associated costs.

Minimum Claim: BF1,100, but BF9,000 for a period less than a year unless for the final period.

Agents: must be authorised by Power of Attorney. If the POA is in a form established in a state bound by the Hague Convention of 5 October 1981, it must be annotated according to the convention. If it is in the form of a private agreement established in Belgium, signatures must be certified by the authorities of the commune or authenticated by a Belgian notary. If it is in any other form, it must be authenticated by the relevant diplomatic or consular agent and the Belgian Ministry of Foreign Affairs.

Method of Payment: credit transfer to a postal account kept in Belgium or abroad by the claimant or his agent, or by transfer to a specific type of bank or financial institution, or by postal order or international money order.

Appeals: within two years of refusal. The options are a formal appeal by serving a writ against the Belgian authorities or an informal written request for reconsideration.

Denmark

13.10

Claim Form: R86 1

Authorities Address: Told-og Skatteregion Sønderborg, Hilmer Finsens Gade 18, 6400 Sønderborg, Tel: +45-74 12 73 00, Fax: +45-74 42 28 09.

Language: Danish.

Additional Non-Deductible Items: entertainment expenses, hotel expenses, car hire.

Minimum Claim: DKR200 but DKR1500 for a period less than a year unless for the final period.

Agents: must be authorised by claimant.

Method of Payment: credit transfer to bank or postal giro account.

Appeals: can be made to the Central Customs and Tax Administration (Told-og Skattestyrelsen) in Copenhagen.

Finland

13.11

Claim Form: available from the address below.

Authorities Address: Uundenmaan verovirasto, Yritsverotoimisto, PL 34, 00521 Verotus, Finland, Tel: +358-973 114311, Fax: +358-973 114392.

Language: Finnish or Swedish.

Additional Non-Deductible Items: entertainment expenses; motor cycles, caravans, private aircraft and related supplies; car hire, fuel and repairs.

Minimum Claim: FIM150 but FIM1,200 for a period less than a year unless for the final period.

Agents: must be authorised by claimant.

Method of Payment: credit transfer to bank or postal account in Finland or to bank account abroad.

Appeals: can be made to the Provincial Court of Uusimaa in writing. Appeal petitions to be submitted to the Provincial Tax Office within three years of the end of the calendar year to which the disputed decision relates.

France

13.12

Claim Form: available from the address below.

Authorities Address: Direction Générale des Impôts, Service de remboursements de la TVA aux assujettis établis a l'étranger, Centre des

Non-Résidents, 9 Rue d'Uzès, 75080 Paris Cedex 02, Tel: +33-144822540 or +33-144822541, Fax: +33-140410536.

Language: French.

Additional Non-Deductible Items: housing, hotel accommodation, lodging, entertainment and restaurant expenses; passenger transport and incidental activities; motor fuel (except diesel on which a proportion can be claimed if solely for business purposes); goods and services supplied free or well below cost except goods at very low value; services relating to non-deductible goods, e.g. car repairs.

Minimum Claim: FF170 but FF 1,400 for a period less than a year unless for the final period.

Agents: must be authorised by claimant.

Method of Payment: credit transfer to bank or postal giro account.

Appeals: details on how to appeal are available from the Paris address above.

Germany

13.13

Claim Form: available from the address below.

Authorities Address: Bundesamt für Finanzen, Friedhofstrasse 1, 53225 Bonn, Germany, Tel: +49-228 406 403, Fax: +49-228 406 661.

Language: German.

Additional Non-Deductible Items: food and accommodation expenses and costs incurred in respect of the travel element for staff vehicles. Furthermore, 50% of expenses relating to means of transport which are not used exclusively for the business is non-deductible as is 80% of VAT relating to business entertainment. Full details of business entertainment expenditure are required and proof that it was for business purposes. Without such details, none of the VAT on business entertainment expenditure can be claimed.

Minimum Claim: DM50 but DM400 for a period less than a year unless for the final period.

Agents: must be authorised by claimant.

Method of Payment: credit transfer to bank or postal account in Germany or abroad.

Appeals: a written request for reconsideration can be submitted or a formal appeal. The time limit is one month from receipt of the disputed decision if it was in writing or one year if not in writing.

Greece

13.14

Claim Form: available from the address below.

Authorities Address: Ministry of Finance, 14th Directorate of VAT and Indirect Taxes, Sina 2-4, 10672 Athens, Greece, Tel: +30-1 364 72 03, Fax: +30-1 364 54 13.

Language: Greek.

Additional Non-Deductible Items: non-business supplies; food, drink and tobacco products; hotel and other accommodation; entertainment, hospitality and amusements; acquisition, leasing or hire, modification, repair or maintenance of passenger motor vehicles, pleasure boats or private aircraft; transport of people who are VAT-registered or of members of their staff.

Minimum Claim: 46,000 Drachmas for a period less than a year unless for the final period in which case the minimum is 6,000 Drachmas, the same minimum that applies to claims for a full year.

Agents: must be authorised by claimant.

Method of Payment: credit direct to claimant's bank account or to an authorised agent.

Appeals: details of how to appeal are available from the Athens address above.

Ireland

13.15

Claim Form: available from the address below.

Authorities Address: The Revenue Commissioners, VAT Repayment Section, Government Buildings, Ennis, County Clare, Ireland, Tel: +353-65 412 00, Fax: +353-65 403 94.

Language: English.

Additional Non-Deductible Items: food and drink; hotel and other accommodation; personal services; entertainment expenses; purchase and hire of passenger motor vehicles; petrol; goods and services used for an exempt activity; goods for supply in Ireland or for hiring out for use in Ireland.

Minimum Claim: IR£19.40 but IR£155 for a period less than a year unless for the final period.

Agents: must be authorised by claimant.

Method of Payment: payable order (cheque) sent by post.

Appeals: can be made to the Revenue Commissioners and the courts. Appeals to the former should be made within 21 days of receiving the disputed decision. Appeals can then be made to the ordinary courts if there is still failure to agree.

Italy

13.16

Claim Form: available from the address below.

Authorities Address: Ufficio Entrate di Roma 6, Via Canton n. 20, 00144 Roma, Italy, Tel: +39-6 520 74217 or +39-6 520 90223, Fax: +39-6 520 39 07.

Language: Italian.

Additional Non-Deductible Items: non-business supplies; food and drink; hotel accommodation; travel; the acquisition or hire of passenger motor vehicles, motorcycles, pleasure boats or aeroplanes; all fuels for the above transport; luxury goods such as furs, sparkling wines and oriental carpets.

Minimum Claim: 25 Euro but 200 Euro for a period less than a year unless for the final period.

Agents: must be authorised by claimant.

Method of Payment: in lire to an account in the claimant's name at an Italian bank or post office.

Appeals: can be made to the Taxation Commission.

Luxembourg

13.17

Claim Form: available from the address below.

Authorities Address: Administration de l'Enregistrement et des Domaines, Bureau d'imposition XI, 17 Avenue Guillaume, BP 31, 2010-Luxembourg, Tel: +352 44 9051 (switchboard), +352 44 905455 (Bureau XI), Fax: +352 25 07 96 (Bureau XI).

Language: French.

Additional Non-Deductible Items: recreation and entertainment expenses.

Minimum Claim: 25 Euro but 200 Euro for a period less than a year unless for the final period.

Agents: must be authorised by claimant.

Method of Payment: credit transfer, cheque or money order in Luxembourg or abroad.

Appeals: can be made to the tax authorities or to the civil courts. If the latter option is chosen, the Director at the Luxembourg address must be notified within three months of the notification of refusal.

Netherlands

13.18

Claim Form: available from the address below.

Authorities Address: Belastingdienst/Particulieren/Ondernemingen buitenland, Postbus 2865, 6401DJ Heerlen, Netherlands. Tel: +31-45 573 66 66, Fax: +31-45 573 66 84.

Language: Dutch, but English, French and German also accepted.

Additional Non-Deductible Items: food and drink for immediate consumption in hotels, cafes, restaurants, boarding houses and similar establishments supplied to persons staying only a short time; goods and services connected with luxuries, amusements and entertainment; goods and services given as gifts to those who cannot recover all or most of the VAT that would have been charged as input tax; goods and services to be used for supplies to staff of housing, wages in kind, sport and recreation facilities, private transport, any other supplies for personal use other than food and drink.

Minimum Claim: NLG60 but NLG470 for a period less than a year unless for the final period.

Agents: must be authorised by claimant.

Method of Payment: credit transfer (or postal order on request) to a Dutch or foreign bank.

Appeals: can be made to the authorities within six weeks of receiving the disputed decision. If the final decision is still in dispute, a further appeal can be made within six weeks to the Tax Chamber of the District Court of Appeal.

Portugal

13.19

Claim Form: available from the address below and from specialist stationers, National Press bookshops and Public Treasury offices.

Authorities Address: Direcção-Geral das Contribuições e Impostos, Direcção de Serviços de Reembolsos do IVA, Avenida João XXI, Apartado 8220, 1802 Lisboa Codex, Portugal, tel: +351-1 795 01 02, Fax: +351-1 793 81 13.

Language: Portuguese.

Additional Non-Deductible Items: the supply, manufacture, importation or hire of private vehicles; petrol (although 50% of gas oil allowed); transport, business trips and tolls; accommodation, food, drinks, and tobacco; entertainment, amusements and luxuries.

Minimum Claim: ESC4,000 but ESC32,000 for a period less than a year unless for the final period.

Agents: must be authorised by claimant.

Method of Payment: payable order to the claimant or agent or by transfer to a Portuguese bank account where the claimant completes section 6 on the form.

Appeals: details available from the Lisbon address above.

Spain

13.20

Claim Form: available from the address below.

Authorities Address: Delegación Especial de Madrid de la Agencia Estatal de Administración Tributaria, Dependencia Regional de Gestión, Sección de Regimenes Especiales, C/ Guzman el Bueno, 139 Planta 1a, 28071 Madrid, Spain, Tel: +34-1 582 67 39, Fax: +34-1 582 67 57.

Language: Spanish.

Additional Non-Deductible Items: accommodation, meals and travel expenses unless deductible for personal and Corporate Income Tax purposes; entertainment expenses; car hire and fuel unless wholly for business purposes.

Minimum Claim: PTAS3,000 but PTAS25,000 for a period less than a year unless for the final period.

Agents: must be authorised by claimant.

Method of Payment: cheque or money order.

Appeals: details available from the Madrid address above.

Sweden

13.21

Claim Form: available from the address below or the Swedish Embassy in London.

Authorities Address: Särskilda Skattekontoret, 77183 Ludvika, Sweden, Tel: +46-240 870 00, Fax: +46-240 103 40.

Language: Swedish or English.

Additional Non-Deductible Items: entertainment expenses; transport unless wholly for business purposes; car hire although 50% allowable if wholly for business purposes.

Minimum Claim: SEK250 if for a year and SEK2,000 if for three months.

Agents: must be authorised by claimant.

Method of Payment: postal giro in Sweden, to a bank account in Sweden or abroad or to the claimant in Sweden or abroad.

Appeals: can be made to the Ludvika address above within two months of receipt.

United Kingdom

13.22

Claim Form: VAT 65 or 65A available from the address below, from main exhibition centres or from any local VAT office.

Authorities Address: HM Customs & Excise, VAT Overseas Repayment Unit, Custom House, PO Box 34, Londonderry, BT48 7AE, Northern Ireland, Tel: +44-1504 37 26 00, Fax: +44-1504 37 25 20.

Language: English.

Additional Non-Deductible Items: non-business supplies (an apportionment can be made where the supplies are used for a mixture of business and non-business purposes); goods and services for use in making UK supplies; purchases and imports of most ordinary business cars although 50% of the VAT is allowed on lease and hire charges where there is some business use; certain second-hand goods where no tax invoices are issued (see Chapter 9); entertainment expenses.

Minimum Claim: £16 but £130 for a period less than a year unless for the final period.

Agents: must be authorised by claimant by Power of Attorney or letter of authority.

Method of Payment: by SWIFT (Society for Worldwide Inter-Bank Financial Telecommunications), to a UK bank account held by the claimant or by payable order in sterling to the claimant or his agent. SWIFT is encouraged by Customs and to pay by this method, they require the following information:

- bank account number
- bank ID code (sort code)
- bank name and address, and
- account name
- a copy of a bank credit slip
- currency of account.

If the claimant prefers to be paid by payable order, it should be cashed at their own bank.

Appeals: can be made for reconsideration to the UK authorities that refused the claim within 30 days of receiving the decision. If the result is still unsatisfactory, an appeal to an independent Tribunal can be made within a further 21 days. Alternatively, an appeal can be made within 30 days direct to the Tribunal.

Claims in the UK by businesses from outside the EC

13.23 Businesses established outside the EC may claim a refund from the UK authorities for VAT they have incurred here (in accordance with the EC Thirteenth Directive). The conditions are:

(*a*) they must not be registered, registrable or be entitled to register in the UK;

(*b*) they must have no business establishment or residence anywhere in the EC; and

(*c*) they must not make any supplies in the UK (other than transport services related to the international carriage of goods, or services where VAT is payable in the UK by the person or business to whom the supply is made i.e. reverse charge services as described in Chapter 12).

The fundamental difference from the rules for businesses established elsewhere in the EC is that a 'reciprocity' rule applies. This means that the claimant's country must allow similar concessions to UK businesses as regards its own turnover taxes. However, the UK refund will only be disallowed if the claimant's country actually operates such a scheme but fails to allow UK businesses to use it.

There are certain items on which a refund is not allowed. These are the items always disallowed along with the additional items disallowed in the UK as described at 13.3 and 13.22.

The reference period and time limits

13.24 Claims must still be made no later than six months after the period to which the claim relates. However, the reference period for non-EC claimants is 1 July to 30 June rather than the calendar year. Hence, the deadline is 31 December.

Other specific rules

13.25 Non-EC claimants use Form VAT 65A to make their claims, rather than Form VAT 65 and instead of a certificate of taxable status accompanying the first claim in each reference period, the claimant must include a certificate from the official authority in its country confirming his registration for business purposes.

Recent developments concerning recovery of foreign VAT

13.26 The European Parliament has endorsed proposals to change the means by which EC businesses reclaim VAT incurred in other member states. If these proposals were adopted, the procedures described in this chapter would be abolished and businesses would be able to reclaim such VAT through their VAT returns. If, however, a UK registered business were to claim, for example, German VAT on its UK VAT return, there would have to be a mechanism for the UK Treasury to recover the amount paid to that business from the German Treasury. Although ideas for such a mechanism were studied, these plans have been shelved for the time being.

Chapter 14

Keeping Records and Accounts

Introduction

14.1 Every VAT registered person is required to keep such books and records as will enable Customs to verify any transaction affecting how much VAT is payable by him or refundable to him (*Sch 11 para 6*).

14.2 All activities that generate positive rated, zero-rated or exempt income must be recorded so that any visiting officer can verify output tax and partial exemption calculations, and confirm the right amount of input tax recoverable in any particular period.

14.3 There is no obligation to record income outside the scope of VAT but quite apart from the unsatisfactory situation which would result through having incomplete records, such income is best recorded within the VAT accounting system so that Customs can check and verify apportionment of input tax based on the split of taxable and non-business income.

14.4 Whilst the VAT law gives Customs the power to direct what records must be kept, those necessary to comply with other statutory obligations such as Companies and Direct Taxation Acts will usually be acceptable.

Statutory requirements are in *Sch 11 para 6* and *SI 1995/2518, Reg 31*. These are reproduced by Customs at Section 8 of Public Notice 700 'The VAT Guide' and in Leaflet 700/21 'Keeping Records and Accounts'. If a taxable person fails to keep records and accounts in a satisfactory manner, Customs have the power to direct him to keep any records they choose. Their requirements would be notified in writing.

General information required by Customs

14.5 As a general rule, Customs require all taxable persons to record all:

- positive rated, zero-rated and exempt supplies made,
- exports,

- gifts or loans of goods by the business,
- self-supplies,
- goods acquired or produced which are subsequently put to private or non-business use,
- imports, EC acquisitions and removals of goods from warehouses,
- services received from abroad subject to the reverse charge,
- purchases of goods and services on which VAT is charged,
- adjustments to accounts and invoices including details of credits allowed and received, and
- any other information which affects the amount of VAT payable to or recoverable from Customs.

The 'six year' rule

14.6 Acceptable records should generally be kept for six years, albeit there is a three-year cap on assessments other than in suspected fraud cases and on the permissible period for which VAT can be recovered. There is also a need to keep records supporting capital goods scheme calculations on relevant property for ten years (see Chapter 7).

The maximum period for which records are to be retained can be reduced if Customs so approve.

Records must be kept for the statutory or the agreed period even if the business is deregistered.

This is not the case for transfers of going concerns (see 14.11) and formal insolvencies.

Calculation of the 'six year' period

14.7 The following rules govern the commencement of the six-year period:

(*a*) For documents which record individual events such as tax invoices, the period starts from the date of issue whether or not the event has happened.

(*b*) For documents which summarise transactions such as the formal accounts of the business, the period starts from the date the document is prepared.

(*c*) For documents which record a series of events such as ledgers, the period starts on the date of the last entry in a bound book or the last entry on a loose-leaf record kept in a binder.

(*d*) Parts of records can be destroyed when they become six years old (e.g. pages of a sales day book) albeit the benefit of doing this is questionable and could create suspicion.

Example 117

On 30 September 2001 Mr Keepsake finds some old business records for which he has been looking. They consist of a notebook listing sales invoices on one page only and copies of the invoices themselves. He had recorded these separately between completing one sales daybook and buying another.

There are five invoices dated as follows:

26 September 1995
28 September 1995
31 October 1995
2 November 1995
5 November 1995

Mr Keepsake may throw away the two September 1995 invoices but the others should be kept for the time being. He may throw away the notebook on 5 November 2001 at the earliest.

Items falling within the definition of 'business records'

14.8 The following fall within the definition of business records:

- original purchase invoices and copy sales invoices
- retailers' records of daily gross takings such as till rolls
- official import entry documents and evidence of exports and EC sales
- 'relevant' business correspondence, notably correspondence with Customs
- copies of orders and delivery notes
- bank statements and paying-in slips
- records of purchases and sales (although for purchases, the strict requirement only covers records of purchases on which input tax is being reclaimed)
- appointment and/or job books and cards if applicable
- credit and debit notes
- the VAT account

- financial statements including profit and loss accounts and balance sheets.

The definition of business records and accounts has been disputed so far as it relates to management accounts. The definition includes financial statements but no specific mention is made of management accounts, albeit the checking process is normally made easier if they are available.

If any non-compulsory records are kept, it is usually advisable to have them available for a visiting officer to inspect so that he can confirm more easily whether or not the right amount of tax has been accounted for.

Computerised records

14.9 Customs require written notification if any business wishes to keep computerised records which must then be kept in a legible format enabling visiting officers to trace a clear audit trail.

Some Customs officers receive additional training in computerised accounting and, if they see fit, will visit a business which has notified its intention to use a computerised system simply to check that it meets with their approval and produces correct calculations of VAT payable and recoverable.

Some software systems are standard, off-the-shelf packages that have been examined by Customs before going on general sale but this does not necessarily mean they are automatically approved for every business. For example, the basic package may calculate VAT on a cash basis assuming use by small businesses operating the cash accounting scheme, whereas the user may be operating the invoice basis. So Customs will exercise discretion as to whether they wish to examine even the most basic systems.

Larger businesses usually have bespoke systems which Customs like to flowchart to ensure all necessary functions produce the correct result. For example, the system must obviously identify the correct VAT liability of all supplies of goods and services made and make sure non-deductible input tax is not reclaimed. The systems of some businesses, perhaps dealing with branches and complex activities, can cause difficulties for their own finance staff, so it is essential for them to agree clear guidelines and conditions with Customs officers, some of whom will only have a basic training, and where misunderstanding can be frustrating and time-consuming.

If there is any part of the system that threatens the accurate declaration of VAT due, Customs will notify the business and necessary modifications to the system must be made.

If a business wishes to issue computerised sales invoices, it must notify Customs in writing at least one month before the proposed start date.

Records on microfilm or microfiche

14.10 These are permissible provided that they can be read easily by visiting officers and copies can be made. Again, written authorisation is required and Customs have the power, if necessary, to refuse or withdraw permission for the protection of the revenue.

For storage purposes, some businesses transfer hard copy records onto microfilm or microfiche.

Even though Customs may on request allow records covering VAT periods within the last six years to be destroyed if they are satisfied there is no revenue threat, the obligation to keep records under other statutory requirements must not be overlooked.

Transfers of going concerns

14.11 The rules are explained at 2.10 and 2.16. When the transferee wishes to take over the VAT registration number of the transferor, Form VAT 68 must be completed and the transferor must hand over to the transferee all records enabling him to calculate VAT correctly.

If the business is partly exempt or is operating the capital goods scheme for relevant computer hardware or property, the transferee must have access to earlier calculations so that subsequent ones can be made accurately. All capital goods scheme adjustments are based on the input tax recovery percentage in the year the item was acquired so if, for example, the business is transferred seven years after the acquisition of a relevant building, the transferee must be given the calculations for those years so that he can calculate adjustments for years 8 to 10. This is especially important bearing in mind the requirement to keep general records for a maximum of only six years.

See 7.22 *et seq.* for a detailed explanation of the capital goods scheme.

The cash accounting scheme

14.12 Special record-keeping requirements apply to businesses operating the cash accounting scheme. These are explained at 15.27–15.35.

Making records available to Customs (Sch 11 para 7)

14.13 Traders who keep adequate records and who have complied with their statutory taxation obligations should not fear visits by VAT inspectors albeit there is usually some apprehension that they have not fully understood VAT law and could hence face a bill because of errors which they have made.

Customs officers have the power to examine any documents relating to goods supplied by a business and to the consideration for any supply of services provided. They can make copies or extracts of the documents and if necessary remove records at a reasonable time and for a reasonable period.

Unless the removal causes disruption to the ongoing business activities, there should normally be no reason to object to it, although the officer should issue a receipt listing exactly which records and documents have been taken. This should be signed by the officer and on behalf of the business.

Customs are entitled to access to all documentation relating to the acquisition of goods and their subsequent removal or sale and if the goods are still held by the business, Customs may inspect them at a reasonable time and in a reasonable manner. This includes taking samples. In order to verify the supply of services, Customs may have access to the name and address of the recipient.

Records kept by professional accountants

14.14 Customs will usually agree in these circumstances to carry out their inspection at the accountant's offices although they may wish to inspect the main business premises separately.

On occasions, Customs may see fit to remove the records from the accountant's premises. They have the power to do this but without prejudice to any lien that may be in place. Consequently, the records should be returned to the accountant and not his client when Customs' work is completed.

A detailed receipt for the records should be requested by the accountant.

If Customs remove records either directly or from the accountant and, for whatever reason, lose or destroy them, compensation should be available to the business involved.

Customs' power to take samples

14.15 Customs officers have the power to take samples of goods from a business or samples of materials which are used to make finished goods in a reasonable form and manner if it appears necessary to them to do so for the protection of the revenue. They do not have to return them but if they are not returned within a reasonable time and in a reasonable condition, compensation may be available which could equal or exceed the cost of the samples taken.

Customs' right of entry to inspect premises

14.16 An authorised Customs officer may, at any reasonable time, enter and inspect any premises where there are reasonable grounds for believing they are used for making taxable supplies of goods. This can include an individual's private residence. Once inside the premises, the officer may carry out inspections of goods as he sees fit.

It is normal for such officers to have written authority to carry out the inspection which the owner of the premises is entitled to see.

Search warrants

14.17 On rare occasions, officers may be issued with search warrants by a magistrate who, on the basis of information given on oath, suspects either that there has been a serious fraud or that evidence of an offence may be found on site.

The warrant specifies the person or persons authorised to make the search and gives the power to:

- seize and remove anything that could be used as evidence including goods, records and other documents;
- search anybody on site suspected of being involved in an offence;
- carry out the above within certain specified times.

The warrant may also indicate that the search may only be carried out in the presence of a uniformed police officer. A copy of the warrant is given to the owner or occupier of the premises.

Special Customs' powers to examine records in the case of suspected offences

14.18 Where Customs suspect that any VAT offence is being, has been or will be committed and they have evidence that key documents or records are held by a particular person, they may apply to a magistrate for an access order empowering them to examine the documents or records and take away any necessary extracts. If the order is granted, the action must be carried out within seven days.

Customs do not in their application have to stipulate the suspected offence but doing so is more likely to convince the magistrate that 'reasonable grounds' exist. Authorised persons within the Inland Revenue may act in similar situations even where they only suspect there might be an offence, whereas Customs must have reasonable grounds for their suspicions.

Since it has been known for Customs to act without reasonable grounds all parties should be aware of the restriction.

Summary of records required or helpful at a VAT visit

14.19 When a Customs officer arranges a routine visit, the following books, records and related documents should be available for inspection:

- certificate of VAT registration and certificate of incorporation if applicable
- all books and records covering the VAT periods being checked (usually all periods since the last visit)
- copy sales invoices and original purchase invoices
- orders and delivery notes
- any other working papers, computer print-outs etc. that will facilitate checking the VAT account audit trail
- relevant correspondence
- financial statements including management accounts.

Other Customs' powers affecting record-keeping and inspection

14.20 Apart from the powers explained earlier in this chapter, an authorised person has the power to:

(*a*) have the following produced for inspection at the trader's premises or off site:

(i) letters and other written documents,

(ii) maps, plans, graphs, drawings, photographs,

(iii) discs, tapes, sound tracks or similar devices,

(iv) film, microfilm, negatives, tapes for visual images;

(*b*) require a trader to account for the whereabouts of goods he has acquired in the UK, acquired from other EC Member States or imported from outside the EC (he may still have them in stock, have sold them, exported them or sold them to a customer in another EC country, put them to private use or they may have been lost or destroyed);

(*c*) have a gaming machine opened;

(*d*) commence prosecution proceedings against anybody who in any way prevents an officer from doing his job whether or not by physical means.

Additional requirements for particular trades, activities and special schemes

14.21 Most of the basic record-keeping requirements are contained within *Regulation 31(1)* of *SI 1995/2518*.

Regulation 31(2) gives Customs the power to set additional rules for particular types of trade, business activity and special scheme.

Retailers

14.22 Most retailers are unable to record and calculate VAT due on sales in the usual way because of the volume and mix of their supplies.

Hence there are special schemes for retailers. Following an overhaul of retail schemes, retailers may now choose from five methods of calculation as follows:

- 'point of sale' — where the liability is identified by separate till buttons for each rate of VAT or similar means;
- an apportionment of takings where goods are sold at different rates of VAT (two schemes); and
- 'direct calculation' based on recording estimated selling prices of goods purchased for resale (two schemes).

All of these schemes require an accurate record of daily gross takings (DGT).

Businesses with a tax exclusive turnover exceeding £10 million are not allowed to use one of the five standard schemes, and must agree a bespoke scheme with their local VAT office.

The definition of DGT is the total takings each day from taxable retail supplies, including all amounts as they are received by the business or on its behalf from cash customers, the full value including VAT of all credit and other non-cash retail sales at the time of supply, and details of any appropriate adjustments.

Technological advancement means that most tills today are electronic and sophisticated. Sometimes sufficient information for VAT purposes is shown on the tail of the till roll or 'Z' print but, before the main roll is discarded, Customs should approve that the 'Z' print information is acceptable.

In any case, full till rolls should be kept for three to six months and 'Z' prints for the full six years unless Customs formally approve a shorter period.

Where approval is given for retailers to keep 'Z' prints only, each one should be dated.

Public Notice 727 explains retail schemes in detail and Leaflets 727/3, 727/4 and 727/5 explain how to work the point of sale, apportionment and direct calculation schemes respectively.

Trading with other EC countries

14.23 Under certain circumstances, additional reports must be prepared by those who trade with other EC countries and submitted to the relevant Customs department. All businesses that sell and despatch goods to customers in other member states and send the goods there must complete summaries of such sales each calendar quarter (EC Sales Lists). Also those who bring in or send goods from or to other member states where the value either way exceeds £233,000 p.a. must complete supplementary declarations for Intrastat purposes. The threshold is increased from time to time. Further details are in Chapter 11.

Sometimes, it will be necessary to appoint a tax representative in a country in which taxable supplies are made but where the supplier does not have business premises (but see also 11.24). Tax representatives may act for more than one principal so it is important for them to keep a proper VAT account for each and supporting records that enable figures to be checked and verified by the relevant authorities. For UK VAT purposes, this applies to overseas businesses with tax representatives in the UK.

VAT account summaries should identify acquisitions of goods from other member states and the VAT should be entered in Box 2 of the VAT Return Form VAT 100. Input tax is then recoverable subject to the normal rules in Box 4. Net EC sales and acquisitions are then recorded in Boxes 8 and 9 respectively (see Chapter 15). All supporting documentation such as invoices, proof of export or acquisition, orders and delivery notes should also be kept.

The following additional records must be kept to support all temporary movements of goods:

Goods despatched

(*a*) materials sent to other member states for performance of processing work;

(*b*) goods sent to other member states for repair or alteration;

(*c*) goods moved to other member states for use in connection with supply of services to be performed in those states;

(*d*) goods sent to other member states under what would be temporary import relief conditions if the goods were imported from a country outside the EC.

Information required in the register:

(i) the date the goods were removed;

(ii) the date the goods are returned;

(iii) a description of the goods;

(iv) the reason for the movement (e.g. process work);

(v) the consideration for the supply, if applicable.

Goods received

(*a*) materials received for processing.

Information required in the register:

(i) the date the goods arrived;

(ii) the date the goods are returned;

(iii) a description of the goods;

(iv) the reason for the movement (e.g. process work);

(v) the consideration for the supply, if applicable.

Concessions for process engravers, typesetters and lithoplate makers

14.24 There are unique problems of record-keeping and liability for this type of business.

Traders are often required by their potential customers (notably advertising agencies) to produce specimens in large quantities.

The final product may or may not be zero-rated and the complex law on printed matter can be confusing and open to misinterpretation. It is normal practice for specimens to be kept only for a short time, which would cause traders VAT compliance problems unless a concession were available.

Customs have agreed a concession with the relevant trade association allowing specimens to be kept for a maximum of three months.

Unless written orders are received demonstrating that the goods will be used for a purpose which allows zero-rating, supplies must be standard-rated. Such orders must be cross-referenced clearly so that officers can easily verify liability.

Keeping records after deregistration

14.25 Businesses which deregister are normally bound by the six-year rule for keeping records except when the business is transferred as a going concern, in which case the transferee takes over the responsibility (see 14.11).

There is a special rule for company liquidations, the liquidator being able to dispose of records one year after the company was dissolved. If Customs wish them to remain in existence after that date, they are responsible for taking possession and arranging and paying for storage.

Authenticated receipts in the construction industry

14.26 These are frequently used in the construction industry, being prepared by those who have received and are paying for construction services. They become valid for VAT purposes once the supplier has signed and 'authenticated' the receipt. They are issued instead of, not as well as, tax invoices. The tax point is triggered by the receipt of the amount due.

Customs encourage main contractors to notify them in writing if they are unable to obtain authenticated receipts from recipients of their services on three consecutive occasions, following which they will normally instigate action against the recipient for breaching regulatory provisions on the issue of tax invoices.

Further details are in Chapters 3 and 8.

Banks

14.27 Special concessions apply to banks as regards the information required on tax invoices. The customer's account number can be inserted in place of their address and the sort code can replace the branch address. Also, this type of invoice need not carry a separate identifying number.

Margin schemes and global accounting

14.28 These are covered in depth in Chapter 9 including the rules regarding the keeping of records and accounts.

The tour operators' margin scheme

14.29 This is covered in Chapter 10 including the rules regarding the keeping of records and accounts.

Property managing agents

14.30 Property managing agents are involved in collecting rents on behalf of landlords. These are exempt from VAT except for commercial property rents where the landlord has exercised the option to tax (see Chapter 8). Three invoicing arrangements are permitted involving landlord, agent and tenant as follows:

- (i) the landlord issues a tax invoice to the tenant (either direct or via the agent);
- (ii) the landlord issues a tax invoice to the managing agent, who then issues a tax invoice to the tenant, in which case the landlord and agent both declare output tax and input tax is recovered by the agent and the tenant subject to their taxable status; or
- (iii) the landlord authorises his agent in writing to issue tax invoices on his behalf stressing clearly who is the principal and who is the agent in the arrangement — the landlord then receives copies of the tax invoices from his agent and declares the output tax thereon.

The third option applies whether the agent is using a manual or computerised accounting system.

Whatever the arrangement, VAT will be payable on the commission charged by the VAT registered agent who will issue an appropriate invoice. It is possible for non-registered agents to use the first or third type of arrangement above, but not the second.

Example 118

Reeves owns five commercial properties and has opted to tax all of them. The quarterly rent on each is £3,000 + £525 VAT. Mortimer acts as managing agent. On 24 June 2001, Reeves issues a tax invoice to Mortimer for £15,000 + £2,625 VAT to cover the five properties. Mortimer then issues five separate tax invoices for £3,000 + £525 on the same day from himself to each tenant.

Mortimer receives payment from one tenant on 1 July. He passes it on to Reeves less his 10% commission and issues a tax invoice to Reeves accordingly. The invoice to Reeves is for £300 + £52.50 VAT and the payment to Reeves is £3,172.50 (£3,525 rent including VAT less £352.50 commission including VAT).

Note that it would also be possible for both Reeves and Mortimer to issue requests for payment on 24 June, i.e. not tax invoices, then issue full tax invoices on receipt of payment under the continuous supplies of services rules (see 3.14).

Other special requirements

14.31 Other types of activity or scheme may also have special record-keeping requirements. If these are significant, they are covered in the chapter dealing with the particular scheme or activity.

Chapter 15

Completing VAT Returns

Introduction

15.1 VAT is a self-assessing tax.

Once a business is registered, it is the responsibility of the 'taxable person' (e.g. the sole proprietor, the partners, the directors etc. depending on the status of the business) to complete VAT returns and send them to Customs. Returns are handled in Southend, not by local offices. Only the return itself along with payment of the net tax due (if output tax exceeds input tax) should be sent to Southend.

The return form (VAT 100) is invariably sent out from Southend well in advance of the relevant period end. All VAT enquiries, whether or not relating to completion of the return should be addressed to the local office. If the business wishes to explain how certain figures have been arrived at, a letter should be sent to the local office, with accompanying schedules although, as a general rule, supporting schedules need not be sent with returns. The return figures themselves are available to local offices on a national computer network.

Tax periods

15.2 When a new business registers for VAT, it will receive a Certificate of Registration for Value Added Tax (Form VAT 4). This form includes information such as the trader's name; the name of the business if different; the address and the periods VAT returns will cover. These periods usually cover three months but in certain circumstances can cover one month, one year or non-standard periods previously agreed with Customs and usually based on quarterly accounting dates rather than month ends (*ss 25 and 96(1)* and *SI 1995/2518, Reg 25*).

Example 119

John Smith registers for VAT on 15 January 2001. If he is to complete returns for the quarters ending March, June, September and December, his Form VAT 4 would say 'Returns to be made in respect of period ending 31 March and quarterly thereafter'. So the first return would cover the period 15 January to 31 March 2001 and ensuing returns would cover the full quarter.

Quarterly returns

15.3 VAT returns cover a 'tax period' or 'prescribed accounting period' (*s 25*). The vast majority of businesses make only or predominantly standard-rated sales and therefore, because they exist to make a profit, their output tax will normally exceed their input tax. These businesses usually complete returns every three months. There are three possible 'staggers' for quarterly returns ending:

- 31 January, 30 April, 31 July and 31 October,
- 28 (or 29) February, 31 May, 31 August and 30 November, or
- 31 March, 30 June, 30 September and 31 December.

When Customs receive new applications for registration, they allocate the staggers evenly to ensure there is not an excessive workload in processing returns for any particular one. However, businesses may apply for a specific stagger if it suits their requirements. This can be done in writing either when the application for registration is submitted or at any later date if there is a valid reason for changing from the existing stagger. For example, many businesses prefer to align their stagger with their accounting date, but it may also be possible to choose a stagger which ensures there is no unreasonable delay in a one-off large input tax claim.

Monthly returns

15.4 Some businesses such as supermarkets, booksellers or exporters have mainly zero-rated income. It is quite normal for their input tax (for example on standard-rated overheads) to exceed output tax. 'Repayment traders', as they are known, may ask Customs' permission to complete monthly returns in order to receive their repayments quicker and improve cash flow. Permission is rarely denied.

Payment traders may also request monthly returns if they so wish but only in exceptional circumstances will this happen because payments would be due earlier than if quarterly returns were made.

Customs have the power to vary the length of tax periods but will only do so in exceptional circumstances where it appears necessary to protect the revenue, e.g. they may cancel approval for a repayment trader to complete monthly returns and instruct him to revert to quarterly returns if he has failed to comply with other areas of VAT law. It would appear that these decisions cannot be appealed to a Tribunal.

Tax periods of other length

15.5 There are two other types of return period:

(1) *Non-standard tax periods* — these still cover more or less a three-month or one-month period but end on the accounting dates used by the registered business, e.g. if management accounts are prepared to 25 March, 24 June, 29 September and 25 December, Customs will normally on written application by the business allow VAT return periods to end on those dates rather than 31 March, 30 June, 30 September and 31 December. Accounting dates may vary each year if they are based on a number of weeks (usually 13) so the non-standard tax periods for VAT returns should also be reviewed annually and agreed with Customs in such cases.

(2) *Annual VAT returns* — these can be used by businesses whose taxable turnover excluding VAT is less than £600,000 (from 1 April 2001, previously £300,000). The procedure is known as the 'annual accounting scheme' and is explained further at 15.36 *et seq.*

Certain businesses which have larger net amounts due to Customs are required to make monthly payments on account even though they still complete returns covering the normal periods. This is covered in more detail at 15.46.

Time limits

15.6 A VAT return must be submitted within one month after the end of the tax period to which it relates. This is called the 'due date' and it is always specified on the return form to avoid any doubt. Customs accept a return is 'on time' if payment is sent first class at the latest one day before the due date or second class two days before. It is essential to send any payment due on time to avoid being in default. If the return is on time and the payment is late, a default has occurred which counts towards the default surcharge system.

Example 120

Just in Time Ltd filed its last four VAT returns as follows:

12/00 — sent 1st class on 30 January 2001 with payment
03/01 — sent 2nd class on 29 April 2001 with payment

06/01 — sent 1st class without payment on 24 July 2001; payment sent 8 August 2001
09/01 — sent 2nd class on 29 October 2001 with payment

Payments for 12/00 and 09/01 are on time but 03/01 is one day late and 06/01 is eight days late. Customs may ignore the 03/01 default, especially if it were the company's first default, but the second would be penalised as described below and in Chapter 16.

After one default, a surcharge liability notice is sent by Customs which effectively constitutes a warning. A further default within the next year is then subject to a surcharge of 2% of net tax due. Subsequent defaults increase in severity to a maximum of 15%. Default surcharges and other penalties are covered in Chapter 16.

It is the responsibility of the registered person to ensure payments are punctual. It is no excuse if, for example, a sole proprietor is out of the country generating new business on the due date. He must make arrangements for the return to be sent with any payment due by the due date. The one month allowed from the end of the tax period is considered sufficient for such arrangements to be made.

It may be that certain vital information is still not available one month from the end of the tax period, so that accurate figures cannot be entered on the return. If this happens, the taxpayer must ask the local VAT office for permission to use estimates, which will be allowed if Customs agree accurate figures could not be obtained. Where a return showing agreed estimated figures is sent to Southend with any payment by the due date, there is no default but if the request to use estimated figures is not made until after the due date, the taxpayer is in default.

As soon as actual figures are available, an adjustment must be made.

The time limits for submission of a VAT return are identified on the Form VAT 100 itself and should not be amended by the taxpayer. Any changes to the figures initially entered in the various boxes may be altered and initialled but information provided by Customs should not be changed, e.g. the dates covered by the return; the due date; sections marked 'for official or office use only'.

How to pay

15.7 The most attractive method of payment for the taxpayer is the credit transfer system. Electronic methods of payment such as the Bankers Automated Clearing System (BACS), the Clearing House Automated Payment System (CHAPS) or Bank Giro Transfer provide an extra seven days from the normal due date for the payment to be considered as on time. Payment by cheque or postal order is also acceptable but this does not give the extra seven days' grace.

Most businesses submitting VAT returns with a due date on or after 31 May 2000 have an extra seven days to pay the amount due to Customs if they submit them electronically. The time extension is not available to businesses paying VAT on account or to those using the Annual Accounting scheme. Most using the Payment on Account method already pay electronically and those using the Annual Accounting scheme get extra time to pay anyway.

The concession is offered on a return-by-return basis offering businesses the chance to change payment methods when they wish. However, if they revert to paying by cheque, they will no longer receive the extra seven days. Business Brief 21/2000, 23 May 2000 refers.

Death

15.8 The last tax period for a sole trade ends on the date of death and a new tax period starts on the following day if the assets of the business are taken over by another person intending to carry on the same business. The personal representatives will usually do this, even if only temporarily.

Final returns

15.9 When a business ceases to be registrable for VAT for whatever reason, an effective date of deregistration is agreed with Customs as explained in Chapter 2. The VAT return for the final period from the normal start of the period to the deregistration date is not submitted on Form VAT 100. Form VAT 193 is used instead and provides a separate box for declaration of output tax on assets on hand at deregistration where the VAT thereon exceeds £1,000.

The VAT account

15.10 Every business registered for VAT must keep a 'VAT account'. This is a summary of all VAT payable for the period including output tax adjustments on items such as credit notes issued and VAT on fuel scale charges; and a summary of all VAT refundable to the business including necessary adjustments, for example, refunds of VAT on bad debts.

The summary should be kept in a file or in a similar place so that it can be made available to a Customs officer on request. Normal procedure is for working papers to be kept in a separate file along with copies of completed VAT returns. Working papers should not be sent to Customs with returns and payments.

Example 121

Sample VAT account for period 09/01:

Output tax	£
Sales July 2001	20,500
Credits July 2001	(2,250)
Sales August 2001	18,360
Credits August 2001	(1,120)
Sales September 2001	24,600
Credits September 2001	(2,800)
Sub-total	**57,290**
Plus fuel scale charge	200
Total	**57,490**

Input tax	£
Purchases July 2001	12,350
Credits July 2001	(1,100)
Purchases August 2001	14,230
Credits August 2001	(1,670)
Purchases September 2001	13,770
Credits September 2001	(850)
Sub-total	**36,730**
Plus bad debt relief	2,625
Total	**39,355**

Net payment due to HM Customs & Excise £57,490 – £39,355 = **£18,135**

Net outputs — **£328,514**

Net inputs — **£224,885**

Declaration

15.11 Each VAT return must be signed and dated by an authorised person such as the sole proprietor, a partner or a director (or another person approved by Customs in writing to do so, e.g. a company secretary). By signing, the signatory is declaring that the return is true and complete. The form does not even contain a phrase such as 'to the best of my knowledge' so it is arguable that initial accuracy is even more important in order to avoid the risk of financial penalties. Some consider the declaration should include a reference to the best of one's knowledge because a subsequent voluntary disclosure of errors found would imply that the taxpayer knew the initial declaration was false, but Customs are unlikely to adopt that interpretation.

A box by box guide to the completion of the return is contained in paragraphs 15.12 – 15.26.

Box 1

15.12 The legend for this box states: 'VAT due *in this period* on sales *and other outputs*'. The stress has been added to demonstrate the most likely areas where errors could occur. Firstly, the output tax to be included in this box is that which falls due in the period covered by the dates at the top of the form. For example, businesses accounting for VAT on the accruals or invoice basis should include the amounts shown on invoices dated within the period whether or not payment has been received. Those operating cash accounting must account for the VAT on payments received during the period and ensure they can be cross-referred to the original sales invoices. Cash accounting is explained further from 15.27.

The words also include 'and other outputs' so the taxpayer must remember to include the less obvious areas which generate output tax such as:

- takings from machines kept on site, e.g. vending machines, laundry facilities — in the case of vending machines, the supplier usually empties it regularly and gives the user a slip showing output tax due
- canteen takings
- fuel scale charges
- asset sales
- hire or loan of goods to others
- individual business gifts costing more than £15 excluding VAT
- standard-rated income from any miscellaneous business activity carried out by the same business during the period
- services imported from abroad where the reverse charge applies (see Chapter 12)
- self-supplies e.g. stationery (see VAT Leaflet 706/1; the self-supply of stationery only affects partly exempt businesses), construction services

- sales of goods to businesses in other EC Member States which are not registered for VAT or do not supply their registration number if they are registered
- goods taken out of the business for private use
- purchases under the gold scheme (which operates in a similar way to the reverse charge and EC acquisitions in that the purchaser accounts for output tax on relevant purchases of gold and claims the same amount back as input tax subject to the normal rules).

The total in Box 1 would be reduced by the VAT on any credit notes falling within the period. Again, the credit note date would apply unless the cash accounting scheme were applied, in which case, the refund date would apply. Further adjustments would be necessary if the taxpayer had found net errors of less than £2,000 in Customs' favour on previous returns which may be corrected on a later return. If net errors exceed £2,000, a separate voluntary disclosure should be made to Customs either by letter or on Form VAT 652. Special rules apply to retailers using a retail scheme to calculate output tax, each scheme having its own explanatory leaflet available from local VAT offices. Any additional amounts of tax notified by Customs as due, e.g. by assessment, should not be included.

Example 122

The following relate to period 12/01:

1. Output tax due — £27,582.13
2. Fuel scale charges due — £416.91
3. Output tax underdeclared in period 09/01 — £1,934.56
4. Assessment received re period 03/00 — £2,978.72 (sale of lorry for £20,000 deemed to be VAT inclusive)

1–3 are included in Box 1 of the 12/01 return (note that the underdeclaration discovered in period 09/01 is less than £2,000) but the assessment is excluded and paid separately.

Box 2

15.13 VAT due on goods acquired from other EC Member States should be entered in Box 2. This effectively works in the same way as the reverse charge for imported services although output VAT under the reverse charge is aggregated with normal output tax in Box 1. When a UK purchaser acquires goods from a supplier in another member state, he must give his UK VAT registration number to the supplier who shows it on his sales invoice preceded by GB. The supplier's own registration number is preceded by the two-letter code for the country in which he is established. Intra-community trade is covered in greater detail in Chapter 11.

If the UK purchaser does not give the supplier his registration number, the supplier must charge his own country's VAT and the UK purchaser would have to claim a refund from the VAT authorities in the supplier's country subject to the conditions described in Chapter 13.

Example 123

A Dutch company supplies goods to a VAT registered UK purchaser who in turn supplies his registration number. The Dutch invoice should show the supplier's registration number with the prefix 'NL' e.g. NL 1234 56 789 B14 and the customer's with the prefix 'GB' e.g. GB 602 1121 20 for the supply to be free of Dutch VAT. If the value were, say, NLG 9,000, the customer would convert it to sterling using the accepted rate of exchange (say, NLG 3 to £1) and add UK VAT at 17.5%. Therefore, VAT would be due on £3,000 i.e. £525. The UK customer would enter this amount in Box 2 of his next VAT return and add the total to output tax in Box 1. The tax point is the 15th day of the month following that in which the goods were despatched.

15.14 Only VAT on acquisitions of goods from other EC Member States is entered in Box 2. VAT on imported services calculated using the reverse charge mechanism is aggregated with other output tax in Box 1. In both cases (imported services and EC acquisitions), the amount calculated and paid as output tax may also be recovered as input tax in Box 4 subject to the normal rules such as a restriction if the UK purchaser is partly exempt.

Box 3

15.15 This is simply the figures in Boxes 1 and 2 added together (unless one of the entries is negative in which case Box 3 would be the difference between Boxes 1 and 2). Businesses which do not buy goods from other EC countries will simply enter the same figure in Boxes 1 and 3, and enter 'none' in Box 2.

Box 4

15.16 The entry in this box is all the VAT in the particular tax period that the business is claiming back from Customs, not just input tax on normal purchases and expenses. The entry also includes VAT on imports of goods from outside the EC, removals of goods from warehouses or free zones and the amounts also paid in Box 2 as output tax on EC acquisitions, imported services and gold purchases under the gold scheme unless the business is partly exempt, in which case the input tax would normally be less than the corresponding output tax.

Bad debt relief

15.17 Adjustments under the refunds for bad debts provisions should also be entered in Box 4. If the business is claiming relief for a six-month-old supply on which it has paid output tax but has not received payment from its customer, it can be claimed as additional input tax. Conversely, if the business has not paid a six-month-old debt owed to a creditor who has sent notification that he is claiming relief, it must reduce input tax by the amount originally claimed on the supply.

Non-deductible items

15.18 When compiling the 'VAT deductible' side of the VAT account, businesses should always ensure they exclude VAT paid on non-deductible items such as:

- new cars bought for the business on which input tax may not be reclaimed if there is any private use whatsoever
- business entertainment
- non-business purchases
- goods bought under one of the second-hand margin schemes — the supplier does not issue a tax invoice and declares output tax on the difference between his buying and selling price (see Chapter 9)
- private accommodation costs of directors of limited companies.

Businesses should remember to include in Box 4 input tax paid on imported services and goods acquired from other EC Member States, output tax on which should have been declared in Boxes 1 and 2 respectively. Partly exempt businesses may not be able to recover all the output tax paid as input tax.

Miscellaneous issues concerning Box 4

15.19 Where input tax has previously been recovered on goods or services received by a business but it later transpires that there has been a genuine mistake or overcharge, the supplier issues a credit note. Unless both parties agree that VAT accounts will not be adjusted, the purchaser must reduce his Box 4 entry by the amount of VAT shown on credit notes received during the relevant period.

Businesses using the cash accounting scheme should ensure they only enter in Box 4 VAT on amounts they have paid their suppliers during the relevant period, provided of course the payments relate to positive rated supplies in the first place and can be cross-referred to tax invoices issued by suppliers.

Payments under assessments issued by Customs and amounts owed by Customs should not be included, but if errors are discovered when completing the return and the net amount of VAT involved is less than £2,000 in the taxpayer's favour, it can be included with other input tax in this box. Net errors in the taxpayer's favour exceeding £2,000 should be notified to Customs on Form VAT 652 or by letter. Input tax which is not claimed in the tax period in which it was incurred may still be claimed in a subsequent period and qualify as tax for that period subject to the three-year cap.

Special rules apply to certain types of business. For example, builders may not recover input tax on certain fixtures and fittings; tour operators may not recover input tax on bought-in margin scheme supplies (see Chapter 10); and businesses operating the margin scheme for sales of second-hand goods may not recover input tax on goods bought for resale (see Chapter 9).

Box 5

15.20 This box is for the net payment due to or from Customs for the period. The amount to be entered is the difference between Boxes 3 and 4. If a payment is due and enclosed with the return, the separate box indicating that fact should be ticked.

If reductions in output or input tax are such that the total for the period is negative, the entry in Boxes 1, 2, 3 or 4 as appropriate should be in brackets. In such cases, where one of Box 3 or 4 is negative, the two figures should be added together.

Example 124

Period 07/01

Box 3 — £5,874.21

Box 4 — £3,211.78

Box 5 — £2,662.43 (due to HM Customs & Excise: Box 3 – Box 4)

Period 10/01

Box 3 — £6,382.55

Box 4 — (£158.79)

Box 5 — £6,541.34 (due to HM Customs & Excise: Box 3 + Box 4).

Box 6

15.21 This entry may not seem so important but it should be accurate so that Customs can make certain checks such as whether all sales within the period were standard-rated. The figure should be all outputs falling within the period less the VAT itself, including the following:

- standard or reduced rated sales to UK customers excluding VAT
- zero-rated sales including exports and sales of goods to customers in other EC countries who have provided their VAT number for inclusion on the sales invoice
- exempt supplies
- sales to customers in other EC countries on which VAT has been charged (perhaps because they are not VAT registered) excluding the VAT
- the value on which VAT has been paid under the reverse charge mechanism (value means the total received less the VAT)
- the value of supplies which are outside the scope of UK VAT but on which associated input tax is deductible
- deposits invoiced excluding VAT
- the value of goods belonging to the business which are transferred to another EC country
- the value of supplies to customers in other EC countries on sale or return.

Box 8 is for sales of goods and related services such as freight and insurance charges to customers in other EC countries only but the Box 8 figure is also included in the Box 6 total.

Box 7

15.22 Net inputs are shown in Box 7. That is, expenditure for the period on positive rated, zero-rated and exempt items excluding any VAT paid. This includes the value of imports, acquisitions of goods from other EC Member States and the value of imported services.

Box 9 is set aside specifically for the value of acquisitions of goods and related services (see 15.25) from other EC Member States but the figure should also be aggregated with other inputs in Box 7.

In all cases, the following items should be omitted from Box 6 or 7 in accordance with VAT Leaflet 700/12 Section 3:

- the VAT itself
- wages and salaries
- PAYE and national insurance contributions
- money put into and taken out of the business by the owner
- loans, dividends, and gifts of money
- insurance claims
- Stock Exchange dealings (unless the business is a financial institution)
- MOT certificates
- motor vehicle licence duty
- local authority rates
- income which is outside the scope of VAT because it is not consideration for a supply.

If credit notes have been issued by suppliers during the period, the value net of VAT should be taken off the total but if cash discounts have been received, they should not be taken off. If it is the practice of the business to record amounts after the deduction of cash discounts, Customs require a reasonable amount to be added back for VAT statistical reporting purposes.

Box 8

15.23 This box is for recording the value of supplies of goods and related services to other member states of the EC. However, it is not totally restricted to sales because the value of goods despatched to other member states must also be included even if the recipient of the invoice is based outside the EC or if no actual sale is involved.

Other items to be included are:

- the value of new means of transport supplied to non-registered customers in other EC countries
- the value of goods sent to other EC countries for installation or assembly there.

Process work performed on goods in the UK is excluded because it is treated as a supply of services.

Distance sales

15.24 If sales to non-registered customers in other member states under the distance selling provisions have exceeded the destination country's distance selling registration threshold, values should be included in Box 8 (and the seller would normally be required to register for VAT in the destination country). However, if such sales are still below the distance selling registration threshold for any particular country, the values are omitted from Box 8 because UK VAT is actually charged and sales are treated in the same way as sales to UK based customers.

Distance sales are explained in detail in Chapter 11.

Box 9

15.25 In a similar way to the rules for Box 8, entries in Box 9 are not confined to purchases from VAT registered suppliers of goods in other EC Member States. Values must be entered even if there is no actual purchase made and if the business invoiced is based outside the EC but the goods have started their journey in another member state.

The special rules for acquisition tax points are explained at 3.22 and 11.3. Goods acquired from other member states for installation or assembly in the UK should be included but process work on goods carried out in other member states is excluded as the supply is treated as a service.

Final checks

15.26 There are a number of checks that can be applied to ensure, to the best of one's ability, that the figures entered on the return are correct. For example, if there is an entry in Box 9 indicating that there have been acquisitions of goods from other EC Member States in the period, there should obviously be a figure in Box 2 for the VAT itself on those acquisitions. Also, if the business only has standard-rated income, Box 3 would normally be 17.5% of Box 6. It is also helpful to double check that allowable bad debt relief has been claimed, net errors of less than £2,000 from previous returns have been included, and adjustments have been made for credit notes issued and received unless both parties have agreed not to adjust the VAT.

The taxpayer should ensure that where no entry is required in any of the Boxes, the word 'none' is inserted. An authorised person (usually the sole proprietor, a partner or a director or any other person the business has authorised so long as Customs have been informed in writing), should ensure they have signed and dated the declaration and printed their name, putting the VAT registration number to which the payment relates on the cheque to Customs if payment is made by that means.

A copy of the return should also be kept and filed with working papers showing how totals have been calculated. This is usually the starting point for Customs officials when making a routine inspection.

The cash accounting scheme (SI 1995/2518, Regs 56 to 65)

15.27 Unless special rules apply, most businesses must use the 'accruals' or 'invoice' method to determine the time when VAT is payable or recoverable. Cash businesses such as retailers account for output tax on the receipt of cash unless, for any reason, an invoice is issued earlier, but purchases for resale and other expenditure are normally covered by credit terms e.g. 30 days for payment, so they reclaim input tax based on the date of the invoice rather than the date of payment. Therefore, a business using the invoice method would pay output tax and recover input tax in any given tax period on all invoices showing tax points falling within the dates shown at the top of the return form.

However, businesses with an annual taxable turnover of less than £600,000 (from 1 April 2001, previously £350,000) may opt for the cash accounting scheme whereby output tax is only payable when payment is received although input tax may only be recovered when purchase invoices are paid. In addition to the obvious cash flow advantage, use of the scheme means output tax is not paid on debts that could become bad.

Example 125

Sales Invoice Date	Payment Received Date	Output Tax	Purchase Invoice Date	Payment Made Date	Input Tax
01/03/01	30/04/01	£1,501	27/02/01	01/04/01	£500
15/03/01	30/03/01	£2,010	28/02/01	31/03/01	£750
22/03/01	22/04/01	£2,350	02/03/01	15/04/01	£1,000
29/03/01	01/07/01	£5,010	31/03/01	31/03/01	£1,500
01/04/01	30/06/01	£4,010	31/03/01	31/05/01	£1,200
Totals		**£14,850**			**£4,950**

The above trader completes VAT returns covering the quarters ending 31 March, 30 June, 30 September and 31 December. Comparing the results for quarter 03/01 under the invoice method of accounting and the cash accounting scheme:

(1) *Invoice method*

Output tax is due on all invoices dated 1 January to 31 March 2001 inclusive. So output tax due is £10,850 because the 1 April invoice falls in the 06/01 quarter.

All of the purchase invoices fall within the relevant dates so £4,950 input tax is recoverable.

Therefore, the net payment due to Customs is £10,850 – £4,950 = £5,900.

(2) *Cash accounting scheme*

Output tax is due on all payments received within the relevant dates. In this example, payment is only received for the second invoice so output tax due is £2,000. Output tax of £5,000 on the fourth invoice will not be due until quarter 09/01 because payment was delayed until 1 July and the same would have applied to the fifth invoice if it had been paid one day later, so the person responsible for credit control could play a key role in cash flow control in that whilst chasing payment it would be advantageous to ask the customer to wait a little longer if settlement is imminent and borderline between tax periods.

Input tax is recoverable on payments made within the relevant dates. The first invoice was paid a day too late to be included so only the second and fourth invoices can be included. So input tax recoverable is £2,250.

Therefore, the net repayment due from Customs is £2,250 – £2,000 = £250.

(3) *Cash flow saving achieved by using the cash accounting scheme*

In this case, the cash flow saving on the March 2001 return is £5,900 + £250 = £6,150.

How the cash accounting scheme works

15.28 The scheme can be particularly advantageous if customers regularly pay late but the scheme user pays suppliers' invoices earlier. If customers pay by return or, say, always within the 30 days allowed, there is no real benefit in using the scheme.

Any VAT registered business may opt for the cash accounting scheme provided that taxable turnover excluding VAT in the 12 months from the date of the option is not expected to exceed £600,000 (from 1 April 2001, previously £350,000). Once the business has opted to use the scheme, it must normally be continued for at least two years. There is a 25% tolerance built into the scheme so that users need not leave it as soon as their taxable turnover exceeds the joining threshold, but they must leave it once taxable turnover has exceeded £750,000 (from 1 April 2001, previously £437,500) in the last 12 months.

Normally, an eligible business will not be denied the use of the scheme so long as all conditions for using it are fulfilled. Customs do have the power to refuse use of the scheme (e.g. because of a poor compliance history) but they rarely exercise it even when return payments have been late and default surcharges have been applied.

Full details about the scheme are in VAT Public Notice 731 'Cash Accounting'.

Conditions for using the scheme

15.29 Apart from the turnover limits and two-year minimum period already explained, users must keep additional records to those normally required for the invoice method. A fully analysed cash book must be kept showing details of payments received and payments made. There must also be a clear cross-reference system allowing a visiting officer to trace payments back to the relevant sales or purchase invoices. The invoice requirements and the tax points are the same. It is only the actual payment or recovery of the VAT involved that is delayed.

The scheme must be used for the whole of the business covered by the VAT registration number (subject to the exclusions in 15.33 and 15.35). This may influence the decision whether or not to use it, especially if there is more than one source of taxable income and not all involve credit sales.

If a computer is used for accounting purposes, the software must also facilitate the correct record-keeping requirements.

When a business starts to use the scheme, it must be from the start of a tax period. It must prepare a separate schedule of all sales and purchase invoices on which output tax has been paid and input tax claimed in earlier tax periods but on which payment has not yet been received or made. These are excluded from the totals in the first return under the cash accounting system so as to avoid duplication of output tax payments and input tax claims. Similarly, schedules must be prepared when the business leaves the scheme so that VAT on unpaid invoices dated before the scheme ended is brought into account in the next period.

The most important other condition is that all purchase invoices settled in cash by a business using the scheme must be receipted and dated by the supplier when payment is made. This condition does not apply to cheque payments. When sales invoices are paid by customers who are themselves using the scheme, the sales invoices must be receipted and dated on request and a copy kept.

When an amount is 'received'

15.30 It is not always obvious when an amount is received because of the different methods of payment available. Clearly, cash is received on the date the money is physically received by the payee. However, a cheque is received on the date shown on it or the date it is received by the payee, whichever is the later. Cheques which are not honoured do not constitute payment so the payee using the scheme need not account for output tax, but if the tax has already been brought into account, the VAT account may be adjusted accordingly.

Credit card payments are made on the date the voucher is made out, not on the date payment is received from the card company. Direct debits, standing orders and bank giro credits are received on the date they are credited to the relevant account. If a deposit is a positive rated supply for VAT purposes, output tax is due on the date it is received.

The above rules trigger the requirement for accounting for output tax assuming the relevant supplies are positive rated.

When a payment is 'made'

15.31 Making a payment under the scheme triggers an input tax entitlement.

Cash is paid on the date the payer receives a receipted tax invoice, and in a similar way to the outputs rules, cheques are paid on the date thereon or the date they are sent to the supplier, whichever is the later. As, in this case, it is the user of the scheme issuing the cheque, there is no entitlement to input tax if it is dishonoured.

Payments by direct debit, standing order or bank giro are made when the payer's account is debited and if deposits paid constitute positive rated supplies in the hands of the recipient, any entitlement to input tax occurs when the payment is made.

International trade

15.32 VAT on goods which are brought into the UK from other EC or non-EC countries or which are removed from a warehouse or free zone must be accounted for subject to the normal rules outside the cash accounting scheme but if they are then sold onwards in the UK, the sale is within the scheme.

If goods are exported to countries within or outside the EC, VAT may be accounted for under the scheme where satisfactory evidence has not been received to prove export. Therefore, when the time limits for receipt of evidence have expired, output tax becomes due on monies received to that point and further output tax is due as and when any subsequent monies are received.

Miscellaneous issues

15.33 In their Public Notice 731, Customs refer specifically to the fact that goods bought or sold under hire-purchase, conditional sale and credit sale agreements must be dealt with outside the cash accounting scheme. They also clarify what to do if a less than full value payment is received or if part payments or payments in kind are received.

A less than full value payment is usually received when commission is due to a third party, such as with credit card transactions and sales through auctioneers. Taxpayers using the scheme must ensure that they account for VAT on the full value before deduction of commission.

If there is any VAT charged on the commission it can be treated as input tax.

If a part payment is received or payment is made in kind (for example a payment which covers more than one invoice), amounts should normally be attributed to invoices in the order they were issued. If they represent supplies at different rates of VAT, a fair and reasonable apportionment should be made (e.g. a pro rata calculation so that the whole payment is not allocated to the zero-rated element).

Example 126

Martin Books & Videos Ltd is a wholesaler of the goods indicated by its name. It operates the cash accounting scheme and completes quarterly returns to the end of April etc. On 28 March 2001, it issues the following invoice to a customer:

Books —	1,000
Videos —	3,000
Net	4,000
VAT	525
Total	£4,525

A payment of £2,500 was received on account on 15 April 2001 and the rest was paid on 15 May 2001. The amount of output tax due on the 04/01 return is:

$$\frac{2{,}500 \text{ (payment received)}}{4{,}525 \text{ (invoice total)}} \times 100 = 55\% \text{ of invoice has been paid}$$

Therefore, £525 × 55% = £288.75 output tax is paid on the 04/01 return (the rest being paid on the 07/01 return).

If, say, the same customer had made exactly the same order twice; received two invoices for £4,525 including VAT, both dated in March, and made a payment on account of £7,000 on 15 April 2001, the calculation would be as follows:

£4,525 of the £7,000 is attributed to the first invoice on which £525 output tax is paid. The remainder follows the same apportionment rules as above:

$$\frac{2{,}475 \text{ (7,000 paid on account less 4,525 attributed to first invoice)}}{4{,}525 \text{ (second invoice including VAT)}} \times 100$$

= 54%

£525 × 54% = £283.50

So output tax paid on the £7,000 received on account is £525 (first invoice) + £283.50 (second invoice) = £808.50.

Leaving the cash accounting scheme

15.34 The scheme must normally be used for a minimum of two years but a user may leave it at any time if he receives no advantage from using it or if he cannot fulfil the conditions.

The user must leave the scheme immediately the £750,000 (from 1 April 2001, previously £437,500) threshold is exceeded so if, for example, the limit was exceeded in period 09/01, the invoice method would apply for period 12/01 onwards.

When a business is sold as a going concern and the new owner takes over the VAT registration number, the seller must inform him that the scheme is in operation.

If a user deregisters, he must complete a final return two months after the effective date of deregistration and account for VAT on all supplies made and received during the last six months of his registration whether or not payment has been received for those supplies. If the period for which the supplies were owing was longer than six months, the bad debt relief rules would apply. Valid tax invoices must be held to support input tax claims.

Anti-avoidance measures

15.35 The scheme is subject to the following anti-avoidance provisions:

- invoices issued where full payment is not due for more than six months from the invoice date must be accounted for outside the scheme;
- invoices issued before a supply of goods or services is actually made must be accounted for outside the scheme;
- Customs can prevent a business starting to use the scheme if they perceive a threat to the revenue;
- a business using the scheme must leave it as soon as taxable turnover in the last 12 months to the end of a tax period has exceeded £750,000 (from 1 April 2001, previously £437,500) (see 15.34);
- when a business stops using the scheme after exceeding the threshold, it must account for all VAT on unpaid invoices at that time which would have been due under the invoice method rather than continue to account for it under the scheme.

A business using the scheme may continue to do so even if some form of civil penalty is incurred (e.g. misdeclaration penalty or default surcharge) or if input tax is claimed in error under the invoice method. A civil *evasion* penalty (i.e. for conduct involving dishonesty (*s 60*)) will, however, normally make the user ineligible to continue using the scheme.

Factored debts (i.e. where the debts are formally assigned to the factor and cease to belong to the scheme user) must be accounted for outside the scheme, so VAT must be paid on the full value of the supply when the debt is assigned.

Where the scheme user adopts a factoring or invoice discounting facility to help obtain payments but retains ownership of the debts, the cash accounting scheme can be used for monies received. It can also be used for previously assigned debts which are subsequently assigned back to the scheme user to the extent of any amount still not received.

The annual accounting scheme (SI 1995/2518, Regs 49 to 55)

15.36 As with the cash accounting scheme, the annual accounting scheme is intended to benefit its users rather than act simply as an alternative accounting method. The main features are the completion of only one VAT return each year with payments on account being made throughout the year. The scheme acts in a similar way to budget payments for domestic utility bills and council tax.

Conditions for using the scheme

15.37 A business may use the scheme if the following conditions are met.

- Customs' written permission has been obtained, normally in response to submission of Form VAT 600 which is available in VAT Public Notice 732 (compare the cash accounting scheme where prior permission is not required);
- the business has been registered for at least one year (because Customs base the payments on account on the previous year's net payments);
- the business expects taxable turnover in the next 12 months to be no more than £600,000 (from 1 April 2001, previously £300,000) excluding VAT;
- there is no group or divisional registration in place; and
- if the business has used the scheme before, there has been a gap of at least one year since ceasing to do so.

15.38 The user first completes a VAT return for a transitional accounting period which will run from the date he started using it to the day before the start of the first full accounting year. The date on which the full accounting year starts is determined by Customs.

The due date for the transitional return and payment depends on the length of the period. If the transitional period covers four months or more, the return and balancing payment are due no later than the last working day of the second month after the period end and if it covers less than four months, the due date is the last working day of the first month after the period end.

Example 127
(1) Transitional period: 1 November 2000 to 31 March 2001 (five months). Due date = last working day in May 2001.
(2) Transitional period: 1 January 2001 to 31 March 2001 (three months). Due date = last working day of April 2001.

15.39 Interim payments on account will be due either monthly, quarterly or not at all, depending on annual turnover levels and the net amounts paid to Customs in the previous year. If annual taxable turnover excluding VAT does not exceed £100,000, but the net amount paid to Customs over the year exceeds £2,000, quarterly payments of 20% of the VAT paid in the previous 12 months (rounded to the nearest £5) will be due by the last working day of the 4th, 7th and 10th months of the annual accounting period.

If taxable turnover was no more than £100,000 and net payments were less than £2,000, interim payments are not required but can be made voluntarily.

If taxable turnover is between £100,000 and £600,000 (from 1 April 2001, previously £300,000), nine monthly interim payments of 10% of the previous year's total payments are made starting in month 4 and ending in month 12.

All balancing payments are then made when the annual return figures are known and submitted at the end of month 14 i.e. two months after the year-end.

Example 128
JKL Ltd pays VAT on account of £3,000 per month from August 2001 to April 2002 inclusive. Total paid is £27,000. It completes its annual return to 30 April 2002 which shows £29,675 due. JKL Ltd pays the balance of £2,675 by 30 June 2002.

15.40 Payments must be made by credit transfer and users may choose their preferred method from standing order, direct debit, bank giro credit, BACS/CHAPS.

15.41 If a user is making quarterly interim payments but taxable turnover goes over £100,000, he may continue to do so until turnover reaches £110,000. Once it exceeds that level, quarterly payments can continue until the end of the current accounting period after which monthly payments must begin. The reverse applies to users making monthly payments whose turnover falls below £100,000.

15.42 As with the cash accounting scheme, there is an overall 25% tolerance built into this scheme so that users need not leave it until their taxable turnover exceeds £750,000 (from 1 April 2001, previously £375,000). Normal accounting for VAT would recommence after the end of the current accounting year.

15.43 The total VAT due for the year is shown on the annual return and the balancing payment due is the amount in Box 5 of the return less interim payments made to date. If interim payments have exceeded the total shown, Customs will automatically refund the difference. The annual return is then used as the basis for calculating interim payments for the next year. Customs inform users in writing of the amounts due.

Example 129

In *Example 128* above, the actual amount due for the year ending 30 April 2002 is £29,675. Therefore, payments on account for the year 2002/03 are £2,967.50 (10% of previous year's liability) starting in August 2002 and ending in April 2003 at which time the next annual return is filed.

15.44 The scheme has advantages other than those already mentioned, such as reduced administrative burdens, often improved cash flow and fewer special scheme calculations (e.g. retail schemes and partial exemption). However, it requires discipline in budgeting for interim payments and especially the balancing payment which could be significant if there has been growth in the current year or increased positive rated sales.

15.45 Users should indicate when they want their accounting year to end for the purposes of the scheme. This could be aligned with the usual accounting year for simplicity. Users should also notify Customs of significant changes affecting either their use of the scheme or the level of interim payments. This could involve negotiations with Customs at the start of an accounting year if interim payments are based on the previous year's trade but activity will significantly decrease. Evidence should be made available to justify reduced payments on account.

Monthly payments of VAT on account by larger businesses (s 28 and SI 1993/2001 as amended and SI 1995/2518, Regs 44 to 48)

15.46 Businesses which pay significant net amounts of VAT to Customs over a year are obliged to make monthly interim payments on account. They still complete quarterly returns and either make a final balancing payment or receive a refund if the interim payments exceed the total due for the quarter. It is estimated that the scheme applies to between 2,500 and 3,000 businesses.

15.47 The scheme applies to all businesses which pay 'true tax' of more than £2 million in a 12-month period. This means the actual net VAT due as shown on returns plus any assessments issued by Customs and errors disclosed voluntarily. The amount also includes VAT paid on imports and removals of goods from warehouses if applicable. Liability to apply the scheme will be notified by Customs in writing.

15.48 As soon as a business has exceeded the threshold and received notification, it is required to make one payment on account by the last working day of the third month of the next tax period and the balancing payment at the end of the following month. Thereafter, two interim payments are due each quarter, by the last working day of the second and third months, then a balancing payment is made at the end of the following month.

Example 130

ABC Ltd has made VAT payments to Customs in the last year as follows:

Quarter	Net VAT Paid
February 2001	£575,000
May 2001	£620,000
August 2001	£700,000
November 2001	£695,000
Total	**£2,590,000**

A payment on account will be made at the end of February 2002 (the third month of the next period) and the balancing payment made or refund received at the end of March 2002 once the February 2002 return has been submitted.

15.49 The scheme also becomes operational if the limit is exceeded in a period of less than 12 months.

15.50 The payments on account are 1/24 of the total paid to Customs in the 'reference period' which is defined according to the stagger used for completing VAT returns as shown in *Example 131*. When a business first uses the scheme, the payments are based on the period in which the threshold was exceeded. If the period was less than 12 months, a proportionate calculation is made. In *Example 130* each interim payment on account will initially be £107,916.66, being 1/24 of £2,590,000, so in the first period when only one payment on account is made, the balancing payment is likely to be higher if turnover levels are fairly constant.

Payments remain the same until the next annual cycle for payments on account begins and the new amounts are based on the 'reference period' or year as shown in *Example 131*.

Example 131

Stagger	**Quarter ends**	**Reference year**	**Annual cycle begins**
1	Mar, Jun, Sep, Dec	Year ending Sep	April of following year
2	Apr, Jul, Oct, Jan	Year ending Oct	May of following year
3	May, Aug, Nov, Feb	Year ending Nov	June of following year

15.51 Payments on account must always be made by electronic means, e.g. bank giro credit, standing order, BACS.

Failure to make any due payment may result in a default surcharge and action by Customs' Debt Management Division to recover the debt. Customs may also insist on monthly returns in future.

Changes in amounts payable

15.52 If there are significant increases or decreases in the actual amounts due to Customs, the amounts due on account will also be changed.

Customs will increase payments due on account by issuing a revised schedule if the actual amount due is 20% or more higher than the amounts calculated from the reference period.

If net amounts due to Customs in the forthcoming year are expected to be less than the previous year, the business may apply for payments on account to be reduced accordingly. Customs themselves may reduce the amounts if the net VAT due for a year after the reference period was less than 80% of the amount due for the reference period, or if they are satisfied that the net amount due for the current year which has not yet ended will be less than 80% of the net amount due for the reference period.

Customs must approve all reductions in writing.

Leaving the scheme

15.53 If net VAT due falls below £2 million during the reference period, Customs will notify the business in writing and the business will leave the scheme six months later. A business will also leave the scheme if net VAT due in any completed year after the end of the reference period falls below £1.6 million.

Option to pay actual monthly VAT due

15.54 Businesses may elect to pay the actual net VAT due for the first two months of the quarter instead of the payment on account. For example, a relevant business completing a return for period 02/02 would pay the actual amount due for December 2001 by the last working day of January 2002 and the actual amount due for January 2002 by the last working day of February 2002. The final payment would then equate to the actual amount due for February 2002.

The Large Payers Unit must be notified in writing and the business must normally continue on this basis for at least a year. Defaults or inaccuracies may result in Customs demanding a return to the standard payments on account system or even monthly returns.

15.55 If a net refund is shown for a particular month, Customs will not repay it but deal with the overall position at the end of the tax period when the return is made. Also, net refunds in one of the first two months cannot be offset against a payment due for the other. If trading patterns regularly involve months where a repayment would be due, businesses should consider opting to complete monthly returns, in which case the repayment would be made promptly.

15.56 Businesses operating the payments on account scheme that have been refused permission to pay actual net amounts due rather than the payments on account calculated by Customs have the right to appeal the decision to a VAT Tribunal.

Recent developments

Payment in euros

15.57 Although the UK was not one of the 11 member states of the EC to adopt the euro on 1 January 1999, Customs can accept payments in euros by methods such as cheque or credit transfer. All declarations including VAT returns and Intrastat forms must still be in sterling. Invoices may be in euros but as with invoices in other foreign currencies, the sterling conversion must be shown with any VAT calculated on that value.

Electronic returns

15.58 Taxpayers may now apply to Customs to file their VAT returns electronically. The principal way of doing this would be via the Internet. The facility became available by the insertion of *Regulations 25(4A) to (4L)* into the *VAT Regulations (SI 1995/2518)* effective from 1 March 2000. An electronic return is only deemed to be filed if it has been successfully recorded by the relevant electronic validation process (*Regulation 25(4F)*). The validation process also identifies the person making the return and that person is also responsible for making an electronic payment. A discount of £50 is given for filing electronically.

15.59 There is an example of an electronic VAT return on Customs' website: www.hmce.gov.uk/bus/vat100.

Chapter 16

Assessments, Penalties and Appeals, Interest on Repayments

Introduction

16.1 The whole subject of disputes and penalties must be put in context.

The majority of assessments issued by Customs are first agreed with the registered person and are accurate.

This chapter seeks to ensure that the taxpayer is confident of the way forward whenever a person authorised by Customs makes a mistake in seeking to raise an assessment or impose a penalty or where there are genuine grounds for appeal.

Before one can hope to successfully appeal against an assessment, it is essential to appreciate the wide-ranging powers of authorised officers. Thus, this chapter will examine the types of assessment and the conditions governing their issue.

16.2 It is possible to avoid assessments by anticipation and close, efficient monitoring of the VAT account, identifying errors and using the voluntary disclosure procedure.

This chapter also reviews the ways errors discovered by the taxpayer should be dealt with so as to minimise or eradicate exposure to penalties and interest charges.

16.3 As there is widespread misunderstanding of taxpayers' rights following the issue of an assessment, the chapter also examines all appeal procedures in detail and clarifies seldom recognised or appreciated available courses of action.

Formal appeals and negotiations which fail at local VAT office level can be taken through the independent Tribunal system and beyond, through the national courts and possibly even to the European Court of Justice. However, many cases heard before a Tribunal should never have gone that far in the first place.

On the other hand, there are other cases where taxpayers accept Customs' decisions without question and pay assessments which should never have been issued. This chapter considers what action to take to achieve a balance between making efficient use of appeals procedures and keeping the cost of professional assistance to a minimum.

16.4 The Statutes are sometimes uncertain or their meaning is disputed by the parties. Since the introduction of VAT into the UK in 1973, the number of Tribunal cases has increased significantly, mainly due to the decriminalisation of certain errors, the introduction of civil penalties and uncertainty as to the interpretation of the law. Thus many appeals are by appellants claiming they have a 'reasonable excuse' for their error, and seeking the withdrawal of the civil penalty.

Although Tribunals are not bound by earlier Tribunal decisions, the issues decided are often invaluable in formulating a later appeal. This chapter highlights situations where it is helpful to be aware of cases which might be used as a precedent.

Customs' powers — failure to make returns, etc. (s 73)

16.5 *Section 73* is the statutory authority for Customs to raise assessments where a taxable person has failed to make returns. A closer look at the section reveals the wide-ranging nature of their powers:

> 'Where a person has failed to make any returns required under this Act (or under any provision repealed by this Act) or to keep any documents and afford the facilities necessary to verify such returns or where it appears to the Commissioners that such returns are incomplete or incorrect, they may assess the amount due from him to the best of their judgement and notify it to him' (*s 73(1)*).

Firstly, the powers are not restricted to the current statutory provisions but cover any provision repealed by the present legislation.

Secondly, Customs are required to make assessments to the best of their judgement but best judgement is not defined. Clearly, it could be interpreted by different people in different ways. In practice, for certain types of assessment, Customs calculate a round-figure estimate based on certain criteria such as trading patterns established by any earlier returns. The point to note is that whenever an authorised officer is dissatisfied with the completeness of records, he can estimate how much tax should have been paid based on the information available to him.

Incorrect refunds

16.6 *Section 73(2)* gives Customs similar powers where the registered business has wrongly received a refund or VAT credit and *s 73(3)* extends that power to enable them to assess after deregistration has taken place.

Assessments must be split correctly between tax periods but *s 73(4)* allows for the combination of assessments under *s 73(1)(2)* and thus simplifies the task of assessment.

EC acquisitions and imported goods

16.7 *Section 73(7)* gives Customs power to take action in respect of the onward supply of EC acquired or imported goods, albeit they rarely need to exercise it. Essentially, if a taxable business acquires goods from an EC supplier or imports them from outside the EC, Customs may require the business to account for them from time to time and if the business fails to prove that they have been passed on either in the UK or abroad, or lost or destroyed, they may raise an assessment for the VAT which would have been due on a supply of these goods.

Higher assessments

16.8 Where an estimated assessment has been issued because of failure to make a return and the taxable business pays the assessed amount but even so fails to make a subsequent return showing the correct figures, Customs may, if they think fit, issue another estimated assessment but for a higher amount (*s 73(8)*).

This further demonstrates the extent of Customs' powers, it being generally accepted that Customs officers have greater legal powers than the police and the Inland Revenue, each subsection within *s 73* supporting that view.

Interest on VAT recovered or recoverable by assessment (default interest) (s 74)

16.9 Interest is seen as commercial restitution rather than open to negotiation and, certainly in the early years, Customs officers tended to take the view that they could not vary the strict calculation of interest. There are many examples where that view was challenged successfully.

There is now a three-year cap on interest charges and it is only applied where it represents genuine commercial restitution and not where there is no loss to the Exchequer.

Example 132
King Holdings Ltd fails to charge output tax on £100,000 management charges to its fully taxable subsidiary Warren Ltd, which in consequence does not claim input tax on those charges. Default interest should not be charged because there is no loss to the Exchequer. King should have paid £17,500 output tax but Warren would have been able to reclaim the same amount as input tax. King Holdings Ltd also fails to account for output tax on a lathe sold to Mr Maloney, a private individual, for £2,000. King would receive an assessment for £350 VAT plus default interest.

Default interest is charged at varying commercial rates and any changes are always from 6th of a particular month. The rate from 6 May 2001 is 7.5%.

Other powers — ss 75 and 76

16.10 Apart from the principal powers already described, Customs may use their best judgement and discretion to assess in a number of other circumstances.

EC acquisitions by non-taxable persons — s 75

16.11 *Section 75(1)* states that if any business, when not a taxable business, acquires goods subject to excise duty or a new means of transport from another member state and fails to:

(i) notify Customs,

(ii) satisfy Customs that particulars provided in the notification are accurate or complete, or

(iii) give Customs sufficient information to verify the particulars of the notification,

Customs may use their best judgement to assess the amount of VAT due on the acquisition and notify the person concerned.

Section 75(2) adds time limits but also enables Customs to raise additional assessments where further evidence comes to their knowledge.

Penalties, interest and surcharges — s 76

16.12 Customs retain the power to assess penalties, interest and surcharges even if the conduct giving rise to such a charge has ceased. Although attribution to relevant tax periods is required where possible, Customs may use their best judgement to allocate charges where direct attribution is not possible.

16.13 Whether or not the Commissioners have the power to raise an assessment in a given situation is not usually the main factor leading to disputes but rather the application of their powers. Inevitably there will be circumstances where an assessment is in order and permissible by law but its issue would be against the spirit of the tax.

On the other hand, it may be clear to a visiting officer that declared outputs and output tax are suppressed by whatever means and his best judgement thus comes into play.

Disputes arise where the taxpayer questions this judgement and carefully thought-out appeals with full explanations as to why it is considered best judgement has not been applied are often successful.

Sometimes, Customs officers have issued assessments based on projected outputs using the simplest method possible, claiming erroneously to have applied best judgement. Proprietors in the licensed trade, fish and chip shops and restaurants are particularly affected. This type of assessment is analysed later in the chapter with comments on how to challenge the amount.

Types of assessment

16.14 There are three principal types of assessment:

(*a*) estimated net tax due when the taxpayer fails to furnish a return by the due date;

(*b*) notice by a Customs official of output VAT underdeclared or input VAT overclaimed; and

(*c*) additional assessment after new information has come to Customs' attention.

These are dealt with at 16.15 – 16.21.

Failure to submit returns — estimated assessments

16.15 Since there is a default surcharge when VAT is paid late (see 16.32 below), it is important for taxpayers not only to submit returns on time but also to pay any tax due by the due date. Failure to do so triggers a default and the surcharge procedure commences.

If Customs do not receive the return and payment on time, they usually issue a reminder. This does not mean a default has been avoided.

Thereafter, an estimated assessment is issued.

Often, the amount of the assessment is less than the actual net tax due but Customs will pursue the difference and amend any default surcharge when the figures are available to them.

Example 133

Hutchinson does not pay the amount due on his VAT return for period 11/01 on time. The VAT owing on the return is £10,000 and it is his third default, so a surcharge of 5% applies (see 16.32). Customs issue an assessment of £8,000, being estimated tax due plus default surcharge of £400.

When Customs become aware of the correct liability of £10,000 they will pursue the extra £2,000 tax and levy an additional surcharge of £100 (as 5% of £10,000 is £500 not £400).

If the return has still not been furnished 30 days after the issue of the assessment, the estimated amount becomes a debt due to the Crown together with any additional amount owing when the return is eventually submitted. Civil action then follows if the trader fails to pay.

Assessments following visits

16.16 All VAT registered businesses should receive routine visits from Customs officers from time to time. The objective of these visits, normally called 'assurance' visits, is to ascertain the credibility of returns submitted from the date of registration or since the last visit, with any errors discovered after all checks have been completed being notified by the issue of an assessment.

The visiting officer does not carry out an audit and control procedures vary according to the type and size of the business but he must satisfy himself that payments made or refunds received genuinely reflect trade over the period in question. He concentrates on the areas of greatest risk to the revenue and consequently may not find all errors, but such as are found are incorporated into an assessment.

This type of assessment is by far the most common. The vast majority are issued for clear-cut errors of output tax underdeclared or input tax overclaimed and are never the subject of a dispute.

A small percentage are issued in error or in cases where the officer's use of best judgement could be brought into question, making a sound knowledge of VAT law and procedures essential so that the business can make effective use of the reconsideration and appeals procedures.

Assessments must be allocated to specific tax periods in order to determine whether a misdeclaration penalty applies (see 16.36) and from what date interest should be calculated. Output tax and input tax errors for the same period are combined but misdeclaration penalties are shown separately. Default interest is shown as a single amount on page 1 of the assessment form (VAT 655).

Where the officer needs to estimate outputs in the absence of satisfactory records, he must exercise best judgement and attribute additional tax fairly between tax periods.

The proposed assessment must be discussed with the trader in advance of its issue so that he understands why it is being issued and the trader must be notified within the time limits set down in *ss 73(6)* and *77* (see below and Public Notice 989 paragraph 1.9).

The basis for the assessment must be explained on the assessment form, an incorrect reason rendering it invalid.

Customs will usually send a letter to traders facing an assessment which will enable them to query the preliminary calculations before the assessment is actually made.

In Business brief 5/2001, 13 March 2001, Customs announced changes in practice as regards making and notifying assessments, effective from 1 March 2001. These are outlined in greater detail in a new publication, VAT Notice 915 'Assessments and Time Limits: Statement of Practice'. The principal changes are as follows:

— pre-assessment letters will be sent to traders before all assessments (the previous practice was not to send them when the content of the assessment was clear or the deadline for making the assessment was imminent);

— legal time limits apply to the 'making' of an assessment, not its notification to the taxpayer, so Customs now apply the time limits for making assessments to their notification to ensure taxpayers know for sure that they are made in time (Customs regard the notification date as the date the assessment is sent by post, hand, fax or e-mail to the last known address of the taxpayer);

— where the normal computer-generated Notice of Assessment is unlikely to be processed within the time limits, Customs now send the taxpayer a letter clearly headed 'Notification of Assessment' and normally send the computer-generated version at a later date to ensure the assessment is not out of time.

Mark-up assessments

16.17 Visiting Customs officers have access to guidelines on mark-ups on cost expected for certain types of business. These guidelines are intended to allow for the effect of certain influences such as the geographical location of the business and a reasonable amount of wastage. For example, it would be unreasonable to expect the same mark-up to apply to a City of London free house as to a tied public house on a Northern council estate.

Mark-up assessments — public houses

16.18 One of the most common types of business on which mark-up exercises are undertaken is public houses. Visits are often carried out by relatively junior officers. Consequently, concern that takings may have been suppressed can occur more readily if lack of experience prevents them from taking all relevant factors into account. They often rely on the internal guidelines which only provide an indication as to expected takings. For the most part, miscellaneous factors such as the experience of bar staff, wastage, and happy hours mean the actual mark-up achieved can be considerably lower.

Mark-up assessments involve use of best judgement and even if an underdeclaration of takings is agreed, the officer must attribute the amount due as accurately as possible between tax periods. For example, an allowance should be made for draught beer lost through pipe-cleaning, pulling off pints at the beginning of each session and beer at the bottom of each barrel which cannot be sold. Other factors that could affect the mark-up achieved include free drinks and theft of stock.

Any assessment based on estimated outputs such as a mark-up exercise can usually be challenged and often reduced on the basis that the officer has failed to exercise best judgement by omitting relevant factors. Strictly, once the result of a local reconsideration has been received, the taxpayer has 21 days to appeal to an independent VAT Tribunal if still dissatisfied but the local VAT office will often itself review the matter again especially if new information is made available to them.

A public house which prepares its own periodical reconciliation of takings with stock purchases, explaining any deficiencies by a contemporaneous note is always in a good position to meet any Customs challenge.

Mark-up assessments — fish and chip shops

16.19 The traditional fish and chip shop has been afforded similar treatment to public houses in that special exercises are often undertaken to establish true takings where visiting officers have reason to doubt VAT return declarations.

The method of arriving at estimated takings is somewhat different, the cost of potatoes and weight of bags of chips being factors used in the past.

This method was used more often before the introduction of tills with buttons for each item sold. Now Customs normally focus on the accuracy of recorded takings compared with till roll readings. They often also check with suppliers of potatoes and fish that all the purchase invoices have been recorded.

As with public houses, there are often grounds for challenging assessments, such as potato price fluctuations, special offers, and wastage through unsold stock or bad buying and inexperience of staff.

Other assessments based on estimated outputs

16.20 Wherever there is doubt as to the reliability of declared outputs, the visiting officer has a number of options available in order to establish what is to him a more accurate figure. Cash or bank patterns are tested against the trader's explanations of how the business is run and the cash managed.

For certain types of service, for example in the motor trade, it is possible to establish a relationship in the pricing system between parts and labour. By establishing the purchase price and mark-up on parts and using the normal hourly labour charge, it is possible to project expected takings. Similar principles are often applied with restaurants. Where a mark-up exercise is inappropriate, officers can establish a relationship between food and drink sold or a relationship between eat-in and take-away sales. Whatever method is used there are usually mitigating factors in favour of the taxpayer, whose cause is always helped by as much back-up evidence of underachievement as possible.

Additional assessments

16.21 Additional assessments are issued where new information becomes available to Customs. A common occurrence is after an initial assessment has been issued for a tax period for which no return has been furnished; the registered business has paid the assessment and a higher actual amount due for the period is subsequently established.

Another situation might be through the exchange of information with the Inland Revenue, who indicate to Customs that a trade has been successfully challenged on the recording of sales, or has used false purchase invoices.

There are certain restrictions and conditions covering the issue of assessments, set out at 16.22 to 16.30.

Time limits for assessments

16.22 The time limits for assessments issued under *ss 73, 75* and *76* (see 16.5–16.8 and 16.10–16.13) are in *ss 77* and *73(6)*.

Assessments under *s 77(1)* cannot be made:

(*a*) more than three years after the end of the prescribed accounting period, import or EC acquisition concerned, or

(*b*) in the case of penalties, surcharges and interest under *s 76*, three years after the event giving rise to the penalty, unless *s 76(3)* applies.

Penalties, interest and surcharges under *s 76(3)* are assessed as amounts due in the prescribed accounting period which, in each of five cases, is known as 'the relevant period'. The five cases are as follows:

(i) default surcharges where the relevant period is the prescribed accounting period in respect of which the taxable person is in default and in respect of which the surcharge arises;

(ii) civil fraud penalties where the relevant period is the prescribed accounting period for which the VAT evaded was due;

(iii) civil fraud penalties for obtaining VAT credit where the relevant period is the prescribed accounting period in respect of which the payment was obtained;

(iv) misdeclaration penalties where the relevant period is the prescribed accounting period for which the VAT liability was understated or input tax was overstated; and

(v) interest charges where the relevant period is the prescribed accounting period in respect of which the VAT was due.

Time limit for penalties, interest and surcharge assessments — s 77(2)

16.23 Penalties, interest or surcharges under *s 76(3)* may be assessed before the end of the two-year period beginning:

(*a*) in the case of penalties for failure to submit or inaccuracies in EC sales statements, on the date when facts available to Customs satisfy them that there has been a default or a material inaccuracy; and

(*b*) in any other case, on the date when the correct amount of VAT due for the relevant prescribed accounting period has been established.

Section 77(3) allows for references to prescribed accounting periods to include relevant periods under *s 76(3)*.

There is a two-year time limit for Customs to penalise the submission of incorrect EC Sales Lists. This was clarified by *FA 1999, s 18* (see also 16.37).

Time limits for fraud assessments — s 77(4)

16.24 If VAT has been lost through civil or criminal fraud or in circumstances giving rise to a penalty for failure to notify or for unauthorised issue of invoices, assessments may be made for 20 years, Customs in these circumstances not being bound by the three-year cap.

Time limits — Assessments after a person's death — s 77(5)

16.25 *Subsections (2)* and *(4)* of *s 77* are both subject to this subsection which imposes time limits for assessments after a person's death. No assessment is permissible later than three years after the person's death, even if the 20-year limit for fraud would apply but for the death. Any assessment which could have been made immediately after the person's death may be made at any time within the next three years.

Time limits for assessments under s 73(1), (2) and (3) — s 73(6)

16.26 Assessments under the first three subsections of *s 73* must be made within the time limits provided in *s 77* and are not to be made after the later of the following:

(*a*) two years after the end of the prescribed accounting period; or

(*b*) one year after evidence of facts, sufficient in Customs' opinion to justify the making of an assessment, comes to their knowledge,

but subject to *s 77*, if Customs acquire further relevant information after issuing an assessment under *s 73(1)*, *(2)* or *(3)*, they may issue an additional assessment.

Notification to the correct person

16.27 Assessments must be notified to the correct person. This is particularly important with group registrations where all taxable supplies by or to members of the VAT group are deemed to be made by or to the representative member.

Where applicable, notification must be made to a personal representative, trustee in bankruptcy, interim or permanent trustee, liquidator or any person otherwise acting in a representative capacity (see for example *s 73(5)* or *(10)*).

16.28 All penalties, interest and surcharges assessed must use the correct relevant period as the basis for the calculation.

Other conditions

16.29 All information shown on an assessment form must be correct, notably the taxpayer's VAT registration number, name and address, the reason code for each error and the attribution to the correct VAT accounting period.

Where the assessment is an estimate of underdeclared tax, the officer must exercise best judgement in apportioning the amount he considers due between VAT accounting periods.

Whenever Customs make a mistake either in their calculations or on the assessment form itself, taxpayers have a strong case for claiming that it is invalid, albeit Customs have been known to obtain payment of VAT due independently of the assessment system, for example, in *International Language Centres Limited (No 2)* (*QB* [*1983*] *STC 394*) their assessment was outside the time limits but they sued successfully as it was recoverable as a debt due to the Crown.

16.30 Customs regularly stress how important it is for taxpayers to submit accurate returns. Although this is sound advice, it is equally important that authorised officers adhere to all the conditions governing the issue of assessments. Accuracy and observance of time limits are essential.

Now that it is regular practice for visiting officers to send written details of their findings before the assessment itself is issued, there will hopefully be fewer unnecessary appeals both at a local level and through the Tribunal and Courts.

Penalties

Introduction

16.31 There is a wide range of penalties available to Customs for various errors covered by *ss 59–69*. Under certain circumstances, they also have the power to mitigate those penalties under *s 70*. These issues are dealt with at 16.32 to 16.43 below.

Default surcharge

16.32 The default surcharge (*s 59*) applies to circumstances described in 16.15 where the amount due on VAT returns is paid late.

A person is deemed to be in default if by the last day on which a VAT return is due to be submitted (i.e. the end of the month following the VAT period), Customs have not received the payment due on that return. Customs have stated that they will accept that a return and the tax due were posted in time if there is evidence that they were despatched one working day prior to the due date if posted first class or two working days if posted second class.

The legislation provides:

(*a*) If a taxpayer fails to submit a return or payment on time, a surcharge liability notice is issued (*s 59(2)*).

(*b*) The surcharge liability notice will remain in force for a period of one year from the end of the late return period and on any default of submission of return or payment within that year, a further surcharge liability notice will be issued for one year from the end of the next late return period and this will be considered a continuous period with the first surcharge notice (*s 59(3)*). An automatic surcharge of 2% of any tax due will apply (*s 59(4)(5)*).

On a subsequent default in respect of payment within the surcharge period, the penalty will be increased to 5% and by a further 5% to a maximum of 15% on any subsequent default (*s 59(5)*).

The surcharge liability notice will lapse if there are no further late payments or returns within the extended period and a new surcharge liability notice will then be issued if a further payment or return is submitted late.

If the amount of the surcharge at 2% or 5% is less than £200 it is not collected. The minimum surcharge at 10% or 15% is £30.

There is no liability to default surcharge if:

- a nil VAT return is submitted late;
- a return is submitted late but the VAT is paid by the due date,

but a default will be recorded, and if a surcharge liability notice is in force it will be extended. Such defaults do not, however, increase the rate of surcharge, which will only increase where VAT is paid late or under-paid.

Example 134

Peter Harris has a successful engineering business. He seeks advice since he is unhappy at the situation that has arisen following the submission of his VAT returns over the past few years. The details of these returns are as follows:

VAT period ended	**Date return submitted and payment made (except as noted below)**	**Payment due**
		£
31 December 1999	15 February 2000	3,250
31 March 2000	27 April 2000	2,850
30 June 2000	18 August 2000	9,575
30 September 2000	20 October 2000	4,400
31 December 2000	29 January 2001	4,950
31 March 2001	27 May 2001	11,200
30 June 2001	31 August 2001	2,750
30 September 2001	17 October 2001	17,800
31 December 2001	30 January 2002	14,900

Cheques for the full amount of VAT payable have accompanied all the returns submitted with the exception of the return submitted on 30 January 2002 when, owing to cash flow problems, a payment of £4,900 was sent and the balance of £10,000 was paid on 22 March 2002.

Peter Harris has commented that he considers it unfair that any surcharge should be payable. Over the past year or so he has been under financial pressure and has always been close to his bank overdraft limit which has prevented him from meeting his VAT liabilities by the due date. His business has now improved but, owing to an increase in the level of activity, he believes that his book-keeper will not be able to prepare VAT returns on time.

(*a*) Calculate the default surcharges that should apply to him.

(*b*) Specify the action that he should take to avoid further surcharges.

(*c*) Consider whether he has any grounds for challenging any default surcharges that have occurred to date or may occur in the future.

Peter Harris — Default surcharge liability

VAT period ended	**Date return submitted**	**Date of payment (if different)**	**Due date**	**Is payment late?**	**Action**
31.12.99	15.2.00		31.1.00	Yes	Surcharge liability notice
31.3.00	27.4.00		30.4.00	No	
30.6.00	19.8.00		31.7.00	Yes	2% penalty i.e. £191 (not collected)
30.9.00	20.10.00		31.10.00	No	
31.12.00	29.1.01		31.1.01	No	
31.3.01	27.5.01		30.4.01	Yes	5% penalty i.e. £560
30.6.01	31.8.01		31.7.01	Yes	10% penalty i.e. £275
30.9.01	17.10.01		31.10.01	No	
31.12.01	30.1.02	22.3.02	31.1.02	Yes	15% penalty i.e. £1,500

(*a*) Peter Harris will receive a surcharge liability notice at the time of the first default, covering the period of 12 months to 31 December 2000.

Since he makes a further payment late in the quarter to 30 June 2000, a penalty arises of 2% of the tax payable on that return, i.e. 2000, £9,575 × 2% = £191. A penalty at the 2% or 5% rate of less than £200 is, however, not collected, which applies to the £191 for the June 2000 quarter, but the penalty *rate* for a subsequent default is increased and the surcharge period is extended for a further 12 months from the end of the second late return period, i.e. to 30 June 2001.

The penalty for the next late return, i.e. that for the quarter to 31 March 2001, is therefore £11,200 × 5% = £560, and the surcharge period is extended to 31 March 2002, with a further increase of 5% in the subsequent penalty level. The penalty further increases to 10% for the return for the quarter to 30 June 2001, and the surcharge period is extended to 30 June 2002.

A surcharge is due on a default (after the first) when any part of the payment due is late. Accordingly, when part of the payment is delayed in respect of the quarter ended 31 December 2001 the penalty is again triggered. However, the penalty only applies to the outstanding tax for the period (*s 59(4)*). For the quarter ended 31 December 2001, therefore, the penalty is based on the outstanding tax, i.e. £10,000 × 15% = £1,500.

The surcharge period is extended to 31 December 2002 and any subsequent penalty within that period will be at the maximum rate of 15%. The surcharge period will only come to an end when four consecutive returns have been paid on time.

(*b*) Peter Harris must take all practical steps to ensure that his VAT returns are submitted on time with full payment. Evidence of posting should be obtained. Sufficient staff or professional assistance must be engaged to complete the return and pay the tax due within the given one-month period. This will be much cheaper than paying surcharges (which are not deductible in calculating taxable profits). Arrangements should be made with his bankers or other financial backers (e.g. factors) to enable funds to be available to meet his VAT liability. If necessary, the level of activity must be restricted to enable the business to meet its obligation. An extension of seven days can be obtained to the normal due date for payment if payment is made by credit transfer.

(*c*) The only grounds on which a default surcharge can be challenged are (*s 59(7)*):

(i) the return was posted at such a time that it would be reasonable to expect that it would arrive on time, or

(ii) there is a reasonable excuse for the delay.

However, it is provided in *s 71* that a reasonable excuse does not include:

- insufficiency of funds to pay any tax, or
- where reliance is placed on any other person to perform any task, their failure to perform that task.

As Peter's reasons for making late returns are financial pressure, and increased activity resulting in failure of his book-keeping staff to meet time limits, both are specifically excluded from being a reasonable excuse and a challenge against the default surcharge would be unlikely to succeed.

Sections 59A and 59B deal with the interaction between the default surcharge and the payments on account scheme (see 15.46 *et seq.*).

Conduct involving dishonesty — civil evasion penalty (CEP)

16.33 Under *s 60*, Customs may issue a civil evasion penalty where they can prove on the balance of probabilities that a trader has knowingly evaded VAT by taking or omitting to take a particular course of action. When an officer becomes concerned that fraud has taken place, he normally refers the case to a special unit within each Collection called the Local Fraud Unit (LFU). Thereafter, a thorough investigation takes place, often involving taped or verbatim recorded interviews and a caution.

When interviewed, a trader under investigation is usually given Notice 730 to read. This explains procedures to ensure he understands what is happening. If dishonesty is proven, the penalty is 100% of the tax evaded although Notice 730 clearly explains the 'discounts' available for co-operation with Customs' investigations. The maximum discount available is 75%, making the penalty 25% of the tax evaded (but see also 16.34 below). However, if a trader accepts a 25% penalty, he is tacitly admitting dishonesty, so if he believes he has not been dishonest, he should appeal further. If the dishonesty charge is then dropped, the *de minimis* limits for misdeclaration penalty would be applied and, if applicable, it would be levied at 15% of the tax due in the periods in which those limits were exceeded.

Example 135

Mr Fudger is accused of suppressing his takings over the period January to December 2001. The VAT underdeclared is £60,000. Customs issue a CEP for £60,000, making the amount due £120,000. Fudger is interviewed and given Notice 730 to read. He co-operates fully with Customs and is offered a 75% 'discount'. The penalty is now £15,000. However, Fudger convinces Customs he did not knowingly underdeclare his takings and they agree. The assessment was spread evenly over periods 03/01 to 12/01 i.e. £15,000 per period. The misdeclaration penalty limits are applied (see 16.36) with the result that the penalty only applies to period 06/01 i.e. £15,000 × 15% = £2,250 (see also 16.34 below immediately after this example).

Section 61 enables Customs to issue CEPs to directors of a company as well as the company itself.

16.34 In Business Briefs 11/2000 and 12/2000, 1 and 8 September 2000 respectively, Customs announced the introduction of a new approach to the investigation of civil fraud to be trialed from 1 September 2000 for one year. This took place in three regions: the East Midlands, London and the North West but also involved the participation of the National Investigation Service (NIS). The new approach involved less formal meetings than those described earlier in this paragraph with the purpose of reaching an early agreement with affected traders and their advisers as to the nature, extent and reason for irregularities. These meetings, at which a trader would be expected to admit dishonest conduct, would be followed by a full disclosure report by the trader and full co-operation was 'rewarded' by a reduction in the penalty from 100% of the tax evaded to 20%. The whole procedure was seen as a way of avoiding in-depth investigations, the cost of long, drawn-out appeals and prosecution in some cases. It is understood that the procedure is to be continued and extended to other regions.

It has always been possible for Customs to instigate criminal rather than civil fraud proceedings in the most serious cases of VAT evasion but they have now also changed their policy as to what constitutes a serious fraud. From 1 September 2000, they normally instigate criminal proceedings only in the following circumstances:

— the evasion involves one or more businesses the activities of which are solely or primarily bogus or undertaken as a systematic fraud against the tax;

— there is a deliberate intent to deceive during a civil investigation;

— the offence is perpetrated by those who would be expected to advise other businesses on VAT matters, e.g. accountants and lawyers;

— the evasion is executed together with other activities where criminal investigation has taken place or is planned;

— there has been a previous VAT or Customs and Excise offence resulting in a penalty, the compounding of proceedings or a criminal conviction.

It should be noted that there is no lower or upper limit that triggers criminal proceedings.

Customs see these new policies as more effective and as a means of working more effectively with other government departments such as the Inland Revenue.

Incorrect certificates

16.35 Where a business issues a certificate to claim zero rating to which it is not entitled, e.g. claiming a building is constructed for a relevant residential or charitable purpose, there is a penalty under *s 62* equal to the amount of VAT that should have been paid.

Example 136
A charity has a building constructed for £1,000,000 and claims it will be used for a relevant charitable purpose so the main contractor zero rates his services. The charity uses the building for non-qualifying purposes. It is liable to a penalty of £175,000.

The penalty does not apply if Customs or a Tribunal can be convinced of a reasonable excuse for the error.

From 27 July 1999, this penalty also applies to incorrect certificates given to obtain fuel and power at 5% VAT rather than 17.5% (*FA 1999, s 17*).

Misdeclaration penalty

16.36 If a business files a VAT return and underdeclares output tax and/or overclaims input tax, or if Customs issue an assessment that is too low and the business does not notify them within 30 days, a misdeclaration penalty could apply under *ss 63 and 64*.

A penalty of 15% of the error applies if that error equals or exceeds the lesser of £1,000,000 and 30% of the 'gross amount of tax' ('GAT'), i.e. the correct output tax and input tax for the relevant period added together.

Example 137
In period 10/01, a haulage company fails to declare output tax of £3,500 on the sale of a lorry. Its return shows the following: Output tax — £6,200 Input Tax — £1,200 Net payment due to Customs — £5,000 GAT is 6,200 + 1,200 + 3,500 (the error) = £10,900 30% of £10,900 is £3,270. The error exceeds £3,270 so a penalty is due. The penalty is £3,500 × 15% = £525.

This penalty applies to specific tax periods, not to assessments as a whole, so it is crucial for errors to be correctly attributed to tax periods because misdeclaration penalties are calculated by computer.

A second test is available to Customs although infrequently used. They may first issue a penalty liability notice serving as a warning that further errors will be penalised. Thereafter, if the business makes a material error within the next eight tax periods, it will receive a penalty.

An error under this provision (*s 64*) is material if it equals or exceeds the lesser of £500,000 and 10% of GAT. The penalty is 15% of the error.

Misdeclaration penalty does not apply if Customs or a tribunal can be convinced of a reasonable excuse for the error.

EC Sales Lists — Inaccuracies and failure to submit

16.37 If a business selling goods to VAT registered businesses in other member states completes inaccurate EC Sales Lists, Customs may issue a warning within six months. If a second inaccurate ECSL is then filed within two years, Customs may issue a second warning. If a third inaccurate ECSL is submitted within two years of the second warning, a penalty of £100 applies (*s 65*).

An inaccuracy is only regarded as material if the incorrect information is misleading and the penalty does not apply if a reasonable excuse is proven.

16.38 Failure to submit ECSLs also triggers penalties under certain circumstances. Customs may issue a default notice giving the business 14 days to file the declaration. If the business then fails to observe the 14-day deadline, a penalty of £5 per day applies up to a maximum of 100 days (*s 66*).

If the declaration is made within 10 days of receipt of the default notice, the penalty is £50. The business must file subsequent declarations on time for a whole year for the system to start again, otherwise subsequent defaults are penalised without prior warning. The second default is penalised at £10 per day and the third and subsequent defaults at £15 per day.

These penalties do not apply if a reasonable excuse exists.

Late registration penalty

16.39 Where Customs are notified of a requirement to register for VAT late, there is a penalty based on a percentage of net VAT due for the period that the business should have been registered up to the date of actual notification (*s 67*).

The penalty is as follows:

- notification up to 9 months late — 5% of net tax due
- notification between 9 and 18 months late — 10% of net tax due
- notification more than 18 months late — 15% of net tax due

If there is a net refund due to the business, there is no penalty.

Example 138

On 30 April 2000 a business exceeds the then registration threshold of £52,000 and notifies its requirement to register on 15 November 2001. Net VAT due is £20,000.

Notification should have been by 31 May 2000 because the business has 30 days to notify, therefore actual notification is just under 18 months late. The penalty, therefore, is £2,000 (£20,000 × 10%).

Other penalties

16.40 Penalties also exist for unauthorised issue of tax invoices, breaches of walking possession agreements and breaches of regulatory provisions (*ss 67–69*) but these are seldom applied.

Miscellaneous issues concerning penalties

16.41 Penalties for more serious errors override lesser errors. For example, a misdeclaration penalty is not applied if a civil evasion penalty is levied and no civil penalty applies if the trader has been convicted of a criminal offence.

16.42 Customs have the power to mitigate penalties for conduct involving dishonesty, misdeclaration, late notification and unauthorised issue of tax invoice. For example, where a sole trader claims 100% input tax without being aware of the changes to partial exemption *de minimis* limits, he may trigger a misdeclaration penalty but Customs could reduce it from 15% to, say, 5% (*s 70*).

16.43 When considering reasonable excuses and possible mitigation, Customs may not take into account the following:

- lack of funds,
- the fact that there may have been no significant loss of VAT,
- reliance on a third party to perform a task, and
- the fact that the trader in question or his representative has acted in good faith.

VAT account monitoring and voluntary disclosures

16.44 The most effective way to avoid penalties is by regular monitoring of the VAT account, highlighting errors and disclosing them voluntarily in writing to Customs.

In order to avoid any liability to a penalty, written notification is compulsory if the total net error (VAT not paid to Customs less overpayments) exceeds £2,000. Net errors involving VAT under £2,000 may be adjusted on the next return.

Example 139
When preparing the 08/01 return, a company accountant realises he forgot to account for £2,100 VAT on the sale of plant in period 11/00. He also discovers that the company paid £350 VAT on the sale of zero-rated books in period 02/01. The net error is £1,750 in Customs' favour but as this is less than £2,000, it can be included with other output tax in Box 1 of the 08/01 return.

Once the disclosure is made, Customs will issue an assessment but will not usually issue a misdeclaration penalty even if the limits have been exceeded, the only possible exception being if the disclosure were made after Customs had initiated the visit process, e.g. made an appointment and believed that the disclosure was only being made because of their involvement.

There is no liability to a misdeclaration penalty if at a time when a trader has no reason to believe that enquiries are being made by Customs into his VAT affairs, he gives Customs full information about inaccuracies.

The voluntary disclosure procedure is not as straightforward as it first seems. Customs must be given 'full information' about the errors involved, but the term 'full information' is not further defined.

There is no guidance as to how the information must be furnished to the Commissioners neither is there an obvious way of proving when a person has no reason to believe that Customs are enquiring into his VAT affairs.

This clause is another example of widely drawn legislation which requires reference to official notices and leaflets for guidance on Customs' interpretation. Leaflet 700/45 'How to correct errors you find on your VAT returns' explains how Customs will treat voluntary disclosures.

Paragraph 2 of the leaflet states that they will accept voluntary disclosures after they have commenced enquiries unless they have reason to believe that:

(*a*) the taxpayer discovered the errors earlier and disclosed them only because a visit had been arranged; or

(*b*) the disclosure during or after a visit was prompted by their enquiries into the taxpayer's affairs.

Net errors of less than £2,000 discovered on previous VAT returns that are adjusted on the next return will be treated as true tax for that period, no interest being charged.

Where net errors discovered exceed £2,000, the taxpayer must notify the local VAT office in writing using Form VAT 652 or in plain letter form so long as full details are given including tax periods concerned, whether relating to input or output tax and whether under or overdeclarations.

Example 140

A sole trader fails to account for £1,600 VAT on the sale of a machine in period 02/01 and £1,200 on the sale of a van in period 05/01. He discovers the error when preparing the 08/01 return. To make a voluntary disclosure using the letter option rather than Form VAT 652, he could use the following words:

HM C & E
VAT Office
Address

Dear Sirs

Name — VAT registration number

I write to disclose errors I have discovered on previous VAT returns as follows:

Period 02/01 — £1,600 output tax due on sale of machine
Period 05/01 — £1,200 output tax due on sale of van
Total underdeclaration — £2,800

Please accept this letter as a voluntary disclosure.

Yours faithfully etc.

For net errors over £2,000, default interest will be charged. As interest is calculated from the date of the error to the date Customs issue a Notice of Voluntary Disclosure, there is scope for challenging the amount charged if there is an unreasonable delay between the disclosure and the issue of the Notice.

A voluntary disclosure, although not actually avoiding assessments, is useful in avoiding misdeclaration penalties and stopping interest accumulating.

Customs have also announced publicly that no interest will be charged where there is no overall loss to the Exchequer, e.g. where an underdeclaration in one tax period becomes an automatic overdeclaration in the next. Businesses should note, however, that if 'compensating errors' are not voluntarily disclosed, Customs may impose a misdeclaration penalty on the underdeclaration in accordance with Leaflet 700/45 paragraph 6.

Appeals procedure

16.45 An air of mystique surrounds this procedure, which is at least offputting and sometimes frightening to the average would-be appellant.

Ignorance of primary VAT law is generally not acceptable as a reasonable excuse for avoiding penalties and surcharges but on occasions the Tribunals have decided that the application of a particular aspect of VAT law is so uncertain that the appellant could be excused for getting it wrong (see, for example, *Silver Knight Exhibitions Ltd, MAN/92/1826, No 10569*).

Pre-assessment letter

16.46 If a visiting officer indicates that he has discovered errors on the returns examined, the taxpayer should request a letter from him explaining his findings in full and supporting his conclusions with statutory references.

As part of his visit, the officer is obliged to discuss with the taxpayer any errors found but many visits move straight from this discussion to the issue of the assessment itself.

If this happens, the taxpayer should ask for the letter before taking any further action, in the meantime appealing specifically against the assessment, the request for the letter itself constituting one of the grounds for an appeal (see also 16.16).

Pre-assessment negotiations

16.47 Most local VAT offices now allow a reasonable amount of discussion and correspondence between visiting officers and taxpayers before the assessment is issued. This is only necessary where there is any doubt concerning the error, only a small proportion of errors being open to debate.

The officer will usually agree to send a draft schedule of errors for the trader to examine and if possible agree, following which the formal assessment is then issued.

Clearly, full agreement before the assessment is issued is preferable but interpretation of law and best interests of the trader sometimes makes this impossible.

Professional assistance should be sought where necessary. It is essential where Customs formally caution the trader in cases of suspected fraud.

Post-assessment negotiations — the local reconsideration

16.48 Once a valid assessment has been issued, the trader has 30 days to appeal formally to an independent VAT Tribunal and/or to request a local reconsideration.

The letter of request for a local reconsideration should be prepared carefully with assistance from professional advisers on complicated technical issues.

The disputed matter is then reviewed by a different officer at the local VAT office and a revised written decision is communicated. Workloads and limited resources at local offices mean that reviews take varying amounts of time but once a decision has been sent to the taxpayer, he has a further 21 days to appeal to an independent Tribunal if he has not already done so.

Even so, VAT offices will often agree to more than one local reconsideration especially if additional information becomes available.

One of the main hurdles the taxpayer must overcome is the problem of making his case to the reviewing officer, who has had no involvement with his affairs until that point.

The emphasis here must be clarity and availability of as much supporting documentation as possible.

Taxpayers often consider submitting a formal appeal to an independent VAT Tribunal as soon as they receive the assessment even though they hope to resolve the matter at a local level. This is because a Tribunal decision in the appellant's favour normally involves an application for costs which, if successful, would be backdated to the date the appeal was submitted. If an agreement is reached without the need for a Tribunal hearing, the taxpayer should withdraw his appeal by informing the relevant Tribunal centre in writing. In such cases, the issue of costs should be resolved between the taxpayer and Customs. If agreement cannot be reached, the Tribunal should be asked for a direction.

Grounds on which to defend assessments

16.49 The procedural and technical grounds on which assessments might be defended are dealt with earlier in this chapter.

Further comment on 'best judgement' is at 16.50 below, and Customs' misunderstanding is dealt with at 16.51.

16.50 There is often a fine line between an officer making effective and efficient use of information and material before him, and reaching a hurried, simple conclusion to avoid an in-depth investigation into the trader's affairs involving considerable time and resources.

That the word 'judgement' is used indicates that there will always be an element of subjectivity involved. A judgement can only be made where there is something available to judge, so in circumstances where no information is made available to a visiting officer, he cannot make an assessment based on best judgement. He must first initiate an investigation into the trader's affairs in an attempt to obtain information.

Essentially, an officer must make a value judgement on all relevant information made available to him, ignore any irrelevant information, and make a reasonable decision, not an arbitrary one. In most decided cases, it has proven difficult for the taxpayer to demonstrate that best judgement has definitely not been exercised but that should not detract from an appeal where there is evidence demonstrating that the officer has ignored key information.

16.51 Until recently, VAT control officers tended to use internal classified instructions and public notices on which to base their judgements and decisions but through regular liaison with representative groups and professional advisers, Customs agreed that they should lay more emphasis on the underlying law rather than its official, internal interpretation. This has led to a marked improvement in the way negotiations are handled and there is now generally greater mutual respect between traders, their professional advisers and Customs.

Even so, just as taxpayers sometimes misunderstand the liability of certain supplies, so do Customs officers. Although training programmes have improved significantly, there is no substitute for experience. Regular legislative changes complicate the issue and mean the chances of error are increased.

As demonstrated in Chapters 3 to 5, VAT law cannot list every type of supply which is standard-rated. Therefore, zero-rated, reduced-rated and exempt supplies are specified. However, commercial and IT developments mean that there are many areas open to interpretation, the underlying law and relevant decided cases being of importance.

Where the taxpayer considers that part or all of an assessment relates to a misunderstanding of the law, he should ensure that his defence is well supported by a full explanation and obtain professional assistance if necessary.

The fact remains that many of the incorrect assessments are those issued to small businesses where the visiting officer has incorrectly determined the liability of supplies but the taxpayer has insufficient knowledge to lodge an appeal and insufficient financial resources to obtain professional assistance. This highlights the need for traders themselves, or through their trade associations, to keep up to date with the law and practice as it affects their business.

16.52 Various types of assessment will be issued after the visiting officer has given the business a deadline for the provision of key information or evidence but which has not been forthcoming.

It is a valid defence against the enforcement of the assessment if this information is subsequently obtained and made available to Customs for examination. The most common occurrences are as follows:

- zero-rating disallowed for exports because no evidence of export is available;
- input tax disallowed because corresponding purchase invoices are unavailable; and

- zero-rating disallowed on construction of buildings designed for a relevant residential or charitable purpose because no certificate confirming eligibility is available from the customer.

If such evidence is furnished after the assessment has been raised, not only should Customs withdraw the assessment but they should also cancel any default interest charged (because there has been no loss to the Exchequer).

Errors following incorrect rulings from previous visiting officers — 'misdirection'

16.53 It may be that a previous visiting officer has given the taxpayer instructions concerning the correct VAT treatment of certain activities. If, during a subsequent visit, this treatment is brought into question and the first officer is proven wrong, there may be grounds for the taxpayer to avoid an assessment through misdirection.

The onus would be on the taxpayer to demonstrate beyond reasonable doubt that his actions were as a direct result of Customs' advice so it is essential to obtain written confirmation of instructions received.

The courts have confirmed that Customs cannot be 'estopped' from protecting the revenue even if one of their authorised persons has given an incorrect ruling to a taxpayer who has acted on it in good faith, but there is still some hope in that misdirection is dealt with in VAT Public Notice 48 'Extra-Statutory Concessions' para 2.5. This concession follows a Parliamentary statement made by Mr Robert Sheldon on 21 July 1978 (Hansard, vol 161, col 426) now commonly known as the 'Sheldon statement'.

The statement runs as follows:

> 'If a Customs and Excise officer, with the full facts before him, has given a clear and unequivocal ruling on VAT in writing or, knowing the full facts, has misled a registered person to his detriment, any assessment of VAT due will be based on the correct ruling from the date the error was brought to the registered person's attention.'

Where the taxpayer can prove misdirection beyond reasonable doubt, Customs should instruct change of practice only from a current date based on the Sheldon Statement.

Tribunal appeals (ss 82 to 85 and SIs 1986/590 and 2288)

16.54 If all efforts to reach an agreement with the local office fail, the taxpayer may appeal to an independent VAT Tribunal. If still unsuccessful, the case may be further appealed on points of law to successively the

High Court, the Court of Appeal, the House of Lords and possibly even the European Court of Justice which has the power to rule that UK national law may be *ultra vires* the EC Sixth Directive.

The main subjects on which a Tribunal may hear appeals are follows:

- registration and cancellation of registration
- the tax chargeable on a supply
- an amount of input tax disallowed
- the proportion of input tax recoverable
- any decision concerning the approval of a person as a fiscal warehousekeeper
- the amount of a refund of VAT on the construction of a dwelling for oneself
- bad debt relief claims
- the cancellation of an election to pay actual VAT due under the payments on account scheme
- refund of input tax in respect of importation for private purposes of goods belonging to another person
- refusal to allow group registration or a change to an existing group
- direction that two or more persons should be registered for VAT as one taxable person
- a notice given by Customs terminating a company's involvement in a group registration
- a refusal to act or continue to act on a request to be registered as an intending trader
- any direction that VAT must be charged on the open market value of a supply
- refusal to allow use of a retail scheme
- any requirement imposed by Customs on the production of tax invoices by a computer
- assessments or the amount charged on assessments
- the requirement to provide security
- any liability to a penalty or surcharge
- the amount of any penalty, interest or surcharge
- the making of an assessment within a twenty-year time limit instead of a three-year limit
- refusal to allow use or termination of the cash accounting scheme.

The ability to appeal is clearly welcome but the potential appellant should always perform a cost benefit analysis before deciding whether or not to proceed because of the often significant cost of professional representation which would be borne if the appeal were lost and on rare occasions even if it were won.

16.55 The following approach to assurance visits and reacting to Customs' findings is recommended:

- take notes during visits
- ask for all findings to be confirmed in writing
- ensure all areas of dispute are agreed and understood by both parties
- make full use of the local review procedure, more than once if necessary
- be aware of statutory and case law relevant to the business
- keep fully abreast of developments and act on relevant issues
- prepare meticulously
- use professional expertise where necessary
- be confident.

16.56 A successful allegation by Customs that sales and/or purchases have been suppressed or that fictitious purchase invoices have been included will have a direct bearing on the liability to direct taxation. The agreement of the amount involved will influence the subsequent settlement with the Inland Revenue, and there is a tendency to forget this, settling for additional VAT of only 17.5% whilst forgetting that direct tax could be as high as 40% on the same figure. Adequate preparation for the control visit and hard negotiating in the face of any challenge is therefore essential.

Interest in cases of departmental error and repayment supplement

Statutory interest

16.57 Subject to the three-year cap, interest is available from Customs in cases where a taxpayer has made a payment because of Customs' error.

In accordance with *s 78*, interest is available where the taxpayer has:

- paid too much VAT,
- underclaimed,
- been prevented from reclaiming VAT at the proper time, or

- been denied a set-off of tax against an amount owing to Customs

as a result of a Customs error.

Taxpayers must claim in writing. The interest rates vary and are normally changed when the rate of default interest in Customs' favour changes. The rate from 6 May 2001 is 4%.

The interest period runs from the date Customs receive the overpayment or from the date of authorisation of a refund claim that is too low. For any other repayment delay, interest runs from the date the taxpayer might reasonably have expected to receive it from Customs. The interest period does not include time taken up by Customs in dealing with reasonable queries or time when the taxpayer's conduct hinders Customs' work.

Repayment supplement

16.58 Under *s 79*, Customs are obliged to pay a repayment supplement on repayment returns that they do not authorise and repay on time. Customs must receive the relevant return by the due date for it to qualify for a supplement, which is then payable if Customs fail to direct the issue of the repayment within the 'relevant period'.

The phrase 'relevant period' means the period of 30 days beginning with the later of:

- the day after the last day of the tax period in question, and
- the date Customs receive the relevant return or claim.

The 'relevant period' provision relates to claims received by Customs on or after 9 March 1999 and was introduced to close a loophole in the legislation that allowed artificial claims prior to that date.

The repayment supplement itself is the greater of £50 and 5% of the refund, but if the relevant return overstates the refund due by more than the greater of £250 and 5% of the true amount of the claim, no supplement will be paid.

Repayment supplement does not apply to the following:

- overdeclarations notified by Customs;
- Eighth Directive refunds paid to businesses from other EC member states (see Chapter 13);
- refunds paid under the DIY housebuilders scheme;
- VAT claimed after deregistration on professional fees;
- bad debt relief claims.

Mixed Supplies

Mayhew operates a retail confectionery and newspaper business. The following figures for his tax period from 1 June 2001 to 31 August 2001 are extracted from his records:

	£
Sales of confectionery	30,200
Sales of newspapers and magazines	16,200
Sale of shop equipment	600
Purchases of confectionery	21,200
Purchases of newspapers and magazines	9,100
Wages	11,300
Other expenses — standard-rated	4,600
— zero-rated	380
— exempt	140
Purchase of a new motor car for manager on 1 June 2001	8,460
No VAT is included in any of the above figures	

The figure of £4,600 for standard-rated expenses includes £2,920 leasing charges on a car used by Mayhew and also includes all petrol used for both business and private purposes by Mayhew and the manager. The fuel scale charge is £453 per quarter for Mayhew's car and £307 per quarter for the manager's car (both inclusive of VAT).

The VAT payable by Mayhew for the period from 1 June 2001 to 31 August 2001 is as follows:

Mayhew — VAT return quarter ended 31 August 2001

	£
Output tax (see below)	5,502
Input tax (see below)	4,515
Payable by 30 September 2001	987
Outputs *	£47,648
Inputs **	£43,880

Computation of Output Tax:	£		£
Confectionery	30,200	@ 17.5%	5,285
Newspapers	16,200	@ 0%	–
Equipment	600	@ 17.5%	105
Petrol £453 × 7/47			67
40/47 =	386		
£307 × 7/47			45
40/47 =	262		
Outputs *	47,648		5,502

Computation of Input Tax:	£		£
Confectionery	21,200	@ 17.5%	3,710
Newspapers	9,100	@ 0%	–
Expenses	4,600	@ 17.5%	805
	380	@ 0%	–
	140	Exempt	–
Capital expenditure on car	8,460	Non-deductible	–
Inputs **	43,880		4,515

Zero-Rating, Exemption and Partial Exemption

N Sawyer, a furniture manufacturer, who is a registered taxable person for value added tax, undertook the following transactions:

(i) Sold furniture for £16,000 less settlement discount of 5% to a UK wholesaler who did not deduct this when making payment.

(ii) Sold furniture (in January 2001) for £3,000 to a UK wholesaler who was declared bankrupt before the payment date on 1 February 2001. The trustee in bankruptcy estimates dividends of 20% will eventually become payable.

(iii) Sold furniture for £10,000 to a customer in the USA.

(iv) Sold furniture (in February 2001) for £30,000 to a customer in France who provided a French VAT number.

(v) Sold machine no longer required for use in the trade to a London merchant for £1,000.

(vi) Sold furniture (in March 2001) for £2,000 to a customer in Germany who is not registered for VAT.

(vii) Sold motor car for £3,000 which had originally cost him £15,000.

(viii) Hired furniture to a nearby factory for use at a staff party, charging hire of £600.

(ix) Rented part of his office accommodation to a business associate for six months at £400 per month commencing 1 September 2000.

(x) Incurred legal charges of £400 for preparation of a rental agreement re the letting of his office accommodation.

(xi) Bought a new machine from Germany for £20,000 in January 2001.

(xii) Bought materials from Norway for manufacturing purposes for £80,000.

(xiii) Incurred £750 bank charges in respect of his business bank overdraft.

All items exclude any addition for VAT.

The amount of VAT chargeable or recoverable by Sawyer in respect of each item is as follows:

N Sawyer — Value added tax chargeable or recoverable

		£
(i)	Where a cash discount is offered, VAT is chargeable only on the discounted amount, whether the discount is taken or not. Sawyer will therefore be liable to account for VAT of 17.5% × £15,200 (£16,000 less 5% thereof).	2,660
(ii)	Sawyer will account for VAT of 17.5% × £3,000 when he makes the taxable supply.	525
	He will be able to make a claim for a refund of this amount six months after the payment date, i.e. 1 August 2001 (reduced if any amount is received from the trustee in bankruptcy). Sawyer must notify the debtor in writing within 7 days of making the claim. The debtor then has to account to Customs for input tax claimed.	
(iii)	Exports to non-EC countries are zero-rated, so no tax will be chargeable on the sale of the furniture to the USA customer so long as satisfactory evidence of export is available.	–
(iv)	Supplies to EC countries are zero-rated providing proof of export is held and the customer provides a valid VAT number which is shown on Sawyer's invoice. The country codes (FR:GB) must be shown before the VAT numbers.	
	Therefore, no tax will be chargeable on the sale of furniture to the French VAT registered trader.	–
(v)	VAT is charged on both revenue and capital items, so Sawyer will be liable to account for VAT of 17.5% × £1,000	175
(vi)	If supplies are made to another EC country and the customer is *not* a registered trader then UK VAT will be chargeable i.e. 17.5% × £2,000	350
(vii)	VAT is not payable on the sale of a second-hand motor car except to the extent if any that the sale price exceeds the cost. No tax will therefore be payable in this case.	–
(viii)	Taxable supplies include the hire of goods, so Sawyer will be liable to account for VAT of 17.5% × £600.	105

		£
(ix)	Rent of land is an exempt item so no VAT is chargeable unless an option to tax is exercised by the landlord or the rent included the use of facilities. VAT of £400 × 17.5% = £70 per month would be due in those cases.	
(x)	Professional charges made by a registered taxable person are liable to VAT in the normal way, even if they relate to an exempt output by the person incurring the expense, thus the person who prepared the rental agreement will, if he is a taxable person, be liable to account for VAT at 17.5% × £400 = £70.	
	Sawyer will only be able to recover the £70 so long as he exercises his option to tax the rents or the rent includes use of facilities or his input VAT does not have to be restricted because of exempt supplies. Assuming the latter	(70)
(xi)	Sawyer will be required to account for output tax of 17.5% of £20,000 = £3,500 on the acquisition of the machine from Germany for use in his business, but as he is fully taxable, he will be entitled to deduct an equivalent amount as input tax in the same VAT return	3,500
	so the net effect will be nil.	(3,500)
	Sawyer must give his VAT number to the German supplier who will show it on his invoice.	
(xii)	The importation of goods from a non-EC country will result in VAT being paid at the border or later under the duty deferment scheme. It is not paid to Customs on the normal VAT return. That VAT may be treated as input tax and therefore Sawyer will be able to recover £80,000 × 17.5% on his VAT return	(14,000)
(xiii)	Bank charges are an exempt item so no VAT is chargeable, or recoverable by Sawyer	–

Supplementary Example 3

New Business Venture

Wilson is in the process of obtaining a lease on premises for a new business venture. The building concerned is currently not in use, having previously been used by its owners as a grocery store. Wilson is purchasing the fixtures and fittings for £75,000 and will pay a rent of £12,000 p.a. No premium will be payable on the grant of the lease.

The vendor is registered for VAT and has not exercised his option to apply VAT to supplies relating to the building in question.

Wilson anticipates using part of the building as an off-licence, part as a delicatessen and the remainder as tea rooms.

The produce sold in the tea rooms, e.g. sandwiches, cakes, etc., will also be available in the delicatessen.

Wilson currently operates a catering franchise at a municipal golf course in another town and is VAT registered.

The goods for resale will be acquired from one source for both businesses.

The VAT implications of

(*a*) commencing the new business venture, and

(*b*) accounting for VAT on outputs will be:

(*a*) A further registration will not be required as Wilson's existing number will be used, only one return being submitted each quarter.

The grant of a lease is exempt from VAT, although the landlord may opt to charge VAT both on any premium for the grant of the lease and on any rents. The landlord has not exercised his option in this example.

The purchase of the fixtures will not be outside the scope of VAT under *Article 5(1)* of the *Value Added Tax (Special Provisions) Order 1995 (SI 1995/1268)* because the business is not being transferred as a going concern.

Accordingly, Wilson will have to pay £13,125 VAT to the vendor on the purchase of the fixtures and fittings (£75,000 × 17.5%) provided the contract describes the price as being exclusive of VAT. Otherwise the price will be deemed to be inclusive of VAT and VAT of 7/47 × £75,000 = £11,170 will be payable to Customs by the vendor out of the £75,000 received.

Input tax will be recoverable on Wilson's next VAT return providing he receives a VAT invoice.

Since the landlord has not exercised his option to charge VAT, the rent is an exempt supply, and will not have VAT added to it.

Wilson must ensure that his records contain the required information in order to complete the return for the combined business.

If the new premises are to become the principal place of business, then the existing VAT local office must be informed in writing within thirty days.

(*b*) The existing business and the new business will both be retail businesses covered by the special schemes for retailers.

The existing business would appear to make all supplies at standard rate, the VAT being calculated as 7/47ths of takings.

The new business will make supplies at standard rate (off-licence and tea rooms) and also at zero rate (certain food sales in delicatessen).

It would be very difficult to split the purchases for the delicatessen, the tea room, and the catering franchise, so that the schemes that rely upon analysis of purchases will not be appropriate.

It would be difficult to estimate zero-rated sales by reference to purchases since the various aspects of the business rely on the same purchases. Schemes which identify supplies at the point of sale would therefore be the appropriate ones to use. In that connection, in the case of the tea room the major difficulty is likely to be a customer who decides to buy food to take out at the same time as consuming goods on the premises.

The delicatessen sales will need analysing between standard-rated and zero-rated sales and some reasonable form of proof of the analysis, like a coded till roll, kept.

General Compliance Issues

John's Jeans, a wholesaler, makes up its VAT returns to 31 July, 31 October, 31 January and 30 April in each VAT accounting year.

Its sales (net of VAT) for the year ended 30 April 2001 were:

		Adult Clothing £	**Children's Clothing £**	**Commissions on Factored Children's Clothing £**
Quarter ended	31 July 2000	21,200	14,750	1,200
	31 October 2000	18,700	12,925	340
	31 January 2001	32,600	21,617	3,780
	30 April 2001	23,900	15,284	1,100
		96,400	64,576	6,420

Its records relating to purchases and general business overheads show the following inputs:

		Invoice Totals (inc VAT) £	**VAT £**	**Petrol for Sole Proprietor (included in Invoices) £**
Quarter ended	31 July 2000	25,165	2,310	204
	31 October 2000	37,952	3,862	287
	31 January 2001	22,137	2,108	228
	30 April 2001	40,478	4,771	240

John had not made any exempt supplies during the year ended 30 April 2000.

During the year John had sold his 1,600cc Ford on 1 October 2000 for £2,000 and purchased a new 1,100cc Metro for £8,000. The purchase and sale are not included in the above figures. By 30 April 2001 the Metro had travelled 6,900 miles. John's mileage had not altered materially during the year. The car is his only motor vehicle.

On 23 December 2000 John presented his manager with a clock as recognition of twenty-five years' service. The clock cost John £140 plus VAT and had a retail value of £235 (including VAT).

Owing to cash flow problems John sold his freehold warehouse on 1 March 2001 for £200,000. The warehouse had been erected ten years previously and John had made no election to waive exemption from VAT prior to the sale. Legal and agent's costs amounting to £12,000 plus VAT of £2,100 are included in the purchase invoices. He now operates from rented premises.

It is the policy of the firm to pay all invoices within seven days of receipt. Clothing debtors take an average of 90 days to pay their accounts. Commission is paid with the tax invoice.

The VAT payable or reclaimable in each of the above quarters and the amounts to be included as outputs and inputs on each of those returns would be as follows:

John's Jeans — Summary of VAT returns

	Q/E 31.7.2000 £	Q/E 31.10.2000 £	Q/E 31.1.01 £	Q/E 30.4.01 £
Output tax — see calculation below	3,968	3,376	6,428	4,413
Input tax	2,310	3,862	2,108	2,671
Payable	1,658		4,320	1,742
Repayable		486		
Outputs – see calculation below	37,426	32,221	58,354	240,501
Inputs – see calculation below	22,855	34,090	20,029	35,707
Computation of output tax				
Adult clothing	21,200	18,700	32,600	23,900
Commission	1,200	340	3,780	1,100
	22,400	19,040	36,380	25,000
At 17.5%	3,920	3,332	6,366	4,375
Gift to employee			24	
Scale charge for petrol — see calculation below	48	44	38	38
	3,968	3,376	6,428	4,413

	Q/E 31.7.2000 £	Q/E 31.10.2000 £	Q/E 31.1.01 £	Q/E 30.4.01 £
Scale charges for petrol				
1,600cc car	48.40	32.27	–	–
1,100cc car	–	12.71	38.12	38.12
	48.40	44.98	38.12	38.12
Computation of outputs (net of VAT)				
Adult clothing	21,200	18,700	32,600	23,900
Commission	1,200	340	3,780	1,100
Children's clothing	14,750	12,925	21,617	15,284
Gift to employee	–	–	140	–
Sale of buildings	–	–	–	200,000
Scale charge for petrol	276	256	217	217
	37,426	32,221	58,354	240,501
Computation of inputs (net of VAT)				
Gross	25,165	37,952	22,137	40,478
Less VAT	2,310	3,862	2,108	4,771
	22,855	34,090	20,029	35,707

Note:
Although the fuel scale charge altered at 6 April 2001, the new rate will only be used from the start of the next VAT quarter.

De minimis limits for input tax attributed to exempt supplies in quarter to 30.4.01:

Attributed input tax re exempt supplies Sale of building	£2,100
De minimis limit is £625 per month × 3 months =	£1,875

(and less than 50% of all input tax, i.e. below 50% × £4,771 = £2,386)

As the attributed input tax exceeds £1,875, no deduction is allowed for that tax. Input tax for the quarter ended 30 April 2001 is therefore:

	£
Total input tax	4,771
Less attributed to exempt supplies	2,100
Attributed to taxable supplies	2,671

As John did not have any exempt supplies in the preceding VAT year then for the purpose of the annual adjustment for exempt supplies the period is limited to the period from the first day of the quarter in which the supply occurs (1 February 2001) to the end of the VAT year (30 April) and where the supply occurs in the last quarter, as it does in this example, then there is no annual adjustment.

If the building had been sold in May 2000, i.e. in the first quarter, the *de minimis* limit would have been the lower of:

(i) £625 per month × 12 months = £7,500, or

(ii) 50% of all input tax

½ × £13,051 = £6,525

The *de minimis* limit for John's Jeans for the year ended 30 April 2001 would therefore be £6,525. The attributed input tax would have been less than that amount and it would therefore have been allowed in full.

As the exempt supply is an isolated supply it is assumed that Customs would not attempt to disallow any part of input tax relating to general overheads.

Using approximate calculations, the effect of adopting:

(*a*) cash accounting for VAT (see 15.27 *et seq.*)

(*b*) annual accounting for VAT (see 15.36 *et seq.*)

on the assumption that the turnover during 2001/02 will be 5% greater than in 2000/01 would be as follows:

(*a*) John's Jeans has made taxable supplies during the year to 30 April 2001, excluding the sale of the building (an exempt supply) of (37,426 + 32,221 + 58,354 + 40,501) = £168,502 with an estimated turnover for the coming year of £176,927. Since this is less than £600,000 (from 1 April 2001, previously £350,000) John may use the scheme.

Since John pays his bills as they arrive he will receive the maximum advantage from operating cash accounting. Using an average figure, he will receive a 'one-off' cash flow gain of:

Taxable supplies on credit (adult clothing) = £96,400 p.a. (year ended 30.4.01)

Credit period three months 3/12 of £96,400 =	
£24,100 × 17.5% =	4,218
Inflation for 2001/02, say 5%	210
Cash flow advantage	£4,428

This advantage will occur in the first quarter that he adopts the scheme as he will only account for VAT output tax in that period on amounts received for goods supplied after joining the scheme, which with 90 days' credit will be a very small amount. John will, of course, account for VAT on commission when received.

In order to claim input tax he will need to show that the invoices are paid. This could be done by adding the cheque number to the invoice with date of payment. If bills are paid by cash then a receipted VAT invoice will be required.

As well as the cash flow advantage mentioned above John will also receive automatic relief for bad debts whilst he is within the scheme.

(*b*) The annual accounting scheme is available to businesses who expect their tax exclusive turnover for the coming year to be not more than £600,000 (from 1 April 2001, previously £300,000). Since this applies to John he is eligible to use the scheme.

If John elected to make annual returns from 1 July 2001 then his monthly payment would be:

VAT paid in previous year (1,658 – 486 + 4,320 + 1,742) = 7,234 × 10% = £723

Payments of £723 per month would be made from the end of October 2001 to June 2002, with a final payment with the VAT return by 31 August 2002.

Motor Vehicles

(*a*) A wholesaler has the following transactions in motor vehicles used in his business during the quarter ended 30 June 2001.

(i) Sale of Mini car for £2,000 (cost August 1998, £3,750)

(ii) Purchase of Morgan car for £24,000

(iii) Purchase of transit van for £11,750

(iv) Sale of Morgan car (purchased above) for £28,700.

VAT liability — quarter ended 30 June 2001

		Output tax (Input tax) £
(i)	Mini cost £3,750, selling price £2,000 — no liability	–
(ii)	Morgan cost £24,000. No input tax deductible	–
(iii)	Transit van cost £11,750 Input tax deductible $\frac{7}{47} \times$ £11,750	(1,750)
(iv)	Sale of Morgan for £28,700 Margin over cost £4,700 $\times \frac{7}{47}$	700

(*b*) A registered trader leased a new motor car in August 2001. The agreement provided for payments of £470 per month. All fuel used in the vehicle and all repairs and servicing required is paid for by the business, and VAT recovered thereon. It has been agreed that two-thirds of the usage of the vehicle is for business purposes.

From 1 August 1995 a leasing company can fully recover input tax on the purchase of a qualifying motor car which is to be leased out. The leasing charges are therefore calculated on the net of VAT price. To that figure is added VAT at 17.5%, i.e. £400 + VAT at 17.5% = £70 = leasing charge £470. To indicate that the lease company had purchased the car on a VAT invoice, and had recovered input tax, the lease invoice must state that the leased car is a qualifying car under *article 7(2)* of the *VAT (Input Tax) Order 1992 (SI 1992/3222)*.

If such a car is leased by a fully taxable trader who uses it *wholly* for business purposes, then the VAT element is recoverable as input tax. If, however, there is any private use of a qualifying leased car by the registered trader, or by an employee, shareholder or associate, then only 50% of the input VAT on the car lease payments is recoverable. A partly exempt business will further restrict the claim if the car is treated as an overhead by reference to the exempt portion. An exempt business, or partly exempt business that allocates the car wholly to exempt supplies, cannot recover any input tax.

In this instance 50% of the VAT will be recoverable, i.e. 50% x £70 = £35 per month. As VAT is recovered on all fuel purchased the fuel scale charge will apply in calculating the trader's output tax. Because the vehicle is used for business purposes, VAT input tax is recoverable in full on the repair and servicing costs, without a private proportion adjustment (Customs Notice 700/64 paragraph 28 as amended).

(*c*) A national company has a fleet of 115 cars used by sales representatives, of which 84 are 1,600cc cars used by higher paid employees, 30 are 1,300cc cars used by lower paid employees and the remaining car is a 2,800cc car used by the sales director.

The VAT implications of:

(i) requiring a contribution from each user of £94 per month in respect of the private use of the car;

(ii) providing all petrol for the cars (including travel from home to office);

(iii) charging each user for all petrol used privately;

(iv) reducing the salary of each user by £94 per month when first provided with a car;

(v) changing to diesel powered cars and providing all fuel as in (ii) above,

are as follows.

From 1 August 1995 no VAT liability arises on contributions made by employees for use of a company-owned car on which input tax has been blocked or a leased car to which the 50% restriction has been applied. (The income tax charge for the provision of the car would be reduced by the employee contribution.)

Any petrol provided for private use of employees constitutes a taxable supply. This is accounted for by applying VAT to the income tax fuel scale charge for all cars (owned or leased) whether provided to higher or lower paid employees, or by not claiming deductible input tax on any fuel purchased.

The output tax for periods starting after 5 April 2001 would be:

	£ p
84 × £45.72 =	3,840.48
30 × £36.04 =	1,081.20
1 × £67.46 =	67.46
VAT payable per quarter	4,989.14

(*d*) If each car user is charged for petrol used privately then 7/47 of the amounts charged is output tax and must be accounted for in the normal manner. If the price charged to the employees for petrol is less than that paid by the employer or does not cover all fuel used privately, then the scale charges still apply.

(*e*) VAT is not payable on a salary sacrifice and therefore no liability would arise. (The full income tax charge would apply on the provision of the car, but as the salary is lower by £94 per month, income tax relief would be obtained for the reduction in salary, rather than the contribution by the employee as in (i) above, leaving the employee in the same position.)

If the company changed to diesel powered cars, the quarterly charge would be reduced by £1,126.41 to:

	£ p
114 × £33.51 =	3,820.14
1 × £42.59 =	42.59
VAT payable per quarter	3,862.73

(*f*) A driving school bought a motor vehicle for use as a car for instruction for £11,750 on 1 August 1997.

The VAT implications if the school sold the car for £7,520 on 31 March 2001 to:

(1) another driving school, or

(2) a member of the public, or

(3) a second-hand car dealer, would be:

(i) A driving school registered for VAT is entitled to reclaim input tax on the purchase of a car to be used for driving instruction, i.e. 7/47 × £11,750 = £1,750.

(ii) Since the driving school recovered the input tax on the car in full, VAT must be charged on the full selling price when the car is sold, no matter who the purchaser is (unless the purchaser is from outside the EC, in which case the export sale would be zero-rated). A VAT invoice must be issued to a buyer who will be able to reclaim input tax, such as a VAT registered used car dealer, or another driving school etc., but need not be issued to a member of the public. Car dealers will deal with such a car outside the margin scheme and when it is sold the dealer will charge output VAT on the full sale proceeds.

(*g*) A garage is not approved to carry out MOT tests but offers to its customers the service of taking the vehicle for test to an approved centre. Set out the VAT implications of:

(i) charging the customer the actual fee charged by the approved centre;

(ii) charging the customer the actual fee for the MOT paid to the approved centre plus a service charge for delivery and collection;

(iii) charging the customer the full statutory fee for the MOT, when the approved centre has charged a discounted price.

Customs have confirmed that charges for MOT tests are outside the scope of VAT as a statutory levy, providing the amount charged by an approved centre does not exceed the statutory maximum fee. Furthermore, any discount offered by an approved centre to an unapproved garage is no longer treated as a taxable supply by the unapproved garage, but as a normal trade discount and therefore it has no VAT effect (i.e. the amount net of discount is outside the scope of VAT). The position in the circumstances indicated is:

(1) If the amount charged by an unapproved garage is exactly the same as that charged by the approved centre, then it can be treated as a disbursement and thus outside the scope of VAT. In order for this to apply, the conditions set out in Customs Notice 700 at paragraph 10.8 must be met.

(2) If the unapproved garage charges an additional amount for arranging the test, for example for delivery and collection, the additional fee is liable to VAT at the standard rate. The test fee may still be treated as outside the scope of VAT providing it is shown on the invoice as a separate amount.

(3) Where an unapproved garage charges its customer a higher amount than that charged by the approved garage, and does not show the additional amount separately on the invoice, the supply does not satisfy Customs' conditions and therefore the whole supply is a composite supply chargeable at the standard rate.

Supplementary Example 6

Groups of Companies and Group Registration

The Johnstone Group is comprised of the following companies:

Johnstone plc — a quoted holding company, which co-ordinates three trading subsidiaries:

Doubles Limited — a manufacturer of dominoes for sale in the UK and export markets.

Excess Limited — an authorised motor insurance company.

Flush Limited — the owner and operator of the 'Full House' casino in London.

Doubles Limited is the only company in the group which is registered for VAT.

The VAT implications of the following transactions, with appropriate planning suggestions, are:

(i) Johnstone plc is the company which handles all the employment matters for the group, entering into contracts of employment with employees. It also operates the payroll and provides benefits in kind. It recharges on a monthly basis to the appropriate company the costs attributable to employees who work for each subsidiary.

(ii) Doubles Limited incurs legal and professional fees of £40,000 plus VAT in arranging a deposit of £2 million from its surplus funds which it places with Excess Limited. Excess Limited then pays interest on the deposit of 10% on 30 June and 31 December each year.

(iii) Flush Limited buys two gaming machines and a new roulette table which it installs in the casino.

(iv) Doubles Limited pays £30,000 to Excess Limited for corporation tax group relief for trading losses of £100,000 surrendered to it by Excess Limited.

Although Doubles Limited is the only company currently registered for VAT, it would appear likely from the information given that Johnstone plc should be registered in respect of the provision of recharged salaries and Flush Limited may be registrable as regards supplies relating to gaming machines.

A penalty will be incurred for non-registration, based upon the VAT due by the relevant company from the date notification should have occurred to the date of actual registration. If that period is under 9 months the penalty would be 5% of the tax payable. For a period over 9 months and under 18 months the penalty is 10%, increased to 15% for a period over 18 months and under three years; thereafter there could be a civil fraud penalty of up to 100% of the tax due if Customs considered the failure to register was conduct involving dishonesty.

(i) *Johnstone plc — recharged salaries*

The provision of staff to another company is a taxable supply, not a reimbursement (*C & E Commrs v Tarmac Roadstone Holdings Limited, CA [1987] STC 610*) so VAT should be added to the recharges.

The VAT charged would be recoverable input tax for Doubles Limited. Flush Limited may be able to recover part of its input tax if it is registered because of its taxable supplies. Excess Limited is wholly exempt and the tax is irrecoverable.

Accordingly the present arrangements give rise to an unnecessary cost of non-recoverable input tax. The simplest way to avoid that cost would be for each company to employ its own staff and bear its own payroll administration costs directly.

(ii) *Doubles Limited — professional costs re loan*

A supply of money (loan to Excess Limited) or credit is an exempt supply. Any costs (professional charges) must be attributed to the relevant supply. Accordingly the VAT input tax of £7,000 is attributed to an exempt supply and is not allowable. This rule applies to all partial exemption tax years starting on or after 10 March 1999 (*SI 1995/2518* as amended by *SI 1999/599*). The regulations previously allowed certain businesses to disregard exempt input tax in specified categories, such as that which was attributable to deposits of money. Therefore, if Doubles Limited had incurred the £7,000 input tax in a tax year ending 31 March, 30 April or 31 May 1999 or before, it would have been able to recover it. It may still be possible to recover such input tax if the supply to which it relates (the supply of money or credit) is considered incidental to the main business activities (*SI 1995/2518, Reg 103*).

(iii) *Flush Limited — gaming equipment*

Normally casinos only make supplies that are exempt from VAT, so the input tax on the roulette table is not recoverable.

Flush Limited may, however, be making taxable supplies in addition to the exempt supplies. The takings from the gaming machines are taxable supplies, as are any admission fees and bar or catering supplies. If such supplies exceed the current threshold (£54,000), then registration will be compulsory. Input tax on the gaming machines would then be recoverable in full (attributable to taxable supplies).

Flush Limited should also agree a suitable partial exemption scheme to maximise its input tax recovery on overheads. This would include the VAT charged by Johnstone plc on the payroll.

(iv) *Doubles Limited — group relief*

A payment for group relief is a movement of funds and not a supply for VAT, so there are no VAT consequences of the payment.

Care must be taken to ensure that no other services (e.g. management charges) are included, as these would be liable to VAT.

FOOTNOTE

A group registration for all companies would not be appropriate to Johnstone plc and its subsidiaries in view of the wholly exempt business of Excess Limited and the partly exempt business of Flush Limited. If those companies were not included in the group registration then only Johnstone plc and Doubles Limited would be grouped. This may be appropriate to ensure that input tax incurred by the holding company is not fully lost.

However, it may then mean that other supplies by the holding company to its exempt subsidiaries would become taxable rather than being made by a non-registered company (if the supplies by the holding company were below the registration limit).

Should any of the members of this commercial group wish to form a group registration, they must apply in writing. Customs then have 90 days from receipt of the application to accept or refuse it. They also have the power to include or remove a relevant company from a group registration where it appears necessary to do so for the protection of the revenue (see 2.35).

Table of Cases

Abbey National plc (C-408/98) 6.29
British Airways plc v C & E Commrs CA, [1990] STC 643 3.52
C & E Commrs v British Telecommunications plc HL, [1999] STC 758 3.53
C & E Commrs v FDR Ltd, CA [2000] STC 672 5.37
C & E Commrs v Plantiflor Ltd CA, [2000] STC 137 3.53
C & E Commrs v Zoological Society of London, CJEC Case C-267/00 5.82
Card Protection Plan [2001] STC 174 3.52, 4.11, 4.30
Century Life plc, CA 2000, [2001] STC 38 5.17
Centrax Ltd, LON/98/218, No 15743 11.5
Chobham Golf Club, LON/96/833, No 14867 5.77
EC Commission v Italian Republic (Case C-45/95) [1997] STC 1062 5.83, 9.38
Goldsmiths Jewellers Ltd v C & E Commrs (Case C-330/95) [1997] STC 1073 3.41
International Language Centres Limited v C & E Commrs (No 2) QB, [1983] STC 394 16.29
Liverpool Institute for Performing Arts, CA [1999] STC 424 7.10
Lubbock Fine & Co, LON/90/1657, No 6242 Chapter 8 Annex
Madgett & Anor (t/a Howden Court Hotel) ECJ Joined Cases C-308/96 and C-94/97 10.36, 10.37
Medical Defence Union v Department of Trade [1979] 2 All ER 421 5.6
Merseyside Cablevision Limited, MAN/85/327, No 2419 2.20
Mirror Group Plc, LON/97/233, No 15443 8.29
Prudential Corporation plc (VTD 17030) 5.41
Rialto Homes plc [1999] VATDR 477 (VTD 16340) 8.16
SEH Holdings Limited (VTD 16771) 8.48
Silver Knight Exhibitions Ltd, MAN/92/1826, No 10569 16.45

Table of Statutes

1907 Limited Partnership Act . . . 2.23

1950 Employment and Training (Northern Ireland) Act 5.57

1960 Professions Supplementary to Medicine Act 5.61

1968 Gaming Act
- s 14 . . . . 5.19
- Pt II 5.20, 5.23
- Pt III 5.20

1968 Medicines Act 4.68

1973 Employment Training Act . 5.57

1982 Insurance Companies Act . . 5.5, 5.11
- ss 2–4 . . . . 5.3
- Schs 1, 2 . . . . 5.3

1983 Medical Act
- s 18(3) 5.62

1986 Financial Services Act 5.42

1988 Income and Corporation Taxes Act
- s 839 . . . . 4.38, 5.16

1989 Water Act 4.20

1990 Enterprise and New Towns (Scotland) Act 5.57

1994 Value Added Tax Act (VATA 1994) 1.4, 6.48
- s 6 . . . . 3.9
- s 7 . . . . 3.1, 3.2
  - (4) 2.6, 2.37
  - (10)(11) 12.29
- s 8 . . . . 3.23
- s 9(a)(b) 2.5
- ss 10–14 . . . . 3.22, 11.3
- s 24 . . . . 6.2
  - (1)(2) 1.22
- s 25 . . . . 6.10, 15.2, 15.3
- s 26 . . . . 6.6, 7.5
  - (2)(b) 6.13
- s 28 . . . . 15.46
- s 30(6) 12.15
- s 33 . . . . 2.34
- s 36 . . . . 3.39
- s 39 . . . . 13.1
- s 40 . . . . 14.18
- s 41 . . . . 2.34
  - (6) 5.69, 5.77
- s 42 . . . . 2.34
- s 43 . . . . 2.25
- s 46 . . . . 2.29
- s 48 . . . . 11.24
- s 49(1)(a) 2.10
- s 50A 9.1
- s 51A 2.31
- s 53 . . . . 10.1
- s 55(1)–(4) 5.84
- ss 59–69 . . . . 16.31
- s 59(2)(7) 16.43
- ss 59A, 59B 16.31
- s 60 . . . . 15.35
- s 61 . . . . 16.34
- ss 63, 64 . . . . 16.36
- ss 67, 68 . . . . 16.40
- s 69 . . . . 13.6, 16.40
- s 70 . . . . 16.31
- s 71 . . . . 16.43
- s 72(3) 4.54
- s 73 . . . . 16.5, 16.8, 16.22, 16.26
  - (1) 16.5, 16.6, 16.26
  - (2)–(3) 16.6, 16.26
  - (4) 16.6
  - (5) 16.27
  - (6) 16.16, 16.22, 16.23
  - (7) 16.7
  - (8) 16.8
  - (10) 16.27
- s 74 . . . . 16.9
- s 75 . . . . 16.10, 16.22
  - (1)(2) 16.11

1994 Value Added Tax Act (VATA 1994)
s 76 . . . . . . 16.10, 16.12, 16.22
(3) 16.22, 16.23
s 77 . . . . . . 16.16, 16.22, 16.26
(1) 16.22
(2) 16.23, 16.25
(3) 16.23
(4) 16.24, 16.25
(5) 16.25
s 79 . . . . 16.58
ss 82–85 . . . . 16.54
s 88 . . . . 3.69
s 94(3) 5.75
(4) 16.43
s 95 . . . . 11.18
Sch A1 . . . . 4.71, 4.81, 5.1
para 1(6) 8.53, 8.54
para 3(2) 4.71
para 6 . . . . 4.78
Sch 1 para 1 . . . . . 2.2, 2.6, 2.13
para 1A 2.13
para 2 . . . . 2.13
para 9 . . . . 2.5
para 14(1)(2) 1.20
Sch 3A 13.6
Sch 4 para 5 . . . . 13.6
(2) 3.57
(2A)(5A) 3.58
Sch 5 . . . . . 12.36, 12.39, 12.40
para 3 . . . . 12.42
para 7A . . . 12.41, 12.42
Sch 7A 4.3, 4.81, 5.1
Group 6 . . . . . 8.3, 8.53
Group 7 . . . . . 8.3, 8.54
Sch 8 . . . . 4.5, 5.1, 5.72
Group 1 . . . . 4.6
Group 2 . . . . 4.17
Group 3 . . . . 4.23
Group 4 . . . . 4.23
Item 1 . . . . . 4.30
Group 5 . . 4.32, 5.2, 8.3, 8.60
Item 1 . . . . . 8.30
Item 2 . . . . 8.10, 8.25, 8.33
Items 3, 4 . 8.10, 8.25
Group 6 . . 4.32, 8.3, 8.27, 8.35
Item 1 . . . . . 8.30
Group 7 . . . . 4.33
Group 8 . . . . . 4.34, 5.60, 5.73, 12.32, 12.34
Items 1–16 . 4.34
Items 1, 2 . . 4.34
Items 2A, 2B . . 4.34, 4.36
Item 3 . . . . . 4.37
Item 4 . . . . . 4.38
(a) . . 4.38
Item 5 . . . . . 4.39
Item 6 . . . . . 4.40
(a) . . 4.40
Item 6A . . 4.34, 4.40
Items 7–9 . . 4.40
Item 10 . . . . 4.41
(a) . 4.40, 4.41
(b)(c) . . . 4.41
Item 11 . . . . 4.40
Item 12 . . . . 4.42
Item 13 . . . . 4.43
Group 9 . . . . 4.45
Groups 10, 11 . . . . . . 4.46
Group 12 . . . . 4.47, 4.54
Item 1 . . . . 4.48
Item 1A . . 4.49
Items 2–20 . . . 4.50
Item 2 . . . . 4.51
Items 3–20 . . . 4.52
Group 13 . . . . 4.58
Items 1–3 . 4.58
Group 14 . . . . 4.59
Group 15 . . . . 4.47, 4.60
Group 16 . . . . 4.69
Sch 9 . . . . 3.7, 7.6
Group 1 . . . 5.2, 5.83, 8.3, 8.8, 8.40
Item 1 . . . . 8.30, 8.34
Group 2 . . . . . . 5.3, 6.13
Items 1–4 . . 5.3
Group 3 . . . . 5.18
Group 4 . . . . 5.19
Group 5 . . . . . 5.30, 7.13
Items 1–8 . . 6.13
Item 1 . . . . . 5.32
Item 2 . . . . . 5.33
Item 3 . . . . . 5.34

Item 4 . . . . . 5.36
Item 5 . . . . . 5.37
Item 6 . . . . . 5.38
Item 7 . . . . . 5.39
Item 8 . . . . . 5.40
Item 9 . . . . . 5.41
Item 10 . . . . 5.42
Group 6 . . . . 5.44
Item 1 . . . . . 5.51
Item 2 . . . . . 5.52
Item 3 . . . . . 5.53
Item 4 . . . . . 5.55
Group 6 Item 5 . . . . . 5.57
Item 6 . . . . . 5.58
Group 7 . . . . 5.60
Item 1 . . . . . 5.61
Item 2 . . . . . 5.62
Item 3 . . . . . 5.63
Item 4 . . . . . 5.64
Item 5 . . . . . 5.65
Items 6–8 . . 5.66
Items 9, 10 . 5.69
Item 11 . . . . 5.67
Group 8 . . . . 5.71
Group 9 . . . . 5.75
Group 10 . . . . 5.76
Group 11 . . . . 5.78
Group 12 . . . . 5.79
Group 13 . . . . 5.80
Item 1 . . . . 5.81
Item 2 . . . . 5.82
Group 14 . . . . 5.83
Group 15 . . . . 5.84
Sch 9A 2.25–2.27
Sch 10 . . . . 8.3
para 2 . . 5.83, 8.30, 8.40
paras 3, 3A 8.40
Sch 11 . . . . 3.39
para 2 . . . . 3.25
(3) 11.26
para 6 . . . . . . 14.1, 14.4
para 7 . . . . 14.13

1998 Finance Act
s 23 . . . . 3.41

1999 Finance Act 2.28
s 13 . . . . 5.82, 5.84
s 15 . . . . 3.39
s 17 . . . . 16.35
s 18 . . . . 16.23

2000 Limited Liability Partnership Act 2.23

Table of Statutory Instruments

1985/1204 Betting, Gaming and Amusements (Northern Ireland) Order 5.19
Ch III 5.23

1987/1806 VAT (Tour Operators) Order 10.1

1992/2790 Statistics of Trade (Customs and Excise) Regulations 11.31

1992/3121 VAT (Place of Supply of Services) Order 12.30

1992/3222 VAT (Input Tax) Order 16.17
art 7(2) 6.21

1995/1268 VAT (Special Provisions) Order 6.28
art 5 .... 2.39, 6.28

1995/2518 Value Added Tax Regulations
reg 3 .... 6.39
reg 10 .... 11.24
reg 14 .... 3.26
reg 15 .... 3.69
regs 21–23 .... 11.26
reg 25 .... 6.10, 15.2
(4A)–(4L) 15.58
reg 29 .... 6.39
reg 31 .... 14.4
(1)(2) 14.21
regs 49–55 .... 15.36
regs 56–65 .... 15.27
reg 65(2) 6.16
reg 98 .... 11.13
regs 99–110 .... 7.5
reg 99 .... 7.7
reg 101 .... 7.8
(2)(d) 7.10
reg 105 .... 7.15
reg 107 .... 7.17
regs 108, 109 .... 7.20
regs 112–116 .... 7.22
reg 113 .... 7.23
reg 114 .... 7.24
reg 115 .... 7.24, 7.34
reg 130 .... 12.19
regs 146–155 .... 11.18
regs 185–197 .... 31.1

1999/438 VAT (Amendment) Regulations
reg 12 . . . . . 12.19

1999/593 Value Added Tax (Buildings and Land) Order 8.45

1999/594 Value Added Tax (Finance) Order 5.37

1999/599 VAT (Amendment) (No 2) Regulations 7.34

1999/1642 Value Added Tax (Abolition of Zero-Rating for Tax-free Shops) Order 4.59

1999/1994 Value Added Tax (Sport, Sports Competitions and Physical Education) Order 5.77

1999/2833 Value Added Tax (Supplies of Goods Where Input Tax Cannot be Recovered) Order 5.83

1999/2834 Value Added Tax (Subscriptions to Trade Unions, Professional and Other Public Interest Bodies) Order
art 4(a) 5.75

1999/3115 Value Added Tax (Importation of Investment Gold) Relief Order 5.84

1999/3116 Value Added Tax (Investment Gold) Order 5.84
art 3 . . . . . 5.84

2000/753 Value Added Tax (Passenger Vehicles) Order 4.38

Index

A

Accountants, records kept by, 14.14
Accounts *See* Records and accounts
Advertising, 5.37
  charity, 4.67
Agents
  acting in own name, 3.73
  acting in principals' name, 3.72
  definition of, 3.71
  disbursements, 3.75
  insurance, services of, 5.15
  intra-community transactions, 3.73
  invoicing, 3.74
  margin schemes, use of, 9.15
  non-EC transactions, 3.73
  securities, dealings in, 5.39
  transport, relating to, zero-rating, 4.41
Air passenger duty, 10.27
Air transport
  composite supplies, 3.52
Aircraft
  ancillary and associated services, 4.40
  qualifying, meaning, 4.35
  zero-rating, 4.35–4.36
Animals
  DIY livery, 4.15
  food for, 4.13
  grazing rights, 4.14
  keep of, 4.14
  See also Pet food
Annual accounting scheme
  conditions for using, 15.37–15.45
  generally, 15.36
  main features, 15.36
Annual adjustment
  calculation, 7.17–7.18
  registration period, 7.19
Annual invoices
  use of, 3.37
Anti-avoidance
  groups, provisions relating to, 2.27
    completing VAT returns, 15.35
Antiques
  imported and reimported, 4.77, 12.5
  meaning, 9.4
  special VAT rate, 12.5
  See also Auctioneers' scheme
Appeals
  procedure, 16.45
  tribunals,
    assurance visits, approach to, 16.55–16.56
    grounds for appeal, 16.54
    luxuries, amusements and entertainment, relating to, 6.27
    right of appeal, 16.54
Apportionment *See* Partial exemption
Approval
  goods supplied on, 3.15, 11.9
Artistic services
  place of supply, 12.35
Assessments, 16.1–16.4
  additional, 16.21
  errors following incorrect rulings, 16.53
  estimated, 16.15
  estimated outputs, based on, 16.20
  failure to submit returns, 16.15
  following assurance visits, 16.16
  grounds on which to defend, 16.49–16.52
  higher, 16.8
  interest on VAT recovered or recoverable by, 16.9
  local reviews, 16.48
  mark-up,
    fish and chip shops, 16.19
    guidelines, 16.17
    public houses, 16.18
  misdirection, effect of, 16.53
  notification to correct person, 16.27–16.28
  other conditions, 16.29–16.30

Assessments *(continued)*
other powers, 16.10
post-assessment negotiations, 16.48
pre-assessment letter, 16.16, 16.46
pre-assessment negotiations, 16.47
restaurants, 16.20
section 73, under, 16.26
time limits for, 16.16, 16.22–16.26
types of, 16.14
See also Appeals
Assets
business assets, use of, 3.64
deregistration, on hand at, 2.38–2.39
Assurance visits, 1.4
approach to, 16.55–16.56
assessments, following, 16.16
Auctioneers' scheme
antiques, meaning, 9.4
calculating output tax due, 9.25
calculations, 9.28
charges to be included or excluded, 9.28
collectors' items, meaning, 9.4
conditions for operating, 9.24
generally, 9.23
purchase invoices, 9.26
sales invoices, 9.27
works of art, meaning, 9.4
zero-rated goods, 9.29
Austria
recovery of foreign VAT, 13.8
Authenticated receipts
construction industry, 3.33, 8.21, 14.26
Authorised unit trusts, 5.41
Azores, 4.43

B

Bad debts
completing VAT return, 15.17
credit notes, issue of, 3.50
deregistered business, refunds to, 3.47
documentation required, 3.42
group registration and refunds, 3.49
insolvent customers, 3.48
mutual debts, 3.45–3.46
part payment, receipt of, 3.43–3.44
records required, 3.42
Bad debts *(continued)*
refunds of VAT on,
credit notes, 3.50
deregistered business, to, 3.47
documentation required, 3.42
generally, 3.38–3.50
group registrations, 3.49
insolvent customers, 3.48
mutual debts, 3.45–3.46
part payment, receipt of, 3.43–3.44
records required, 3.42
tour operators' margin scheme, 10.28
Bank notes
zero-rating, 4.46
Banks
record-keeping requirements, 14.27
Baptist Union
ecclesiastical exemption, 8.37
Belgium
recovery of foreign VAT, 13.9
Betting and gaming
bingo,
cash bingo, 5.25
generally, 5.23
prize bingo, 5.24
value of exempt supply,
cash bingo, 5.25
prize bingo, 5.24
casino card room games, 5.22
exemption, generally, 5.19–5.21
game of chance, meaning, 5.21
Bingo *See* Betting and gaming
Blind
talking books for, 4.31
wireless sets for, 4.31
Book tokens
zero-rating, 4.29
Booking fees
output tax, 3.66
Books
blind, talking books for, 4.31
leaflet, meaning, 4.25
liability of common items of printed matter, 4.25
printed matter,
liability of common items of, 4.25
services associated with production of, 4.26–4.28
zero-rating, 4.23–4.25

British Retail Consortium, 4.69
Brokers
  insurance, services of, 5.15
Building materials
  meaning, 8.17
  zero-rating, 8.17–8.18
Buildings
  annexes constructed for relevant charitable purpose, 8.12
  change of use,
    disposal or letting, 8.22
    occupier, by, 8.23
  commercial, 8.7, 8.50
    sale of, 8.26
  converted, sale of, 8.28
  exempt land, 8.19
  new, 8.15
  option to tax, 8.7, 8.45–8.46, 8.50
  owned by pension fund, 8.50
  protected, 4.32
  qualifying, 8.7
    sale of, 8.25
      renovated, sale of, 8.28
  tax invoices, 8.19
  See also Construction services, Listed buildings
Burial and cremation
  corpses, removal of, 5.73
  exemption, generally, 5.71
  exhumation, 5.74
  monumental masons, services of, 5.72
Business entertainment
  non-deductible input tax,
    generally, 6.24
    staff parties, 6.25–6.26
    subsistence expenses of staff distinguished, 6.24
    tribunal appeals, 6.27
Business records
  items falling within definition of, 14.8
Business splitting, 2.13
Businesses
  foreign,
    distance sellers to UK, 2.32
    group registration and, 2.28
  gifts, 3.57–3.60
  larger, monthly payments of VAT on account by,
    changes in amounts payable, 15.52
    generally, 15.46–15.51
    leaving scheme, 15.53
Businesses *(continued)*
  larger, monthly payments of VAT on account by, *(continued)*
    option to pay actual monthly VAT due, 15.54–15.56
  stocks and assets, use of, 3.64
  transport, services relating to, 4.41
  See also Business entertainment, Deregistration, Transfer of going concern

C

CD Roms, rating of, 4.24
Call-off stocks, consignments distinguished from, 11.8
Cancellation charges
  output tax, 3.66
Capital goods scheme
  adjustment,
    calculations, further issues concerning, 7.34
    periods, 7.32
    responsibility for, 7.35
  computer hardware, individual items of, 8.6
  construction, 8.4–8.6
  date of acquisition, 7.33
  generally, 7.22–7.27
  input tax on capital goods, 7.35
  land, 7.30, 8.4–8.6
  mechanics in detail, 7.28–7.35
  property, 7.30, 8.4–8.6
  record-keeping, 7.35
  value, how to determine, 7.31
Capping, partial exemption, 7.21
Caravans
  zero-rating, 4.45
Card Protection Plan, 3.52
  zero and reduced rate, 4.11, 4.30
Care
  meaning, 4.64
Care in the Community programme, 5.64
Cars
  accessories, 6.19
  demonstration, 9.38
  fuel scale charges, 3.76
  leased, 6.21
  maintenance, 6.20
  modifications, 6.19
  new rules from 1 August 1995, 6.18

Cars *(continued)*
  non-deductible input tax,
    accessories, 6.19
    leased cars, 6.21
      qualifying, 6.21
    maintenance, 6.20
    modifications, 6.19
    new rules from 1 August 1995, 6.18
    rebates of rentals, 6.22
    repairs, 6.20
    short-term car hire, 6.23
  rebates of rentals, 6.22
  repairs, 6.20
  second-hand, for subsequent export, import VAT repayments on, 12.12
  second-hand goods margin scheme,
    demonstration cars, 9.38
    driving schools, 9.40
    exports, 9.42
    generally, 9.5, 9.35
    imports, 9.41
    incomplete records, 9.36
    mechanical breakdown insurance (MBI), 9.43
    new cars, recovery of input tax on, 9.39
    private taxi firms, 9.40
    road fund licences, 9.37
    self-drive hire firms, 9.40
    self-supplies, 9.38
    trading at auctions, 9.40
    warranties, 9.43
  short-term car hire, 6.23
Cascade taxes
  inherent weaknesses, 1.12
  transaction chain, example, 1.13
Cash accounting scheme
  accruals method, 15.27
  anti-avoidance measures, 15.35
  change of VAT rate, 3.69
  completing VAT return,
    amount received, 15.30
    conditions for using scheme, 15.29
    generally, 15.27
    international trade, 15.32
    invoice method, 15.27
    leaving scheme, 15.34
    miscellaneous issues, 15.33
    when payment made, 15.31
    workings of, 15.28
Cash accounting scheme *(continued)*
  conditions for using, 15.29
  international trade, 15.32
  leaving, 15.34
  record-keeping requirements, 14.12
  recoverable input tax, 6.16
  when amount received, 15.30
  when payment made, 15.31
  workings of, 15.28
Cash and carry wholesalers
  tax invoices, 3.30, 6.45
Casino card room games
  exemption, 5.22
Catering
  business splitting, 2.13
  food distinguished from, 4.6
Catholic Church *See* Roman Catholic Church
Central heating, 4.74
Change of use
  disposal or letting, 8.22
  occupier, by, 8.23
  partial exemption, 7.20
Channel Islands
  exports, 12.15
Charities
  advertising, 4.67
  construction services, 8.14
  donated goods, sales or exports of, 4.61
  exports,
    donated goods, of, 4.61
    other, 4.62
  fund-raising events by, 5.79
  handicapped persons, supplies for use by, 4.50–4.55
  medicinal products, supplies of, 4.68
  mixed standard and zero-rated services apportionment, 8.14
  nominated eligible bodies, supplies of relevant goods to, 4.63–4.66
  sea, provision of rescue or assistance at, 4.37
  zero-rating,
    charity advertising, 4.67
    exports of donated goods, 4.61
    generally, 4.60
    medicinal products etc., supplies of, 4.68
    nominated eligible bodies, supplies of relevant goods to, 4.63–4.66

Charities *(continued)*
  zero-rating, *(continued)*
    other exports, 4.62
    relevant goods, supplies of, 4.63–4.66
    sales of donated goods, 4.61
Children
  clothing and footwear, 4.69
Chronically sick
  chronically, meaning, 4.50
Church of England
  ecclesiastical exemption, 8.37
Church in Wales
  ecclesiastical exemption, 8.37
Churches
  ecclesiastical exemption, 8.37
Civil engineering works
  new or partly completed, sale of, 8.33
  sewerage services, supplies of, 4.20
  treatment of, 8.33
  VAT liability of typical transactions, 8.9
  water, supplies of, 4.20
Civil proceedings, 16.34
Clothing and footwear
  protective boots and helmets, 4.70
  young children, 4.69
  zero-rating, 4.69
Clubs
  exemptions, 5.77
Collectors' items
  imported and reimported, 4.77, 12.5
  meaning, 9.4
  special rate VAT, 12.5
  See also Auctioneers' scheme
Commercial buildings
  sale of, 8.26
Competitions
  exemptions, 5.77
Completing VAT returns *See* VAT returns
Composite supplies
  air transport, 3.52
  Card Protection Plan, 3.52
  non-profit making bodies, 3.52
  opticians, 3.52
  mixed supplies distinguished from, 3.51–3.52
Computer hardware
  capital goods scheme, 8.6
Computer invoicing
  use of, 3.34
Computerised records
  requirements relating to, 14.9
Consideration
  meaning, 12.1
Consignment stocks
  call-off stocks distinguished from, 11.8
Construction industry
  authenticated receipts, 3.33, 8.21, 14.26
Construction services
  annexes constructed for relevant charitable purpose, 8.12
  authenticated receipts, 8.21
  building materials, 8.17–8.18
  capital goods scheme, 8.4–8.6
  charities, 8.14
  definitions, 8.7
  educational institutions, 5.59
  further comment, 8.10
  generally, 8.1–8.8
  landscaping, 8.16
  mixed standard and zero-rated services, apportionment and, 8.14
  new building, 8.15
  output tax, 3.24
  residential property, 1.19, 3.7, 4.3, 4.79, 8.7
  services ancillary to, 8.16
  subcontractors, 8.20
  urban regeneration schemes, 1.19, 3.7, 4.3, 4.79
  VAT liability of typical transactions, 8.9
  zero-rating,
    annexes constructed for relevant charitable purpose, 8.12
    exclusions from, 8.13
    extent of, 8.11
    generally, 4.32
    mixed standard and zero-rated services, 8.14
    zero-rated supplies, 8.16
Containers
  output tax, 3.54
Control visits *See* Assurance visits
Converted buildings
  sale of, 8.28
Corporate hospitality, 4.42
Corpses, removal of, 5.73
Credit
  granting of, exemption, 5.33

Credit card vouchers
  tax invoice, as, 3.28
Credit cards, exemptions, 5.30–5.31
  services to banks for, 5.37
Credit management, 5.37
Credit notes
  bad debts relief and, 3.50
Cremation *See* Burial and cremation
Criminal proceedings, 16.34
Crown
  registration, 2.34
Crown land
  buildings on, 8.38
Cultural services
  exemption, 5.80–5.82
  place of supply, 12.35
Current accounts
  operation of, exemption, 5.40

D

Data processing services, 5.37
Day centres
  relevant establishments, meaning, 4.64
  zero rating, 4.52
De minimis limits, 7.21
  application of, 7.16
Death
  payment of VAT, 15.8
  time limit for assessment after, 16.25
Debts
  mutual, 3.45–3.46
  See also Bad debts
Declarations
  completing VAT return, 15.11
Default surcharge
  completing VAT returns, 15.6
Default surcharge liability
  introduction of, 16.15
  surcharge liability notice, issue of, 16.15
Definitions *See* Words and phrases
Delivery charges
  output tax, 3.53
Denmark
  recovery of foreign VAT, 13.10
Deposit accounts
  operation of, exemption, 5.40
Deposits
  output tax, 3.16
Deregistration
  assets on hand at, 2.38–2.39
Deregistration *(continued)*
  circumstances requiring, 2.35
  distance selling, 2.40
  EC acquisitions, 2.41
  expenditure incurred after, 6.36
  generally, 2.35
  keeping records after, 14.25
  optional, 2.36–2.37
  post-deregistration input tax, 2.43
  record-keeping after, 14.25
  refund to deregistered business, 3.47
  registration void *ab initio*, 2.42
  retention of records after, 2.44
  stock and assets on hand at, 2.38–2.39
See also Registration
Direct attribution
  introduction of, 7.8
Disbursements, 3.75
Disclosures
  voluntary, 16.44
Distance selling
  completing VAT return, 15.24
  deregistration, 2.40
  exciseable goods, and, 11.16
  generally, 11.13
  group registration, and, 11.17
  sales to UK, 2.7, 2.32
  voluntary registration under, 11.15
  workings of, 11.14
Divisional registration
  nature of, 2.29
Documentation
  bad debts, 3.42
  input tax claims, evidence required to support,
    acceptable forms of evidence, 6.39–6.48
    acquisitions from other EC countries, 6.43
    alternative evidence, 6.47
    cash and carry invoices, 6.45
    generally, 6.38
    imports from outside EC, 6.42
    pro-forma invoices, 6.41
    reclaims without supporting invoices, 6.46
    self-billed invoices, 6.40
    services acquired from abroad, 6.44
Donated goods, 4.61
Donations
  output tax, 3.67

Drugs and medicines
  acquisitions from other EC countries, 4.57
  charities, supplies to, 4.50–4.55
  goods dispensed on prescription, 4.48
  handicapped persons, supplies to, 4.50–4.55
  imports of eligible goods from outside EC, 4.56
  other goods, 4.49
  zero-rating, 4.47–4.57
Duchy land
  buildings on, 8.38
Dwellings
  meaning, 8.7
  See also Property

E

EC *See* European Community
EFL courses, 10.37
E-mail invoicing
  use of, 3.36
Ecclesiastical exemption, 8.37
Education
  construction of new buildings, 5.59
  EFL courses, 10.37
  educational institutions, 5.59
  eligible body, provision by, 5.49, 5.51
  establishments outside scope of VAT, 5.46
  establishments providing exempt education, 5.45
  examination services,
    meaning, 5.54
    provision of, 5.53
  exemption, generally, 5.44
  exemption, partial, 5.47
  goods closely related to exempt service, 5.55–5.56
  physical, 5.76
  private tuition, supply of, 5.52
  services closely related to exempt service, 5.55–5.56
  vocational training, provision of, 5.57
  youth club, provision of facilities by, 5.58
Election to waive exemption *See* Option to tax
Electricity *See* Fuel and power
Electronic VAT returns, 15.58–15.59
Ending businesses *See* Deregistration
Energy-saving materials, 4.74
Engineering insurance
  exemption, 5.11
Entertainment, business *See* Business entertainment
Entry of premises
  Customs' right of entry to inspect, 14.16
  search warrants, 14.17
Errors
  EC sales lists, 11.29
  incorrect rulings from previous visiting officers, 16.53
  supplementary statistical declarations, in, 11.41
European Community (EC)
  acquisitions,
    imported goods, and, 1.10, 16.7
    non-taxable person, by, 16.11
    trading in goods within EC, 11.3
  background to VAT, 1.5–1.9
  deregistration, EC acquisitions and, 2.41
  distance selling,
    exciseable goods, and, 11.16
    generally, 11.13
    group registration, and, 11.17
    voluntary registration under, 11.15
    workings of, 11.14
  drugs acquired from other countries, 4.57
  EC sales lists,
    branches, 11.30
    errors, 11.29
    generally, 11.26
    groups, 11.30
    methods of submitting, 11.28
    working of, 11.27
  effect of VAT system on UK, 1.26
  input tax claims, evidence required to support,
    acquisitions from other EC countries, 6.43
    imports from outside EC, 6.42
  installed or assembled goods, 11.5
  introduction of VAT system in UK, 1.5

European Community (EC) (continued)
medicines acquired from other EC countries, 4.57
non-registered persons, acquisitions by, 2.33
non-taxable persons, acquisition by, 16.11
partial exemption, 7.4
penalties,
acquisitions and imported goods, 16.7
non-taxable person, acquisition by, 16.11
purchase of goods from other member states, 3.22
repair services, 11.5
sales, 11.2
Sixth Directive, 1.26
system of VAT, 1.26
traders with other EC countries, record-keeping requirements, 14.23
trading in goods within,
approval, goods sold on, 11.9
call-off stocks, 11.8
consignment stocks, 11.8
distance selling,
exciseable goods, 11.16
generally, 11.13
group registration, and, 11.17
voluntary registration under, 11.15
workings of, 11.14
EC acquisitions, 11.3
EC sales, 11.2
EC sales lists,
branches, 11.30
errors, 11.29
generally, 11.26
groups, 11.30
methods of submitting, 11.28
working of, 11.27
generally, 11.1
goods supplied and installed in other EC countries, 11.7
Intrastat, 11.31
simplification, 11.43–11.46
new means of transport,
bringing into UK from other member states, 11.23
date of first entry into service, 11.19
definitions, 11.18

European Community (EC) (continued)
trading in goods within, (continued)
new means of transport, (continued)
new vehicles used in UK before taking abroad, 11.22
sales in UK for removal to other member states, 11.20
type approval, 11.21
processing, goods sent to other EC countries for, 11.6
record-keeping, 11.25
repairs, goods sent to other EC countries for, 11.6
reporting requirements, 11.25
sale or return, goods sold on, 11.9
supplementary statistical declarations (SSDs),
correcting errors and omissions, 11.41
frequency of, 11.33
generally, 11.31
header information, 11.37
in detail, 11.32
information required on, 11.36
item information, 11.38
low value consignments, 11.39
nil returns, 11.40
responsibility for submitting declaration, 11.34
visits by Customs to check, 11.42
when movement must be recorded on, 11.35
tax representatives, 11.24
transferring own goods to another EC country, 11.5
triangulation,
generally, 11.10
procedure without simplification, 11.11
simplified procedure, 11.12
values on which acquisition calculated, 11.4
Treaty of Rome, 1.6, 1.8
triangulation,
generally, 11.10

European Community (EC) *(continued)*
  triangulation, *(continued)*
    procedure without simplification, 11.11
    simplified procedure, 11.12
  See also Recovery of VAT, Tour operators' margin scheme
Examination services
  meaning, 5.54
  provision of, 5.53
Exempt supplies
  time of supply rules, 3.18
  See also Exemption, Partial exemption
Exemption
  betting and gaming,
    bingo,
      cash bingo, 5.25
      generally, 5.23
      prize bingo, 5.24
      value of exempt supply,
        cash bingo, 5.25
        prize bingo, 5.24
    casino card room games, 5.22
    game of chance, meaning, 5.21
    generally, 5.19–5.21
  blocked items, 5.83
  burial and cremation,
    corpses, removal of, 5.73
    exhumation, 5.74
    generally, 5.71
    monumental masons, services of, 5.72
  categories of, 5.1
  charities, fund-raising events by, 5.79
  clubs, 5.77
  competitions, 5.77
  credit cards, 5.30–5.31
  cremation *See* burial and cremation, *above*
  cultural services etc., 5.80–5.82
  data processing services, 5.37
  education, 5.44–5.59
    construction of new buildings, 5.59
    educational institutions, 5.59
    eligible body, provision by, 5.49, 5.51
    establishments outside scope of VAT, 5.46
    establishments providing exempt education, 5.45

Exemption *(continued)*
  education *(continued)*
    examination services,
      meaning, 5.54
      provision of, 5.53
    generally, 5.44
    goods or services closely related to exempt service, 5.55–5.56
    new buildings, construction of, 5.59
    partial exemption, 5.47
    private tuition, supply of, 5.52
    vocational training, provision of, 5.57
    youth clubs, provision of facilities by, 5.58
  finance,
    administrative arrangements and documentation, provision of, 5.36
    advance, making of, 5.33
    agent, services of, 5.39
    authorised unit trust, management of, 5.41
    banks, 5.37
    credit, granting of, 5.33
    credit management, 5.37
    current account, operation of, 5.40
    Customs Leaflet 701/29 paragraph 20, 5.43
    deposit account, operation of, 5.40
    finance company, finance terms separately supplied by, 5.35
    financial services excluded from exemption, 5.37, 5.43
    generally, 5.30
    instalments, terms require payment by, 5.34
    issues, transfers, receipts of money, 5.32
    management services, 5.37
    open-ended investment company, services of authorised corporate director of, 5.42
    savings account, operation of, 5.40
    secondary securities, dealings in, 5.38
    securities, dealings in, 5.38

Exemption *(continued)*
finance, *(continued)*
trust based scheme,
management of, 5.41
unit trusts, 5.41
fund-raising events by charities,
5.79
generally, 1.20, 5.1
gold, investment, 5.84
health and welfare,
dental services, 5.62
doctors' deputising services,
5.65
generally, 5.60
human blood and products,
5.66
pharmaceutical chemists,
services of, 5.63
recognised hospital, treatment
provided by, 5.64
registration, categories of, 5.61
restrictions to exemptions, 5.68
transportation of sick or injured
people, 5.67
welfare services, 5.69–5.70
input tax not recoverable, 5.83
insurance,
agents, services of, 5.15
brokers, services of, 5.15
business permitted to provide
exempt insurance, 5.5
engineering insurance, 5.11
exclusions, 5.17
export insurance, 5.10
generally, 5.3–5.4
intermediaries,
exclusions, 5.17
other rules and exceptions
for, 5.16
services of, 5.15
MAT insurance, 5.9
main types covered by
exemption, 5.7
pension review services, 5.17
reinsurance, 5.8
self insurance schemes, 5.14
supply of insurance, meaning,
5.6
warranties, 5.12–5.13
investment gold, 5.84
land, 5.2
lotteries,
generally, 5.26

Exemption *(continued)*
lotteries, *(continued)*
prizes,
goods, 5.28
services, 5.29
value of exempt supply, 5.27
management services, 5.37
non-profit making bodies, 5.75
patriotic bodies, 5.75
philanthropic bodies, 5.75
philosophical bodies, 5.75
political bodies, 5.75
postal services, 5.18
professional bodies, 5.75
religious bodies, 5.75
sport,
Customs Leaflet 701/45
paragraph 18, 5.77
non-profit-making members
clubs, 5.77
physical education, 5.76
sports competitions, 5.76
trade unions, 5.75
voluntary staff, 5.82
works of art etc., 5.78
See also Non-profit making
bodies, Partial exemption
Exhumation, 5.73
Expenditure
generally, 6.1–6.3
non-deductible input tax,
expenditure after registration,
6.34, 6.36
expenditure prior to
registration, 6.34–6.35
See also Input tax
Export insurance
exemption, 5.10
Exports
acceptable evidence of, 12.24
accounting issues concerning,
12.25
Channel Islands, 12.15
consolidation, supplies to overseas
business for export after,
12.21
direct, 12.16–12.17, 12.22
evidence of, 12.24
export houses, 12.20
exporters' obligations, summary
of, 12.23
generally, 12.15

Exports *(continued)*
incorporation, supplies to overseas business for export after, 12.21
indirect, 12.16, 12.18, 12.22
Isle of Man, 12.15
overseas visitors, 12.19
processing, supplies to overseas business for export after, 12.21
retail, 12.16, 12.19
second-hand cars, 9.42
time limits for zero-rating of, 12.22
Customs Information Sheet 2/00, 12.22
proof of export, 12.22
types of, 12.16
zero-rating, 4.58, 12.22

F

Farmers
registration, 2.30
Farmhouses
non-deductible input tax, 6.33
Faxed invoices
use of, 3.35
Final consumers
meaning, 1.13
Finance
administrative arrangements and documentation, provision of, 5.36
advance, making of, 5.33
agents, services of, 5.39
authorised unit trusts, management of, 5.41
credit, granting of, 5.33
current accounts, operation of, 5.40
Customs Leaflet 701/29 paragraph 20, 5.43
deposit accounts, operation of, 5.40
exemption, generally, 5.30
finance companies, finance terms separately supplied by, 5.35
financial services excluded from exemption, 5.37, 5.43
instalments, terms require payment by, 5.34
issues, transfers, receipts of money, 5.32
issues, underwriting, 5.37

Finance *(continued)*
open-ended investment companies, services of authorised corporate director of, 5.42
savings accounts, operation of, 5.40
secondary securities, dealings in, 5.38
trust based schemes, management of, 5.41
Finland
recovery of foreign VAT, 13.11
Fish and chip shops
mark-up assessment, 16.19
Food
animals, for,
DIY livery, 4.15
generally, 4.13
grazing rights, 4.14
keep of animals, 4.14
pet food, 4.16
assortments, 4.11
catering distinguished from, 4.6
mixtures, 4.11
packaging, 4.12
standard-rating, 4.9
zero-rating,
animals, food for,
DIY livery, 4.15
generally, 4.13
grazing rights, 4.14
keep of animals, 4.14
pet food, 4.16
assortments, 4.11
generally, 4.6–4.10
mixtures, 4.11
packaging, 4.12
Footwear *See* Clothing and footwear
Foreign businesses
distance sellers to UK, 2.32
group registration, and, 2.28
Foreign VAT *See* Recovery of VAT
France
recovery of foreign VAT, 13.12
Fraud
time limits for, 16.24
Free zones and warehouses
workings of, 12.14
See also Imports
Freehold sales
VAT liability of typical transactions, 8.9

Freight transport
  intra-community transport, 4.43–4.44
  place of supply, 12.33
  zero-rating, 4.39
Fuel and power
  landlords, supplies by and to, 4.75
  reduced rate, 1.19, 3.7, 4.3, 4.71–4.76
  schools, supplies to, 4.76
  small quantities, automatic reduced rate for, 4.73
Fuel purchases
  receipts for, 3.29
Fuel scale charges, 3.76
Fund-raising events
  charities, by, 5.79
  qualifying bodies, by, 5.79

G

Galleries, 6.48
Games of chance
  meaning, 5.21
Gaming *See* Betting and gaming
Gas *See* Fuel and power
Germany
  recovery of foreign VAT, 13.13
Gifts
  business, 3.57–3.60
Global accounting
  calculating output tax due under, 9.21
  eligible goods, 9.19
  generally, 9.18
  record-keeping requirements, 9.20, 14.28
  starting to use, 9.22
Going concern transfer *See* Transfer of going concern
Gold
  investment, 5.84
  zero-rating, 4.46
Goods
  actual and basic tax points, 3.10–3.11
  approval or similar, supplied on, 3.15, 11.9
  basic tax point, 3.10
  EC trade in,
    approval, goods sold on, 11.9
    call-off stocks, 11.8
    consignment stocks, 11.8
    EC acquisitions, 11.3
Goods *(continued)*
  EC trade in, *(continued)*
    EC sales, 11.2
    goods supplied and installed in other EC countries, 11.7
    processing, goods sent to other EC countries for, 11.6
    repairs, goods sent to other EC countries for, 11.6
    sale or return, goods sold on, 11.9
    transferring own goods to another EC country, 11.5
    values on which acquisition calculated, 11.4
  loss of, 3.61
  place of supply, 3.2
  private use, taken for, 3.19–3.21
  purchase from other EC Member States, 3.22
  sale or return, supplied on, 3.15, 11.9
  tax point, 3.10–3.11
  theft of, 3.62
  See also Capital goods scheme, Second-hand goods margin scheme
Government departments
  registration, 2.34
Grazing rights
  zero-rating, 4.14
Greece
  recovery of foreign VAT, 13.14
Group registration
  anti-avoidance provisions, 2.27
  application to form VAT group, 2.26
  bad debt refunds, and, 3.49
  distance sales, 11.17
  expulsion, 2.28
  foreign businesses and, 2.28
  generally, 1.16, 2.25
  ineligibility, 2.28
  option to tax, 8.46
  tour operators' margin scheme, 10.11
Guides
  tour operators' margin scheme, 10.29

H

Handicapped persons
  aids for, 4.50–4.55

Handicapped persons *(continued)*
charities, supplies to, 4.50–4.55
meaning, 4.50
talking books for, 4.31
vehicles for, 4.51
Health and welfare
dental services, 5.62
doctors' deputising services, 5.65
exemption, generally, 5.60
human blood and products, 5.66
pharmaceutical chemists, services of, 5.63
recognised hospitals, treatment provided by, 5.64
registration, categories of, 5.61
restrictions to exemptions, 5.68
transportation of sick or injured people, 5.67
welfare services, 5.69–5.70
Helmets, protective, 4.70
Hire-purchase transactions
exemption, 5.34
output tax, 3.63
second-hand goods margin scheme, 9.16
Holding companies *See* Transfer of going concern
Horses
second-hand goods margin scheme, 9.44
Houseboats
zero-rating, 4.45
Houses *See* Dwellings, Property, Renovated houses
Housing associations, 8.28

I

Imports
bulked entries, 12.11
deferring duty and VAT, 12.7
drugs, 4.56
free zones and warehouses, 12.14
from inside and outside EC, 1.10, 4.56–4.57
generally, 12.2
input tax claims, evidence for, 12.8
medicines, 4.56
overseas business importing goods into UK, 12.9
permanent, relief on, 12.13
postal, 12.10
repayments on second-hand cars for subsequent export, 12.12
Imports *(continued)*
reverse charge for imported services, 12.40
second-hand cars, 9.41, 12.12
services imported from abroad, 3.23
temporary, relief on, 12.13
time VAT is payable on, 12.6
valuation, 12.3–12.5
works of art, antiques and collectors' items, 4.77, 12.5
zero-rating, 4.58
Input tax
blocked items, 5.83
documentary evidence required to support claims,
acceptable forms of evidence, 6.39–6.47
acquisitions from other EC countries, 6.43
alternative evidence, 6.47
cash and carry invoices, 6.45
generally, 6.38
imports from outside EC, 6.42
pro-forma invoices, 6.41
reclaims without supporting invoices, 6.46
self-billed invoices, 6.40
services acquired from abroad, 6.44
galleries, 6.48
imports, evidence for claims, 12.8
meaning, 1.22, 6.4–6.9
museums, 6.48
new cars, 9.39
non-deductible,
business entertainment,
generally, 6.24
staff parties, 6.25–6.26
subsistence expenses of staff distinguished from, 6.24
tribunal appeals, 6.27
cars,
accessories, 6.19
leased, 6.21
maintenance, 6.20
modifications, 6.19
new rules from 1 August 1995, 6.18
qualifying, 6.21
rebates of rentals, 6.22
repairs, 6.20
short-term car hire, 6.23

Input tax *(continued)*
non-deductible, *(continued)*
expenditure,
incurred after registration, 6.34, 6.36
incurred prior to registration, 6.34–6.35
farmhouses, 6.33
generally, 6.17
non-business activities, input tax used for, 6.37
transfer of business as going concern, 2.16
arranging business transfer, 6.29
generally, 6.28
holding company,
not carrying on separate business, 6.30
registered, input tax recovery by, 6.32
registration, 6.31
post-deregistration, 2.43
reclaims without supporting evidence, 6.46
recoverable,
cash accounting scheme, 6.16
circumstances, 6.11–6.12
late claims, 6.14
method, 6.10
research and development costs, 6.15
special circumstances,
cash accounting scheme, 6.16
generally, 6.13
late claims, 6.14
research and development costs, 6.15
Inputs
meaning, 1.22
Insolvent customers
bad debt relief, 3.48
Inspections
Customs' right of entry to inspect premises, 14.16
other Customs' powers, 14.20
Instalments
terms require payment by, exemption, 5.34
Insurance
agents, services of, 5.15
brokers, services of, 5.15
businesses permitted to provide exempt insurance, 5.5
Insurance *(continued)*
engineering insurance, 5.11
exemption,
exclusions, 5.17
generally, 5.3–5.4
main types covered by, 5.7
export insurance, 5.10
holiday and travel, 10.26
intermediaries,
exclusions, 5.17
other rules and exceptions for, 5.16
services of, 5.15
MAT insurance, 5.9
mechanical breakdown, 9.43
reinsurance, 5.8
self insurance schemes, 5.14
supply of, meaning, 5.6
warranties, 5.12–5.13
Intangible services
place of supply, 12.36
Intellectual services
place of supply, 12.36
Intending traders
registration, 2.20
Interest
assessment, VAT recoverable by, 16.9
penalties, interest and surcharges, 16.12
time limit for assessment, 16.23
VAT recovered, on, 16.9
Intermediaries *See* Insurance
International services
accounting for VAT, 12.37
business status, evidence of, 12.38
cultural, artistic and similar services, 12.35
freight transport, 12.33
generally, 12.26
hire of means of transport, 12.34
intangible, intellectual, professional services etc., 12.36
Internet services, 12.42
land, 12.31, 12.39
passenger transport, 12.32
place of supply,
accounting for VAT, 12.37
basic rule in UK, 12.29
business status, evidence of, 12.38
cultural, artistic and similar services, 12.35

International services *(continued)*
place of supply, *(continued)*
exceptions to basic rule, 12.30–12.39
freight transport, 12.33
generally, 12.27
hire of means of transport, 12.34
intangible, intellectual, professional services etc., 12.36
land, services relating to, 12.31, 12.39
law, 12.28
passenger transport, 12.32
reverse charge for imported services, 12.40
telecommunications, 12.36, 12.41
transport,
freight, 12.33
hire of means of, 12.34
passenger, 12.32
zero-rating, 4.33
International trade
cash accounting scheme, 15.32
consideration, meaning, 12.1
generally, 12.1
reverse charge for imported services, 12.40
telecommunications services, special treatment of, 12.41
See also Exports, Imports, International services
Internet services, 12.42
Intrastat regime, 11.31
simplification, 11.43–11.46
See also Supplementary statistical declarations (SSDs)
Investment gold, 5.84
Investment management services, 5.41
Invoices *See* Purchase invoices, Tax invoices
Ireland
recovery of foreign VAT, 13.15
Isle of Man
exports, 12.15
Italy
recovery of foreign VAT, 13.16

J

Joint owners
option to tax, 8.46

L

Land
capital goods scheme, 7.30, 8.4–8.6
co-owners of, registration and, 2.24
definitions, 8.7
election to waive exemption *See* option to tax, below
exemption, 5.2, 8.19
freehold, 4.61
generally, 8.1–8.8
grant of interests in and rights over, 8.34
international services, 12.31, 12.39
meaning, 8.34
option to tax,
effect of, 8.42
generally, 8.40
group registration, 8.46
joint owners, 8.46
miscellaneous issues concerning, 8.47–8.51
notification of, 8.43
owned by pension fund, 8.50
transfer of going concern, 8.44
workings of, 8.41
services relating to, 3.24
transfer of business as going concern, 8.34
VAT liability of typical transactions, 8.9
See also Civil engineering works, Leases, Listed buildings, Property

Landlords
fuel and power, supplies of, 4.75

Landscaping, 8.16
Leaflets
meaning, 4.25

Leases
generally, 8.29
rental income, 8.30
service charges, 8.31
VAT liability of typical transactions, 8.9
variations, 8.32

Letters
pre-assessment, 16.46

Lifeboats
meaning, 4.37

Limited liability partnership *See* Partnership
Limited Liability Partnership Act 2000, 2.23
Limited partnerships *See* Partnership
Limited Partnerships Act 1907, 2.23
Listed buildings
  approved alterations, 8.36–8.38
  Crown land, 8.38
  Duchy land, 8.38
  ecclesiastical exemption, 8.37
  qualifying as, 8.35
  sale of, 8.27
  substantially reconstructed, main interests in, 8.39
Lithoplate makers
  record-keeping requirements, 14.24
Local authorities
  registration, 2.34
Loss
  goods, of, 3.61
Lotteries *See* Betting and gaming
Luxembourg
  recovery of foreign VAT, 13.17

M

MAT insurance
  exemption, 5.9
Madeira, 4.43
Management services, 5.37, 5.41
Margin schemes
  fundamental principle, 9.1
  generally, 9.1–9.6
  international trade, and,
    EC countries,
      purchases from, 9.31
      sales to buyers in, 9.32
    exports, 9.34
    generally, 9.30
    imports of goods from outside EC, 9.33
  operation since 1 January 1995, 9.2
  record-keeping requirements, 14.28
  tangible movable property, 9.3
  See also Second-hand goods margin scheme, Tour operators' margin scheme
Market research, 5.37
Mark-up assessments
  fish and chip shops, 16.19
  guidelines on, 16.17
  public houses, 16.18
Medicinal products
  charities, supplies to, 4.68
  meaning, 4.68
Medicines *See* Drugs and medicines
Methodist Church
  ecclesiastical exemption, 8.37
Microfilm or microfiches
  records on, 14.10
Misdirections
  incorrect rulings from previous visiting officers, 16.53
Mixed supplies
  composite supplies distinguished from, 3.51–3.52
  including zero-rated printed matter, 4.30
Monitoring
  VAT account, of, 16.44
Monthly payments on account
  changes in amounts payable, 15.52
  larger businesses, by, 15.46–15.56
  leaving scheme, 15.53
  option to pay actual monthly VAT due, 15.54–15.56
Monumental masons, 5.72
Motor cars *See* Cars
Museums, 6.48
Mutual debts
  bad debt relief, 3.45–3.46

N

NMT *See* Transport
National Listening Library
  zero-rated supplies to, 4.31
Negotiations
  local review, 16.48
  post-assessment, 16.48
  pre-assessment, 16.47
Netherlands
  recovery of foreign VAT, 13.18
New means of transport (NMT) *See* Transport
Non-deductible input tax *See* Input tax
Non-profit making bodies, 5.69–5.70, 5.75–5.77, 5.79
  composite supplies, 3.52
Northern Ireland
  ecclesiastical buildings in, 8.37
Notification
  registration, of,
    going concern transfers, 2.16
    other matters, 2.17

Notification *(continued)*
registration, of, *(continued)*
procedures relating to, 2.14–2.34
Numbers *See* VAT numbers

O

Occupiers
change of use by, 8.23
Offences
suspected, special Customs' powers to examine records, 14.18
Open-ended investment companies
services of authorised corporate director of, 5.42
Opticians, 3.52
Option to tax
conversion to residential use, 8.48
effect of, 8.42
generally, 8.40
group registration, 8.46
joint owners, 8.46
miscellaneous issues concerning, 8.47–8.51
notification of, 8.43
property owned by pension fund, 8.50
transfer of going concern, 8.44
workings of, 8.41
Output tax
accommodation tax points, 3.17
actual tax point
goods, 3.11
services, 3.13
approval or similar, goods supplied on, 3.15
auctioneers' scheme, 9.25
bad debts, refunds of VAT on,
credit notes, 3.50
deregistered businesses, refunds to, 3.47
documentation required, 3.42
generally, 3.38–3.50
group registrations, 3.49
insolvent customers, 3.48
mutual debts, 3.45–3.46
part payment, receipt of, 3.43–3.44
records required, 3.42
basic tax point,
goods, 3.10
services, 3.12, 3.14
booking fees, 3.66
business gifts, 3.57–3.60

Output tax *(continued)*
business stocks and assets, use of, 3.64
cancellation charges, 3.66
cash accounting, 3.69
change of rate,
cash accounting, 3.69
generally, 3.68
retail schemes, 3.70
second-hand schemes, 3.70
composite supplies, 3.51–3.52
containers, 3.54
credit notes, 3.50
delivery charges and postage, 3.53
deposits, 3.16
donations, 3.67
exempt supplies, 3.18
fuel scale charges, 3.76
generally, 3.1
global accounting, 9.21
goods, 3.2
actual and basic tax points, 3.10–3.11
approval or similar, supplied on, 3.15
loss of, 3.61
private use, taken for, 3.19–3.21
purchases from other EC Member States, 3.22
sale or return, supplied on, 3.15
theft of, 3.62
hire purchase and similar transactions, 3.63
land, property and construction services, 3.24
loss of goods, 3.61
meaning, 1.22
miscellaneous issues, 3.77
mixed and composite supplies, 3.51–3.52
packaging, 3.54
part-exchange transactions, 3.56
payphones, 3.65
phonecards, 3.65
postage, 3.53
private use, goods taken for, 3.19–3.21
retail schemes, 3.70
sale or return, goods supplied on, 3.15
second-hand goods, sales of, 3.55
second-hand schemes, 3.70
self-supplies, 3.19–3.21

Output tax *(continued)*
services, 3.3
actual and basic tax points, 3.12–3.14
continuous supplies of, 3.14
imported from abroad, 3.23
land, property and construction, 3.24
tax points, 3.9–3.14
accommodation, 3.17
actual and basic,
goods, 3.10–3.11
services, 3.12–3.14
theft of goods, 3.62
tips, 3.67
UK rate, 3.7
when output tax is due, 3.6
zero-rated supplies, 3.18
See also Agents, Tax invoices
Outputs
generally, 3.1
meaning, 1.22, 3.1
See also Output tax
Overseas visitors, 12.19

P
Packaging
food, 4.12
output tax, 3.54
Part payments
bad debt refund, entitlement to, 3.43–3.44
Part-exchange transactions
output tax, 3.56
second-hand goods margin scheme, 9.17
Partial exemption
annual adjustments,
generally, 7.17–7.18
registration period, 7.19
apportionment,
calculations, 7.13–7.15
excluded items, 7.13–7.15
generally, 7.9
incidental items, 7.13–7.15
special methods, 7.11–7.12
standard method of, 7.10
capping, 7.21
change of use, 7.20
consequences of, 7.7–7.15
de minimis limits, 7.16, 7.21
direct attribution, 7.8
European law, 7.4
Partial exemption *(continued)*
exempt input tax, 7.3
exempt supplies, 7.6
generally, 7.1–7.6
intended use, change of, 7.20–7.21
meaning, 1.25
mechanics of, 7.7–7.15
partly exempt business, 7.2
tax year, 7.7
trade bodies, 7.12
UK law, 7.5
VAT year, 7.7
See also Capital goods scheme, Exemption
Partnership
business splitting, 2.13
group registration, 2.23, 2.25–2.28
limited and limited liability, registration of, 2.23
registration,
generally, 2.22
transfer of going concern, 2.16, 2.23
Passenger transport
place of supply, 12.32
wheelchair access, 4.38
zero-rating, 4.38
Patriotic bodies, 5.75
Payphones
output tax, 3.65
Penalties
assessment,
additional, 16.21
civil evasion penalty, 16.33
civil proceedings, 16.34
criminal proceedings, 16.34
default surcharge, 16.32
departmental error interest, 16.57
EC Sales Lists, 16.37–16.38
errors following incorrect rulings, 16.53
estimated, 16.15
estimated outputs, based on, 16.20
failure to submit returns, 16.5, 16.15
following assurance visits, 16.16
generally, 16.31
grounds on which to defend, 16.49–16.52
higher, 16.8
incorrect certificates, 16.35

Penalties *(continued)*
  assessment, *(continued)*
    interest on VAT recovered or recoverable by, 16.9
    late registration penalty, 16.39
    local review, 16.48
    mark-up,
      fish and chip shops, 16.19
      guidelines, 16.17
      public houses, 16.18
    miscellaneous issues, 16.41–16.43
    misdeclaration penalty, 16.36
    misdirection, effect of, 16.53
    notification to correct person, 16.27–16.28
    other conditions, 16.29–16.30
    other penalties, 16.40
    other powers, 16.10
    post-assessment negotiations, 16.48
    pre-assessment letter, 16.46
    pre-assessment negotiations, 16.47
    repayment supplement, 16.58
    section 73, under, 16.26
    time limits for, 16.22
    types of, 16.14
  civil proceedings, 16.34
  criminal proceedings, 16.34
  default surcharge liability, 16.15, 16.32
  EC acquisitions,
    imported goods, and, 16.7
    non-taxable persons, by, 16.11
  failure to make returns, 16.5, 16.15
  generally, 16.1–16.4
  higher assessments, 16.8
  incorrect refunds, 16.6
  interest,
    surcharges, and, 16.12–16.13
    VAT recovered or recoverable by assessment, on, 16.9
  mark-up assessments,
    fish and chip shops, 16.19
    guidelines on, 16.17
    public houses, 16.18
  misdeclaration, 16.36, 16.44
  post-assessment negotiations, 16.48
  pre-assessment,
    letter, 16.46
    negotiations, 16.47

Penalties *(continued)*
  returns, failure to make, 16.5, 16.15
  time limits,
    assessment under section 73, for, 16.26
    assessments, for, 16.22
    death, assessment after, 16.25
    fraud, for, 16.24
    penalties, interest and surcharge assessments, for, 16.23
  VAT account monitoring, 16.44
  voluntary disclosures, 16.44
  See also Appeals, Assessments
Pension review services, 5.17
Pensioners, 4.74
Pet food
  zero-rating, 4.16
  See also Animals, food for
Pharmaceutical chemists
  services of, 5.63
Philanthropic bodies, 5.75
Philosophical bodies, 5.75
Phonecards
  output tax, 3.65
Physical education
  exemption, 5.76
Place of supply
  generally, 3.1
  goods, 3.2
  meaning, 3.1
  services, 3.3
  tour operators' margin scheme, 10.7–10.9
  See also International services
Political bodies, 5.75
Ponies
  second-hand goods margin scheme, 9.44
Portugal
  recovery of foreign VAT, 13.19
Postage
  output tax, 3.53
Postal imports
  treatment of, 12.10
Postal services
  exemption, 5.18
Printed matter
  liability of common items of, 4.25
  services associated with production of, 4.26–4.28
  See also Books
Private tuition
  supply of, 5.52

Private use
goods taken for, 3.19–3.21
Pro-forma invoices
input tax claims, evidence required to support, 6.41
use of, 3.31
Process engravers
record-keeping requirements, 14.24
Processing
goods sent to other EC countries for, 11.6
supplies to overseas business for export after, 12.21
Product design, 5.37
Professional bodies
exemption, 5.75
Professional services
place of supply, 12.36
Property
alteration, 1.19, 3.7, 4.3, 4.79, 8.52–8.59
capital goods scheme, 7.30, 8.4–8.6
change of use,
disposal or letting, 8.22
occupier, by, 8.23
conversion, 1.19, 3.7, 4.3, 4.79, 8.52–8.59
definition of terms, 8.53
definitions, 8.7
election to waive exemption *See* option to tax, *below*
freehold sales, VAT liability of, 8.9
generally, 8.1–8.8
option to tax,
conversion to residential use, 8.48
effect of, 8.42
generally, 8.40
group registration, 8.46
joint owners, 8.46
miscellaneous issues concerning, 8.47–8.51
notification of, 8.43
owned by pension fund, 8.50
transfer of going concern, 8.44
workings of, 8.41
renovation, 1.19, 3.7, 4.3, 4.79, 8.52–8.59
residential, 1.19, 3.7, 4.3, 4.79, 8.52–8.59
miscellaneous issues, 8.56–8.58
supply of related goods, 8.55
transitional rules, 8.59

Property *(continued)*
sale of renovated houses, 8.28, 8.60
sales,
commercial buildings, 8.26
converted buildings, 8.28
generally, 8.24
housing associations, 8.28
listed buildings, 8.27
person who has constructed, 8.25
qualifying buildings, 8.25
services relating to, 3.24
urban regeneration schemes, 1.19, 3.7, 4.3, 4.79, 8.52–8.59
See also Civil engineering works, Construction services, Land
Property managing agents
record-keeping requirements, 14.30
Protected buildings
zero-rating, 4.32
Public bodies, 5.69
Public houses
business splitting, 2.13
mark-up assessment, 16.18
Public interest bodies, 5.75
Purchase invoices
auctioneers' scheme, 9.26
post-deregistration input tax, 2.43
second-hand goods margin scheme, 9.8–9.9
Purchase tax
replacement of, 1.11

Q

Qualifying buildings
sale of, 8.25

R

Racehorse owners
registration, 2.31
Rates of VAT
change of,
cash accounting, 3.69
generally, 3.68
retail schemes, 3.70
second-hand schemes, 3.70
generally, 1.19
works of art, etc., 12.5
See also Reduced rate, Zero-rating

Receipts
  authenticated, construction industry, 3.33, 8.21, 14.26
  fuel purchases, for, 3.29
  See also Tax invoices
Records and accounts
  additional requirements,
    banks, 14.27
    construction industry, authenticated receipts in, 14.26
    deregistration, keeping records after, 14.25
    generally, 14.21
    global accounting, 14.28
    lithoplate makers, concessions for, 14.24
    margin schemes, 14.28
    other special requirements, 14.31
    process engravers, concessions for, 14.24
    property managing agents, 14.30
    retailers, 14.22
    tour operators' margin scheme, 14.29
    traders with other EC countries, 14.23
    typesetters, concessions for, 14.24
  bad debts, 3.42
  banks, 14.27
  business records, items falling within definition of, 14.8
  capital goods scheme, 7.35
  cash accounting scheme, 14.12
  computerised records, 14.9
  construction industry, authenticated receipts in, 14.26
  deregistration, retention after, 2.44, 14.25
  exports, accounting issues concerning, 12.25
  general information required by Customs,
    business records, items falling within definition of, 14.8
    cash accounting scheme, 14.12
    computerised records, 14.9
    generally, 14.5
    microfilm or microfiche, records on, 14.10

Records and accounts *(continued)*
  general information required by Customs, *(continued)*
    six year rule,
      calculation of six-year period, 14.7
      generally, 14.6
    transfer of going concern, 14.11
  global accounting, 9.20, 14.28,
  international services, 12.37
  keeping, 14.1–14.31
  lithoplate makers, concessions for, 14.24
  making records available to Customs,
    generally, 14.13
    premises, Customs' right of entry to inspect, 14.16
    professional accountants, records kept by, 14.14
    record-keeping and inspection, other powers affecting, 14.20
    samples, Customs' power to take, 14.15
    search warrants, 14.17
    suspected offences, power to examine records in case of, 14.18
    VAT visit, summary of records required or helpful at, 14.19
  margin schemes, 9.7, 14.28
  microfilm or microfiche, records on, 14.10
  premises,
    Customs' right of entry to inspect, 14.16
    search warrants, 14.17
  process engravers, concessions for, 14.24
  professional accountants, kept by, 14.14
  property managing agents, 14.30
  retailers, 14.22
  samples, Customs' power to take, 14.15
  search warrants, 14.17
  second-hand cars, 9.36
  six year rule,
    business records, items falling within definition of, 14.8
    calculation of six-year period, 14.7

Records and accounts *(continued)*
six year rule, *(continued)*
computerised records, 14.9
generally, 14.6
suspected offences, special powers to examine records in case of, 14.18
tour operators' margin scheme, 10.21, 14.29
traders with other EC countries, 14.23
trading in goods within EC, 11.25
transfer of going concern, 14.11
typesetters, concessions for, 14.24
VAT visit, summary of records required or helpful at, 14.19
Recovery of VAT
foreign VAT,
anti-avoidance measure, 13.6
claim procedure,
non-deductible items, 13.3
receiving refunds, 13.5
recent developments, 13.26
time limits, 13.4
workings of, 13.2–13.6
claims in UK by businesses outside EC,
generally, 13.23
other specific rules, 13.25
reference period, 13.24
time limits, 13.24
generally, 13.1
reference period, 13.24
specific rules for each member state, 13.7–13.22
time limits, 13.4, 13.24
See also Input tax
Reduced rate
consolidation of legislation, 4.81
fuel and power, 1.19
generally, 4.3, 4.71–4.72
landlords, supplies by and to, 4.75
schools, supplies to, 4.76
small quantities, automatic reduced rate for, 4.73
generally, 4.3
urban regeneration schemes, 1.19, 3.7, 4.3, 4.79, 8.52–8.59
women's sanitary products, 1.19
Registration
anti-avoidance provisions, 2.27
businesses, overseas, 2.7
co-owners of land, 2.24
Registration *(continued)*
Crown, 2.34
distance sellers to UK, 2.7, 2.32
distance selling, voluntary registration under, 11.15
divisional, 2.29
EC acquisition by non-registered person, 2.33
expenditure incurred prior to, 6.35
farmers, 2.30
foreign business and group registration, 2.28
generally, 2.1–2.13
going concern transfers, 2.10
group,
anti-avoidance provisions, 2.27
application to form VAT group, 2.26
bad debt refunds, and, 3.49
distance selling, 11.17
foreign businesses and, 2.28
generally, 2.25
option to tax, 8.46
tour operators' margin scheme, 10.11
intending traders, 2.20
land, co-owners of, 2.24
local authorities, 2.34
non-registered persons, EC acquisition by, 2.33
notification procedures,
generally, 2.14–2.34
going concern transfers, 2.16
other matters, 2.17
numbers,
receiving, 2.18
recognising valid VAT numbers, 2.19
other relevant supplies, 2.7, 3.4
partnership,
generally, 2.22
limited and limited liability, 2.23
period, 7.19
place of supply,
generally, 3.1
goods, 3.2
services, 3.3
racehorse owners, 2.31
receiving VAT registration numbers, 2.18
taxable supplies, 2.6, 3.1
thresholds, 2.2–2.9
tour operators' margin scheme, 2.8, 10.10

Registration *(continued)*
valid VAT numbers, recognition of, 2.19
values,
generally, 3.5
margin schemes, 2.8–2.9
void *ab initio*, 2.42
waiver of, 2.21
who must register, 2.11–2.13
See also Deregistration
Reinsurance
exemption, 5.8
Relevant goods
meaning, 4.63
Religious bodies, 5.75
Renovated houses, sale of, 8.28, 8.60
Rental income
exemption, 8.30
Repairs
goods sent to other EC countries for, 11.6
Reporting
trading in goods within EC, 11.25
Representatives and guides
tour operators' margin scheme, 10.29
Research and development costs
recoverable input tax, 6.15
Residential property *See* Property
Retail schemes, 14.22
change of rate, 3.70
See also Exports
Retailers
record-keeping, 14.22
Returns *See* VAT returns
Reverse charge
imported services, for, 12.40
Roman Catholic Church
ecclesiastical exemption, 8.37
Royal National Institute for Blind (RNIB)
zero-rated supplies to, 4.31

S

Sale or return
goods supplied on, 3.15, 11.9
Sales invoices
auctioneers' scheme, 9.27
second-hand goods margin schemes, 9.10–9.14
Sales taxes
cascade taxes, 1.12
compared with VAT, 1.13–1.25
Sales taxes *(continued)*
purchase tax, 1.11
Samples
Customs' power to take, 14.15
Sanitary products (women), 1.19, 3.7, 4.3, 4.78
Savings accounts
operation of, exemption, 5.40
Schools
fuel and power, supplies of, 4.76
Scotland
ecclesiastical buildings in, 8.37
Sea
charities providing rescue or assistance at, 4.37
lifeboats, 4.37
Search warrants, 14.17
Second-hand goods margin scheme
agent, use by, 9.15
antiques, meaning, 9.4
auctioneers' scheme,
calculating output tax due, 9.25
calculations, 9.28
charges to be included or excluded, 9.28
conditions for operating, 9.24
generally, 9.23
purchase invoices, 9.26
sales invoices, 9.27
zero-rated goods, 9.29
basic conditions, 9.6
cars,
demonstration cars, 9.38
driving schools, 9.40
exports, 9.42
generally, 9.5, 9.35
imports, 9.41
incomplete records, 9.36
mechanical breakdown insurance (MBI), 9.43
new, recovery of input tax on, 9.39
private taxi firms, 9.40
road fund licences, 9.37
self-drive hire firms, 9.40
trading at auctions, 9.40
warranties, 9.43
change of rate, 3.70
collectors' items, meaning, 9.4
generally, 3.55, 9.1–9.6
global accounting,
calculating output tax due under, 9.21
eligible goods, 9.19

Second-hand goods margin scheme *(continued)*
global accounting, *(continued)*
generally, 9.18
record-keeping requirements, 9.20
starting to use, 9.22
hire-purchase sale, 9.16
horses, 9.44
part-exchange, 9.17
ponies, 9.44
purchases and purchase invoices, 9.8–9.9
record-keeping requirements, 9.7
sales and sales invoices, 9.10–9.14
works of art, meaning, 9.4
Secondary securities
dealings in, exemption, 5.38
Securities
dealings in, exemption, 5.38
Security goods, 4.74
Self insurance schemes
exemption, 5.14
Self-billing
business operating, 3.32
input tax claims, evidence required to support, 6.40
Self-supplies
cars, demonstration, 9.38
output tax, 3.19–3.21
Service charges
tenants, levied on, 8.31
Services
actual and basic tax points, 3.12–3.14
continuous supplies of, 3.14
imported from abroad, 3.23
land, property and construction, 3.24
place of supply, 3.3
printed matter, production of, 4.26–4.28
tax point, 3.12–3.14
telecommunications, special treatment of, 12.41
See also Construction services, International services
Sewerage services
civil engineering works linked with, 4.20
zero-rating, 4.17–4.18
Sheltered accommodation, 4.52
Ships
ancillary and associated services, 4.40
qualifying, meaning, 4.35
zero-rating, 4.35–4.36
Shoes *See* Clothing and footwear
Shops, tax-free, 4.59
Six year rule
calculation of six-year period, 14.7
generally, 14.6
See also Records and accounts
Spain
recovery of foreign VAT, 13.20
Sport
competitions, 5.76–5.77
Customs Leaflet 701/45 paragraph 18, 5.77
non-profit-making members clubs, 5.77
physical education, 5.76
Staff parties
non-deductible input tax, 6.25–6.26
Sticking tax
meaning, 1.13
Stocks
business stocks, use of, 3.64
deregistration, on hand at, 2.38–2.39
Subcontractors
services provided by, 8.20
Subsistence expenses, 6.24
Supplementary statistical declarations (SSDs)
correcting errors and omissions, 11.41
frequency of, 11.33
generally, 11.31
header information, 11.37
in detail, 11.32
information required on, 11.36
Intrastat regime, 11.31
simplification, 11.43–11.46
item information, 11.38
low value consignments, 11.39
nil returns, 11.40
responsibility for submitting, 11.34
visits by Customs to check, 11.42
when movement must be recorded on, 11.35
Supplies, exempt *See* Exemption
Surcharges
penalties, interest and, 16.12

Surcharges *(continued)*
time limit for assessment, 16.23
Surrenders
VAT liability of typical transactions, 8.9
Sweden
recovery of foreign VAT, 13.21
SWIFT, 13.22

T

TOMS *See* Tour operators' margin scheme
Tax free shops, 4.59
Tax invoices
annual, 3.37
authenticated receipts, 3.33
cash and carry wholesalers, 3.30, 6.45
characteristics of, 3.26
computer invoicing, 3.34
credit card vouchers, 3.28
e-mail invoicing, 3.36
faxed invoices, 3.35
fuel purchases, receipts for, 3.29
generally, 3.25
less detailed, 3.27–3.30
modified, 3.27–3.30
pro-forma, 3.31, 6.41
self-billing, 3.32, 6.40
supporting, input tax reclaims without, 6.46
tour operators' margin scheme, 10.16
Tax periods
annual VAT returns, 15.5
generally, 15.2
monthly returns, 15.4
non-standard, 15.5
quarterly returns, 15.3
Tax points, 3.9–3.18
accommodation, 3.17
actual and basic,
goods, 3.10–3.11
services, 3.12–3.14
goods, 3.10–3.11
refunds, 3.39
services, 3.12–3.14
tour operators' margin scheme, 10.12–10.15
Tax representatives
trading in goods within EC, 11.24
Tax-free shops, 4.59
Taxable persons
intending traders, 2.20
meaning, 1.13, 1.24
registration, 2.11–2.13
Taxable supplies
meaning, 3.1
place of, 3.1
registration and, 2.6
Telecommunications services, 12.36
special treatment of, 12.41
Television, 4.30
Tenants
service charges, 8.31
Theft
goods, of, 3.62
Thresholds
registration and, 2.2–2.7
Time limits
assessment, for,
death, assessment after, 16.25
fraud, 16.24
generally, 16.22
penalties, interest and surcharge, 16.23
section 73, assessment under, 16.26
completing VAT returns, 15.6
exports, zero-rating of, 12.22
foreign VAT, recovery of, 13.4, 13.24
fraud, for, 16.24
Time of supply *See* Tax points
Tips
output tax, 3.67
Tour operators' margin scheme
air passenger duty, 10.27
bad debt relief, 10.28
business customers, supplies used by, 10.19
calculation of VAT due under,
Customs' Leaflet 709/5, 10.35
generally, 10.31–10.32
provisional value, 10.33
simplified formula, 10.34
calculations under, 10.4–10.6
total purchase price, 10.24
total selling price, 10.22–10.23
costs charged in foreign currency, 10.25
Customs' Leaflet 709/5, 10.35
EFL courses, 10.37
European case law, 10.36
extra costs, 10.30

Tour operators' margin scheme *(continued)*
- generally, 10.1
- group registration, 10.11
- holiday and travel insurance, 10.26
- mechanics of, 10.2–10.16
- nominal margin scheme supplies, 10.20
- place where margin scheme supplies provided, 10.7–10.9
- provisional value, calculation of, 10.33
- record-keeping requirements, 10.21, 14.29
- registration, 10.10
- representatives and guides, 10.29
- specific exclusions from,
  - business customers, margin scheme supplies used by, 10.19
  - generally, 10.17
  - nominal margin scheme supplies, 10.20
  - wholesale supplies, 10.18
- tax points, 10.12–10.15
- VAT invoices, 10.16
- values, 2.8–2.9
- wholesale supplies, 10.18

Trade bodies, 7.12

Trade unions, 5.75

Traders
- other EC countries, with,
  - record-keeping requirements, 14.23

Trading in goods within EC *See* European Community (EC)

Transfer of going concern
- holding companies
  - not carrying on separate business, 6.30
  - registered, input tax recovery by, 6.32
  - registration, 6.31
- keeping records and accounts, 14.11
- land, 8.34
- non-deductible input tax,
  - arranging business transfer, 6.29
  - generally, 6.28
  - holding company,
    - not carrying on separate business, 6.30
    - registered, input tax recovery by, 6.32

Transfer of going concern *(continued)*
- non-deductible input tax, *(continued)*
  - holding company, *(continued)*
    - registration, 6.31
- option to tax, 8.44
- record-keeping requirements, 14.11
- registration,
  - generally, 2.10
  - notification of, 2.16

Transport
- agents, 4.41
- air passenger
  - composite supplies, 3.52
- ancillary and associated services, 4.40
- business services, 4.41
- designated travel services, 4.42
- freight, 4.39, 12.33
- hire of means of, 12.34
- intra-community, 4.43–4.44
- new means of (NMT),
  - bringing into UK from other member states, 11.23
  - date of first entry into service, 11.19
  - definitions, 11.18
  - sales in UK for removal to other member states, 11.20
  - type approval, 11.21
  - using new vehicles in UK before taking abroad, 11.22
- passenger, 4.38, 12.32
  - wheelchair access, 4.38
- place of supply,
  - freight transport, 12.33
  - hire of means of transport, 12.34
  - passenger transport, 12.32
- qualifying ships and aircraft, 4.35–4.36
- sea, supplies to charities providing rescue or assistance at, 4.37
- sick or injured people, of, 5.67
- zero-rating,
  - agents, 4.41
  - ancillary and associated services, 4.40
  - business services, 4.41
  - designated travel services, 4.42
  - freight transport, 4.39
  - generally, 4.34

Transport *(continued)*
- zero-rating, *(continued)*
  - intra-community transport, 4.43–4.44
  - passenger transport, 4.38
  - qualifying ships and aircraft, 4.35–4.36
  - sea, supplies to charities providing rescue or assistance at, 4.37

Travel
- designated services, 4.42
- *See also* Transport

Treaty of Rome, 1.6, 1.8

Triangulation
- generally, 11.10
- procedure without simplification, 11.11
- simplified procedure, 11.12

Tribunal appeals
- assurance visits, approach to, 16.55–16.56
- grounds for appeal, 16.54
- luxuries, amusements and entertainment, relating to, 6.27
- right of appeal, 16.54

Trust based schemes
- management of, exemption, 5.41

Typesetters
- record-keeping requirements, 14.24

U

Unit trusts, 5.41

United Kingdom
- recovery of foreign VAT, 13.22

United Reformed Church
- ecclesiastical exemption, 8.37

United States, 1.26

Urban regeneration schemes, 1.19, 3.7, 4.3, 4.79, 8.52–8.59

V

VAT accounts
- requirement to keep, 15.10

VAT Central Unit
- returns handled by, 15.1

VAT numbers
- receiving registration number, 2.18
- valid, how to recognise, 2.19

VAT returns
- annual accounting scheme,
  - conditions for using, 15.37–15.45
  - generally, 15.36
  - main features, 15.36
- anti-avoidance measures, 15.35
- bad debt relief, 15.17
- box by box guide to completion, 15.12–15.26
- cash accounting scheme,
  - accruals method, 15.27
  - anti-avoidance measures, 15.35
  - conditions for using, 15.29
  - generally, 15.27
  - international trade, 15.32
  - invoice method, 15.27
  - leaving, 15.34
  - miscellaneous issues, 15.33
  - payment made, 15.31
  - when amount received, 15.30
  - working of, 15.28
- completing,
  - annual accounting scheme,
    - conditions for using, 15.37–15.45
    - generally, 15.36
  - bad debt relief, 15.17
  - box by box guide to completion, 15.12–15.26
  - cash accounting scheme,
    - accruals method, 15.27
    - conditions for using, 15.29
    - generally, 15.27
    - international trade, 15.32
    - invoice method, 15.27
    - leaving, 15.34
    - miscellaneous issues, 15.33
    - payment made, 15.31
    - when amount received, 15.30
    - working of, 15.28
  - declaration, 15.11
  - default surcharge, 15.6
  - distance sales, 15.24
  - final checks, 15.26
  - freight and insurance charges, 15.21
  - generally, 15.1
  - how to pay,
    - BACS, 15.7
    - CHAPS, 15.7
    - death, 15.8
    - electronic, 15.7
    - Euros, 15.57

VAT returns *(continued)*
completing, *(continued)*
how to pay, *(continued)*
final returns, 15.9
generally, 15.7
monthly payments on account by larger businesses,
changes in amounts payable, 15.52
generally, 15.46–15.51
leaving scheme, 15.53
option to pay actual monthly VAT due, 15.54–15.56
non-deductible items, 15.18
tax periods,
annual VAT returns, 15.5
generally, 15.2
monthly returns, 15.4
non-standard, 15.5
quarterly returns, 15.3
time limits, 15.6
VAT account, 15.10
declaration, 15.11
distance sales, 15.24
electronic filing, 15.58–15.59
failure to make, 16.5, 16.15
final, 15.9
final checks, 15.26
how to pay,
BACS, 15.7
CHAPS, 15.7
death, 15.8
electronic, 15.7
final returns, 15.9
generally, 15.7
monthly payments on account by larger businesses,
changes in amount payable, 15.52
generally, 15.46–15.51
leaving scheme, 15.53
option to pay actual monthly VAT due, 15.54–15.56
non-deductible items, 15.18
payment in Euros, 15.57
prescribed accounting period, 15.3
recent developments, 15.57–15.59
tax periods,
annual VAT returns, 15.5
generally, 15.2
monthly returns, 15.4
non-standard, 15.5
quarterly returns, 15.3
time limits, 15.6

VAT returns *(continued)*
VAT account, 15.10
VAT Central Unit, 15.1
VAT visits *See* Visits
Value added tax
cascade taxes, 1.12
EC system, 1.26
generally, 1.1–1.9
introduction to, 1.1–1.32
misleading nature of term, 1.15
nature of, 1.10–1.25
purchase tax, replacement of, 1.11
sales taxes, compared with, 1.13–1.25
scope in UK, 1.27–1.32
Value Added Tax Act 1994, 1.4
Values
margin schemes, 2.8–2.9
meaning, 3.5
See also Imports
Visitors, overseas, 12.19
Visits
assurance, 1.4
approach to, 16.55–16.56
assessments, following, 16.16
summary of records required or helpful at, 14.19
supplementary statistical declarations, relating to, 11.42
Vocational training
provision of, 5.57
Voluntary disclosure
full information, of, 16.44
Voluntary staff, 5.82
Vouchers
credit card sales, 3.28

W

Warehouses, workings of, 12.14
Warranties
exemption, 5.12–5.13
second-hand cars, 9.43
Water
civil engineering works linked with, 4.20
meters, 4.21
zero-rating, 4.17, 4.19
Welfare services
exemption, 5.69–5.70
meaning, 5.69
See also Health and welfare

Wheelchair access
  passenger transport, 4.38
Wireless sets
  blind, for, 4.31
Words and phrases
  antiques, 9.4
  building materials, 8.17
  business records, 14.8
  call-off stocks, 11.8
  care, 4.64
  chronically, 4.50
  collectors' items, 9.4
  consideration, 12.1
  consignment stocks, 11.8
  construction services, 8.7
  dwelling, meaning, 8.7
  eligible bodies, 4.63
  examination services, 5.54
  final consumers, 1.13
  game of chance, 5.21
  handicapped persons, 4.50
  input tax, 1.22, 6.4–6.9
  inputs, 1.22
  land, 8.7, 8.34
  leaflets, 4.25
  lifeboats, 4.37
  medicinal products, 4.68
  output tax, 1.22
  outputs, 1.22, 3.1
  partial exemption, 1.25
  place of supply, 3.1
  property, 8.7
  public bodies, 5.69
  qualifying, 4.35
  relevant establishments, 4.64
  relevant goods, 4.63
  sticking tax, 1.13
  supply of insurance, 5.6
  taxable persons, 1.13, 1.24
  taxable supplies, 3.1
  welfare services, 5.69
  works of art, 9.4
Works of art
  exemption, 5.78
  imports and reimports, 4.77, 12.5
  meaning, 9.4
  special VAT rate, 12.5
  See also Auctioneers' scheme

Y
Youth clubs
  provision of facilities by, 5.58

Z
Zero-rating
  auctioneers' scheme, 9.29
  bank notes, 4.46
  books,
    blind,
      talking books for, 4.31
      wireless sets for, 4.31
    book tokens, 4.29
    CD-Roms, 4.24
    Card Protection Plan, 3.52
    generally, 4.23–4.25
    leaflets, 4.25
    liability of some common items of printed matter, 4.25
    production of printed matter, services associated with, 4.26–4.28
    talking books for blind, 4.31
    wireless sets for blind, 4.31
  building materials, 8.17–8.18
  caravans, 4.45
  charities,
    advertising, 4.67
    donated goods, sales or exports of, 4.61
    generally, 4.60
    handicapped persons, use by, 4.50–4.55
    medicinal products etc., supplies of, 4.68
    nominated eligible bodies, supplies of relevant goods to, 4.63–4.66
    other exports by, 4.62
  clothing and footwear,
    generally, 4.69
    protective boots and helmets, 4.70
    young children, 4.69
  construction services,
    annexes constructed for relevant charitable purpose, 8.12
    exclusions from zero-rating, 8.13
    extent of zero-rating, 8.11
    generally, 4.32
    mixed standard and zero-rated services, 8.14
    zero-rated supplies, 8.16
  corporate hospitality, 4.42
  drugs and medicines,
    acquisitions from other EC countries, 4.57

Zero-rating *(continued)*
drugs and medicines, *(continued)*
charities, supplies of medicinal products etc. to, 4.68
generally, 4.47
goods dispensed on prescription, 4.48
handicapped persons, aids for, 4.50–4.55
imports of eligible goods from outside EC, 4.56
other goods, 4.49
exports, 4.58, 12.22
Customs Information Sheet 2/00, 12.22
proof of export, 12.22
food,
animals, for,
DIY livery, 4.15
generally, 4.13
grazing rights, 4.14
keep of animals, 4.14
pet food, 4.16
assortments, 4.11
generally, 4.6–4.10
mixtures, 4.11
packaging, 4.12
footwear and clothing,
generally, 4.69
protective boots and helmets, 4.70
young children, 4.69
freight transport, 4.39
generally, 4.1–4.5
gold, 4.46
handicapped persons, aids for, 4.50–4.55
vehicles for, 4.51
helmets, protective, 4.70
houseboats, 4.45

Zero-rating *(continued)*
houses, renovated, sale of, 8.28, 8.60
imports, 4.58
international services, 4.33
intra-community transport, 4.43–4.44
medicines *See* drugs and medicines, *above*
mixed supplies, 4.30
Card Protection Plan, 3.52
passenger transport, 4.38
protected buildings, 4.32
protective boots and helmets, 4.70
sewerage services and water,
civil engineering works, 4.20
generally, 4.17
miscellaneous issues, 4.22
nature of sewerage services, 4.18
supplies of water, 4.19
water meters, 4.21
tax-free shops, 4.59
time of supply rules, 3.18
transport,
agents, 4.41
ancillary services, 4.40
associated services, 4.40
business services, 4.41
charities providing rescue or assistance at sea, supplies to, 4.37
designated travel services, 4.42
freight, 4.39
generally, 4.34
intra-community, 4.43–4.44
passenger, 4.38
qualifying ships and aircraft, 4.35–4.36
sea, supplies to charities providing rescue or assistance at, 4.37